Bureau of International Research
Harvard University and Radcliffe College

THE FRENCH FRANC
1914-1928

THE MACMILLAN COMPANY
NEW YORK · BOSTON · CHICAGO · DALLAS
ATLANTA · SAN FRANCISCO

MACMILLAN & CO., Limited
LONDON · BOMBAY · CALCUTTA
MELBOURNE

THE MACMILLAN COMPANY
OF CANADA, Limited
TORONTO

THE FRENCH FRANC

1914-1928

The Facts and Their Interpretation

BY

ELEANOR LANSING DULLES, Ph.D.

BRYN MAWR COLLEGE

New York

THE MACMILLAN COMPANY

1929

Printed in the United States of America by
J. J. LITTLE AND IVES COMPANY, NEW YORK

To

E. F. D. AND A. M. D.

PREFACE

The book aims, first, to present historically the facts concerning the fluctuation of the French franc between 1914 and 1928 and attendant economic and psychological conditions, and second, to test prevailing monetary theories in the light of what actually occurred in France. The facts have been compiled in a comprehensive and impartial manner and primarily from original sources, in the hope that they may serve others also in formulating or testing economic principles, particularly those dealing with money.

The research was begun in 1924 and continued through the four years of crises till after legal stabilization in 1928. The material was collected while there was still much secrecy and ignorance. By compiling the material in "the present," however, it has been possible to give due account to the psychological factors which, in the opinion of the author, have never been given their proper weight.

It is important that the conflicts of opinion and policy of postwar years should be recorded. How will future governments meet emergency demands for funds? How can depreciation be checked? How can national credit be safeguarded? The answers to these and to many such questions are to be found in a study of the unsuccessful and successful efforts in France.

My debt of gratitude is very great. Professor Rist of the Faculté de Droit, vicegovernor of the Bank of France, has been an unfailing source of encouragement and suggestions. Professor Allyn A. Young has been both an inspiration and guide, giving most generously of his time. He has followed the work from the beginning reading the entire manuscript and criticizing from the wealth of his knowledge and experience. Professor Schumpeter of the University of Bonn read considerable parts of the manuscript. Professor Taussig made some suggestions as to the treatment of an early portion of the book. My brother, John Foster Dulles, has made comments on those questions which approached the practical problems he has dealt with. To these and others who have been interested in these problems I wish to express my very genuine appreciation. Many French officials, bankers and members of the United States diplomatic service have been most considerate in facilitating the necessary research. The particular views here expressed are, however, to be attributed to the author alone.

The work would have been impossible without the financial assistance of the Harvard and Radcliffe Bureau of International Research. I wish to thank them for giving me this responsibility and opportunity.

ELEANOR LANSING DULLES.

January 1, 1929.

CONTENTS

INTRODUCTION

Miss Dulles's book has a twofold significance. In the first place it is a history. It gives an account of an important episode—or series of episodes—in the recent history of France. In the second place, it is an essay in monetary theory. It presents the results of an inquiry into the behavior of prices, exchanges, production, and trade under a régime of inconvertible paper money. But the reader will find that Miss Dulles draws no sharp line between her account of the various specific factors which shaped the fortunes of the franc and her analysis of the quantitative relations between the variations of the currency and the fluctuations of other economic phenomena. This, I think, is one of the principal merits of her book.

It is no longer profitable to inquire into the working of a depreciated currency with no other end in view than that of finding a fresh confirmation of established monetary principles. No intelligent person who has given any attention to the matter any longer doubts that there is a fairly dependable relation between the amount of a country's currency and the purchasing power of a currency unit. An inquirer's time and energy can be given more profitably to problems which as yet have not been so fully disposed of. Among these problems are such matters as the degree of rigidity or elasticity which may appear under particular conditions in the relation between the quantity of money and prices, the nature of the mechanism by means of which —again under particular conditions—that relationship is maintained or changed, the direction in which the controlling forces run and the way in which they get their initial impulse, the manner in which the whole interrelated system of prices is affected, and the resulting effects upon different forms of economic activity. It is to difficult questions such as these that Miss Dulles, so far as she deals with monetary theory, has addressed herself. When one pursues questions of this order at all closely one inevitably passes from the field in which general theorems, of the nature of economic "laws," are applicable to a field in which the search must be for the particular explanations of particular happenings.

Moreover, when a country's money is depreciated and is fluctuating in value, and most of all when its future depends upon the needs of the government and the nature of the financial expedients to which the government resorts, the behavior of producers and consumers, traders and bankers, lenders and borrowers, in transactions which involve transfers of money, is affected. The ordinary practices which lie back of and which, in a sense, give meaning to theorems which express the necessary mathematical relations between the quantity of money and the level of prices are not wholly to be relied upon. The theorems remain true, but when severed from their factual background they become mere truisms. There is the danger that if they are pressed into service in the study of the phenomena of depreciated currencies they will carry their old associations with them and will suggest wrong inferences with respect to the nature of the forces at work and the order of causal sequences. The task which confronts the investigator, therefore, is not that of putting the new body of experience into the old formulas, but involves a mixture of historical appraisal and economic analysis. There must be an account of what was done and, so far as possible, of why it was done, and there must also be an examination of the interrelations of the different things which were done and of their visible consequences. Such considerations both explain and justify the methods which Miss Dulles has used and the general course which her inquiries have taken.

The stress which Miss Dulles puts upon psychological attitudes, particularly as they manifest themselves in speculative operations, is, I believe, not disproportionate to their real importance. It will be understood, of course, that Miss Dulles has in mind something much more far-reaching than the technical processes of organized speculation or the transactions of professional speculators. Just as the housewife who buys sugar in advance of her needs because she thinks that if she waits she will have to pay a higher price is a speculator in sugar, so every person who spends or accumulates money or who borrows or lends with a view to securing gains or avoiding losses attaching to changes in its purchasing power is a speculator in money. The most striking instances of speculation in money occur when a sudden loss of confidence in the stability of its value, arising from the disclosure of a disappointing budgetary situation or from other developments which are likely to affect the national finances adversely leads to a "flight" from a country's money in the form of the precipitate buying of foreign exchange. The return movement which sets in when stability appears to be in a fair way to be achieved or even when the financial prospect is in any considerable degree altered for the better is of course also speculative in character. In the early stages of currency depreciation, when hope of a fairly early return to the former gold parity has not yet been abandoned, forces which again are properly to be called speculative, showing themselves in an increased demand for money for holding rather than for spending, sometimes help to bolster up its value. Monetary speculation appears in domestic markets—in the markets for commodities, for land, and for equities in industrial undertakings—as well as in the markets for funds payable in the moneys of other countries. For various reasons, however, these last markets are more quickly sensitive to shifts of speculative opinion. It is possible, of course, to put all of these phenomena into the conventional formulas, and to dispose of them as changes in the demand for money or in the velocity of its circulation. But we get closer to the roots of the matter if we put our emphasis in the first place upon changes in the hopes and fears and in the calculations of those who use money rather than upon the formal consequences of such changes.

One should beware of thinking that speculation in a depreciated money and speculation in a commodity must operate in much the same way and have much the same sorts of effects. It is not true, for example, that the effects of speculation in money are necessarily short-lived and that the ultimate determinants of its value remain unaffected. Under the conditions which usually attend the use of inconvertible paper money there are no fixed limits to the amount which can be supplied. A fall in its value, whether attributable to speculative operations or to any other cause, leads to a larger volume of expenditures and hence to a demand, on the part of the government as well as on the part of industrialists and traders, for larger supplies of money. Larger advances by the banks to industry and trade will be justified by the increase (in terms of money units) of their assets, of the volume of their transactions, and of their prospective profits. The amount of advances which will be made to the government will depend upon its needs, and what its needs are will depend in considerable part upon what its fiscal policy is. But they will always be increased by a fall in the value of the currency unit. There is no "limiting" or "ultimate" supply of inconvertible money apart from such restrictions as the government may choose to impose upon itself or upon the banks. Speculation in an inconvertible currency, therefore, by helping to bring about the result which it anticipates, may sometimes operate cumulatively in one direction, in a way for which speculation in wheat or cotton affords no parallel.

The results of two years of residence and study in France show themselves not only in Miss Dulles's knowledge of details and in her command of sources of information but also in her interpretation of the character of the problem with which she deals. That problem, as she sees it, is not merely a matter of the changing quantitative relations of certain economic variables. It is first of all a problem of public policy, and it is a problem which is related to the interests of the country and of its people in many different ways. Impressions and appraisals, as well as economic inferences, have their place—and a proper place—in her book. It adds to the value of her work that she writes as a friendly and sympathetic historian. I wonder, however, whether she does not at some points go rather too far in her defense of the fiscal policies of the French government. The economist, if he is to fulfil his own proper function, cannot deliver himself over completely to historical determinism. It is not for him to say that conditions being what they were all doors were closed to any better solutions than were reached. I have no patience, I confess, with those who say that during the war and the years immediately following it France, or any other country similarly circumstanced might have got along without inflation. Such a statement either is a pointless platitude or is nonsense. But there were times, I think, when French fiscal policy was not shaped entirely by the compulsion of circumstances, but was built partly upon illusions—as, for example, in respect of recoverable reparations or the possible return of the franc to the prewar gold parity—which were clung to even after they were known to be illusions.

The stabilization of the franc might not have had to wait until 1928 if the problem had been attacked in the same way and with the same determination six years earlier. But these are matters of conjecture. What is certain is that the monetary experience of France since 1914 affords a particularly inviting opportunity for the study of the behavior of an instrument which men have created for their own purposes, but which they have not yet fully learned how to control and to use. Miss Dulles has made good use of that opportunity.

ALLYN A. YOUNG.

London School of Economics.

ANALYSIS

A. THE PROBLEM

CHARTS

TABLES IN THE TEXT [1]

[1] See appendix for other statistical data.

STATISTICAL APPENDIX

THE FRENCH FRANC
1914-1928

THE FRENCH FRANC
1914–1928

CHAPTER I

THE SIGNIFICANCE OF DEPRECIATION

THE French franc lost eighty per cent of its value as a
result of the World War. It fell from an exchange value of
19.29 cents in 1914 to 3.90 cents in 1928,[1] and its internal
purchasing power fell to the same extent. Such depreciation,
bound to have serious consequences in the financial, economic, and social life of any nation, has caused notable
changes in France. In the first place, the temporary loss in
financial prestige and power has been considerable. In the
second place, production has come to be dominated more
and more by large manufacturing units and corporate forms
of enterprise.[2] The results of this change are likely to persist. In the third place, the shift of power from the middle
classes to the industrial leaders and to those with more
flexible incomes [3] appears to have changed the character of
French life and ideals to a notable extent. Other results of
depreciation might be mentioned, but these are perhaps the
most striking.

The harm which has been wrought in the way just indicated will become less serious as stable money values follow

---

[1] See table of dollar rates for the franc, appendix.

[2] *Bulletin de la statistique générale de la France* (April-June, 1927), p.
277. Figures indicate changing size of industrial concerns.

[3] Flexible incomes are those incomes which vary more or less directly
with prices and other economic conditions. Fixed incomes are those dependent on long-time contract, such as salaries or interest on bonds.

the period of rapid change, and as various phases of economic life become adjusted to new conditions. On the other hand, all the changes in the economic and social aspects of life are not yet fully revealed, and may be cumulative.

The balance sheet of the war cost will be made out in time, and the results of depreciation are bound to become evident. Its causes are somewhat more difficult to ascertain. At first glance the problem may seem simple; depreciation often follows war, and heavy government expenditures, debts, and inflation are all influences which undermine money value. But many countries fought in the World War, increased their debts, bought goods abroad, and inflated their currencies. Some currencies regained par shortly after the peace was signed, some remained in a state of uncertainty and changing depreciation for years, and others fell rapidly towards zero. Why was France able to keep a middle course and yet not able to bring her currency back to par? There must have been special reasons which did not operate either in the case of England, on the one hand, or in that of Germany, on the other.

Reconstruction the Cause of Depreciation

The special fact in the French case was the size and urgency of her reconstruction problem. This led to her policy on reparations, the growth of the internal debt, and most of the important events in her foreign and domestic history after the war.

It is true that, even apart from reconstruction expenditures, the French had large foreign debts, both public and private. It is probable, nevertheless, that France would have been able to bring the franc to par if her reconstruction needs had been smaller. It is noteworthy that her private creditors did not show any pressing intention to collect their debts or refuse new loans until after the serious reparation muddle in 1922. Moreover, the largest govern-

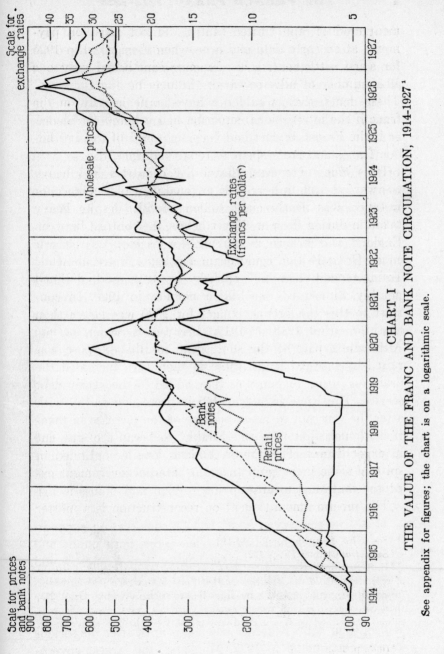

THE VALUE OF THE FRANC AND BANK NOTE CIRCULATION, 1914-1927 [1]

CHART I

See appendix for figures; the chart is on a logarithmic scale.

3

ment creditor, the United States, did not insist on payments at an early date and even when they asked in 1925 for some settlement, such demands constituted only one of a number of adverse factors influencing the currency.[1] These debts, then, would not have borne heavily on the franc if the international situation had inspired confidence, or if the French budget had been lightened of the 100 billion francs and more spent to repair damages.[2]

It is true, of course, that other countries had heavy postwar burdens to bear. The internal debt of England, for instance, was nearly eight billion pounds, despite heavy taxation during the war. Nevertheless, the contrast between England and France is striking, for as soon as the war ended Great Britain could begin a policy of retrenchment.[3] Total expenditures fell slightly in 1919 and declined notably, almost by one billion pounds, in 1920. In contrast to this the French budget for 1920 was larger than that for either 1918 or 1919,[4] because of reconstruction. Although a part of the sum spent for this purpose was raised by internal loans, these in their turn increased the drain on future revenues as they added to the yearly debt service. The English budget deficits were done away with after the war, not so much because of the increase in taxation, though that was considerable, as because of the cut in expenditures. The French budget deficits continued in spite of some increase in taxation because government expenses continued to grow.

The precise amount spent on reconstruction is a matter

[1] See *infra,* Chapter V, pp. 181–183.
[2] See *infra,* Chapter IV, p. 132.
[3] U. S. Senate, *Commission of Gold and Silver Inquiry Report,* pursuant of resolution 469, 67th Congress, entitled *Foreign Currency and Exchange Investigation,* Serial 9, vol. i, by John Parke Young (Washington, 1925), (hereinafter cited as U. S. Senate *Foreign Currency and Exchange Investigation.* The second volume is cited only in the later chapters as specified), p. 469, table 29.
[4] *Ibid.,* p. 493.

of considerable dispute. In the first place, the technical question of what damages should be included under this heading is not easy to solve. For instance, the allowances for personal damages and pensions formed a considerable part of the French bill against Germany and these, for the most part, should not be considered as reconstruction charges.[1] However, granted that every warring country suffered some of these losses, in the case of France a part was due primarily to invasion, and the material and bodily harm done to noncombatants was certainly a special burden. Then again, one must admit that a part of the money spent cannot be counted as an unavoidable burden on France, since there was a considerable amount of extravagance and waste. Nevertheless, even after all possible account is taken of these complicating factors, the sums expended by France were large. The government asserted that it had spent 129 billion francs up to 1924.[2] At this date considerable work was still to be done, but the further repairs were less urgent and constituted a comparatively light budget charge. If the amount said to have been spent is reduced by 30 billion francs to make a considerable allowance for sums which either should not have been included under this heading or were attributable to waste and graft, there still remains the very large expenditure of about 100 billion francs, or three times the former internal debt of France.[3]

If one takes into account the broader aspects of this situation, it is obvious that the fact that France wished to collect reparation payment from Germany to meet an immediate need, and that she was the main creditor nation,

---

[1] Bernard Baruch, *The Making of the Reparations and Economic Sections of the Treaty* (New York, 1920), pp. 28-33.

[2] *Documents parlementaires, Chambre,* annexe no. 537, 1924, p. 2109. See also *infra,* Chapter IV.

[3] Henry Chéron, *Rapport au Sénat,* February 22, 1926, annexe no. 84, p. 277. The total government debt of France (internal) was 32,594 million francs on December 31, 1913. See also *infra,* Chapter VI.

placed her in a peculiar position.[1] It was to her interest more than to that of any other country to see that Germany paid. It is possible that the complete default of Germany would have forced France to repudiate, in one form or another, her internal debt, and probably also her external debt. The result was an immediate and inevitable conflict of interest between France and England.[2] France needed money or goods to replace the destruction of her northern departments. England needed money but, even more than increased revenue, she desired the reëstablishment of foreign markets and the recovery of international trade on a normal basis. Moreover, her claim on Germany was less than half that of France, and her interest in collecting it was comparatively slight. Even though her exchequer would suffer through the failure of reparations, her commerce was apt to benefit. France, however, had little to gain in the way of expanding her foreign commerce, and she had much to lose through national bankruptcy. The result was tension, misunderstanding, and divided interests.

In regard to the relations of France with the United States, there might not have been so wide a cleavage if the United States had not determined to withdraw from European controversies. If, for instance, the United States had allowed some connection between reparation payments and the debts of England and France, there would have been a common interest with France in a rapid solution of the reparation problem. It was considered likely for a time that the United States might advance money on easy terms to pay for reconstruction [3] and this would have mitigated

[1] France is entitled under the Spa agreement, July 5, 1920, to fifty-two per cent of reparation payments; England, the second largest creditor, was to receive twenty-two per cent; Italy, the third, ten per cent; Belgium, the fourth, eight per cent. See Karl Bergmann, *History of Reparations* (London, 1927), p. 43.

[2] Alpha [George P. Auld], *Foreign Affairs,* vol. ii. no. 1 (September 15, 1923), pp. 82, 83.

[3] See *infra,* this chapter.

somewhat the desire of France to collect from Germany. However, this second alternative was, like the first, inconsistent with the policy of the government at Washington. The United States withdrew from the field when the war was over and appeared only occasionally in later councils as a creditor or mediator.

It is neither wise nor necessary to judge between nations as to their reparation policies. The situations of the countries involved differed very widely. Under the most favorable conditions, it is hard to see how there could have been complete harmony and understanding. The evident fact is that France paid her reconstruction bills herself for the first years after the war and that the motive for collecting from Germany increased in intensity as the internal debt grew larger. Moreover, as this insistence became stronger, her political isolation increased.[1] Speculators became pessimistic because France was playing a lone hand and because, in case of failure, the budget problem seemed insoluble. Thus, the inability of the government to get money from Germany or loans from the United States led directly through speculation and indirectly through inflation to the extreme depreciation of the franc.

Such comparisons of the various countries at the close of the war are difficult, but it seems clear that the needs of France were the most urgent, excepting, perhaps, those of Germany. It should be remembered that reconstruction began before the war was over. Many peasants were back in their trench-scarred villages before the armistice was actually signed. The government was faced with the necessity of getting food supplies to the north or allowing whole communities to suffer disease and starvation during the winter months. There was some attempt to delay the return of the peasants to the most badly devastated areas,

[1] Karl Bergmann, *op. cit.*, p. 168. In speaking of conditions in 1923, he speaks of "the deep-seated discord among the Allies, and especially between France and Britain."

but this was of little avail. For the good of the country as a whole, the resettlement of the industrial regions and the rebuilding of the factories and railroads were most urgent. These huge tasks demanded money at a time when budget deficits were already very large. The only possible solution seemed to be to advance money and then to see if the defeated nation could meet the bill. It is true that Germany was temporarily faced with famine in 1919 and that the allies had to take steps to alleviate the immediate need. This German situation, however, did not call for such large capital expenditures as those needed in France; the German railroads were still in existence, the factories were standing.

Then again, it might be thought by some that Belgium and Italy were in the same position as France. They were faced with the problem of reconstruction, it is true, but their losses had not been on so large a scale. This fact is indicated by the larger percentage of reparations allotted to France; her part was more than five times the shares to go to Belgium and to Italy. Belgium, moreover, may have profited to a slight extent by the German occupation; a great deal of money had been spent in her cities, and some capital equipment had been put at her disposal. It is true that portions of the battlefields in Belgium could probably never be cultivated again, but her industrial and commercial losses were much less than those of France.

The situation of France, then, as regards reparations, was exceptional. In judging the bearing of this fact on the franc, one should remember that the problem of depreciation is a quantitative one. It is important to make a careful study of the size of debts and budgets and the actual sums of money needed to balance an unfavorable commodity trade. It is necessary, besides, to survey briefly the situation of France at the close of the war in order to understand the cause of subsequent depreciation. It should be recalled, for example, that the franc was not far from its normal gold value at the close of the war. It had been kept at a high percentage of its prewar value both by pegging operations and also by the general expectation that the currency would eventually be able to return to its former value; thus the supporting influences were both material and psychological.

The question naturally arises in this connection as to whether it might have been possible for the franc to return to par. There are some who say that complete restoration might have been possible if the radicals had not gained control in 1924. Others say it would have been possible if the conservatives had understood the fundamentals of reparations. This is, to a considerable extent, political propaganda. In any case, the answer to the question must be sought in the reconstruction-reparation problem. A study of the factors influencing the franc makes it apparent that if this problem could have been solved to the satisfaction of the French, the franc might conceivably have returned to par. The study of the history of the depreciation of the franc and the part played by speculation should make this possibility clear.[1]

THE HOPES OF FRANCE DISAPPOINTED

At the close of the war, the most immediate influence working against the franc was the unfavorable balance of trade. The second in direct relation was the internal debt, which bore with it the threat of inflation or repudiation, and, therefore, of depreciation on both the commodity and the foreign exchange markets. As matters stood in 1919, the French seemed to be faced with a difficult but not impossible task. The unfavorable commercial balance might to a certain extent have been offset by additional outside loans until French industry and exports could again become normal. This would have meant the continued extension of credit to France for a period of three or four years and, in

[1] See *infra,* Chapters IV-VI.

view of the addition of territories and resources through the peace treaty, it is reasonable to suppose that such credits could have been obtained. Of course, the increase in the internal debt of France was a serious matter; it had risen from 32½ billion francs to 140 billion francs at the end of 1918.[1] This would under any conditions have constituted a heavy burden, but not an impossible one. A glance at budget receipts for the following years indicates that revenues would have met the service of the debt if the debt had remained at the 1918 level. Thus it was the two-fold strain of interest and capital expenditures which made necessary the inflation of later years. The internal debt practically doubled during the eight years following the armistice.

France, in 1919, anticipated a far different development of economic affairs from that which took place. In the first place, the French expected, or at any rate they hoped, that the United States would advance money to finance reconstruction.[2] Such expectations were based more on vague prophecies by unofficial Americans in France than they were on official statements. It is not always realized that some of the statements of foreign residents were responsible for serious misunderstandings. Nevertheless, in view of the resources in America and the evident need of France, it is not surprising that these ideas were generally accepted. It was not until the presidential message of December, 1919 stated that Europe must look out for her own needs, that these hopes were abandoned.[3] In the second place, the French confidently expected that every cent that went to pay for rebuilding the North would come eventually from Germany. And in addition to this, they hoped that some of the other war expenditures, which had led to the in-

[1] See *infra*, Chapter VI. The debt situation for the end of each year from 1914-27 is here given.

[2] *Le Pour et le contre* (Paris, December 1, 1919).

[3] See *infra*, Chapter IV.

crease in the debts, would be covered by reparation payments.

According to such an optimistic view of the future, the obligations of the French government, as well as the budget expenditures, would have decreased very soon after the war. Granted such an improvement in public finance, a certain amount of deflation of both currency and the credit seemed possible. Although it was conceivable that foreign private creditors would press their claims before the receipts from Germany had become large, such difficulties were not expected. Moreover, it seemed likely that floating credits of a commercial origin could be refunded into long-time obligations and that the indebtedness of France could gradually be wiped out by payments from Germany and by increase in export trade.

Shortly after the armistice the complexities of the problem began to be seen.[1] The United States did not come forward with offers of reconstruction help, and England and France had serious differences in regard to the peace treaty and reparations. Furthermore, the troubles in Germany made it apparent that she could not pay the reparation bill at once. These political events so absorbed the ablest statesmen that the first decline of the franc, unpegged in 1919, passed almost unnoticed. The sudden drop, due in the first instance to the technical situation of the foreign exchange markets, was accentuated as the general position of France appeared in a more unfavorable light. The increased insistence on reparations, which became more and more important in French internal politics, led to ever-growing friction without. France went on spending money on reconstruction with a growing debt and a diminishing prospect of financial recovery, and the turn of speculation against France was the direct result.

It was natural that, as the size of budget expenditures

[1] See *infra,* Chapter IV. The sequence of events after the war is discussed in more detail in that chapter.

and loans for reconstruction purposes increased, there were heated political struggles over questions which should have been settled mainly by impartial technical experts. The party or group in power, the *Bloc national*, bidding for popular favor, promised that the cost would be met by Germany, just as Lloyd George had previously sworn to hang the Kaiser. As the difficulties became more evident, efforts to overcome them became all the more desperate. Meanwhile, relations between England and France were strained to the danger point on several occasions, and various unsound financial measures were used to postpone the bitter disillusionment of the French electors. The complications thus introduced into the external and internal political situations cannot be measured and appraised in the same manner in which one can measure the volume of trade or the level of prices. They were, none the less, the most important result of the reconstruction tangle, and a prime cause of the depreciation of the franc.

The difficulties in French foreign relations have been more widely understood than have the internal struggles. This is natural, because it has not been generally known to what an extent French political life is inherently unstable.[1] Ministries have been short-lived and majorities have rested on uncertain compromises between small and shifting groups ever since the constitution of 1875. There

[1] A. L. Lowell, *Greater European Governments* (Cambridge, Mass., 1918), p. 182. "Now the fact that the fall of a cabinet does not involve a change of party has two important effects: by removing the fear that a hostile opposition will come to power, it destroys the chief motive for discipline among the majority; and by making the Chamber feel that a change of ministers is not a matter of vital consequence, it encourages them to put them out with rash indifference . . . during the last forty years between 1875 and 1914 there were fifty of them, so that the average duration of the French cabinet has been a little less than ten months. . . . (pp. 175, 176) A cabinet which in the morning sees no danger ahead, and enjoys the confidence of the Chamber and the nation, may be upset before nightfall by a vote provoked in a moment of excitement on a matter of secondary importance."

have been, in recent years, eleven distinct political parties, which unite in varying combinations to form shifting majorities in the Chamber of Deputies. Instability was the result, in part, of the method of electing representatives, which was based on a form of proportional representation, and, in part, on the frequency with which the adverse result of a vote of confidence on minor issues precipitated the fall of ministries.

Such a changing system makes it difficult at any time to institute a vigorous policy of taxation or to carry out any thorough measure of financial reform. When one adds to these uncertain elements in French political life the state of mind in Europe at the close of the war and the general misunderstanding of Germany's power to pay, it is evident that only an unusually wise and powerful ministry could have imposed heavy taxes in France. It is probable that no ministry could have survived such an unpopular program and that if there had been several successive political reversals revolutionary movements might have gained ground in France.

Attempts to conjecture the result of a different policy are of little use. It is important, however, to indicate some of the less evident lines of causality between the reconstruction burden, political programs, and the financial policy. It is generally admitted that the basis of French monetary difficulties was to a considerable extent political. These difficulties should be considered not only from the more coldly detached point of view which now prevails, but also with due allowance for the passions and confusions which dominated public opinion in most countries immediately after the war.

The financial policy which the French actually adopted in 1919 made the subsequent monetary difficulties unavoidable. First it should be noted that from the outset mistaken emphasis focused attention exclusively on the amount of reparations at a time when one of the critical questions for the French was the financing of foreign purchases and the refunding of foreign credits. With such credits France might have been successful with pegging operations through 1919. It is true that the help of the English treasury was withdrawn, but French credit might have been good for private loans in various other financial centers if the government had given its support to traders. If so, the French would have saved in the cost of goods purchased something toward the cost of interest on the new debts.

Then, in the second place, there was no clear understanding of the monetary changes even when depreciation had gained considerable headway. Few people had anticipated the rapid fall in the value of the franc and there was little agitation to prevent the continued decline. This was partly because there were no recent French precedents for this widespread inflation which could be used as a basis for policy and prophecy. There was no clear body of monetary theory to guide financiers and there was, on the contrary, a tone of optimism not justified by the facts. The widespread purchase of francs and marks in the postwar period by people unaccustomed to speculation is evidence of this blind optimism, when the actual value of the mark and the franc might well have incited caution in a money-wise public. The franc lost half its value in 1919, the dollar cost doubled.[1]

1919	Jan.	1	5.45 francs per dollar
	Apr.	1	6.75 " " "
	Dec.	31	11.00 " " "

Since there had been in the previous hundred years no comparable change in European money, new explanations of causes and relationships have to be found.

The French policy seemed to be one of "watchful waiting," when vigorous action was needed. The clearest evi-

[1] See appendix for daily dollar rates in Paris, from 1919-27.

dence of this is found in the very large increase in the internal debt. Figures for this period are as follows: [1]

Dec. 31	1918..............	140,794	million francs
	1919..............	181,872	" "
	1920..............	215,192	" "

The addition of 75 billion francs in two years to the internal debt shows a total lack of an adequate policy to face reconstruction. The cause of serious difficulties lay not merely in the size of the debt, but also in the bad arrangement of repayments and the large percentage of short-time obligations. The maturity dates on loans floated during and after the war were not scattered over the postwar years in an even way; for instance, in 1925, the indebtedness to be paid off was approximately 22 billion francs, a sum which could not be met from normal resources.

As the obligations of the government increased in this manner, and its control over the financial situation diminished, the way was opened for speculation, which was to continue the depreciation begun in 1919. The first collapse, due to the technical situation of the exchange markets,[2] was followed by a growing distrust of the French currency. This speculative influence must be distinguished from the concentrated speculative drives which were later to dominate, for short periods, the movement of foreign capital and dictate the values of European currencies. These more impelling forces were not active in France until late 1922,[3] and were not generally recognized until the deliberate bear movement against the franc threatened it with complete collapse in 1924.[4] The force of speculation was to be the dominant one, once depreciation had become severe. It is well before considering this powerful influence, to discuss the more concrete elements which are usually given as the determinants of monetary value.

[1] See *infra*, Chapter VI, for complete debt statement.
[2] See *infra*, Chapter IV.   [3] See *infra*, Chapter V.
[4] See *infra*, Chapter V.

The main economic factors which influence the value of a monetary unit are the basis for three related bodies of theory; these are, first, the quantity of money in circulation; second, the relative purchasing powers of various monetary units; and third, the movements of commerce and credit between countries. These three groups are closely interrelated but they are given different importance in different monetary theories. They are called *quantitative* factors, by Professor Aftalion;[1] the *qualitative factors,* on the other hand, are the psychological influences. We shall consider, in turn, the quantity theory, the purchasing power parities doctrine, and the balance of trade theory. The failure of these theories to explain the French case of depreciation during this short and troubled period could not have been anticipated before the fact. It is not so much the validity of the general contentions which has been called to question as it is their applicability to particular situations. The two main tests for any economic theory are, first, usefulness as a basis for prophecy—and in this respect all three theories are woefully inadequate—and second, as a basis for constructive policy—and here they prove positively misleading in certain instances. The reason for this inapplicability must be sought not in the logical inaccuracy of the doctrines but in the extensive qualifications which are necessary to make them applicable to severe depreciation.

QUANTITY THEORY DOES NOT EXPLAIN DEPRECIATION OF FRANC

Let us consider first the quantity theory. In its simplest form it states a general truth as to the direct relation of the price level to the means of payment,[2] and changes in

[1] Albert Aftalion, *Monnaie, prix et change* (Paris, 1927), p. 208.

[2] See any standard economic text for an explanation of the quantity theory. J. M. Keynes gives an interesting discussion of recent modifications in his *Monetary Reform* (New York, 1924), pp. 81–95.

the level of prices over long periods have been in accordance with this theory, prices rising as money has increased. The emphasis of the theory was placed, at the beginning, on the amount of metallic money, then on credit as of equal or nearly equal importance as money, and later on the influence of the velocity of the turnover of the means of payment. These amplifications of the quantity theory came as the result of the natural desire to make it fit the complex business world of today. In adding the various complicating elements, however, the theory was pressed beyond its original claim. It was used as an explanation for things which it could not rightly explain, that is, as the sole or main explanation of price changes.

Definite expression of this change in the development of the quantity theory is found in the changing forms of the equation of exchange and other formulations. In its first form it was simply stated as:

$$M \text{ (money)} = P \text{ (prices)} \times T \text{ (goods exchanged)}$$

It was then elaborated to such forms as Fisher's: [1]

$$MV + M'V' = PT$$

in which M' stands for credit and V and V' for the velocity of circulation of money and credit, and which is intended to express more accurately and completely the quantity theory relationship; but in increasing its scope, the theory loses significance. Let us consider this in the light of the French case. The amount of money and credit increased enormously during and after the war. At certain periods, notably during the war, the price level rose in direct proportion to these increases; but at other times, such as in 1921, the price level was considerably higher or notably lower than

[1] It is not necessary to discuss other formulations such as those of Keynes, Hawtrey, Marshall and others, since the point here raised is not as to the validity of such theories but the usefulness of applying a simple quantity theory to the French case.

the money and credit situation would have justified. This can be seen by a comparison of the curves on Chart No. I. This difference is accounted for, according to the theory, by changes in the velocity of circulation of money and credit, and if the formula holds good the velocity of circulation in France must have changed just enough to explain this discrepancy.

The net result of this reasoning is that we can assume that prices in France varied with money when the velocity of circulation remained constant. Since, however, the velocity of circulation changed very markedly and in an unpredictable way in cases of severe depreciation, one could not anticipate the future value of money from the amount in circulation, nor control its value by controlling the amount of money or credit. In other words, the quantity theory so modified fails in our case to meet either of the two tests of a valid theory. Although it was interesting to study the changing relationships of M, M', and V in France, it could be done with profit only after the event. Probably the most striking examples of the divergence of the price level and exchanges from the values dictated by currency and credit occur in 1921, 1924, and 1925,[1] because of the exchange crises in those years and in spite of fairly steady means of payment.

Changes in the velocity of circulation at these times offset the discrepancy, and these changes were dictated by extra-economic influences, forces in the main psychological, a reflection of changing states of public confidence. In fact, politics played a larger part than did paper notes. Those who controlled the issue of francs were helpless until those who controlled the Chamber of Deputies adopted a reasonable, constructive policy. It must be remembered that the velocity of circulation has not been neglected by economists. Mill saw that it was the use of money, rather than its existence, which was significant. Hawtrey has carried

[1] See *infra*, Chapter V.

this emphasis farther,[1] and Keynes has stressed this factor in his analysis of recent currency problems.[2] It is the change in velocity of circulation which makes possible the cumulative decline of money, such as occurred in Germany, Russia, and other countries, when the loss in value outran the ability of the printing press to keep pace. It is the unknown and uncontrollable factor and, in case of extreme depreciation, the most important element; a quantity theory which depends on this factor, velocity, cannot serve as a satisfactory explanation of the causes of extreme depreciation.

It is true that, under certain conditions, in France the effort to decrease the circulation strengthened the value of money; it is even more true that at times the threat of large and continued inflationary issues of money led to rapid depreciation. But the reason for this state of affairs lay not so much in the mechanical influence of the money on the price level as on the evidence it gave of the weak position of the French government, and its inability to meet its need by taxation, to honor its debts, and to conduct its affairs in a sane way. This is seen, for instance, in the varying influence of the deflation attempted in pursuance of the 1920 convention. This had, for a time, a slight influence in steadying the franc, but when it was discovered that other obligations more dangerous than paper notes had piled up for the government in the form of debts, the value of money fell precipitately before there was any notable increase in the circulation. The cause of this situation was only indirectly the quantity of money, and directly the public estimate of the government financial policy.[3] The limitations of the quantity theory as an

[1] R. G. Hawtrey, *Currency and Credit* (London, 1923), pp. 41-45.

[2] J. M. Keynes, *op. cit.*, pp. 51-52. See especially note 1, p. 51.

[3] See *infra*, Chapter VI. Of course, all the adverse aspects of government finance pointed to the possibility of further inflation, but they were not considered exclusively or mainly in this light; possible note issues were discounted, so were tax increases and other economic difficulties.

explanation of the depreciation of the franc are indeed
many. It is obviously too mechanical a theory to express
the shifting complex of economic and psychological relationships which governed short-run value in France. It became apparent that the value of money must be influenced,
first through moral channels, and then, in the second instance, through economic channels.

PURCHASING POWER DOCTRINE ADDS LITTLE

The purchasing power parities doctrine was not useful
in explaining the value of the depreciated franc. This doctrine, a natural extension of the quantity theory, emphasizes the significance of the relative price levels of different
countries. It purports to establish a normal par for inconvertible money on the foreign exchanges; that is, it states
that the exchange rate tends to vary so that a unit of currency has the same purchasing power at home and abroad,
or that, at any rate, the variations of purchasing power of
money in different countries will be kept in alignment. The
main difficulties fall into two groups. The first objections
to the theory are largely technical. They are based on the
impossibility of securing perfect measures of the level of
prices [1] and the difficulty of averaging all possible two-
country relationships so that the various pars will be in
harmony with each other. The second type of objections is
more serious. It strikes at the very root of the theory, for
it denies that prices are the cause and exchange rates the
effect. In fact, it asserts that causality for short times runs
more often from the exchange rates to the price level than
it does in the opposite direction.

It will be recalled that suggestions of the purchasing
power parities doctrine are found in the writings of the
classical economists. But it was Professor Gustav Cassel
who first gave this idea prominence and expressed it in a

[1] See *infra,* Chapter VII.

definite and striking way. Since then, his formulation has been accepted in one of its various forms by such eminent economists as Mr. J. M. Keynes and Professor T. E. Gregory, and has been used to bolster up proposals for inflation or deflation in various countries. Certainly it helps to define the issue in the consideration of monetary policy, and it has brought clearly into the foreground the varying alternative possibilities, control of the exchanges, control of the price level, or the attempt to condition both through more general influences. This difference of emphasis is illustrated by the views, on the one hand, of Keynes, an advocate of the doctrine, who said that the control of the internal price level was the key to the exchange situation, and on the other hand, by Hawtrey, who advised the attempt to control the exchange directly. The theory may best be expressed in the words of Cassel.

When two currencies have undergone inflation, the normal rate of exchange will be equal to the old rate multiplied by the quotient of the degree of inflation in the one country and in the other.[1]

Keynes restates the same theory more briefly.

This ratio between the respective home purchasing powers of the two currencies is designated their "purchasing power parity."[2]

The "degree of inflation" spoken of in Cassel's statement and the "home purchasing powers of the two currencies" referred to in Keynes' explanation are to be estimated by the wholesale price indices in the respective countries. On the basis of purchasing powers, for instance, the par of the franc and the dollar in January, 1919, would have been 11.03 cents per franc, whereas the actual value was 18.35 cents per franc.[3]

---

[1] Gustav Cassel, *Money and Foreign Exchange After 1914* (New York, 1923), p. 140.　　[2] J. M. Keynes, *op. cit.*, p. 97.

[3] U. S. Senate *Foreign Currency and Exchange Investigation*, p. 478. The result was obtained by dividing 199, the wholesale index for the United

Unit: francs per dollar

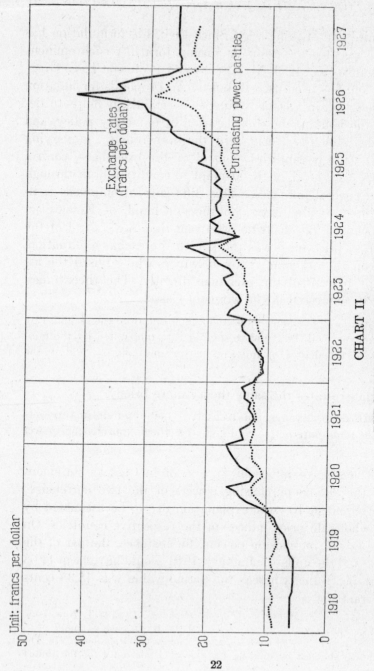

CHART II

PURCHASING POWER PARITIES

FRANCS AND DOLLARS [1]

[1] See appendix for exchange rates, wholesale prices, and purchasing power parities.

22

The practical difficulties in applying such a theory are indeed great.[1] The index number of wholesale prices has been the usual basis on which to reckon this par, but no one index number can be complete. Moreover, there is no clear reason why wholesale prices should be preferred to retail prices. There is, on the contrary, some argument in favor of choosing the retail index number for the par between France and the United States. For if the franc was undervalued in New York, as it was during most of the postwar period, the practical result would be that with dollars one could secure more goods of a given kind by buying francs and spending the francs for goods than one could obtain by spending those dollars in America. As long as this was true, and other things being equal, the undervaluation of the French money would lead to the increased demand for francs and would tend to swing the franc's value upwards. If most foreign exchange purchases were made with a view to the commodity markets, it is probable that some such reaction would usually take place, and if one is mainly interested in France, there is some reason for the preference of the retail index instead of the wholesale index because American importers buy large quantities of finished goods from France and practically no raw or semi-finished products, and these latter count most heavily in the wholesale index. There is room for some doubt on this point and the difference in the result would be considerable, since there is frequently a wide gap between wholesale and retail prices, and between raw and finished goods.[2]

States, by 348, the French wholesale index. This gives a quotient of .571, which is multiplied by the par of exchange, 19.29 cents per franc, a purchasing power par of 11.03 cents. (Our result differs slightly from that here given.) The purchasing power parity was therefore sixty per cent of 18.35 cents the actual rate of exchange, and the franc was overvalued in the United States. When pegging ceased, the relationship changed.

[1] T. E. Gregory, *Foreign Exchange* (Oxford, 1925), pp. 88-90.

[2] *Bulletin de la statistique générale de la France* (October-December, 1927), p. 7. See curve 3 based on retail prices, chart VIII.

It is not important for us to determine here just what index number is best suited for such a purpose, but it is well to note the problem. To take a random comparison of the two indices, one might calculate two different parities for January, 1924, a date just previous to the rapid speculative decline of that year. On the basis of wholesale indices, the parity indicated as normal for the franc and the dollar would be 5.88 cents per franc,[1] while on the basis of retail indices, the par indicated is 3.98 cents per franc.[2] Since the actual par was 4.67 cents per franc, it will be seen that the parity derived from the retail indices is considerably nearer the actual par than that derived from the wholesale indices. This might not always be the case, but the wide divergence of purchasing power parities from actual parities suggests that some further adjustment must be made in the application of the theory. There is so much ground for difference of opinion, and the results reached on slightly different assumptions vary so widely, that there is no sure ground for prophecy and policy in the purchasing power parity theory until statistical science applied to economic data has been farther developed.

There is also the added difficulty of reaching a harmonious adjustment between the parities derived for different countries. It is obvious that the franc may be undervalued in New York and overvalued in Germany. For instance, when the relative price levels continued to give France a slight advantage in exporting to the United States in 1927, the still lower prices in some of the neighboring countries put France in a disadvantageous position in trade with them. At this time the exchange values of the currencies placed the franc at about the same level in New York, Berlin, Rome, and other centers. Thus any practical attempt

[1] U. S. Senate, *Foreign Currency and Exchange Investigation*, p. 478.
[2] *Monthly Labor Review*, U. S. Dept. of Labor, vol. xxv, no. 1, July, 1927, p. 173. This result is obtained by dividing the United States index of retail prices, 146, by the French index, 366, both indices on a 1914 basis.

to adjust the franc with prices in New York would have led to a maladjustment with some other country.

Purchasing power parities theory is usually too complex to be a basis for political action, and too ambiguous to guide the practical financier. Even if statistical methods should progress to a point where the theory may be of use, there would still be serious limits to the validity of the concept. These rest on the assumption of a causal influence running quickly from prices to exchange rates. It is clear in the French case that the divergence of actual foreign exchange rates from price ratios has been greater than the mere imperfections of statistical method would account for. It is true that in the case of England, where the pound sterling never lost more than about a third of its value, purchasing power parities corresponded to exchange rates much more closely than in the case of France.[1] Where depreciation is more marked the divergence is apt to be greater. In France it was more than ten per cent during most of the period under consideration. Here causality ran distinctly from exchange rates to prices. In the first place, during the war years pegging operations prevented the decline of the franc and made the theory inapplicable. It is important to remember that exchange rates can be controlled much more successfully than price levels, since the market for exchange transactions is narrower and the dealings are in the hands of professionals. It is, therefore, possible for long periods to keep the exchange quotation considerably above or below what would be considered normal on the basis of price relations. Then in the second place, the franc fell rapidly after it was unpegged in 1919, and was undervalued in New York, so that it was worth one or two cents less than its purchasing power would have justified. This would have led normally to an increase of exports from France and a

[1] U. S. Senate, *Foreign Currency and Exchange Investigation*, p. 457. See also chart on p. 293. J. W. Angell, *The Theory of International Prices* (Cambridge, Mass., 1926), pp. 430, 431.

decline in imports, raising the franc and lowering the dollar until an equilibrium was reached; but there were several serious disturbing factors. One of these was the imperative need of France for imports and another the relative inelasticity of her exports. This particular situation points to a second important limitation of the theory; it can be applied only to situations in which changes in foreign commerce are possible on a scale sufficient to right the balance once it has been disturbed. This is not possible in the case of serious upsets to the exchanges and price levels; the mechanism of foreign commerce is not sufficiently elastic. In the third place, when in later years France, like some other countries, went through a period of severe depreciation, the important factor both from a quantitative and from a psychological point of view is the movement of capital. In fact, the export or import of capital, in the form of deposit credits, of international securities, or of actual cash, assumes such large proportions when a country is threatened with bankruptcy that the relative importance of the flow of trade governed by commodity price levels is very slight. It is true that the price of securities and some of the other factors which govern the movements of capital might be included in price indices as well as commodities. Such is, however, neither the intention nor the practice of those who uphold the theory. Moreover, a price index which included everything would be meaningless.[1] We must conclude, then, that important economic and political changes first showed in the foreign exchange quotations; they gained magnitude as large sales were made by the outsider who followed "the men who knew." Thus there were wholesale shiftings of balances from one financial center to another and, when these short-time changes led to new levels for exchange and security values, the effects tended to be carried over to the commodity markets. If the cost of the dollar went up, the cost of imports rose, the price of all

[1] See *infra*, Chapter VII.

finished products, which included certain raw materials, rose likewise, and the general level of prices became higher. There was then a slight tendency to cut down the volume of imports and use substitutes, so that the demand for dollars for commercial purposes diminished, and a lesser influence worked towards an upward movement of the franc; but these favorable commercial influences would be much weaker than the unfavorable speculative influences if there were real distrust of the franc. Thus, the invisible items far outweighed the visible ones.

BALANCE OF TRADE HAD LITTLE INFLUENCE ON THE FRANC

This last objection to the purchasing power parities doctrine is the reason why one must turn from the theories of exchange values based on trade movements to speculation theories which rest on intangible but very real forces. It will be noted by the reader that there is no detailed study of the French balance of trade given in this history of French depreciation. This may seem to be a radical departure from the usual analysis of monetary problems. Prewar studies of exchange problems would very naturally have included a careful study of the inward and outward movements of trade, and would have related exchange fluctuations to some particular change in commerce or some concrete invisible item; but the postwar situation requires different treatment. It would undoubtedly be interesting to include a detailed study of the balance of trade with other material bearing on the subject of money value, but the long labor involved in such a task would not be warranted in the present case because the normal items in the balance of accounts of France sank to relative unimportance. Moreover, material is lacking for an adequate quantitative statement. There are a number of complicating factors which cast doubt on many of the figures available. One of these is the rapid change of habits in commerce, and of prices,

which makes those items which are based mainly on estimates, such as freight charges and immigrant remittances,
extremely hard to determine. Another is that the method
of valuing French commerce has been changed by law, so
that year to year comparisons are difficult. Then again, the
fluctuations of prices have made deception in valuation on
the part of importers and exporters very easy. But more important than these difficulties is the fact that capital movements far outweighed commerce in value. In order to justify
this omission of a detailed discussion of commerce it is
well to look at some of the existing estimates of the French
balance of trade and compare their results with what
is known of the speculative movements of balances and with
exchange fluctuations.

Let us compare the three most important items in the
balance of payments: capital items, tourist expenditures,
and commodity trade. Figures for the commodity balance
of trade are easily available and fairly accurate; those for
the years 1913 through 1926 are given below.

A study of this table and chart indicates that, with
the exception of the war years, the difference between the
exports and the imports was not very great. Before the war
the balance had been unfavorable.[1] During the war, of
course, the excess of imports over exports was very large,
but this "unfavorable" trade situation was not permitted
to affect the exchanges directly. The difference was met by
loans, and the franc pegged, as has been explained above.
To be sure, the unbalanced war-time trade influenced the
exchanges later through the pressure of capital items, such

---

[1] Henry Bérenger, "L'Accord franco-américain sur les dettes de guerre,"
note communiquée le 30 avril, 1926, par la présidence du conseil sur le
règlement de la dette française envers les Etats-Unis, *L'Europe nouvelle*,
9th year, no. 429 (May 8, 1926), p. 660. "Avant la guerre, le commerce
extérieur de la France se soldait par un léger déficit, ses exportations
s'élevant a 80-85% de ses importations . . . ce défecit était plus que com-
pensé par l'excédent des 'exportations invisibles'." See also *l'Annuaire
statistique,* 1922, p. 92.

TABLE I

FRENCH COMMODITY TRADE[1]

1913–1926

(In millions of francs)

	Imports	Exports	Excess of Imports over Exports	Excess of Exports over Imports
1913............	8,421	6,880	1,541	.....
1914............	6,402	4,869	1,533	.....
1915............	11,036	3,937	7,099	.....
1916............	20,640	6,215	14,425	.....
1917............	27,554	6,013	21,541	.....
1918............	22,306	4,723	17,583	.....
1919............	35,799	11,800	23,919	.....
1920............	49,905	26,895	23,010	.....
1921............	22,068	19,773	2,295	.....
1922............	23,930	21,379	2,551	.....
1923............	32,689	30,433	2,256	.....
1924............	40,132	41,454	.....	1,322
1925............	44,095	45,755	.....	1,660
1926............	59,515	59,535	.....	20
1927............	52,853	55,228	.....	2,375

as unfunded foreign credits and very large government debts.

It is evident that the commodity balance alone had a slightly depressing immediate influence on the franc. The favorable balances from 1924 to 1927 cannot be considered normal; it is possible that they represent a retarded response to the bonus on exports, but it should be noted that in 1927, the year when this premium on exports had disappeared, the favorable excess was greatest. However this may be, the excess of imports over exports is usually more than offset by the expenditures of tourists in France. This item, which has righted the balance and permitted France to build up her foreign investments to a considerable figure, cannot be measured accurately. Bérenger estimates the

[1] Henry Bérenger, *op. cit.*, p. 660. This gives the years 1913 through 1924. *Statistique mensuelle du commerce extérieur de la France* (1926), no. 12, p. 8, and (1927), p. 7. These give the years 1925, 1926, 1927. Adjustment should be made for commerce with the colonies. Bérenger gives material for this in his report, p. 662. The difference is not very large.

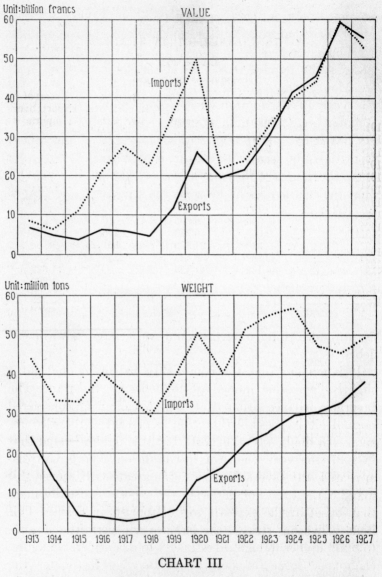

CHART III

FOREIGN COMMERCE—WEIGHT AND VALUE, 1913-1927[1]

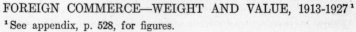

[1] See appendix, p. 528, for figures.

amount spent in 1924 as 3,125 million francs,[1] a figure
lower than that given by Pierre Meynial [2] and some others
who have studied the matter. It is not necessary to compare all the important studies of the subject; those made
by Moulton and Lewis, and by Meynial will suffice. For
the year 1924, Moulton gives 5,000 million francs [3] and
Meynial gives 4,800 million francs. Since each of these writers has made a searching critical appraisal of the other's
work the approximate agreement is reassuring. Let us take,
then, the figures of Meynial as correct, though it is possible
that the real figures lie between his statement and that of
M. Bérenger.

TABLE II

AMOUNTS SPENT BY TOURISTS IN FRANCE

(In millions of francs)

	Meynial [4]	Bérenger [5]
1913	600	1,325
1920	2,220	....
1921	2,800	....
1922	3,000	1,727
1923	4,000	2,584
1924	4,800	3,125
1925	9,000	....
1926	13,000	....

The figure for 1926 might seem at first glance to be excessive, but it must be remembered that the exchange situation was more than usually abnormal then,[6] and that large
numbers of tourists rushed to Paris to spend money lavishly
for goods and services when the franc fell to two cents.

The importance of the tourist trade as a balancing item

[1] Henry Bérenger, *L'Europe nouvelle, loc. cit.*, pp. 663, 664.

[2] Pierre Meynial, *Revue d'économie politique* (January-February, 1925),
p. 19.

[3] Moulton and Lewis, *The French Debt Problem* (New York, 1925),
p. 370.

[4] Pierre Meynial, *Revue d'économie politique* (March-April, 1927), p.
279.

[5] Henry Bérenger, *L'Europe nouvelle, loc. cit.*, pp. 663, 664.

[6] See *infra,* Chapters V and VIII.

is clear; it overshadows all the other items except capital. The relative unimportance of ocean freight receipts, for instance, is evident when one considers estimates of about 2,000 million francs, or only about twenty per cent of the 1926 tourist receipts; [1] then again, receipts from transit commerce through France are placed at only about 100 million francs. The movements of the precious metals were very small after the war. There is no other item to challenge the importance of tourist expenditures except the dominant group of capital and credit items.

Capital Items the Most Important

Under normal monetary conditions the movements of capital between countries cannot be measured accurately. They are doubly hard to determine when strong speculative influences are at work. Some of the elements can, of course, be estimated with a reasonable degree of accuracy, but most are purely conjectural. One of the elements included under capital movements, the remittances of laborers into or out of France, can be judged approximately from the number of nationals who reside abroad and the number of foreigners in France. It is possible to make reasonable assumptions as to how much wage earners can afford to send, and a knowledge of the average size of postal drafts and of other forms of remittances helps check such an estimate. Bérenger places this on the debit side of the account to the extent of 1,170 million francs in 1924. [2] The other capital items are not so easy to estimate. For instance, it is even difficult to distinguish capital from interest in this case, since interest reinvested is capital, and bank balances may be either. It is possible, it is true, to note large repayments on

[1] Henry Bérenger, *L'Europe nouvelle, loc. cit.,* p. 663.
[2] Henry Bérenger, *L'Europe nouvelle, loc. cit.,* p. 666. His figure for 1923, 384, agrees approximately with Meynial's figure. Moulton seems to accept Meynial's estimate. See *The French Debt Problem,* p. 359.

maturing debts and to list the more important new loans. It is utterly impossible, on the other hand, to know how many American securities are owned in France or what balances in London or Amsterdam are at the disposal of French financiers. In fact, there are many reasons for concealing these figures and no sure way of finding them out. It is probable that the laws prohibiting the export of capital have made it harder to get exact information on this point, in the case of France, than it would otherwise have been; [1] even without such laws, the effort to evade taxation would lead to concealment.[2] There were, moreover, ever-increasing ways of acquiring foreign credits of various sorts —to methods growing out of normal trade or security transactions were added many fictitious transactions. As speculation increased capital movements increased, but the total cannot be determined. There are two clear indications that they were large enough to outweigh all other influences. These are, first, the striking effect of capital movements on the exchange rate of the franc, and second, the rapid increase of *divers*,[3] or miscellaneous assets, in the Bank of France statement for 1927, when the bank began to take over foreign capital which Frenchmen were selling.

It is obvious that the decline of the franc was an evidence of the unbalanced condition of French capital dealings with the outside world. From one point of view, of course, the payments between one country and all other countries must be in balance, since all debts must have their counterpart in credits. It is current usage, however, to list the

[1] See *infra*, Chapter VI. See also J. Laurès, *Le Problème des changes* (Paris, 1926), pp. 91-123.

[2] Edgar Allix and Marcel Lecerclé, *L'Impôt sur le revenue* (Paris, 1926), p. 306. The simple tax, without adding the *décimes* or taxes on sales or inheritance, amounted to eighteen per cent of the interest on foreign investments. A further tax was imposed on the exchange profit due to the conversion of the interest into francs.

[3] In the statement of January 12, 1928, this item stood at more than 27 billion francs. *The New York Times* (January 13, 1928). See *infra*, Chapter VI.

concrete items in the balance of payments first and then to proceed gradually to the items which are less calculable. In the course of this consideration there is, then, one form of credit which stands out clearly as the balancing item.[1] This is the shifting mass of floating credits, short-time loans, book credits, and bank balances granted to the trader or financier. Any difficulty in obtaining these credits is registered either in money rates on loans, or to a much greater extent in the exchange rates—for credits are granted to the trader by those anxious for his trade only if interest rates are good or foreign currency undervalued on the exchanges. This increased demand for short-time credits leads, thus, to stiffer terms and a higher premium on gold currencies expressed in the exchange rate.

After a period of temporary financial calm, on the other hand, considerable shifts in international indebtedness can take place without causing marked variations in interest or in the exchange rates.[2] It is not possible to discover the quantitative relationship between exchange rates and capital movements, for the effects depend partly on attitudes and interpretations. Compare, for instance, the situations in 1924 and in 1925, times when causes and mechanisms differed markedly. It is probable that more capital left France in the downward plunge of the franc during the speculative drive in the early part of 1924 than returned in its recovery towards the end of March. This assumption is borne out by the ease and rapidity with which the reserve fund derived from the Morgan loan of 100 million dollars was reconstituted, that is, the net government outlay was

---

[1] Gold has been considered the balancing item in many discussions of foreign exchange values. It seems more accurate at the present time to give short-term credits this rôle. In one sense any item may be considered as balancing. J. M. Keynes, "Balance of British Trade, 1925-27," *Economic Journal* (December, 1927), vol. xxxvii, no. 148), p. 565. Keynes says liquid balances are used as settlement instead of gold.

[2] See *infra,* Chapter X, for conditions in 1927.

small in amount.[1] It would be possible for pressure on the exchanges to have more influence in one case than in the other, for smaller funds backed by government determination and coördinated financial effort would tend to influence public opinion more than the efforts of a loose combination of financial adventurers. Demand is never purely quantitative. The terms on which balances would be shifted were more favorable to the franc in one case than in the other. In the fall of 1925, on the other hand, there is no clear evidence of large capital movements out of France. Neither the money markets, banking, nor trade situation showed any great changes. It seems likely that the movement of capital, which had been considerable since 1923, continued as distrust grew, but it was not until the end of the year that the rapid decline of investments in *bons de la défense nationale* indicates that the sums being transferred were large.[2]

After the spring of 1926, it became easier to arrive at an estimate of the value of the net capital movement in or out of France.[3] It is evident that in July, 1926, the actual volume of credits must have run into billions of francs, when the millions of dollars remaining in the so-called Morgan loan were thrown on the market without checking the tide moving against the franc.[4] There was a 100 per cent rise in the foreign exchanges despite the use of perhaps a

[1] *Revue d'économie politique* (March-April, 1925), p. 276. There seems no reason to doubt this statement. See *infra*, Chapter V.

[2] See *infra*, Chapter V.

[3] It must be realized that the expression *capital export* can not represent directly an outflow of capital. That is, the exchange of deposits in France for deposits in London means actually that the deposits in France are the same in amount but the title to them is transferred. The crux of the matter lies in whether the Frenchman is more eager for pounds than the Englishman is for francs. If this is the case, the *gold value* of franc deposits shrinks, and we speak of an export of capital from France. It would be just as accurate, however, to say that there had been an import of pounds into France.

[4] See *infra*, Chapter V.

billion francs in the support of the franc.[1] After the crisis
was passed the Poincaré ministry brought confidence,
which made possible the pegging of the franc. The permission granted the Bank of France to issue new paper notes
against foreign exchange made it easy for the Bank to buy
almost all the foreign credits offered, at the prevailing rate
of exchange.[2] The sums thus taken over by the Bank were
indicated by the growth of the item *divers* among the assets.[3] Since it amounted to 3 billion on August 5, 1926, and
nearly 20 billion francs more in August, 1927, 20 billion
francs was a major part of the capital brought back to
France. It must be considered only a part, for the treasury also accumulated several billion francs, and private
speculators and French companies probably took considerably more. The total may have been as high as 35 or 40
billion francs, and was certainly well over 25 billions.

Such estimates, however unsatisfactory, serve as warn-
ings against dogmatic statements, and as evidence of the
overwhelming importance of capital movements. By all the
indications available, the shift of short-time credits has
been the decisive factor in every exchange crisis. The sharp
fluctuations of exchange rates, when commerce, travel, shipping, and investment conditions remained fairly constant,
the large volume of money known to have been moved from
one centre to another, all bear out this conclusion. If the
movement of capital can rise above 25 billion francs a year,
it is obvious that changes in commodity trade are of rela-

[1] *Revue de science et de législation financières* (October-December,
1926), vol. xxiv, no. 4, p. 674. In one single day the treasury funds diminished by more than 100 million francs. This was due in large measure to the
withdrawal of funds from *bons de la défense* to buy foreign exchange. The
sums spent by the government in support of the franc previous to this date
are not known. They probably amounted to about 1,500 million francs,
since that was the part of the Morgan loan reputed to be in the hands of
the government in the spring of 1926.

[2] See *infra*, Chapter VI.

[3] Pierre Bayart, *La stabilisation française, Revue des sciences économiques*, no. 3 (April, 1917), p. 7, note 1.

tively little influence in the *short-run*. Commerce is of necessity less elastic than capital, except perhaps in emergencies such as war. The corollary is, if capital is the determinant and if concrete factors are almost negligible, then confidence and speculation, rather than commerce and prices, must determine the fate of any monetary unit.

SPECULATION THE DOMINATING FACTOR

We must come, then, quite definitely to speculation as an explanation of *short-time* depreciation; a theory not new, but differing in emphasis from former interpretations. One of the first clear statements of the power of speculation was made by Professor Allyn A. Young, in his article on "War Debts, External and Internal," where he explains the relation of Germany's burdens to the collapse of the mark. His further comment is:

I have reviewed these matters again in order to give point to the emphasis I shall put upon what I believe to be the indispensable key to an understanding of the vagaries of the depreciated currencies of Europe. I refer to the dominating part played by speculation.[1]

He explains why and how "inflation has been the result rather than the cause of depreciation," an idea which was not generally understood at that time.

The same emphasis on speculation is evident in de Bordes' study of the Austrian crown. He says in his conclusions that the expectation of decline caused the decline.

The extraordinary depreciation of the Austrian crown was at bottom a psychological development. There was a total lack of confidence. In view of the situation of Austrian State finances it was generally expected that the crown would continue to plunge farther and farther down. This was the cause of the flight from the crown.[2]

[1] A. A. Young, *Economic Problems New and Old* (Boston, 1927), p. 30. First printed in *Foreign Affairs*, vol. ii, no. 3 (March, 1924).

[2] J. van Walré de Bordes, *The Austrian Crown* (London, 1924), p. 197.

Katzenellenbaum, writing at a somewhat later date on the Russian currency gives great importance to confidence though he differs in applying it only to the external value of money.[1]

Nogaro, in discussing various aspects of depreciation in France, says repeatedly that speculation is the powerful link connecting the various forces bearing on the exchanges.[2] Then again, Aftalion says that the theory of the exchange rates, like that of value and price, must rest on an analysis of complex and changing psychological forces.[3]

Such interpretations as these have been suggested in the discussions of a hundred years of monetary studies, but the present emphasis and application are to a considerable extent different. They embody an attempt to pass over inflation as the prime cause and to stress the more general financial and economic conditions, and so they lead inevitably to new lines of policy and action. This shift in emphasis must be attributed in part to the fact that recent cases of depreciation have been more severe and the causes behind them different from those hitherto studied. The financial chaos has been more widespread; the uncertainty for the future of Russia, Germany, Italy, France, and other countries has led to quick changes in speculative positions as to the future of monetary units. Monetary theory can hardly fail to take slightly new lines in the light of such events.

The development of thought on the theory of the exchange is hampered, however, by limited and ambiguous phraseology. The citations given above indicate the terms which are most generally current. There is objection to each of them on the grounds of vagueness. For instance, *speculation* is the best word to indicate the influences which

[1] S. S. Katzenellenbaum, *Russian Currency and Banking, 1914-1924* (London, 1925), p. 41.

[2] Bertrand Nogaro, *La Monnaie et les phénomènes monétaires contemporaines* (Paris, 1924), pp. 89, 109, 192-195.

[3] Albert Aftalion, *op. cit.*, pp. 345-347.

determine short-run exchange value but there is some uncertainty as to the meaning of this word. It has been used
frequently in a narrow sense to indicate deliberate drives
against a currency for the sake of making gains out of a
sudden rise or fall in its value, as, for example, in January,
1924.[1] If *speculation* is used only in this way, it cannot
well describe the general forces at work. Professor Angell
indicates this difficulty and substitutes the word *anticipation* in his exposition,[2] but this word has not as yet gained
any currency and has not connotations which adapt it readily to economic uses.

Even the term *psychological* cannot be used without
giving false suggestions. It has served of late years to cover
up an immense amount of vague conjecture and ignorance, and must therefore be used sparingly in a scientific
discussion. Aftalion's distinction between *qualitative* or
psychological factors and *quantitative* factors is very useful
but does not do away with our need for a more specific
word. Both Nogaro and Aftalion use the word *prévisions* to
indicate general forecasts as to the future value of money.
This word calls to mind the original sense of *speculation,*
and yet it remains free of some of the objections which now
attach to the latter term. It is possible that *prévision* might
be anglicized and so might serve as a tool in monetary ex-
positions. At the present time, however, *confidence* comes
closest to expressing the nature of the forces behind exchange values and here again, one must note the vagueness as to *what* inspires confidence. In former times it was
mainly an expectation of a return to full gold value for
paper money; now it is more confidence in the general economic and financial situation.[3] There is one objection to
the term, but it does not seem to be serious: it is that *con-*

[1] See *infra,* Chapter V.

[2] J. W. Angell, *The Theory of International Prices* (Cambridge, Mass.,
1926), p. 195.

[3] Professor Schumpeter has indicated to the writer the importance of
finding the object of confidence.

fidence implies active support and not a state of mind which may be unfavorable as well as favorable. It is possible, however, to think of confidence as a mental attitude which can sink almost to zero; whereas, if money circulates at all, some confidence must exist. Certainly the value of a monetary unit is related to the state of confidence; and in the case of the severe depreciation of the franc confidence has been the main short-time determinant of value. Speculation, in the widest sense of the term, has pushed the franc up and down until it has finally come to rest at 3.90 cents per franc.

It is not possible here to solve problems of terminology, but it is necessary to note these limitations. The worst confusion can be avoided if one keep in mind the wider interpretations of the words used. The study of the franc indicates that its depreciation varied with changing opinions, once inconvertibility had opened the gate to uncertainty and the rapid decline had done away with the traditional limits of fluctuation. It was necessary to speculate; for any transaction in goods or in foreign currencies involved estimation as to the future relation of the franc to these things. Speculation, then, takes on a new importance and affects different people as money enters the phase of severe depreciation.

This new situation, which often follows inconvertibility, has sometimes been overlooked. Nogaro is emphatic in stating the marked change with the abandonment of the gold standard. He says:

> The exchanges, once they have left the normal limits set by the ability to change the national money into exportable money without loss, are not kept within any limits whatsoever.[1]

Aftalion says much the same thing.[2] Angell, on the other hand, takes a slightly different attitude when he says that "it is not the fact of inconvertibility but . . . instability it-

---

[1] Bertrand Nogaro, *op. cit.*, p. 206.   [2] Albert Aftalion, *op. cit.*, p. 288.

self that gives the exchanges their peculiar significance." [1]
He goes on to point out that there are instances of inconvertibility without depreciation but the distinction is not
of very great importance, perhaps.[2] It is true that speculation does not become of great importance until after depreciation has passed beyond the limits of variation set
normally by the gold standard; but it is none the less'
true that those who are well versed in financial affairs increase their speculative transactions whenever the legal and
practical certainty of free exchange for gold is done away
with. Even though they speculate on the speedy return of
the gold standard, there is a new influence at work in their
minds, and one which introduces potential instability even
before that instability is registered in actual depreciation.

The dominating influence of confidence in the general
financial situation is, then, the outstanding lesson learned
from a study of the franc. It has been at one and the same
time the cause and the expression of most other influences.
It has made possible prolonged overvaluation of the franc
interrupted by shorter periods of undervaluation and finally
brought the franc to a value in harmony with the number
of notes in circulation, the condition of foreign trade, and
the size of the budget burden.[3]

A different interpretation and emphasis is made by
Professor T. E. Gregory in his clear discussion of foreign
exchange problems. He was arguing against the very patent
evil of inflation, not sufficiently understood at the time of
writing (1921). In stressing this factor he assigns a limited
influence to speculation, saying that speculation has been
used too frequently as an explanation of depreciation. He
continues:

[1] J. W. Angell, *op. cit.*, p. 424.
[2] It is interesting to note that the Turkish pound which is strictly fiat
money and not definitely limited as to numbers in circulation has been relatively stable through 1926 and 1927 when many other monetary units were
fluctuating wildly.
[3] See *infra*, Chapter X.

But it is quite easy to stop the evil of speculation in foreign exchange. All that is required is to cease the creation of the instrument of speculation. Until this is done, to prevent the export of these speculative instruments is like altering the thermometer because it registers too much warmth. . . .[1]

This statement is true and useful when applied to certain situations; frequently inflation must be stopped in order to calm speculation. It is important to realize that inflation has often been a symptom, rather than a cause, of financial ills. It is not true, in France, that speculation was dependent on inflation alone. Moreover, it is clear that once depreciation has become severe, it is not easy to stop speculation by limiting the instruments of speculation. This is true for two reasons. In the first place, the instruments of speculation are various and consist not only in legal tender money but in all those things which can give rise to credits. Exportable goods, become, for instance, a source of speculative credits. In the second place, even if speculation were based primarily on bank notes, variation in the velocity of circulation would make the effectiveness of those notes change very rapidly with changing opinion. Therefore, speculation in the foreign exchanges can be stopped, but only by controlling and adjusting the more important economic and political factors that lie behind the credit of a government.

How Speculation Worked

It is well to examine briefly the ways in which psychological influences affected the franc; there were three main channels of influence. In the first place, opinion was often reflected directly in the pressure of French demand for foreign balances and thus in the fall of the franc on the exchanges. In the second place, pessimism as to the value of the franc expressed itself in the rising price level within

[1] T. E. Gregory, *Foreign Exchange* (Oxford, 1925; first published 1921), p. 79.

France. In the third place, the fear of the future was expressed by the declining value of French securities and in particular the failure of investors to place money in the *bons de la défense*.[1] Each of these three influences reacted on the others and made it increasingly hard for the government to avoid further inflation of the currency. Then, in addition to this, speculation acted in such a way that neither of the normal remedies for depreciation, an increase in the discount rate or an increase in taxation, could improve the situation.[2] The government made considerable effort to lessen the direct influence of speculation on exchange rates, but it was almost powerless to prevent it.[3] French financial affairs could not be surrounded by an insurmountable wall. Exports led to foreign balances and imports required foreign credits, and the state could not control the use of the proceeds. It was easy for individuals to hasten or delay the transference of these balances from one center to another in accord with their estimates of future exchange values. Although the direct sale or purchase of foreign exchange was subject to government supervision and banks were prohibited from selling foreign exchange without permits from the ministry of finance, any individual who could not secure permission to buy exchange directly could buy some security quoted on other European exchanges and so equivalent to a purchase of foreign exchange.[4] The purchase of Suez Canal shares, for instance, represented an exchange transaction since the dividends were payable on a gold basis. Moreover, through such transactions public appraisal of the debates in Parliament were sometimes reflected in the quotations for the dollar and the pound more quickly than newspapers could give the news to the public. It was at the *Bourse* and not at the *Palais Bourbon* that one could

[1] These were short-time treasury notes. See *infra,* Chapter V.
[2] See *infra,* Chapters V and VI.
[3] See J. Laurès, *op. cit.,* p. 97, for regulations regarding export and import credits and other laws in this study.   [4] See *infra,* Chapter V.

judge most accurately the prospects of a political crisis. The
rates for foreign exchange were more than once referred to
as the plebiscite on political affairs, and direct speculation
was an increasingly important factor.[1]

In the second place, the commodity markets came to be
influenced by indirect and unconscious speculation in the
value of French money. During the early years of depreciation, French retailers and to a considerable degree French
wholesalers seemed unconscious of the relation between exchange rates and prices. It is true that commodity prices
rose rapidly during the war, but this was due to the war-
time maladjustments of production, and not to a conscious
analysis of the financial situation. Raw materials were
scarce and labor was lacking, prices rose for various reasons
but not from any conscious discounting of the future value
of the franc. After the war, price movements were various [2]
and there was at first little comparison of prices and
exchange rates. Then the sharp upward turn of prices and
exchange rates, in 1922, led to a clearer realization of the
situation. The purchasing power of the franc became a very
uncertain quantity; raw materials, imported and domestic,
were rising in price, and apparent profits on transactions
often turned into losses. This realization led inevitably to
a larger demand for present goods to avoid higher prices in
the future, and the rising price level, like rising exchanges,
led to an increased need of money and tended to prolong
inflation of the note circulation.

The internal debt, in the third place, was directly affected by the estimated future of the franc in two ways.
The quotations for the *rentes* were an indication of the
situation of government credit, to a considerable extent,
and the floating debt reacted quickly to changes in the attitude toward the franc. This later effect resulted from the
fact that liquid funds flowed rapidly from the exchange
market to the *bons de la défense* and back, and also because

[1] See *supra,* this chapter.   [2] See *infra,* Chapters IV and VII.

those who distrusted government credit would shift their balances from government notes to industrial securities or even commodities if these offered hope of gain. This link between the debt and confidence placed the government in a very embarrassing position in many instances, for the slightest check in political plans led to a movement away from government securities equivalent to a "run on the bank." [1]

Looking at the matter historically, one sees that it was not until after the war that these speculative forces in France were to be reckoned with as dangerous. In fact, after the sharp decline of the franc in 1919 there was considerable speculation in favor of its recovery. But after June, 1922,[2] the drift of opinion was increasingly unfavorable. In the first instance, the effect was mainly on the exchange; then, in 1923 and 1924, the wholesale price curve began to fluctuate in harmony with exchange rates, and still later, in 1925, the subscriptions to the *bons de la défense* varied inversely with the exchange rates, and the movement of prices was in close accord with that of the exchanges.[3]

The ever-closer link between debts and foreign exchange rates is a clear indication of the increasing numbers of people who became involved willingly or unwillingly in *speculation*. Whereas, from 1914 to 1919 the financial problems which had to do with the value of the franc were left in the hands of those professionally equipped to handle such affairs, in 1925 and 1926 every groceryman was considering the effect of the exchange rate on coffee, every stenographer was trying to build up a savings account in a gold standard country. It is hardly possible to exaggerate the extent to which the general public concerned themselves with such matters. The cost of the dollar was the subject of conversation in every corner café and one could hardly

[1] See *infra*, Chapter VI.   [3] See *infra*, Chapters V and VI.
[2] See *infra*, Chapter V.

make a purchase without some discussion of the exchange rate. There was, in fact, a general increase in money consciousness, which made the situation peculiarly hard for the government to handle, and this growing feeling of uncertainty as to the future of all kinds of wealth and on the part of all classes of people led eventually to the hysteria of July, 1926.

There is real significance in this invasion of the financial markets by the outsider; for just as the nonprofessional upsets to a certain extent the dealings of the stock market, so the inexperienced dealer in foreign exchange increases rather than diminishes the amplitude of fluctuations in value. In situations where the old-time dealers in foreign exchanges might look to a careful analysis of bank statements and of foreign commerce, the novice might be influenced by trifling circumstances; and as the number of dealers increased, the number of influences affecting them multiplied. It is in part because of this influx of highly impressionable buyers of exchange that those measures, generally considered inflationary, came to have a disproportionate influence on the franc.

The French bourgeois had come to fear increases in the supply of paper francs. Lessons built on catastrophic declines in Russia and Germany had been heeded. As time went on they made an increasing impression on public sentiment; unfortunately, these lessons were taken too literally, so that the number of notes in circulation came to be a decisive factor to those considering purchase of foreign currencies. In fact, this one item in the Bank of France statement was capable of precipitating a panic, even though the circulation was sometimes barely sufficient for the needs of business. In December, 1925, for instance, there was quite an unreasonable opposition to a much needed increase in the note circulation. This increase, when actually voted, caused no noticeable decline in the franc, although the political uproar which preceded the increase by some weeks

seriously impaired its value.[1] Such influences led to the
cumulative effects which have come to be recognized as
characteristic of severe depreciation. France barely entered
this dangerous territory of collapse and never reached the
point where the printing presses could not keep pace with
depreciation and the gold value of money in circulation
diminished at a rapid rate as it did in Germany.[2] Nevertheless, these cumulative effects began to be evident in 1926
when the gold value of the franc circulation, normally
worth about two billion dollars, fell to almost one billion
dollars in July.[3]

It has long been recognized in banking circles that severe
shocks to confidence are apt to precipitate a wild panic
and that people will take enormous known losses to escape
an unknown future loss. The most interesting study of this
kind of situation is that made by Professor Taussig in his
discussion of values in connection with the penumbra
theory.[4] Professor Taussig here describes the market situation in which a fall in prices leads to an increase in demand.
This situation in the commodity markets occurs in short
periods within the broader limits of value set by prime
costs, and by demand which depends on actual and pressing
needs. Such a situation prevails, too, on a much larger
scale in the stock markets when the conditions become abnormal and the future is uncertain. Similarly, the rise in the
cost of foreign exchange leads to a further rise, when the
first is taken as the beginning of a larger movement, and
buyers rush in to anticipate the later increases. The increase of demand with the rise in cost can go on in the

[1] See *infra*, Chapter V.
[2] U. S. Senate, *Foreign Currency and Exchange Investigation*, p. 538.
The value of the mark circulation declined from more than a billion dollars'
worth in January, 1921, to the low point of 75 million dollars' worth in
November, 1922. The gold value in 1913 was about 500 million dollars.
[3] See *infra*, Chapter V. See Chart No. XXIX, p. 415.
[4] F. W. Taussig, "Is Market Price Determinate?" *The Quarterly Journal
of Economics* (May, 1921), pp. 394-411.

monetary field almost without limit. This is true because cost factors do not determine the supply of currency as they set limits in the commodity markets, and there is no absolute stop to the increase in the amount of the depreciating currency which can be printed and offered in exchange for foreign credits. Even if there are factors tending to set limits to the note circulation, the situation often becomes so confused by the larger number of dealers and the varied interpretations of events and motives in selling francs that such limiting forces do not necessarily stay the tide of opinion.

France Reached the Danger Point

There is a point where this cumulative action cannot be checked. It is, however, impossible to say *a priori* just where that point will be. It is probable that France reached the very edge of the precipice in the last decline in 1926. That the franc did not take the vertical drop expected by many was due not to any immediate financial measures, but to a change in political front and the grim uncompromising attitude of M. Poincaré. The result was a sudden and complete change of confidence; with unbelievable suddennesss the money and exchange markets returned to their normal condition. Demand no longer increased with price. The *penumbra,* if it still existed, was important only for the narrow range of professional dealings which are well within the limits set by what are considered the *real* values. The general public ceased to concern themselves with the intricate problems of exchange value.

It is evident that such a tremendous increase in speculation as preceded Poincaré's return to power upsets the normal activities of a nation and introduces many disturbing factors. It is not the temporary panics, however, that are the most significant, but rather the slow drain of wealth from one group into the hands of others. It is the decline of such things as the habit of saving which took place over a period of years, and the effects upon productive machinery, financial practices, and social institutions which have made the financial aftermath of the war as costly, perhaps, as the war itself.

Unfortunately, it is not possible to consider in detail what all these effects have been. Moreover, it is probably too soon to appraise them in the case of France, since stability has so recently become an actual fact. It would be equally foolish, however, to omit all mention of those general changes which are common knowledge, even though they cannot be thoroughly analyzed at this time. It is probable that these changes will be more evident in a few years than they are at the present time. It is certain that the France of prewar days will never be found in the France of later years. The changes which have taken place in France are similar in kind to those that occur in the so-called business cycle. They differ in that the instability has been so much greater, and so has led to more revolutionary changes. The fall in the value of money, for instance, always brings about changes in the relative power of creditor versus debtor; but it is true to an even greater degree when, as in France, the gold value of government bonds is reduced by approximately two-thirds.[1] In these circumstances there results the partial impoverishment of a certain class of the population, that is, those who had invested moderate savings in conservative securities with fixed income. It is certain that the influence and living standards of this class in France have been seriously threatened. Bérenger stresses the increase of the lower ranges of income. While it is also true that there have been notable changes at the upper extreme, the decline of moderate fortunes has been more detrimental to the national well-being.[2] The results can be traced, to a certain extent, in

[1] Henry Bérenger, *op. cit.*, pp. 640-641.

[2] *Ibid.*, pp. 645. "Economic events of the last ten years have resulted in a redistribution of large fortunes and an increase of the resources of the poorer classes, thus increasing the equality between individuals."

some of the more subtle indications of an increasing emphasis on material values. It is no longer generally practicable
for the professional man to educate his sons to follow the
more liberal callings, the tendency is to send them into
business, so they can help rehabilitate the family fortunes.
All those with fixed incomes, whether from salaries or from
securities, have suffered, since they have not been in a position to insist on an increase in pay commensurate with the
increase in the cost of living.

In line with this general change in French life, one must
consider the increasing power of financial interests and a
certain venturesome attitude which is the natural outgrowth of instability. As some of the more conservative
business men have been crowded to the wall by the decline
in the real value of their fortunes, speculators and inno-
vators have taken their places. Large fortunes have been
built on changing prices, and those who were flexible enough
to understand new conditions and take chances have profited handsomely. There has been a notable increase in the
importance of banking operations, the members of the Paris
Clearing House are much more numerous, and the use of
credit has been greatly stimulated by recent events. In
industry as well as in finance, the daring leaders of new
enterprises have seized their opportunities, and many large
industrial units have grown up as the result of price changes
and reconstruction. It would be difficult to measure the
gains and losses due to such changes, for it is sometimes advantageous to have old plants and customs wiped out so
that new undertakings may be carried on unhampered. That
gains have occurred may be judged from the fact that, according to the index number of production, the real wealth
created each year is above the 1913 level.[1] It is certain that
profits made during 1925 and 1926 were very large, and

---

[1] The Dessirier Index in *Bulletin de la statistique générale de la France*
(October, 1924), pp. 73–101. See later issues. Account is taken of the addition of Alsace-Lorraine.

that they made possible to a considerable extent the ease with which France surmounted the depression that came with stability. It is possible that the advantages of these changes are very great in a material way, whereas, intellectually and socially, France has lost certain valuable forces.

There has undoubtedly been a marked change in the attitude of the French towards the future. They have been forced to see the real value of their savings diminish while taxes rose. They have found nowhere assurance that hard work in the present would bring ease and comfort in the future. The result has been twofold. There have been, on the one hand, feverish attempts either through speculation, adventurous industrial enterprise, or the purchase of land and real goods, to provide for the future; and there has been, on the other hand, much suffering among the aged and those who could not take advantage of speculative opportunities. This suffering, though often hidden, has led to a new cynicism and a defensive and, at times, hostile attitude towards other countries who have been more fortunate since the war.

Some of these ill effects of depreciation will pass, while others may remain as permanent scars to hamper the further growth of the nation. It is impossible at the present time to measure either the loss or the gain; it is sufficient to note, that, despite the difficulties and blunders, France has escaped the very real danger of bankruptcy. She has weathered the storms of the depression and has put in order her budget and her internal debts. Financial factors will come to be less and less disturbing in her productive life. It is to be hoped that she will be free of these extra burdens, to develop commerce and industry with the uninterrupted application of her great energy and her inventive genius.

In the pages which follow we have attempted to describe in some detail the up and down swings of the value of the franc. After a brief discussion of general conditions in

France before and during the war,[1] we have analyzed in more detail the main financial crises from 1919 to 1928.[2] The facts here related have been placed before the reader as impartially as possible. The later chapters, written from a slightly different point of view, attempt to distinguish between internal and external depreciation, and comment somewhat critically on the causes of changes in the value of the franc and the measures used to gain stability.[3] The elements involved in such a study are taken from all phases of French life; for instance, it is necessary to discuss political problems more than is usual in a study which is intended to deal with economic material. The war, reparations, internal struggles between different wings of French politics have determined her policy in taxation, in reconstruction, in Bank procedure, and in the various measures affecting commerce and industry. The inclusion of such varied elements means necessarily that some of them cannot be analyzed in detail.

The conclusion resulting from the study just outlined is that confidence was the principal short-run determinant of the value of the franc. This emphasis on psychological factors should not lead either to skepticism or to inertia in the attempt to control financial forces. Even though the psychological forces are complex and intangible, they are subject to a considerable measure of influence. It is obvious, for instance, that the general public prefers to ignore the problem of money if it is at all possible, and they will not engage in speculation unless instability is very marked and the fears for the future are very great. Moreover, it is possible in times of both slow and rapid fluctuations in the value of money to educate public opinion so that it will have a clearer conception of the real factors on which monetary value rests. It is possible to bring about a better understanding of the place of gold in a monetary system, of

[1] See *infra*, Chapters II and III.   [3] See *infra*, Chapters VI through X.
[2] See *infra*, Chapters IV and V.

the meaning of the quantity of notes in circulation, and the expansibility of foreign credit as a means of paying foreign debts.

As war finance passes into history, one becomes aware of a degree of elasticity in the credit system which would not have been dreamed of before 1914. This means an increase in both the power and the opportunity of central banks. It means an increasing responsibility on the part of financiers and statesmen to look to the effects of depreciation on social welfare, and also to educate the public to meet times of stress in a clear-sighted and understanding fashion.

CHAPTER II

FRANCE IN 1914

FRANCE in 1914 was not well equipped financially to meet
the strains of a long war.[1] There was too little elasticity in
the systems of public and private finance. The taxation and
budget methods were notably antiquated. It was obvious at
the outbreak of the war that revenues could not be increased quickly. Moreover, the credit mechanism was imperfectly developed; it has been generally recognized that
banking operations were incompletely centralized under
the control of the Bank of France. These and other features
of French economic life hampered her when she was faced
with the tremendous expenditures of war and reconstruction. It was with difficulty, and not without heavy cost,
that France weathered the financial stress of the war.

In the case of the War of 1870, on the other hand, the
conservative nature of French financial policy [2] helped her
to bear the reparation burdens imposed. The difference
in the financial situation in 1914 lay mainly in the length of
the struggle and the greater costs of war and reconstruction as compared with 1870. It must be realized, however,
that even in 1870 France found it inexpedient to discharge
(in the economic as contrasted with the legal sense) all
the debts imposed by the Treaty of Frankfort. Though the
burden was so much smaller in amount than the sums
needed during and after the recent war, a very large part

[1] Hon. George Peel, *The French Financial Crisis* (London, 1925), pp. 1-14.
[2] Germain Martin, *Les Finances Publiques de la France* (Paris, 1925),
pp. 15-18. Germain Martin here gives the salient characteristics without
showing their relation to the war emergency in particular.

of the payments was met by borrowing.[1] It is true that in this earlier instance France reaped the benefit of the large holdings of high-grade foreign securities and the considerable gold reserves. These and other characteristic features of French finance aided her both in her cash payments and in the borrowings which helped to make up the total. The net result was the rapid cancellation of Germany's claims on the French government.

After the recent war a different situation existed. Even though France was a victor, she found herself in worse financial straits than in the defeat of 1873. The strain on her resources had been too long. Her foreign securities had lost their value in part and the piling up of internal and external debts had been the result of the inability to increase normal revenues. It had been realized for some time before the war that taxation was not well adjusted to the needs of the nation. The important changes involved could not be made quickly, however, and France had to go through the war period with her cumbersome indirect taxes. It had been common knowledge, too, that the internal debt was heavy compared with that of other nations, but here again, there was no way of preventing the situation from becoming worse at the time of extreme need. Foreign investments, made with a view to political interests rather than security of value, melted away as the war progressed.

These and other handicaps under which France labored must be discussed briefly in order to understand the depreciation of the franc. The more important group themselves naturally under four headings. In the first place, we must consider the budget and taxation. In the second place, we must comment on the internal debt. Then, thirdly, we must describe briefly the investment situation before the war.

---

[1] Germain Martin, *op. cit.*, p. 44. Germain Martin estimates 14 billion francs, or half the sum of the subsequent internal debt, as that part of the costs of the war which were not paid off at once but were carried as a permanent charge on the nation. See also Léon Say, *Les Finances de la France sous la troisième république* (Paris, 1898), pp. 363-451.

And, in the fourth place, we must discuss the position of France in international credit and the nature of her foreign commerce. These aspects of French financial life are all subjects deserving thorough study and analysis. It is impossible to give them more than passing reference here. It is hoped, however, in this brief treatment to help account for the measures adopted by France during and after the war and so to make more clear the forces bearing on the franc.

BUDGET IN BAD SHAPE

Budget deficits were no uncommon thing in France before the war. In the twenty-four years ending 1913 there had been deficits in eleven years and surpluses in thirteen. While these deficits were not large, they indicate the existence of unsound practices which were to cause more trouble later. It is probable that the complex system of accounting for government expenditures was in part to blame for this situation. There were, before the war, more than ten special accounts and budgets.[1] Moreover, these publicly acknowledged accounts do not include all the government expenditures. This confused practice continued through the war and one of the most important budgets after the war was the so-called recoverable budget, which included items charged to the account of Germany. Sums spent under this heading were very large and were not covered in any way by normal revenues. This particular account was not done away with until 1925. There were also in 1925 and 1926 other serious efforts to simplify this very confusing handling of public finance.[2]

These obstacles in the way of good budget practices were

---

[1] Edgar Allix, *Traité élémentaire de la science des finances et de la législation financière française* (Paris, 1921), pp. 68, 69. The list includes the ordinary, extraordinary, and annexed budgets, the service of the treasury, *dispositions spéciales,* and *moyens de services et dispositions annuelles.*

[2] Henry Chéron, *Rapport au Sénat,* December 10, 1926, no. 656, p. 52. See *infra,* Chapter IX.

increased by the customary delay in voting the budget.
This fault in the French political procedure became a very
serious handicap as the expenditures of the government
changed rapidly. It was based on a long-standing tradition.
When Parliament refused to pass the regular budgets before the beginning of the year, provisional grants were made
on the basis of the past needs of the various branches of
the government. Since it was impossible to make this an
accurate estimate of future needs, there was every excuse
and temptation for the different departments to exceed
the amounts granted. Extravagance was the natural result
of such a state of affairs. It was not even possible to judge
accurately at the end of a year what expenditures had been
made, since the various accounts were kept open for several
years. Supplementary appropriations for a given year could
be made some years later and the accounts for any year
were not finally closed for a period of ten years. It will be
readily seen that such a system could not be controlled by
public opinion nor even by parliamentary action. The intricacies of the system were too great, publicity was made
impossible, and extravagance was invited by the method of
keeping the accounts.

The delays and complications which were responsible
to a certain extent for the budget deficits during and after
the war were less significant, however, than were the more
serious difficulties growing out of the system of taxation.
The first main characteristic of the French taxation was
its complexity, the second was the large proportion of
indirect taxes. This situation was the result of a long-standing tradition and was presumably fairly well adapted to
prewar France. Even if this is granted, however, there can
be no justification for the large number of nuisance taxes,
such levies as those on doors and windows [1] and the long

---

[1] Germain Martin, *op. cit.*, p. 59. The tax on doors and windows, one of the
quatre vieilles contributions, was not finally abolished till 1917. The others
of the four were those on land, movable property, and occupations. **They**

lists of small *contributions.* There were innumerable tax laws, many of them placing levies on commodities and most of them indirect in form, that is, taxes that are shifted to the consumer. It is difficult to draw the line between direct and indirect taxation, particularly as the French use the phrase in a way different from that familiar to American economists.[1] Moulton says that eighty-two per cent of the total taxation is indirect, but he seems to be following the French classification.[2] It is probable that the percentage is lower than eighty-two because some taxes included under indirect by the French, such as the *registration* tax, seem to be essentially direct taxes according to American usage. The French distinction is based on the method of administering the taxes rather than on where the ultimate burden is borne. Two of the largest later sources of revenue, the income tax and the business turnover tax,[3] did not exist before the war. The addition of these taxes and the very considerable increase in the levies on inheritances changed the balance from indirect to direct taxation. After the war the resources from the two kinds were almost equal and formed for this reason a much more stable basis for the budget than did the former system with its very large preponderance of indirect taxation. A small part of the income of the state was derived from the state *domaine,* lands and forests, and from state monopolies, such as the tobacco and match. Other

had been condemned before but the legislation doing away with them was not quite complete at the outbreak of the war. See also Edgar Allix, *op. cit.,* p. 136.

[1] Edgar Allix and Marcel Lecerclé, *L'Impôt sur le revenu* (Paris, 1926), vol. i, pp. 9, 10.

[2] Moulton and Lewis, *The French Debt Problem* (New York, 1925), pp. 53, 412.

[3] Etienne Clémentel, *Inventaire de la situation financière de la France au début de la treizième législature* (Paris, 1924), p. 130. The business turnover tax, or *chiffre d'affaires,* was first collected in 1921. There is some question as to whether this should be considered as a direct or as an indirect tax. A part of the burden is undoubtedly passed on to the consumer in the form of increased prices. A part, however, is a deduction from the profits which the business man would otherwise pocket.

enterprises of the government, such as the post and the telegraph, on the other hand, were liabilities and not assets,
since they had to be aided by substantial subsidies. A glance
at the intricate French official statement of revenues leaves
one in a state of great confusion.[1] It is obvious, however,
after analyzing prewar resources, that the larger part of
the income of the government was derived from the taxes
on various commodities, which are clearly indirect taxes;
that some came from registration taxes and others which
may be considered direct; that a smaller part was derived
from the state monopolies and *domaines;* and that no net
revenue accrued from the state enterprises.

Let us consider briefly the practical significance of the
dependence on indirect taxation. In the first place, the
large number of tax laws involved made it difficult, from
the point of view both of legislation and of collection, to
make any notable change in these laws when war expenditures led to increasing budget deficits. In the second place,
the taxes which influenced very directly the price of commodities were peculiarly difficult to alter when the cost
of living was rising rapidly and when a serious social disturbance would have hampered the chance of military victory. There were difficulties in the way of increasing the
percentage of taxation on commodities. It must be admitted, on the other hand, that there was some automatic
increase of revenue from this source, since the rise in prices
increased the yield of the taxes in some cases. This advantage was more than offset, however, by the loss which resulted from the invasion of the North.

It is quite obvious, in retrospect, that if the government
had put the income tax into operation before the war,
France would have been able to increase this tax in the time
of greatest need, and would have found revenues greatly
augmented. The increase in an income tax, once the princi-

[1] *Bulletin de statistique et de législation comparée* (January 1, 1913),
pp. 71-77.

ple has been accepted, is easier to put into effect and less objectionable politically than are taxes on commodities which are consumed by the public in general. England was equipped with such a system of taxation. France had already passed the legislation necessary to put it into effect before the war. The income tax was voted only after a long struggle. It had been proposed as long ago as 1848, but not until 1907 was the project seriously advocated. It was then that Joseph Caillaux, Minister of Finance, tried to reorganize the financial system.[1] The proposal met with severe opposition and was not passed till March 29, 1914. It was passed too late to be of any considerable use in the war, which broke out so soon after. Surely it was very difficult to institute radical change in the financial system during the early years of the war. It would have been quite possible, on the contrary, for the French to have increased existing levies, if, as in England, the income tax had been in good running order for some time. In this fact lies a considerable part of the difference between French and English finance. The very great need of the treasury, however, led the French to put this tax into effect in 1916.[2] It did not become a very large source of revenue, however, until after the armistice. It is conceivable that this tax might have cut the budget deficits by eight or ten billion francs if it had been passed a few years earlier.

In spite of the inadequacy of methods in public finance, the complex body of laws, and methods of administration, it is nevertheless true that the Frenchman was heavily taxed before the war. The total revenue derived from taxation in 1913 was more than four billion francs and the total public revenue including the income from monopolies and other sources was more than five billion francs.[3] If this

[1] Edgar Allix, *op. cit.*, vol. i, pp. 141, 150.

[2] Edgar Allix, *op. cit.*, vol. ii, p. 332.

[3] *L'Annuaire statistique de la France*, 1924, pp. 160, 173. Figures given for total receipts are: central government, 5,091 million francs; departments, 612 million francs; communes, 1,071 million francs.

sum is reduced to a per capita basis by dividing by 39 millions, the estimated population of France, the taxation amounts to 104 francs per person and the total revenues to 130 francs per person.[1] The figures as here given include only the revenue of the central government and not that of the departments and communes. If this burden is compared with that of other countries, it is apparent that the French paid a large part of their income to the government. The per capita taxation, for instance, without any allowance for the very great difference in the per capita income, was higher than that in the United States. Professor Seligman estimates the French per capita tax at $25.00 and that in the United States as $22.95. That of Great Britain was but slightly higher than that of France, $26.89, and Germany collected a much smaller sum than the other three, $15.98 per person.

It is necessary to carry the comparison of tax burdens further in order to see the full significance of the sums collected in the various countries. It is customary to present the figures as percentages of the national income. This practice is subject to the criticism that the national income is itself a figure very hard to arrive at. The significance of such a comparison will be realized when one considers that the prewar per capita income of the United States is generally estimated as more than twice that of France. It is obvious, therefore, that the same per capita taxation would bear much more heavily on the poorer nation than it would on the United States. Even though it is impossible to arrive at precise figures for these ratios, it is well to consider

[1] Some of the estimates found in other sources differ from those given here. This is in the main due to the difference in including or excluding the *domaine,* exceptional resources, departmental or communal receipts. Some of the figures given are: Clèmentel, *Inventaire,* p. 106, 104 francs; National Industrial Conference Board, *Inter-Ally Debts* (New York, 1925), p. 82, 128 francs; E. R. A. Seligman, *Essays in Taxation and Public Finance* (New York, 1926), pp. 35, 41, $25.00; Moulton and Lewis, *op. cit.,* p. 56, 131 francs.

the estimates made, since the difference is so great as to demand attention. Harvey E. Fisk of the Bankers Trust Company has made a study which gives the comparative burdens in terms of the national income.

TABLE III

PERCENTAGES OF INCOME ABSORBED BY TAXES[1]

1913

	Taxes	Total Revenues
France	9.04	11.71
Great Britain	7.03	7.13
Belgium	6.27	9.36
Germany	4.84	5.33
United States	1.95	2.03

The National Industrial Conference Board gives an even higher estimate than Fisk's of the amount paid by the French in taxes before the war. It states that 13.3 per cent of the national income was paid in to the government.[2] The difference is apparently due to the inclusion in the latter case of local taxes. In both studies, however, France stands at the head of the list as the heaviest taxpayer.[3] Professor Seligman, who estimates the tax burden as 14.1 per cent of the national income[4] differs from the others in using a lower figure for the French income. Despite the small difference between the various studies, the general conclusion is the same in every case. France was very heavily taxed before the war. The investigations of the French Service on Reparations are to the same effect. The condition of government finance was not favorable to the as-

[1] H. E. Fisk, *Inter-Ally Debts* (New York, 1924), pp. 322–323.
[2] National Industrial Conference Board, *Inter-Ally Debts* (New York, 1925), p. 82.
[3] J. C. Stamp, "National Wealth and the Income of the Chief Powers," *Journal Royal Statistical Society* (July, 1919), p. 491. Stamp accepts the estimate for the national income of France as 1,500 million pounds in 1914. This is based on the work of Pupin and Théry.
[4] E. R. A. Seligman, *Political Science Quarterly* (March, 1924), p. 142. He estimates the national income as 36,000 million francs in 1913.

sumption of new burdens. There was very great danger
that further increases in the budget might lead to national
bankruptcy.

One further fact must be noted in connection with the
budget and taxation. This is the loss of resources due to the
invasion of the north of France. The ten departments invaded represented before the war approximately four and
a half million people.[1] Moreover, many of the more important industries as well as some of the best agricultural
lands were cut off by the war. The textile interests of Lille,
Roubaix, Reims; the mines of Lens and the North; the
sugar refineries, and steel mills of the northern provinces
were either devastated or in the hands of the Germans.
The revenues which had come from these active industries
had been a considerable part of the total. The most productive regions lay near the frontier and, therefore, were subject to the losses of war. The effort which France made to
increase taxes barely offset the losses due to invasion. Expenditures were increasing by leaps and bounds, and the
deficits were inevitable.[2]

The main economic difficulties which circumscribed
French action in public finance were, then, the badly arranged system of taxation, the fact that budget burdens
were already excessive, and the loss of some of the most
productive frontier territory. In addition to these limiting
factors, the political situation which always affects finance
so directly was quite unsatisfactory. The National Industrial Conference Board Report and the others have explained the low taxation during the war partly on the
grounds of the loss of territory and partly by the political
difficulties.

[1] E. Michel, *La Situation financière et l'achèvement de la reconstitution
au 31 décembre, 1925* (Paris, 1925), p. 51.
[2] A. Ribot, *Exposé des motifs, Bulletin de statistique et de législation
comparée* (November-December, 1914), p. 456. There was a marked decline
in tax receipts at the beginning of the war.

A more significant factor [than the invasion] in explaining the slowness with which the French fiscal system responded to the war needs was the unsatisfactory political situation which persisted throughout the period.[1]

This state of affairs has been indicated in the discussion of the instability of the French government [2] and in the brief mention of the long struggle necessary to put through the legislation on the income tax. There was in addition to this a degree of sectionalism in France which one might not expect in so small a territory. Some regions were less disturbed by war than others, and so were less interested in making the sacrifices which were demanded of them.

THE HEAVY INTERNAL DEBT

The second main characteristic of French financial life was the very heavy internal debt. This constituted a most unfavorable influence. It was in part responsible for the heavy budget requirements referred to above, and it limited the ability of the government to tax and to borrow. The debt amounted to 32,594 million francs in 1913,[3] and was larger than the debt of England, Germany, Belgium, or the United States. It absorbed 27.3 per cent of the budget expenditures in France in 1913.[4] Nearly half the capital sum of this debt was the heritage of the Franco-Prussian War,[5] but it had been augmented by reason of unsound budget practices and large military outlays.[6]

There had been a measure of public approval of the debt situation, despite the fact that it bore heavily on the people in the form of taxes. It is sometimes said that a gov-

[1] National Industrial Conference Board, *op. cit.*, p. 84.

[2] See *supra*, Chapter I.

[3] Henry Chéron, *Rapport au Sénat*, no. 84, 22 février, 1926, p. 277.

[4] Morgan and Company, *Statistical Atlas* (unpublished, Paris), p. 5. Of the rest of the budget, military expenses took 31.1 per cent and 41.6 per cent went to the other departments and services.

[5] See *supra*, Chapter II.   [6] Hon. George Peel, *op. cit.*, p. 41.

ernment benefits from a large debt held in the form of
government securities well distributed throughout the
population. It was thought in France that the habit of subscription to public loans was a good one to form in the
nation. Thus, it was argued, there was an increase in stability and the interest of the people in the affairs of the state.
Later events, however, proved these advantages to be illusory. There was a very small margin of savings for the
government to count on. When the treasury floated its
loans it found that they were supported almost entirely
by war inflation. They were financed in very small part by
new and voluntary savings. It was inevitable that this
should be so. The state had already absorbed a large part
of the national income. In 1914 it could seize the real
wealth of the country only by the roundabout method of
inflation and through loans which brought back a considerable number of the new notes to the treasury. The situation
which had been viewed complacently aggravated the serious difficulties in time of war.

One further fact in regard to the debt should be noted
at this point. Although the paper or nominal value of the
prewar debt was a small part of the total indebtedness after the war, it formed a serious obstacle in the way of rapid
stabilization of the depreciated currency. Those who had
subscribed to the 32 billion francs' worth of prewar *rentes*
and other securities had bought them with gold francs.
They had invested their hard-earned savings in these gilt-
edge securities in order to be able to live on the income in
their old age. There were large numbers of such people.
They constituted in some respects, then, the backbone of
the French nation. They were not the rich but were, rather,
the farmer, the wage earner, the petty official, and the
intellectual worker. When it began to be apparent that the
paper value of their holdings had diminished to a gold value
of one-fifth in comparison with prewar value—to say nothing of the depreciation of the market value of such gov-

ernment holdings, which fell to very low levels in Paris—
they felt very bitter against the parties in control. It became difficult or impossible for any government to handle
the situation in a purely rational way. Although it is probable that stabilization a few years after the armistice, certainly by 1925 or 1926, would have led to greater productive power and to less financial unrest, it was impossible
for the government to alienate the large number of investors in the prewar debt. It was difficult enough to face the
loss involved in the depreciation of investments in industrial concerns, but the deliberate devaluation of the government debt seemed like a dishonorable act. It was not till
stability at a low level had been an accepted fact for two
years that the government could recognize this fact by the
laws necessary to preserve stability.

France before the war had the heaviest debt of the western European nations. After the war she was more heavily
burdened than any nation except Germany, in terms of
her national income. If the prewar debt is calculated on
its former gold value, it is evident that it represented half
the crushing burden which brought France so near to bankruptcy. If this debt had been smaller, it is probable that
France could have met the demands for interest payments
on the rest of the debt, let us say 150 billion paper francs
capital value, after the deduction of 150 billions as the
equivalent of the prewar debt in gold. The government
might even have brought the franc part of the way back
towards its prewar value. Since this was far from the actual
situation, however, she found herself faced with billions of
dollars of interest charges and a very intense feeling of
bitterness on the part of those who had lost through their
investment in government bonds.

Condition of Private Finance Not Favorable

The condition of French private finance in 1914 was not
favorable to the prosecution of a long war. This was a re-

sult both of the general nature of the credit structure and financial practices, and also of the unsettled state of affairs existing in the months just prior to the war. So striking is this latter fact, that it is hard to refrain from the comment that wherever the blame for the war may lie, August, 1914 was extremely unpropitious for France so far as finance is concerned. However this may be, one must focus on the most important facts bearing on the franc, essentially various and complex, and leave outside this field all questions of "war guilt."

It is necessary first to consider briefly some of the characteristics of banking and credit in France. The general nature of the prevailing financial practice is well known. The check, for instance, was little used in France. A comparatively large number of payments were in fact made in gold. Most of the rest were made in the notes of the Bank of France, or in silver which circulated side by side with gold. Deposits in French banks were not large in 1914.[1] Before the war comparatively few banks belonged to the Clearing House and most of the clearing was done through the Bank of France. It was not until 1926, in fact, that the Paris Clearing House rivaled the Bank of France in the total value of checks cleared.[2] The growth in clearings since 1913 is a striking indication of the gradual increase in transferability of bank deposits as compared with currency. Nevertheless, even after the war the French still used checks very much less than the Americans or the English. This state of affairs, while it is somewhat adapted to the French

[1] Germain Martin, *op. cit.*, pp. 18, 19. Deposits in the five large London banks were 31 billions, whereas the four large French banks had only 5 billions in 1914.

[2] Fisk gives the value of checks cleared by the Bank of France as 310 billions in 1913 (*French Public Finance*, New York, 1922, p. 249), whereas the clearings of the *Chambre de Compensation* were slightly over 18 billions (*Bulletin de la statistique générale*, vol. xvi, no. 2, 1927), p. 147. In 1926 the clearings of this Paris Clearing House were approximately 546 billions. The clearings of the Bank of France had increased but not in the same proportion.

temperament and manner of doing business, shows a lack of the most economical methods of handling gold reserves and of canceling credits throughout the country. It is obvious that the more highly developed banking procedures are efficient both in their sparing use of the precious metals and in the speed with which credits and debts are offset even over large territories. There are, moreover, great possibilities of expansion in a system of payment which is based mainly on credit. Such a system is free, to a certain extent, from political hindrances and is not subject to so much interference as is the note circulation.

Another feature of the French financial life before the war was the stability of the discount rate of the Bank of France.[1] The Bank did not use this instrument in an aggressive way either for the control of internal credit or for the regulation of the flow of gold in and out of the country.[2] The rate was three per cent most of the decade preceding the war.[3] The French were not used to frequent changes in the bank rate, nor did they like to use it to bring about pressure on the internal credit situation. It was for this reason, perhaps, that the changes in the rate during and after the war were not well received and did not help the Bank in its efforts to lessen speculation or solidify the credit situation. The policy of France was notably different from that of England. It is not possible to say just what she could have done had she used this banking instrument frequently before the war. It is obvious that she could not use it to any considerable extent in view of her long tradition of discount rate stability.

[1] Charles Dunbar, *The Theory and History of Banking* (New York, 1922), pp. 175, 192.

[2] Auguste Arnauné, *La Monnaie* (Paris, 1926), p. 193. M. Arnauné states that the Bank of France used the premium on gold rather than the increase in the discount rate at times when the metal was leaving the country too fast, in order to avoid the apprehension caused by changes in the discount rate.

[3] *L'Annuaire statistique*, 1922, p. 2.

It is safe to conclude that credit before the war was comparatively little under the control of the Bank of France. There was a natural caution in business and financial dealings which made possible a stability which might not otherwise have prevailed. Despite this conservatism, however, there had been a considerable mushroom growth of small banks before the war. Many of these had sprung up suddenly outside the system which was controlled to a considerable extent by the few large banks.[1] The very fact that credit instruments had not been used as much as in other countries left the way open for many adventuresome and perhaps irresponsible men to go into banking. Often they began business with limited resources and were not subject to adequate control, so that their aims were not harmonized with those of the more responsible banks.[2] Moreover, the situation of one of the large banks, the Société Générale, was very weak in July, 1914.[3] It escaped a serious catastrophe by the aid of the Bank of France. There had been a quite unwarranted withdrawal of funds from this bank in the spring of 1914, which threatened the security of the other large banks because of its effect on confidence. The fact that the situation of the large and small banks was unsatisfactory threw an added burden on the Bank of France, or rather on the treasury, for it was the treasury which came to dominate French financial life as the expenditures and borrowings of the government increased.

The financial situation was further complicated in 1914 by the flotation of the 3½ per cent *amortissable* government loan. The decision had been made early in the year to borrow 805 million francs, a fairly large sum for the pre-war period, to cover outlays for national defense and for

---

[1] Germain Martin, *op. cit.*, p. 18. The importance of the four leading banks, the *Crédit Lyonnais, Comptoir d'Escompte, Société Générale,* and the *Crédit Industriel,* is here indicated.

[2] Hon. George Peel, *op. cit.*, pp. 1-9.

[3] Germain Martin, *op. cit.*, p. 105.

use in Morocco.[1] The success of this issue seemed assured in the first few days of public subscription. It was reported that it was many times oversubscribed. It is possible, indeed, that the fact that requests for shares had to be refused [2] may have been one of the things which led to the subsequent reaction. In any case, the securities were mainly in the hands of speculators and of banks and had not been absorbed by the general public at the time the war broke out.

Ribot described the situation in his 1914 budget report.

> At the moment of declaration of war the loan was for the most part a heavy charge on the credit institutions or on those who had bought for future payment and had great difficulty in meeting their obligations. . . . Payments made to the treasury on the loan amounted to 387 million francs on September first . . . and to 515.7 millions on November thirtieth. . . .[3]

The embarrassment of the banks due to this and other causes made it necessary, in fact, for the central bank to extend them credits and, on the other hand, it definitely limited their power to help the government. The Bank of France increased its discounts by about three billion francs in order to relieve the situation. It thus furnished the banks with cash in return for commercial paper and made a considerable number of loans to *agents de change*.[4]

In regard to private as well as to public loans the situation was not very sound in 1913 and 1914. The *Bourse* had been rather troubled for political and economic reasons.[5] The new government loan was looked on with some disfavor. The impending income tax law and the general discussion of public finance had had an unsettling effect. There was some distrust of the market situation and, although

---

[1] Germain Martin, *op. cit.*, p. 53.

[2] *Le Pour et le contre* (Paris, July 12, 1914).

[3] A. Ribot, *Exposé des motifs, Bulletin de statistique et de législation comparée* (November–December, 1914), pp. 452, 453.

[4] *Ibid.*, p. 453.   [5] *The Economist* (London, April 4, 1914), p. 828.

the discount rate was low, investment in securities was not very active. Germain Martin sums up the situation in his discussion of French finance.

The Paris market from January, 1914 on had, then, plenty of idle funds and it had placed them freely in foreign government securities. There was difficulty, on the contrary, in floating a French loan on our market because, although the technical situation was not bad, there was a rather unpromising political state of affairs.

The capitalists were put out with the government and doubted the future measures of a parliament which would discuss ways of putting in force a tax on personal property.[1]

If internal politics were uneasy, the situation in foreign politics was even more alarming. There had been war in Mexico and the Balkans and the increase in the armaments in many countries was most alarming. Altogether, it was a time of change and uneasiness rather than of sound and confident economic activity.[2]

The nature of French foreign investments should be considered at this point. The importance of capital investments abroad has already been alluded to.[3] The French had accumulated a large number of foreign investments which furnished a substantial income before the war. The sum is variously estimated as about 45 to 50 billion francs.[4] The unfortunate fact about these investments was that they had been influenced to a considerable extent by certain government policies. Even though the placing of the investments was determined by the individual, government influence had led to the choice of a considerable number

[1] Germain Martin, *op. cit.*, pp. 54, 55.

[2] *The Economist* (London, May 23, 1914), p. 1183. "The existence of a critical state of affairs on the Bourse is generally recognized."

[3] See *supra*, Chapter I.

[4] Germain Martin, *op. cit.*, p. 33. Germain Martin here gives 50 billion francs. Moulton, *op. cit.*, p. 20, gives 45 billions. Other estimates are in substantial agreement with these two.

of Turkish, Austrian, and Roumanian securities, and a very large number of Russian investments. Eleven billion francs are said to have been placed in Russia alone and approximately ten billion in the other countries mentioned here. It may be seen readily that even if war had not directly involved all of these countries the investments were not well placed with a view to security. With the particular alignment of warring countries which followed the declaration of war with Germany, the larger part of these investments was a total loss. Whereas investments which had been better distributed might have been a means of paying for foreign purchases, France was suddenly deprived of a very important part of her yearly income. They could not help either to right the balance of payments or to swell the income of individuals.[1]

The loans which the government had made before the war were in character much like those of its citizens. They were placed with a view to cementing political alliances rather than in the interests of security. These government loans were not large compared with those of private investors. They would not have caused the state any serious difficulty if it had not been for considerable sums advanced to Russia,[2] both before and after the outbreak of the war. These advances might have been looked at in a different light if the war on the eastern front had continued till the armistice. Since Russia capitulated before the most critical months of the struggle, however, the original investment was of little avail. Germain Martin criticizes the government, not only for favoring such large investments in Russia, but also for permitting the loans to be diverted from constructive purposes to unproductive uses, so that, even if Russia had been a permanent ally, she would not

---

[1] The government has taken some responsibility in regard to Russian investments, paying a certain small percentage of the original value to those holding Russian securities. This relieved to a slight extent the hardship resulting from these unsound investments.

[2] Moulton and Lewis, *op. cit.*, p. 17, especially note 3.

have owed her strength to a very great extent to these loans. He sets the amount of public and private loans at 12 or 13 billion francs. More than 6 billion francs were advanced by the government, making a total of about 20 billion francs.[1]

Moulton estimates that "something like 23 billions—namely, those invested in Russia, the Succession States, and the Levant—have been rendered valueless for many years if not permanently."[2] Some of the weakness in this investment situation could not be realized before the war. There were sufficient indications, however, to warn a government against such heavy loans to eastern Europe.

FRENCH TRADE SUBJECT TO OUTSIDE INFLUENCES

It is necessary to note that French commerce in goods as well as in capital was not independent of outside influences. There has been a fairly generally accepted notion that France was less dependent on foreign trade than other comparable nations. In fact, it is sometimes said that France is self-sufficient and can go her way alone without many imports from other countries. These ideas misrepresent the real state of affairs. It is true that in comparison with England, a country that would starve if isolated, France might be considered self-sufficient. The value of her foreign commerce, however, has been very large. It amounts to a larger per cent of her national income than does that of the United States and three-fourths that of England. Meynial gives the following comparison:

PERCENTAGE OF PRODUCTS EXPORTED [3]

United States	9
France	18
Great Britain	25

[1] Germain Martin, *op. cit.*, p. 38; Etienne Clémentel, *Inventaire de la situation financière de la France au début de la treizième législature* (Paris, 1924), p. 271. [2] Moulton and Lewis, *op. cit.*, pp. 26, 333.

[3] Pierre Meynial, *Revue d'économie politique* (November, December, 1927), p. 1565. This estimate for the United States ten per cent of export-

As far as the imports are concerned, France was dependent on a number of basic commodities for normal industrial production. Such things as cotton, oil, rubber, coffee, copper, leather, and hides, and countless other staples came to her in large amounts from other countries. A number of the metals were practically unattainable in France. Oil was found only in small quantities. The development of colonial rubber and cotton, and other tropical commodities, had only begun and was negligible from a quantitative point of view. France was very far from being self-sufficient and, with the outbreak of war, which deprived her of fertile land and productive industries, she was more than ever in need of imports. In the changed circumstances, she imported huge quantities of wheat and other foodstuffs which she did not normally get from other countries.

It must be granted, therefore, that France suffered as did other countries from the interruption of normal commercial relations during the war. The impression that she did not need imports is based undoubtedly on the fact that her production is fairly well balanced between agriculture and industry. Moreover, the prevalence of the small farm and the universal interest in market gardening gives an appearance of economic sufficiency which is not borne out by a more careful analysis. When one looks not to the little plots of ground which supplement the income of the factory worker, but to the larger estate cultivated with imported agricultural machinery and fertilized with imported chemicals, one realizes that the situation is not so simple as it seems at first glance. The clothes, for instance, that the peasants wear are largely made from foreign cotton or wool, the shoes of foreign leather, and a considerable number of the instruments and much of the capital equipment are made of foreign metal.

In fact, France is more dependent on foreign trade than

able products exported is frequently given, though some consider it too high. See *Commerce Yearbook,* 1926 (Washington, 1927), vol. i, p. 90.

many other nations, if one considers the invisible items as well as the visible. The importance of the tourist expenditures in France has already been stated.[1] It should be remembered in estimating the effect of the war on her economic life, that the dependence of France on the tourist made her particularly vulnerable, since it cut off a large part of her revenue and led to the inactivity of some of her important industries. It is true that a number of other countries had enjoyed this same type of income, but most of them not to the extent to which France did. They were not, perhaps, so seriously affected by the sudden cessation of this form of commerce. It is true that France gained some revenue from the expenditures of foreign troops on her territory. Nevertheless, the interruption to an important economic enterprise was a serious affair.

Some Good Aspects of French Economic Life

There were, however, certain elements of strength in the organization of French economic life. There were certain advantages in the small productive units, in the general interest in agriculture, in the conservative, careful workmanship and in the way in which different industries and interests were well distributed throughout the country. There may have been some good features, even, in the credit system, despite the inadequate development of some aspects. One such element of strength was the large amount of gold and silver in the country at the outbreak of the war. The reserves of the Bank of France and the gold and silver in hoards represented a fairly large amount of wealth. Little of this was used effectively during the war. A considerable amount of that in private hands was hidden or exported secretly. Some of it, however, was paid into the treasury, and the Bank of France. The government made its appeal to patriotic sentiments and passed laws aimed to

[1] See *supra*, Chapter I.

prevent the private circulation or export of the precious metals. Even though these measures were only partially successful, France, after the war, very soon came to have the second largest gold reserve in the world.[1] While the importance of idle reserves is sometimes questioned, it is probable that they formed a basis of monetary stability in France which would have been sorely missed. It is possible that as conditions began to return to normal after the panic of July, 1926, the amount of gold in the Bank of France increased the optimism of the speculator in francs.[2]

There were, moreover, certain characteristics, hard to analyze or describe, which stood France in good stead during the difficult years of the war. It is not possible here to discuss such intangible forces as the character and intellectual gifts of the French nation. In view of what has been said as to the economic unpreparedness of France—using the term unpreparedness in the broadest possible sense—it must be evident that other influences less easy to measure and appraise were supporting the nation through the terrific struggle. It is probable that it will never be realized how difficult was that struggle. Those who saw worn old men entraining for the front after a few brief days of *permission,* who saw slender boys going off in their crude ill-fitting uniforms to fill the gaps in the front lines, realize, perhaps, to what extent France was pushed to the wall. Few know, however, of the threat of revolt and the actual signs of internal disaffection and conflict which were most alarming in 1917. It is difficult or impossible to find in print any reference to events which were fairly generally known to have taken place. It is probable that the full story will never be revealed.

[1] A. Ribot, *op. cit.*, pp. 463, 464. Apparently the gold drawn from hand to hand circulation at the beginning of the war helped to pay some of the government expenses during those first months.

[2] *Le Pour et le contre* (December 26, 1926). This periodical gives the following estimate. The value is expressed in gold francs: United States, 14 billions; France, 7 billions; and Great Britain, 5 billions.

That there was considerable determination of leadership and a rugged fortitude among the rank and file of the people must be generally admitted. So strong were these forces that they offset the economic disadvantages. Despite the bad condition of the budget, taxation, and debt, France came through the war and reconstruction without bankruptcy and without any general repudiation of her obligations. Even in face of a poorly developed credit system, the lack of use of discount rate policy, and many unsound banking institutions, industry managed to carry on and there was no serious crisis of unemployment and no prolonged financial panic. Even though there were tremendous losses of foreign investments, France managed after the war to build up again a considerable sum of foreign credits. The political situation, which was difficult before the war, got worse after the temporary union was dissolved. The temporary truce between the various warring parties was unpalatable and unnatural. It ceased abruptly when the immediate crisis was over. In the years after the armistice, one sees French political life at its worst. There was a complete inability to form a solid majority and, although this was not new, it was particularly distressing. These various handicaps took their toll from the wealth of the French nation. They paid in money, in prestige, and in well-being. It was inevitable that France should suffer from the fact that she had neglected to put her financial house in order in the years preceding the war.

CHAPTER III

War Finance and the Franc

A GENERAL survey of French economic life leaves a clear impression of a nation which had devoted thought and money to cementing certain political alliances and to keeping armaments in condition, but which was singularly ill adapted to finance war. It is not surprising, therefore, to find that many of the measures adopted during the war were ill-fitting expedients which increased the future burdens of the nation. It would be a mistake, of course, to exaggerate the extent to which nations can prepare for emergencies, and their ability to draw up financial programs in a constructive way once war is in progress, even when conditions are sound. Nevertheless, the contrast between France and England after the war has been emphasized so frequently that it is well to remember that their situations at the outset of the war were not strictly comparable.

With a study of the war period, begins the analysis of the causes and effects of depreciation. In a sense, such a study is still introductory. During the war the situation was abnormal and freedom of action and trade were interfered with by many factors. So great was the interference in economic life, for instance, that internal depreciation went to considerable lengths while external depreciation was comparatively slight, because of pegging. Under more normal conditions it can scarcely be as great as it was during the war.[1] Because of these unusual circumstances,

[1] The cost of the dollar increased about 8 per cent and the cost of commodities in France about 248 per cent.

78

consideration of the war period is primarily an attempt to explain what came after. War measures cannot be analyzed in great detail. We shall attempt to pass them rapidly in review.

In considering the war period it is well to keep in mind the relation of various laws and provisions to the forces which have determined the value of the franc.[1] These forces, it will be recalled, are three: quantity of money, balance of trade, and speculation or confidence. One can see the very direct bearing of war measures on these three influences. In the first place, the increase of the quantity of money and the increased purchases of goods and securities at the very outbreak of hostilities had a very rapid effect on prices, or the internal depreciation of the franc. In the second place, the disturbance to French exports and the rapid increase of imports was inevitably a factor in the temporary as well as the later decline in the exchange value of the franc. In the third place, confidence, both in the success of the French armies and in the working out of French financial plans, influenced very greatly both aspects of the value of the franc. It is obvious that one must assign some importance to each of these factors. The study of causes is limited by the unusual interference with economic life, but the general influence of these factors on the franc must be observed throughout these years.

The problem of the depreciation of the franc is a large one. It is possible to distinguish at least three degrees of depreciation—mild depreciation, severe depreciation, and collapse.[2] There might be some criticism of the use of the

[1] See *supra,* Chapter I, pp. 17, 20, 27, 32, 37.

[2] J. W. Angell, *The Theory of International Prices* (Cambridge, Mass., 1926), p. 425. Angell says of the phrases of depreciation that they are four: "moderate depreciation, severe depreciation, extreme depreciation and collapse, and finally—a stage which may happily intervene at any point in the cycle—recovery and stability. . . ." It seems best to the writer to exclude recovery as being rather distinct from depreciation, and not to posit any theory of a cyclical movement in depreciation.

word mild for any of the recent war-time depreciation, but, in comparison with the other stages under consideration, it seems justifiable. Mild depreciation, then, we may say took place in England, and in France during the early years of the war. If, in the case of France, one emphasizes external as contrasted with internal depreciation, the whole war period can be put in the first, or mild, phase. It is not possible to measure the exact limits where one degree ends and the next begins. In general, however, one may make one's meaning clear by indicating that in the case of mild depreciation the return to par is usually desirable or at least possible. According to this use of the term mild depreciation, one must include most of the cases where depreciation has not led to a 200 per cent rise in prices and exchange rates. There was, for instance, very little serious doubt of the return of the pound sterling to par,[1] even though depreciation carried it as low as $3.22, the average for February, 1920.[2] There was, it is true, considerable disagreement as to the means and the date of returning to par, but with one or two striking exceptions most people confidently relied on a return to the former gold value till after 1926.

During the war, then, whether one judges from the attitude which prevailed as regards the franc or from its value on the foreign exchanges, one may call depreciation moderate. After the war, on the other hand, there came a striking change. It is well, at this point, to look ahead to the very different conditions which prevailed in France from 1919 on. The first year after the armistice was a critical one, also, for other European countries. Those who were destined to stabilize their currency later at a low value suffered very marked depreciation at this time. The German mark fell from 9.64 cents in February, 1919, to 7.95 cents in March,

---

[1] There was considerable agitation against the return to par but official and banking opinion was practically unanimous.

[2] U. S. Senate, *Foreign Currency and Exchange Investigation*, p. 453.

1919.[1] By the end of the year it was worth only 2.10 cents, or, to express the values in another way, the cost of the dollar had increased 350 per cent in about twelve months, and about 1000 per cent since 1913; recovery was scarcely possible. The Italian lira also fell sharply during 1919. It fell from 15.75 cents to 7.66 cents.[2] The course of the exchange rates of the other belligerents was similar.

Severe depreciation such as followed the war will be considered in the chapters which follow. It is mentioned here in order to throw into relief the two degrees of depreciation. It must be remembered that even the very marked changes in value which came with the war were moderate in comparison with the later declines. It is very necessary to distinguish as far as possible between the different economic relationships which prevail with different degrees of depreciation. Even though definite mathematical limits cannot be set, the difference in types is distinguishable. In so far as a quantitative measure can be used, one may say tentatively, as above, that return to par is hardly possible after the exchanges and price levels have increased more than two or three hundred per cent. Such a figure is suggested with many reservations and is based almost wholly on a study of the French case. It is not set forth as a positive or clear-cut limit, nor one on which later argument should stand or fall. It gives merely a hint of the extent to which, it seems, depreciation may go without making a return to par impossible. This figure has been chosen because it seems, from a close observation of French life, that the value relationships, the condition of industry and public finance, were not thrown hopelessly out of joint until, in 1919, depreciation had passed this point. It is, of course, impossible to offer incontrovertible proof. This much, however, will be

[1] U. S. Senate, *Foreign Currency and Exchange Investigation*, p. 531. What really happened was that a *new* mark was substituted when the *old* mark had fallen to about one trillionth of its former value.

[2] *Ibid.*, p. 506.

admitted by all students of recent cases of depreciation—
that there is somewhere a point where the relationships of
various economic factors change sharply. There is a point
where speculation becomes extremely important and all
other factors become relatively unimportant, although the
exact moment at which the transition takes place must be a
matter of some doubt. Moreover, if one carries the analysis
into the next phase, the period of collapse, or near collapse,
one finds still different influences and connections. In the
time of wild panic, the extreme shortage of monetary medium, as compared with the level of prices despite the rapid
increase of notes, is indicative of the cumulative force driv-
ing a currency to destruction. Such a situation was evident
in Germany. The discussion of the later phases of depreciation must, however, be postponed. It is necessary to consider first the causes and conditions of the first decline of
the franc. Depreciation in France during the war was similar in many respects to other cases which have been subjected to careful scrutiny, such cases as the greenbacks and
the pound during the restriction period, for instance.[1]

A general survey of war conditions must be based to a
considerable extent on the various laws, loans, and changes
in the price structure which are to be observed from 1914
to 1919. The steps taken by the government to protect the
franc and to increase its resources are first in importance.
The more general economic influences will be considered after these have been summarized.

THE DESPERATE EFFORTS OF 1914

The war-time depreciation of the franc may be divided
conveniently into three main periods. The first, which is

[1] The National Industrial Conference Board, *Inter-Ally Debts and the
United States* (New York, 1925), pp. 140-186. This study gives a convenient
summary of five such cases. W. C. Mitchell's books are the forerunners
of other later works and supply much valuable material for a study of
conditions of depreciation.

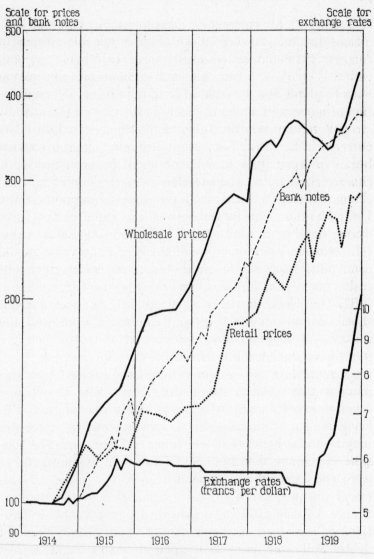

CHART IV

PRICES, DOLLAR RATE AND NOTE CIRCULATION, 1914-1919 [1]

[1] See appendix for figures.

characterized by emergency measures and abnormal conditions in almost every phase of economic life, began in August, 1914 and lasted until April, 1915.[1] The second, which is marked by an increase of financial coöperation with England, the flotation of long-time loans, the resumption of more normal conditions in industry, and the difficult struggle to maintain the value of the franc, lasted until the entrance of the United States into the war. The third period began in April, 1917 and lasted until the armistice. It is characterized by a complete change in the import and exchange situations, because of the financial support of the United States. The movements of the value of the franc during these years were various but at no time did its value fall below 18 cents on the exchanges and the value in the commodity markets, though declining, caused no great confusion nor fear of future collapse.

The outbreak of the war in August came as a great shock, despite all the fears and rumors. The news of the invasion of Belgium, the mobilization of troops, and the immediate inauguration of emergency measures paralyzed for several days the economic life of the nation. A serious panic was avoided with difficulty. Every possible step was taken to avoid the failure of banks and business men and to keep industry running. Some of the various measures may be listed here; the more important ones must be considered in more detail below. Of the very first importance were the laws which suspended specie payment and allowed the increase of the note circulation of the Bank of France. Closely allied to these provisions were the declarations of moratoria on bank deposits and various kinds of debts. Following very soon upon these laws and decrees came the internal loans, first short-time and, in the later period, long-time loans. As time went on, many regulations were put in force which aimed to keep down the cost of

[1] Jules Décamps, *Les Changes étrangers* (Paris, 1922). M. Décamps divides the war period into three periods much as we have done here.

living and prevent suffering among the poorer classes. Such were the fixing of certain prices; the rationing of coal, sugar, gasoline, and various other commodities; the taxing of certain luxuries; and relief allowances to the families of soldiers, to refugees, and to other victims of the war. There were also arrangements to encourage certain industries, subsidies to wages in some cases, and the suspension of import duties on some important commodities. In addition to this, the government took an unusual interest in what concerned transportation, foreign commerce, and the production of the necessities of life.[1]

Let us recall briefly the situation in August, and then proceed to the analysis of the laws of August 5, 1914. On August 1 the Germans mobilized on the French frontier.[2] On August 2 the French were mobilized. The *Bourse* was in violent commotion and the exchanges were very high.[3] On August 3 Germany sent an ultimatum to Belgium. On August 4 the British declared war on Germany, after declaring an ultimatum. The Germans crossed the frontier of Belgium on the following day and attacked Liége. Meanwhile, the French had called an extraordinary session of Parliament, and on August 5 most of the emergency measures were passed.[4] The next day the British called 500,000 men into the field and the Germans retired from Liége; meanwhile the French gained a little ground at Mulhouse. The break between France and Austria came on August 10. It must be remembered that it was not until September that

[1] H. E. Fisk, *French Public Finance* (New York, 1922), pp. 69-83. This book gives a clear and simple statement of the more important measures. Those which demand special attention here will be mentioned later with reference to the French sources.

[2] *Le Pour et le contre* (Paris, August 9, 1914). This weekly financial journal is the source of this description of events.

[3] *Journal officiel, Chambre,* December 29, 1919, p. 5402. "L'Allemagne réalisait son agression en pleine crise de trésorie, d'emprunt et aussi en pleine crise du marché."

[4] *Bulletin de statistique et de législation comparée* (Paris, 1914), p. 135. See also below.

the Germans penetrated so far into French territory that they came almost within gunshot of Paris. During August the *Bourse* remained open,[1] the government remained in Paris, and there was no realization of the probable length of the war. In September, however, the situation grew worse and the *Bourse* was closed on the third of that month. The French government moved from Paris and the next laws were promulgated from Bordeaux.

The first period of severe strain was eased after the battle of the Marne. The financial and industrial mechanisms had withstood it well. After the first drive was over, however, the country had to look for the resources to keep up the long struggle. The more permanent measures were quite different in their nature and importance from the early ones.

The laws of August 5, 1914, in addition to declaring a moratorium on debts coming due, provided for family allowances, raised the upper limits of the circulation of the Bank of France and the Bank of Algeria, and established *cours forcé* for the money.[2] The London *Economist* gives a convenient list of the main laws and provisions which are of interest here.[3] It classifies these as economic and financial.

A. Economic
    I. Suspension of import duties on wheat, barley, oats, maize, and hay
    II. Free importation of frozen meats and potatoes
    III. Embargo on salt exports and foods
    IV. Embargo on exportation of contraband of war

B. Financial
    I. Declaration of temporary moratorium
    II. (a) Deposits of less than 250 francs may be withdrawn
        (b) Deposits over 250 francs, only 5 per cent could be withdrawn

[1] *The Economist* (London, August 22, 1914), p. 353. The markets which remained open "were reduced to impotence."

[2] *Bulletin de statistique et de législation comparée, loc. cit.*, pp. 135, 136. Decrees of July 31 and August 1 had put into force similar moratoria.

[3] *The Economist* (London, August 15, 1914), p. 321.

(c) Moratorium extended to insurance contracts
(d) Relaxation of installment payments on French
   3½ per cent loan
III. Savings bank withdrawals limited to 50 francs a fort-
   night
IV. The issue of 5 and 20 franc notes
V. Suspension of specie payments

All these laws were aimed to strengthen the position of banks and industries so that production could go on uninterrupted. Along with these financial changes came the increase of advances of the Bank of France to the state, but no public statement of this was made until December.[1] The regular statements of the Bank of France were omitted during this period.

INCONVERTIBILITY

The importance of inconvertibility at such a time is universally realized. The purposes were two. In the first place, it was necessary to prevent the flow of gold into hand to hand circulation. Paper money would otherwise have been presented to banks for redemption and the large amount of wealth in this form would not have been at the disposal of the state. In the second place, it made it easier to increase the currency if the changing relation of gold to paper were not clearly evident. With no legal connection between the precious metals and the paper money, it was not clear to all concerned that the paper was losing a considerable part of its value. This fiat money was therefore received without objection when it was tendered in payment of debts. The value of money, once the link with gold is broken, is a matter of speculation to a considerable extent; the situation becomes different from that most often explained by the English classical theory. This theory relies on the effect of gold exports or imports on price levels to bring about a reaction, once the value of money has departed far from its norm. That is to say, if the value of the franc

[1] *Bulletin de statistique et de législation comparée, loc. cit.,* p. 463.

has declined in comparison with the pound, in the first place, gold would be exported to London, and English prices would rise. French prices, on the other hand, would tend to be depressed by the contraction of the means of payment. Then, in the second place, imports from France to England would increase because they became cheaper as compared with the rising English commodities. This would cause the value of the franc to rise again as the balance of payments became more favorable to it. In the case of inconvertible money, on the contrary, no such sequence of events can take place. This is mainly because *gold* exports do not affect prices in the same way; there is no mechanism present to bring about a reaction. There is no decline of prices in France and no marked rise in prices in the other country. It is possible, in fact, that the *credits* granted to France to meet the payments which she finds in excess of her normal supply of credits will have an inflationary— not a depressing—effect on prices. It is not possible, however, to prove that these will cause inflation in one country alone. They are apt to have some effect on price levels in both countries. The credits do not leave the country as definitively as does the gold in the illustration. They may remain for a long period in France, and, if this be the case, there is no force which will swing export trade the other way, since the price differential does not necessarily favor France. Such a state of affairs we find during the war. It is true that hostilities interfered very much with trade, but it is also evident that even after the war there was no force working strongly through price levels to bring the franc back to par. Inconvertibility sets up a special situation for which theory has not yet offered completely satisfactory explanation though the need for such explanation is recognized.[1]

The most serious attempt to find new limits which define the zone of fluctuation of inconvertible money is prob-

[1] See *supra*, Chapter I, p. 40.

ably that of Cassel.[1] He says that new determinants that
restrict the variation of exchange values are price levels
within and without a country. These, he claims, bring about
a reaction in the value of depreciated money. If its external
purchasing power is out of harmony with its internal purchasing power—that is, if the franc should become so cheap
in dollars that it would pay those with dollars to buy francs,
and those with francs to buy French goods rather than
American goods—the favorable turn in French export trade
would lead to an increase in the value of the francs. This
explanation, the purchasing power parities doctrine, has
been considered in Chapter I.[2] It need not be described
further at this point, except to note this aspect of it, that
it is an attempt to substitute a new par for the old par based
on gold. Keynes and Gregory are among the important
economists who follow Cassel in holding this theory of the
exchanges.[3] We have cast doubt as to the working of such
limiting factors in the French case. The internal purchasing
power in France did not govern to any considerable extent
the value of the franc on the exchanges. Although both
phases of value act on each other, the exchange rates seemed
to dominate the price level within France. It is obvious,
then, that if gold values no longer set limits to the fluctuations of a currency, if the external and internal values inter-
act in a very complex and incalculable way, neither setting
any outside limits on the value of the other, the outstanding characteristic of inconvertibility is the uncertainty
of future values. On this fact rests the very great influence
of speculation, which has been discussed in Chapter I.

INFLATION

Inconvertibility is a necessity, because without it the
inflation of the note circulation would be much more diffi-

[1] Gustav Cassel, *Money and Foreign Exchange After 1914* (New York,
1923), pp. 140, 147-162. [2] See *supra*, Chapter I.
[3] J. M. Keynes, *Monetary Reform* (New York, 1924), p. 96. T. E.
Gregory, *Foreign Exchange* (Oxford, 1925), pp. 82-85.

cult. Every country of importance went off the gold standard for a part of the war period. Every country inflated its
circulation to a certain extent. As for belligerent countries,
war could not have been carried on very long without inflation. It was used, both directly to pay the bills of the
government, and indirectly to help the flotation of loans
which brought money into the treasury. As far as concerns the neutral countries, inflation was forced on them
by price conditions at home or abroad, and, in some cases,
by the inflow of gold.

There are various definitions of inflation, but though
in practice there is usually little doubt as to when it occurs there is no entirely satisfactory statement as to just
what it is.[1] Some use the term as if they had in mind
primarily the quantitative aspects of the situation, that is,
the number of notes existing at a given time in comparison
with some other time.[2] Others seem more concerned with
the causal relation of money and prices. The difficulty in the
use of the word arises because those who are talking of
causes frequently speak as if an overissue of notes led to
a rise in prices, which process they call inflation. In reality,
the matter is far from being so simple. Suppose, as occurred
in certain cases in France, through scarcity, goods rose in
price, and this increase in value led later to an increase in
the money to buy these goods, is this to be called inflation?
Even though this represents a case which lies outside the
simpler statements of the quantity theory, it is apparent
that, in the broadest sense, this is inflation. The word becomes almost unusable for general purposes if it is taken
to imply that any increase in currency must necessarily
affect prices.

[1] A. C. Pigou, "Inflation," *Economic Journal* (December, 1917), vol.
xxvii, 486-494.

[2] Professor Joseph Schumpeter has defined inflation as the disturbance
of the relation between the stream of consumable goods and money
incomes per unit of account. (Lectures, unpublished, Harvard University,
April, 1928).

On the other hand, a definition of inflation must take account both of the means of payment and of prices. Hawtrey says that a definition is hardly necessary.[1] Cassel attempts to view the matter on an arithmetical basis. He defines inflation as "the actual creation of artificial purchasing power." [2] He then goes on to say in a later chapter that the "price level becomes under all circumstances the measure of inflation." [3] Keynes calls inflation an "expansion in the supply of money to spend relative to the supply of things to purchase." [4] In his later discussion he considers inflation as a means of taxation.[5] This emphasis on motive has a real value, for in cases of very great extension of purchasing power it is usually to fill some extraordinary need. The likeness of the two phenomena, taxation and inflation, however, stops at this point. The diffusion of inflation through the community is slow, and the effects on different kinds of incomes differ greatly from those of taxation. Moreover, it is not necessarily true that the goods which the government buys with the printed notes are a net deduction from the consumption of the community, as compared with the pre-inflation consumption. Inflation is a dynamic phenomenon. It may lead to the production of greater volume of goods to be consumed. Taxation, on the other hand, is apt to repress production and so to mean a definite curtailment of consumption on the part of the public, at least to the amount of money taken in taxes, perhaps more.

As the word *inflation* is used here it refers to deliberate increases of the means of payment, made mainly by the government. The stress on the conscious act involved is in line with that made by Keynes, though we differ with his further conclusions; and by Pigou in his article in the *Economic Journal*.[6] There is no attempt made here to

[1] R. G. Hawtrey, *Monetary Reconstruction* (London, 1923), p. 33.
[2] Cassel, *op. cit.*, p. 11. [4] J. M. Keynes, *op. cit.*, p. 6.
[3] *Ibid.*, p. 62. [5] J. M. Keynes, *op. cit.*, p. 46.
[6] Pigou, *loc. cit.*, "A way out of this impasse, at all events in modern communities where bankers if left to themselves, may be presumed to

offer a definition; perhaps Hawtrey is right in saying that it is not necessary. There is a fairly general understanding of what the term means. It seems well, however, to point out that there is a clear distinction which may be drawn between the relationships and circumstances in the different cases of increase in the means of payment; there is, first, the situation such as existed in France during the war, where a persistent need of funds led the government to push new notes into circulation; and, in the second place, a situation in which rising price levels in other countries or any change in reserves or prices within a country lead to a drawing out of money or credit from banks.

In the case of France, inflation as it is referred to here may be represented roughly by the advances of the Bank of France to the state. These rose to the high point of 35,950 million francs in December, 1925.[1] This must be taken as a minimum figure for inflation at that time as some of the other increases in the note circulation may be considered inflationary, according to the basic reason for the issues and the effect on prices which can be traced to them. The inevitability of inflation cannot be stressed too much. According to a statement made by Sir Arthur Salter in 1925:

. . . there is still too great a disposition to regard inflation merely as a financial vice. . . . Inflation is, in my view, the practically inevitable complement of war or postwar loans after these pass a certain proportion of the annual taxable capacity of a country.[2]

It will be noted that he included postwar as well as war inflations in this statement. As far as France is concerned, postwar inflation was more dangerous than that during the war because of the tremendous needs for reconstruction as

act in accordance with recognized rules and customs, is to distinguish between movements which are and those which are not, made possible by overt government interference with the banking and monetary machine."

[1] See appendix for table of advances.

[2] Sir Arthur Salter, U. S. Senate, *Foreign Currency and Exchange Investigation* (1925), p. 135.

well as on account of political and other difficulties. As Rist
has so clearly pointed out, in most countries the reversal
of prices in 1920 checked inflation, whereas in France, because of rebuilding, this meant only a temporary decline in
the means of payment and had no substantial effect on the
situation.[1]

Inflation, then, accompanied by inconvertibility, was
one of the most necessary and immediate measures adopted
at the outbreak of the war. It continued to play an important part in French finance till the end of 1925. In order
to make this less alarming to the public, the Bank of France
was permitted to omit its regular weekly statements. These
statements ceased at the end of July, and were not resumed during 1914.[2] It was announced, however, at the end
of the year, that the circulation had increased from 6,683
million francs on July 30 to 9,986 million francs on December 10, 1914. This increase was in part called for by the
disappearance of gold from circulation. It is not possible to
state exactly how much difference the gold made, but it
may easily have amounted to half the increase in the paper
circulation. In other words, some of the new paper merely
displaced gold. The convention of September 21 increased
the legal limit of advances by the Bank of France to the
state to 3,000 million francs, thus leaving the way open for
further inflation.[3]

FURTHER PROVISIONS FOR WAR FINANCE

Immediately following on these first desperate measures
to meet the sudden demand for funds came others in the
nature of loans external and internal, and various forms
of control and price fixing. The Battle of the Marne had in-

[1] Charles Rist, *La Déflation en pratique* (Paris, 1924), pp. 70-71.
[2] See appendix.
[3] See tabular statement of the legal limits and actual amounts of advances and note circulation *infra*, Chapter VI.

dicated the serious need for resources to carry on what might be a protracted war. The French government, from Bordeaux, issued certain decrees. One of the most important of these was that of September 13, concerning the sale of *bons de la défense nationale*.[1] These notes were to be issued in denominations of 100 and 1,000 francs through post offices and banks. They were to yield an interest of five per cent. They became so popular and formed such a ready resource for the government, that they were usually very close to, or even in excess of, the authorized total. The number outstanding on December 15 amounted to more than one billion francs. These were short-term credits, to run for a year or less. A large number of these notes were taken up by banks and insurance companies, in some cases as a productive use of temporarily idle funds, and in some instances because of laws or indirect pressure brought to bear on these institutions by the government. The importance of this source of credit was very great as can be judged by figures for the total in circulation.

TABLE IV

BONS DE LA DÉFENSE OUTSTANDING AT THE END
OF THE YEAR [2]

(In millions of francs)

1914	1,619	1919	46,140
1915	6,963	1920	48,938
1916	12,574	1921	65,420
1917	19,522	1922	56,431
1918	22,335	1923	54,423

It was due to the help of these *bons* that the advances of the Bank of France to the state were kept at a comparatively low figure.[3] This was in spite of the fact that the French war expenditures reached their maximum at the

[1] A. Ribot, *Exposé des motifs, Bulletin de statistique et de législation comparée* (Paris, 1914), p. 462. See also *infra* Chapter VI.

[2] Henry Chéron, *Rapport au Sénat*, no. 84, Paris, February 22, 1926. For later figure see Chapter VI.

[3] *The Economist* (London, October 3, 1914), p. 569, and (October 17) p. 643.

very outset of the war, and that her tax receipts fell off.[1]
The issue of the *bons* was, perhaps, the most important
financial event of the fall.

External loans were important as well as internal loans,
but their special significance was not evident in the first
months of the war. This was because the franc was at a
premium in New York. It was natural that the sudden demand by American tourists for money to return to the
United States caused large offerings of dollars for francs.
Another reason was the maturing bonds of the New York
City Bank, which had to be paid off in francs. The net result of these facts was that gold imports into France exceeded exports in this year.[2] Even with the inflow of gold,
however, the franc was above par in terms of dollars, so
the foreign loans were urgently needed at this time to meet
exchange demands. Such loans were of importance as an addition to the resources of the government, and they came
to be indispensable as a means of protecting the exchange
when in January, 1915 the franc fell below par in terms
of dollars.[3]

There was no adequate arrangement for financing external purchases during this first period. It was largely a
matter of chance that the flow of funds was towards
France at the outbreak of the war.[4] After the tide turned [5]
it was extremely difficult for France to finance her foreign
trade, whereas imports became increasingly necessary.
There were a number of small loans floated outside the coun-

---

[1] Gaston Jèze, *Les Finances de guerre* (Paris, 1920), pp. 24, 40.

[2] U. S. Senate, *Foreign Currency and Exchange Investigation*, p. 486.

[3] *Ibid.*, p. 475.

[4] Georges Pallain, Governor of the Bank of France, "Compte rendu de
la Banque de France, 1915," *Bulletin de statistique et de législation comparée* (February, 1916), pp. 227, 228. "Depuis le début des hostilités
jusqu' aux premières semaines de 1915, les changes étrangers nous étaient
favorables."

[5] *Le Pour et le contre* (Paris, February 21, 1915). The United States
debt to France is here given as 2,000 million francs. It was liquidated
before the end of the year.

try. Décamps says that about 400 million francs' worth
of treasury bills were sold abroad in December, 1914. It is
evident that the government had resources abroad at the
beginning of 1915, for gold flowed into the country in January. Since these resources were not large, a more thorough
and far-seeing plan had to be worked out to meet the growing needs of the nation.

CLOSE COÖPERATION WITH ENGLAND

It was not until April, 1915 that the difficulty of maintaining the exchange rates was fully realized. It was then
that the flow of gold outward became apparent,[1] and all
hope of an early termination of the war was abandoned.
In view of these facts, arrangements were made with the
British treasury on April 30 for loans to France in return
for which the Bank of France sent a small amount of gold
to London.[2] This eased the situation temporarily but further negotiations had to be initiated in the summer. They resulted in the agreement between England and France on
August 15 and the Boulogne conference of August 29, at
which further plans for financial coöperation were made
definite.[3] The result of all this was the floating in America
in September and October of a loan of 500 million dollars,
one half of the proceeds of which were to go to France.
Meanwhile France sent more gold to London in exchange
for larger commercial credits.

The drawing together of the two strongest allies to arrange their finances in common was a very important tendency. Without the help of England, France could hardly
have bought the large amounts of American wheat, cotton,
steel, and other necessities which made her balance of trade

---

[1] U. S. Senate, *Foreign Currency and Exchange Investigation*, p. 487.
Décamps, *op. cit.*, p. 283. Décamps, whom we follow in his division of
the war period, characterizes the years 1915-17 as those of greatest gold
exports.

[2] "Compte rendu de la Banque de France, 1915," *loc. cit.*, p. 230.

[3] *L'Economiste français* (August 21, 1915), p. 236.

so unfavorable during the war years. In order to control to better advantage the value of the franc on the foreign exchanges, the Bank of France sold exchange to meet commercial needs, thus centralizing and coördinating the important dealings. During 1915 another prohibition of private exports of gold was decreed in the summer, and ratified by law in the fall. To meet the needs of the treasury the limit of the amount of *bons de la défense* was raised several times.

This reliance on short-term credit alone could not go on indefinitely. In November, the first consolidation issue was floated. It netted the government a nominal 13 billion francs, but of this only 6 billions was paid in cash.[1] The rest was paid in short-term obligations and a small fraction in the troublesome 3½ per cent 1914 *rente*. The issue took the form of a 5 per cent fifteen-year bond, sold at 88 to yield about 5.70 per cent. The loan was fairly well received, though it strained to the limit the funds of the money market, particularly since there had been a general liquidation of debts which had held over from 1914. There were five other consolidation loans.

TABLE V

AMOUNTS RECEIVED BY THE GOVERNMENT FROM INTERNAL LOANS[2]

1915–1920

(In millions of francs)

Year	Cash	Total	Per Cent	Yield
1915	6,285	13,308	5	5.73
1916	5,425	10,082	5	5.71
1917	5,174	10,209	4	5.83
1918	7,246	22,163	4	5.68
1919	7,035	15,941	5	5.75
1920	11,278	28,089	6	6.00

[1] Etienne Clémentel, *Inventaire de la situation financière de la France au début de la treizième Législature* (Paris, 1924), p. 29. See also "Compte rendu de la Banque de France, 1915," *loc. cit.*, p. 231.

[2] *Ibid.*, p. 29. For the yield, see Germain Martin, *op. cit.*, p. 163. The rest of the payments were made largely in *Bons du Trèsor, Bons de la défense nationale, Obligations de la défense nationale*, and *rentes*.

The year 1916, like 1915, was marked by various arrangements increasing the credit extended to France by England. Treasury bills were discounted in London and gold was sent as the basis of credit. A second conference was held, this time in Calais, to reach an agreement on details.[1] The French tried in other ways to build up foreign credits. One method adopted was the calling in of foreign securities held by individuals which were paid for by the French government in *rentes*. This move was not very successful.[2] In addition to this, the French borrowed small sums in the United States. They borrowed several million francs in Japan, Switzerland, and other countries. The total of these various loans probably came to less than a billion francs. Some account should be taken, however, of the fact that various cities borrowed considerable money in the outside markets in addition to that secured by the central government.[3]

It is difficult to weigh and compare the various kinds of dangers through which France passed. The first months of the war were critical, so assuredly were the last months, when in the spring and summer of 1918 Germany made her desperate effort to break the French line. It is probable, however, from a financial point of view, that the first months of 1917 were the most difficult.[4] It was at this time that the miscellaneous foreign credits which France had been using became very scarce. England was feeling the burden of helping France supply herself with imports; it was doubtful where either of them could turn for further aid. It was only by extensive use of English credit that the franc had been pegged from October, 1916 to April, 1917. It would not have

---

[1] Jules Décamps, *op. cit.*, p. 323.

[2] U. S. Senate, *Foreign Currency and Exchange Investigation*, p. 309.

[3] "Compte rendu de la Banque de France, 1916," *Bulletin de statistique et de législation comparée*, vol. 81 (1917), pp. 208-210. The commercial deficit was about fourteen billion francs in 1916. The exchanges were steadied with miscellaneous credits. Considerable gold was exported.

[4] Auguste Arnauné, *La Monnaie* (Paris, 1926), p. 205.

been possible in the ensuing period, without the credits opened by the American treasury, to finance exports to France.

Before we pass from the second to the third war period, it is well to note the course of prices during these years of inflation, inconvertibility, and exchange disturbance. The index number of wholesale prices shows a steadily upward trend. The increase from 100 in July, 1914 to approximately 300 in 1919 was considerable.[1] The increase of retail prices, on the other hand, was, as could be expected, less marked. During the first months of the war the increase in prices as expressed in the wholesale index was to 144 per cent of 1914. The further ascent forms a nearly straight line on a logarithmic scale, showing that the *rate* of increase was almost uniform. The following figures will indicate in a general way the nature of these changes. Further detail as to prices will be found in Chapter VII. The lag of retail prices in Table VI given on page 100 noted is usual during periods of marked change. Furthermore, the cost of living was kept down by the sluggishness of certain commodities, and in particular by rent, which was fixed by law. It is best not to enter into a detailed discussion of the price increase here. It is well to note in passing, however, since price change was one of the important characteristics of the war period. It also stimulated production [2] to the extreme effort necessary to furnish the army with supplies.

That the needs of the army were very great and that productive resources were strained to the limit may be inferred from the size of the imports in the early months of 1917. In January, 1917, for instance, the value of imports was 2,179 million francs, as compared with 1,180 million francs in January, 1916. The imports in March, 1917 rose

[1] See appendix.

[2] "Compte rendu de la Banque de France, 1917," *Bulletin de statistique et de législation comparée* (April, 1918), p. 671. The increase in coal consumption is here noted as an indication of commercial activity.

TABLE VI

WHOLESALE AND RETAIL PRICE INDICES[1]

1914–1919

(1914 = 100)

Year	Quarter	Retail	Wholesale
1914	1st	...	....
	2nd	...	....
	3rd	100	100.0
	4th	...	112.8
1915	1st	122	132.3
	2nd	116	140.3
	3rd	122	147.5
	4th	120	166.7
1916	1st	137	189.9
	2nd	135	192.4
	3rd	132	192.7
	4th	138	207.8
1917	1st	139	233.6
	2nd	147	271.8
	3rd	183	285.9
	4th	184	279.0
1918	1st	191	319.5
	2nd	218	340.5
	3rd	306	344.5
	4th	237	367.6
1919	1st	248	355.0
	2nd	257	339.0
	3rd	261	356.0
	4th	283	390.0

to 3,035 million francs, the highest figure for the war period.[2] In face of the heavy unfavorable balance of trade, it is no wonder that France was finding it extremely difficult to secure foreign credits. Left to herself, it is doubtful if she would have succeeded. Fortunately, however, help from the United States was at hand.

[1] *Bulletin de la statistique générale,* 1918, April, pp. 251, 260, October, p. 145; 1919, April, pp. 296, 310, October, p. 12; 1920, July, pp. 300, 323.
[2] See appendix.

The United States as a Source of Credits

The third period of war finance is that from April, 1917 to the end of the war. It is characterized by the dependence of France on America rather than on England for foreign credits. It was possible, after the United States declared war, with the aid of a drawing account in Washington to maintain the franc through all the trying months which followed. Even though the outcome of the fighting was often uncertain, relief from the necessity of paying for imports made the immediate financial situation of France secure. There are many interesting and provocative questions connected with these credits extended by the United States government to France, for instance the manner in which imports to France were checked off against these credits. There are serious problems in regard to debts and international relations that hinge on the intention of the government in granting these loans. It is not possible to consider here the circumstances in which the arrangements were made.[1] Various interpretations have been put on the speeches and government pronouncements.

The main fact to be noted in considering the value of the franc is that France was becoming a very poor risk from the banker's point of view but the United States government supported her with credit. The foreign exchange problem of France practically disappeared in April, 1917.[2]

To return to the situation of commerce, the unfavorable balance of commodity trade which had been 14 billion francs in 1916 was 21 billion francs in 1917. The exhaustion of some of the sources of external credit to pay for these imports has been referred to. In addition to this, there was a growing tendency in the United States to look unfavorably

[1] W. R. Batsell, *The Debt Settlements and the Future* (Paris, 1927), pp. 49, 50.

[2] "Compte rendu de la Banque de France," *Bulletin de statistique et de législation comparée* (April, 1918), p. 672.

on new issues of French securities. With the new resources
offered by Congress, the purchase of supplies by France was
limited only by the means of transport; as a result of this,
pressure on the exchanges was entirely relieved.[1] A total of
nearly three billion dollars' worth of goods was bought between 1917 and 1920 without the purchase of any dollar
exchange by France.[2]

The goods bought, however, were not limited to the
amounts covered by treasury credits; the monthly average
of credits used was about 100 million dollars from May, 1917
to September, 1920.[3] The excess of imports over exports, on
the other hand, amounted to about 300 million dollars
throughout this period.[4] Some of the difference must have
been paid by private credits extended by American and
other business men to individuals in France. In this way
there accumulated a large mass of floating credits which was
an important factor in the reversal of the franc when in
1919 and later years American business men wished to liquidate these credits.[5] Imports had to be authorized and in
this way the state prevented the accumulation of debits for
unnecessary things; it also kept the means of transportation
free for the most important commodities. This regulation of
import trade became very strict when it was reënforced by
the restrictions on the purchase of foreign exchange.[6] The
Bank of France sold about 15 billion francs' worth of credit
for commercial needs.[7] In September, 1917, the United
States put an embargo on gold exports,[8] which is reflected

[1] U. S. Senate, *Foreign Currency and Exchange Investigation,* p. 327. The
power of the treasury to grant such credits was voted by Congress, April
24, 1917.

[2] Etienne Clémentel, *Inventaire,* p. 65.   [3] See appendix.

[4] U. S. Senate, *Foreign Currency and Exchange Investigation,* p. 483.

[5] See *infra,* Chapter V.   [6] See *infra,* Chapter VI.

[7] "Compte rendu de la Banque de France, 1917," *loc. cit.,* p. 673. From
the beginning of the war until December, 1917, the Bank of France
put ten and a half billion francs at the disposal of French commerce. Jules
Décamps, *op. cit.,* p. 338.

[8] Gustav Cassel, *op. cit.,* p. 75.

to a certain extent in the decline of imports into France in 1918.[1] In many respects, coöperation of the United States in financial matters counted more than government credits alone would indicate. For instance, the large amount of private credit extended would not have been forthcoming if the political situation between the two countries and the military prospect had been different. The problem of winning the war became from 1917 one of military power and strategy, and only to a small extent a matter of finance.

The Franc Was Steady on the Exchanges

During these three periods, the first emergency period, the time of reliance on England, and the months of American financial aid, the franc remained fairly steady on the exchanges. Pegging was one explanation for the surprising stability of the French exchange, but it was not the only reason. Confidence in the military and financial outcome of the war played its part. Without such confidence it is possible that the pegging operations of the government would not have been successful. It is certain that during the times when the franc was not definitely pegged it would have broken if there had not been a feeling of assurance as to the future. It must be remembered that the volume of commerce paid for by private credits was greater than that financed directly by the government. The action of business men was, therefore, a very great aid to the government, which would have been considerably embarrassed if it had been forced to find all the credits to finance imports for French industry. It is not possible to study all the political and military events which influenced the exchange rate at such times as it was not pegged, or why the franc varied within the zone of fluctuation which the government permitted to remain. The Bank of France did not attempt to set

[1] See appendix, p. 528.

up a gold exchange standard.[1] It merely furnished such a
large part of the exchange credits at rates near par that the
fluctuations were almost negligible during the greater part
of the war. Confidence influenced the franc in its variation
within this zone of fluctuation and also helped to maintain
the franc at those values near the old par which the government wished to prevail.

The internal value of the franc was not as stable as its
value on the exchanges; the steady rise in prices and depreciation of the value of the franc has been indicated in
Table VI given above. Despite a rate of depreciation which
in comparison with normal life was certainly extreme, there
was no serious dislocation of French productive life, nor was
there any clear consciousness on the part of the French as to
what was happening to their money. The rapid rise in certain wages, the expectation of hardship under war conditions, and the attempt by the government to relieve the
most acute suffering prevented any general alarm.

The two aspects of the value of the franc, its relation to
foreign currencies and its power over goods in France, therefore give different indications of what it was worth. The
chart indicates this notable contradiction. There was an attempt to control the franc on both the internal and the external markets, but, as has been indicated, because of the
different natures of the two markets only the exchange control was successful. It was to a certain extent inadvisable
to prevent the upward tendency of prices. This is true because, if price control had been pushed farther it would have
repressed industry to a dangerous extent. However this may
be, it was not feasible to enforce many of the price regulations in a drastic way. Prices, then, since they were less concentrated in one market, represented the *real* value of the
franc more than did the exchange rate. This fact does not

---

[1] "Compte rendu de la Banque de France, 1917," *loc. cit.*, pp. 673, 674.
The *commission des changes* instituted July, 1917, and various other steps
taken to meet the situation are here described.

hold true of the postwar period, when the exchange rate was usually the better indication.[1]

The interrelation of economic factors during the war has been called the characteristic of mild depreciation. This is true even in spite of a considerable degree of interference. Although the various laws and regulations make a comparison with more normal times difficult, there seems no clear evidence that it changed the effect of one factor on another in kind. It certainly changed in degree the influence of one price on other prices. Price control delayed, though it did not prevent, the diffusion of inflation throughout the community. It was responsible for the lags of one price behind another, notably in the case of rents. As some laws kept prices down, so subsidies increased the production of certain commodities, but in neither case did government effort do more than accelerate or retard a tendency already existing. Control of the exchanges, on the other hand, was the one artificial element in the situation which made a profound difference in economic life in general. In spite of all this, however, economic life seemed to be, in the main, free, and very few people realized that the exchange control ran counter to a profound tendency of the franc to decline on the exchanges. This being the case, the situation was decidedly that of moderate depreciation, and had in it practically no elements of panic.

FOUR FACTORS INTERFERING WITH ECONOMIC LIFE

The productive life of France was circumscribed by four types of forces. These were, in the main, evident and unavoidable results of the war situation. First, there were the obvious consequences of *invasion*, the loss of territory, of workers, of morale, and the crippling of production in a number of ways. This was particularly serious because of the loss of territory, which has already been discussed in

[1] See *infra*, Chapter VIII.

Chapter II.[1] In the case of France, many of the key industries were located in the northern departments. In addition to invasion, there was, in the second place, the interruption to *international trade.* The exchange of goods between France and other countries was so completely under control that it was almost like a government monopoly. Some trade was, of course, completely impossible because of the danger to shipping and the inaccessibility of certain markets. These facts were essentially extra-economic and affect the situation so very much that a detailed analysis of economic relations during these years would be useless in view of them.

The two other groups of influences were rooted more firmly in economic life and were typical war phenomena. These were various influences on demand and prices. *Demand,* then, the third abnormal factor, was distorted partly by patriotism and propaganda. There were other changes in demand which grew out of rapid changes in incomes and a different attitude toward spending and saving. We see another aspect of demand as an interfering factor evident in the large requirements of the government for certain commodities irrespective of cost. The states' need both for imports and for home products was highly inelastic. Since the upward pressure on prices is almost always more effective than the downward, such changes necessarily lead to an upward trend of prices.[2] The fourth main change, which worked counter to the third, was *price control,* already mentioned. It has been said above that this was not very effective in the French case; bread, coal, and a few other basic commodities were kept down with reasonable success, it is true, but such cases of control acted to only a slight de-

[1] See *supra,* Chapter II.

[2] The interaction of prices and wages on each other may be represented by a spiral. Since rising prices give reasons for higher wages, and increased spending by wage earners, the tendency naturally continues, unless offset by some drastic change in money or some great improvement in the arts.

gree on the whole upward tendency.[1] Price control had
some social significance, for it was operative in the case of
some necessities of life, but from a purely economic point
of view its importance was slight.

Those who wish to interpret the war situation in terms
of the quantity theory will find it easy to do so. There was a
fairly close correspondence between the increase in the
note circulation and the rise in prices.[2] It is not possible
from this general upward tendency of the two factors to
judge that note increases were generally the cause of price
increase. The cause of the latter lay in the general condition of war demand, of which note circulation was merely
an expression or phase. Moreover, an exact measure of increase in money is not possible, since it is not known how
much gold was in circulation. The increase in note circulation was probably less than increase in prices by a considerable sum. The former increased to 30 billions by December
26, 1918,[3] the latter increased to 355 per cent by the beginning of 1919. In order to make a comparison it is necessary to give the means of payment as a relative on a 1913
base, and this cannot be done accurately. The Bank of
France *Service d'Etudes* gives the 1913 circulation as 12 billion francs of gold, silver, and paper notes,[4] but this is an
estimate of an uncertain quantity. Earlier estimates place
the number between ten and twelve. In any case the increase is barely 300 per cent as compared with 350 per cent
for prices. The comparison cannot be exact, however, because the amount of gold in circulation and in hoards is not
known with any degree of accuracy. One must be content,
therefore, with the general statement that wholesale prices
rose more than did the note circulation.

The precise manner of the inflation behind the price in-

[1] Lucien March, *Mouvement des prix et des salaires pendant la guerre*
(Paris, 1922), pp. 172, 182, 183.   [2] See Chart IV.

[3] See *infra*, appendix. The note circulation is given here for each week
of the period under consideration.

[4] *Service d'études de la Banque de France* (unpublished, Paris, 1927).

creases is not always easy to distinguish. The government
borrowed large sums from the Bank. The total at the end
of the war was 16 billion francs.[1] This money passed at
once into general circulation through the payment for supplies, relief, and other things. In addition to this, the Bank
of France put other notes in circulation through the discounting process. For this reason the increase in notes was
larger than the increase in advances to the state. This discrepancy must have amounted to approximately three or
four billion francs, if the total *increase* in circulation is
taken as approximately nineteen or twenty billion francs,
as is given above. Paper money, however, covered only a
small part of the war-time expenditures of the government.
Another small fraction was met by taxation, the rest was
covered by government loans, the means whereby the government turned over several times the sums secured from
the bank—drawing them back from circulation by the sale
of securities after they had been spent once for goods.
Short-time loans served over and over again to bring in the
needed money. This flow of funds from the treasury to the
public and back into loans would not have moved so fast
unless it had been urged along by the free spending of inflationary notes by the government. A larger and larger
quantity of notes was passing into circulation and only a
part came back as the result of the sale of securities. The
very large amounts of money needed by the government
must be borne in mind; deficits during the war amounted to
more than 144 billion francs.[2] This lack was met by advances from the Bank of France to the extent of 16 billion
francs, by consolidated loans to the sum of 55 billion
francs,[3] by *bons de la défense* up to 22 billion francs.[4] The
rest of the resources came from outside the country, since

[1] Germain Martin, *op. cit.*, p. 238.
[2] Etienne Clémentel, *op. cit.*, p. 14.
[3] See *supra*, this chapter.
[4] George-Edgar Bonnet, *Les Expériences monétaires contemporaines*
(Paris, 1926), p. 92. See *supra*, this chapter.

there was no increase in the income received from normal revenues.[1]

The cost of the war to France is estimated at 268 billion francs by Michel.[2] This figure includes the following items:

Reconstruction	100,000	million francs
Allocations (Relief allowances).......	85,000	" "
Defense	83,000	" "
Total...........................	268,000	" "

Such a sum could not have been recovered by taxation. Even the smaller item given as the cost of defense alone was too great to be met by normal revenues. The increases in rates of taxation did little more than serve to offset decreases from other causes.[3] Other nations managed to increase their revenues, but their internal economic life was not disturbed in the same way by invasion. Schacht gives the following figures, showing how England and Germany met this problem:

PART OF THE WAR COST MET BY TAXATION [4]

England	20 per cent	
Germany	6	" "
France	0	" "

Certainly the course taken by England was the wisest, but it was not possible in all cases.

It is probable that a stronger effort at taxation, though it might not have increased revenues very greatly, might have brought a clear realization that war expenses would have to be paid, and therefore might have lessened ex-

[1] H. Schacht, *The Stabilization of the Mark* (London, 1927), p. 14. Schacht gives the following figures for the financing of the war:

Internal loans	43%
Foreign loans	21%
Floating debt	36%

[*Bons*, advances by Bank of France, etc.]

[2] E. Michel, *La Situation financière et l'achèvement de la reconstitution au 31 décembre 1925* (Paris, 1925), p. 73.

[3] U. S. Senate, *Foreign Currency and Exchange Investigation*, p. 493.

[4] H. Schacht, *loc. cit.*, p. 14.

travagance.[1] The habit of easy spending which was bad
during the war became a serious menace to state finances
during the reconstruction epoch. The effort to tax is first
apparent in the application of the income tax levies in
1916.[2] The changes in the taxation system at this time
were notable, though the yield from the new levies was small
till after the armistice.[3] There were serious efforts to tackle
the problem of taxation toward the very end of the war,
but it was not until 1924 that the income from normal
revenues was really high in France.[4] In the meantime the
internal debt grew to the very large sum—about 300 billion
francs—which was to oppress the government with a crushing interest charge.[5]

One other fact must be noted before concluding this
chronicle of war finance—an account which has been essentially brief and is aimed merely as an introduction to postwar problems. This other possible influence on the financial
situation was the discount rate of the Bank of France. After
the first increase in the rate at the outbreak of the war,
it was lowered to five per cent, where it remained for several
years.[6] This rate was certainly not repressive, though it is
doubtful to what extent it influenced the money market
in any case. Credit expansion, however, was not as great as
one might expect from the large number of notes in circulation. It was not until after the armistice that the notable
increase of bank clearings and other indications of a large
use of credit were strikingly evident.[7] The rate of interest
on government loans was well above the official rate of dis-

---

[1] Seymour Harris, *The Assignats* (thesis, unpublished, Harvard University, 1926), p. 80. Note the percentage of Revolutionary expenses
financed by taxation was considerable.

[2] See *supra,* Chapter II; E. Clémentel, *op. cit.,* p. 123.

[3] Germain Martin, *op. cit.,* p. 133.

[4] See *infra,* Chapter IX.   [5] See *infra,* Chapter VI.

[6] See *infra,* Chapter VI. *Le Pour et le contre* (Paris, December 19, 1927).
The discount rate of the Bank of France was raised to 4½ per cent on
July 30, to 6 per cent on August 1, and then on August 20 was lowered
to 5 per cent.   [7] See tables, appendix, p. 499.

count.[1] Germain Martin concluded after considering various aspects of the money market that these high rates were inevitable:

The policy of high interest rates has grave dangers both social and economic. But was it possible to pursue any other policy? . . . If the state wishes to secure money it must attract funds to the treasury by offering advantages equal to those of the market.[2]

It was difficult for the Bank of France to make a lower rate effective with a rising price level. It was practically impossible to do so when increased production was urgently desired and one means to this end was inflation.

It is wisest, then, to view most of the war measures in France as predetermined by conditions existing at the outbreak of the war, or by the urgent requirements that came with war itself. Some of the expedients adopted by France, such as inflation and control of various aspects of economic life, were common to all warring countries. Others, such as the extensive recourse to short-time loans, were more characteristic of French method as distinguished from those of most other countries. Enough has been said here to make it clear that financing the war by taxation was impossible. Such a conclusion does not, however, preclude the criticism that higher rates early in the war period might have saved France future trouble, since, even if no notable gain had been apparent during the war itself, it would have led to increased revenues immediately after the war. It is apparent now that the large part of the debt which consisted of short-time credits referred to above, approximately a third in *bons de la défense* alone, was a troublesome factor. All this could not have been clearly seen at the time. Moreover, criticisms made by those outside of France often disregard the difficult political situation prevailing within the coun-

---

[1] See *supra,* this chapter. Germain Martin, *op. cit.,* p. 163.

[2] Germain Martin, *op. cit.,* p. 168.

try.[1] Even though the temporary union effected for carrying on the war lessened the instability of the government during hostilities, this union was not on a very sound basis, and existed partly because of the easy makeshift methods which prevailed at certain times in finance.

During the war period, France, and therefore the franc, was dependent first on her own scattered resources, then on England, then on America. Without the help of these two countries the French army could not have been kept in the field in good fighting condition. With this financial backing to make imports possible and protect the exchange rate, the rest of the struggle hinged on the efforts of the French to maintain their own productive powers and a fairly normal economic life within the country in spite of all difficulties. This they managed to do. There were many unnecessary losses, and some serious blunders, but the war was won. In considering the methods used it is well to remember:

The French government knew that it was engaged in a war of extermination. It was necessary above all to assure the triumph of the nation and in comparison with this the sacrifice of money mattered little.[2]

The scars of the war will remain for many years, but despite economic difficulties and mistakes, France managed to maintain her political and territorial integrity.

[1] See *supra*, Chapter I.   [2] Germain Martin, *op. cit.*, p. 165.

CHAPTER IV

Monetary Chaos, 1919–1922

The transition from mild to severe depreciation is usually sudden. It is possible for the money of a nation to be relatively stable through months of slight depreciation and then suddenly break away from its former limits and decline with lightning rapidity. Such was the case for short periods in many European countries. Depreciations at unprecedented rates continued even for longer periods in central Europe. During the year 1919 the rise of the foreign exchanges in Italy, Germany, and France was about 100 per cent.[1] When the various governments withdrew their artificial support as, for instance, in 1919, there was a sudden sharp turn upward of foreign exchange rates. At this time Americans and others who had extended large private credits to foreign buyers were less eager to increase their holdings when they saw that foreign governments no longer intended to control the foreign exchange markets. These credits supplied by individuals and banks during the war period had been approximately as large as government credits.[2] From 1914 to 1918 speculators and traders had assumed that the currencies of the victorious countries would return to par. They had felt that German efficiency and determination would succeed in overcoming the serious obstacles confronting that country. Merchants were predisposed to such

[1] See charts, U. S. Senate, *Foreign Currency and Exchange Investigation* (France, p. 326; Italy, p. 371; Germany, p. 411).

[2] *L'Europe nouvelle* (February 18, 1919), vol. ii, no. 7, pp. 328, 329. Professor William Oualid discusses here the menace of the large commercial debts which he states amounted to about 33,000 million francs in the years 1917 and 1918 alone. See also Chapter III, p. 102, and VIII, pp. 326, 327.

opinions by the fact that only by extending credits could they continue to sell large quantities of products abroad,[1] and the fever of productive activity made them uncritical of the exchange risk.

The continuance of such optimism at the close of the war is astounding as one views it in retrospect. It is hard to remember now the extravagant hopes that Germany could pay billions of dollars to rebuild the devastated regions of France and Belgium. Reparation payments were counted on to reduce the external and internal debts of the victorious countries to prewar figures. Finance Minister Klotz' financial program was summed up in the hopeful formula, "Taxpayers need not worry, Germany will pay." [2] Although it was realized that this would be a heavy drain on German resources, it was assumed that the sums demanded could be secured by increased production and by transfer of large portions of accumulated capital to other countries. Men thought in terms of the indemnity of 1870, which had been paid without striking detriment to France in a short period of time.[3] There was at this time also a natural desire, fulfilled in many cases, to do away with war regulations and restrictions. In England, especially, the extraordinary measures controlling capital, the high rate of interest on French deposits, and the regulation of commerce were terminated early in 1919.[4] In France, too, there was a considerable relaxation of price control [5] and a strong movement to end inflationary methods of government finance. This movement ran counter to various policies of Finance Minister Klotz.

The tendency to end war restraints, however sound in principle, was based on a misunderstanding of postwar con-

---

[1] R. G. Hawtrey, *Monetary Reconstruction* (London, 1923), p. 105.

[2] *L'Europe nouvelle* (February 22, 1919), vol. ii, no. 8, p. 346. Editorial opinion was beginning to question this unbounded optimism.

[3] See *supra*, Chapter II.

[4] *The Economist* (London, January 4, 1919), p. 33.

[5] *Ibid.*, p. 44.

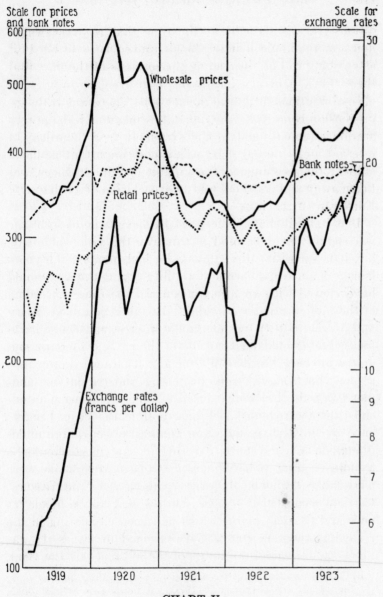

Scale for prices and bank notes

Scale for exchange rates

Wholesale prices

Retail prices

Bank notes

Exchange rates
(francs per dollar)

CHART V

PRICES, DOLLAR RATE, AND NOTE CIRCULATION, 1919-1923 [1]

[1] See appendix for figures.

115

ditions. It was thought at the time that recovery was a much more simple matter than it proved later to be. It is astonishing to find, in reading the journals of the day, that there was a general expectation of an easy resumption of normal relations in international trade. There was little apprehension concerning the difficulties inherent in large reparation payments and in the extremely heavy burdens of internal and external debts. The most important artificial aid to foreign commerce, the support of the exchanges, was taken away and yet there was no expectation of a collapse of European currencies.

It is natural that the feeling of relief at the close of the war should have obscured in this way the vision of many, but it is surprising that those who had handled the problems of finance and currency stability during the war should have viewed with apparent unconcern the sudden freedom of the foreign exchange markets. The situation in February and March of 1919 was extremely interesting. Opinion was focused on the troubled sessions of the peace conference and on the internal disorders of Germany. There were, of course, a few who from the very beginning understood the complexity of the indemnity problem.[1] The realization intensified the controversies in France both at the Peace Conference and in Parliament, when financial policies were under discussion. Critics of the government said there should be a more vigorous policy and higher taxes. Meanwhile there were heavy drains on the existing resources of the treasury. Certain reconstruction expenditures had to be made at once and German marks which had been circulating in the recovered territory had to be redeemed in francs. It was necessary to extend the limits of the advances by the Bank

[1] *The Economist* (London, February 1, 1919), p. 135. An editorial states that the French were beginning to recognize, first that it was useless to force Germany into bankruptcy, second that there must be a revision of the estimates of German wealth, and third, that the Allies must prepare a bill and then arrange a means of payment. (The problem of transfer of wealth was beginning to be realized.)

of France to the state, and of the note issues; [1] the limit of advances was raised to 24 billion francs. [2] The danger of continued inflation was pointed out at this time, but inflation was feared because of its effect on prices and not because of possible trouble with the foreign exchange rates. There was talk of a capital levy to meet the large budget deficits, but the consensus of opinion was in favor of a waiting policy and reliance on German payments. Political and economic doubts which grew out of the peace treaty struggles undermined any serious attempts to cut down expenses and increase revenues. The Bourse was affected adversely but there was no apparent interest in the future of the franc on the exchanges. [3]

SUDDEN DEPRECIATION

The crisis came in March, 1919. The tension at the Peace Conference in Paris was very great, while famine and disorder in Germany were so alarming that the Allies arranged for food shipments to that country. The return of President Wilson to Paris early in March was the occasion of much speculation as to what he would accomplish. [4] The United States delegates to the conference tended to favor more lenient terms to Germany than had been originally suggested. Meanwhile, Great Britain was becoming im-

[1] The convention between the Bank of France and the state signed on February 13 was to increase the advances on February 25. The limit for the note issues was raised from 33 to 36 billion francs. The law approving these conventions was passed March 5, 1919. The discussion in the Chamber of Deputies is an indication of what vague ideas as to the monetary situation were prevalent. *Documents parlementaires, Chambre,* 1919, annexe no. 5771, pp. 895-99. This gives a report on the monetary situation during the war. See also the *Journal officiel, débats, Chambre,* March 5, 1919, pp. 997-1006. See Table XIV and Chart XV, Chapter VI.

[2] Germain Martin, *Les Finances publiques* (Paris, 1925), p. 305.

[3] *Le Pour et le contre* (February 23, 1919).

[4] *Le Temps* (March 7, 1919). On March 4 the U. S. Senate voted that the League and the peace treaty should be considered separately. This was known as the Lodge resolution.

Unit:francs per dollar

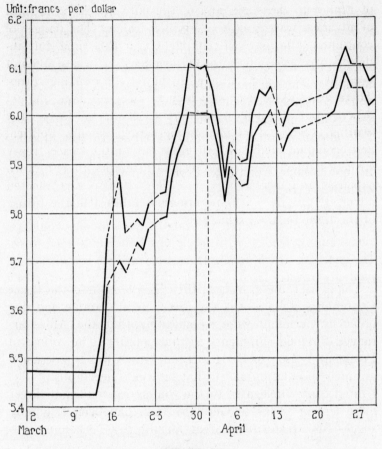

CHART VI

DOLLAR EXCHANGE, MARCH AND APRIL, 1919 [1]

patient because of the attitude of France towards the indemnity,[2] and no satisfactory solution of the question was

[1] See appendix, p. 455, for figures.

[2] *The Economist* (London, 1919), vol. lxxxviii, p. 408. "There are signs of
dissatisfaction as to the delay in arriving at a settlement and the estimates
that are put out as to what Germany can pay are absolutely unofficial.
I am informed on good authority that Germany will be asked to pay an
indemnity of 15 millards [billions] of francs a year for a period of 50
years."

in sight. The only indication of a realization of the danger of depreciation was that the French were considering in a general way the necessity of improving their foreign trade position by reducing imports.[1] There were, on the other hand, frequent statements of editorial opinion that America would continue to grant credits in some form because it was to her interest to foster her export trade. There was little apprehension when the crisis broke. In fact, the decline of the franc was hardly noticed for several days, and it did not become front page news, even though the loss in value was extreme.

The franc was unpegged March 14. This followed the announcement on March 13 that the government would no longer supply traders with foreign exchange at a fixed price. The markets which had been resting in false security were suddenly roused from their apathy.[2] Despite the realization that Great Britain was anxious to return to the freedom of prewar trade, there was little preparation made for this new condition by the French financial interests. It is true that the actual announcement of the cessation of British credits was sudden and unexpected. It is even conjectured that the move was precipitated by the desire in certain countries to put additional pressure on France and bring her to a policy more in harmony with the British views at the Peace Conference. This motive may have been partly responsible for the sudden break of financial solidar-

[1] *Documents parlementaires, Chambre,* 1919, annexe no. 5455, pp. 165-188. *Rapport supplémentaire fait au nom de la commission du commerce et de l'industrie.*

[2] *Le Pour et le contre* (Paris, March 23, 1919). "Les importateurs de marchandises britanniques et les intermédiaires du marché du change ont été informés vers la fin de la semaine dernière que la trésorie anglaise avait suspendu ses avances à l'Etat français et que dès lors le ministère des finances ne pourrait plus concourir à approvisionner de livres sterling le commerce de l'importation. Du jour au lendemain, par conséquent, sans qu'aucun avertissement préalable ait permis aux intéressés de prendre leurs dispositions et d'essayer de se retourner, plus d'intervention du trésor sur le marché du sterling. . . ."

ity, but the withdrawal was consistent with the British
moves toward freer conditions throughout the months of
January and February. The French seemed to rely on the
hope that even if Britain no longer furnished credits, the
United States would find it to her interest to make some arrangements to steady the exchanges.[1] This hope and the
idea that the United States would take over a large part
of the reconstruction of the devastated regions were doomed
to disappointment.

It is possible that the French government was not averse
to a slight depreciation of the franc at this time. *The New
York Times* mentioned the desire expressed in French commercial circles to reduce imports and increase exports.[2]
In any case, they took no immediate steps to prevent depreciation.[3] In New York, as well as in London, the exchange was freed of official intervention.[4] Unfortunately, it
is not possible to weigh against each other the different
motives, partly political and partly economic, behind these
actions. The outstanding fact, however, is that there was no
expectation of a precipitate and continued drop and no
general fear that the franc would get out of control. The
potential ill effects of the large note circulation, high prices,
and heavy external debts, individual and governmental, was
not realized. The surprising calm with which the announcement and the first decline of the franc were received is
sufficient evidence of the lack of understanding.

Whatever the reasons have been, the rise of the exchange
in 1919 was rapid and continuous. The dollar rate had been

[1] *L'Europe nouvelle* (Paris, March 8, 1919), vol. ii, no. 10, p. 476.
See other articles by Léon Polier published previously.

[2] *The New York Times* (March 18, 1919), p. 15.

[3] *The Economist* (London, March 15, 1919), vol. lxxxviii, p. 434. *The
Economist* blames the French government for precipitate action. It could
probably have given some warning.

[4] U. S. Senate, *Foreign Currency and Exchange Investigation*, p. 327.
Credits established up to July, 1919, by the United States treasury con-
tinued to be utilized until September, 1920. The franc was not pegged in
New York, however.

kept at 5.45 francs. It moved to 5.53 on March 14; to 5.70 on March 15. The rate at the end of the year was about 11.00 francs to the dollar. The rise did not stop, except for a few short reactions, until April 27, 1920, when the dollar cost 17.08 francs in Paris.[1] The sudden break in the curve is indicative of the unexpected shortage of foreign credits to meet French payments abroad.

Even after the exchanges had begun to fluctuate wildly, there seemed to be little understanding of what was taking place. The *Journal de Genève* of March 15, in discussing financial affairs, stated:

Without doubt the wind has changed. Good omens are evident, bringing with them more activity and exerting a favorable influence on all quotations. . . . The foreign exchange situation is particularly favorable.[2]

On March 16 it speaks of the animation of the exchanges, and on March 18 of the dissolution of the Interallied Committee on Foreign Credits, resulting in complete freedom of most of the foreign exchange markets. It was not until March 21 that the situation was noted as in any way remarkable—"one can feel a real change in international relationships." It was on this date that London ceased to support sterling in New York.[3]

This lack of apprehension indicates that the first decline was due mainly to the technical condition of the market rather than to panic. The fact that government credits were not forthcoming meant that the demand for foreign credits would only be met with difficulty and at high rates. When later, public opinion in France and without became

---

[1] *La Cote officielle* (Paris, 1919). The figures for the daily quotations for the dollar in Paris are given in the appendix, see *infra*.

[2] *Journal de Genève* (Geneva, March, 1919). See particularly the numbers from March 10-22. It is true that the fall of the franc meant a rise of the Swiss franc, but these discussions usually are international in their point of view. The New York papers show a similar lack of concern.

[3] *The New York Times* (March 21, 1919), p. 16.

aware of the serious obstacles in the way of balancing exports with imports, and a real shortage of means of meeting foreign payments, the psychological factors, as well as the technical, caused rising exchange rates and a falling franc. Moreover, political disturbances, the threat of a capital levy,[1] and disappointment over the treaty, all aggravated the situation; but they were not the main causes. Such were, rather, great needs for foreign goods at a time when the foreign credit mechanism was impaired.[2] The situation was similar in some ways to that at the outbreak of the war. But in 1914 the situation in Paris was quite the opposite—there had been too many dollars and too few francs. The result had been a premium on francs unjustified by the real economic conditions.[3] In 1919, on the other hand, the technical and temporary situation was that which was also dictated by the *real* commercial and credit factors. For that reason there was no significant reaction.

With the greatest possible suddenness, then, after a period of stability on the exchanges, the French franc entered on a period of severe depreciation. From March, 1919, on, there was a growing tendency for value to be determined by powerful psychological forces, by estimates and interpretations of economic and political events. The limits to the range of fluctuations were fixed not by the uncovered volume of trade, nor by the usual transactions in international securities, but by the whole mass of capital which might flow in or out of a country. In other words, there were no effective limits to restrict changes in the value of the franc. War-time measures had established an ex-

[1] *The Economist* (London, March 15, 1919), p. 446. See also March 22, p. 469.

[2] There was a large increase in imports both in quantity and in value compared with those of the previous year:

1918	293	million metric quintals
1919	384	" " "

Bulletin de la statistique générale de la France, U. S. Senate, *Foreign Currency and Exchange Investigation,* pp. 483-4.

[3] See *supra,* Chapter III.

change standard of value for the franc to which it was held
in a general way by the selling—buying was not actually
necessary but would have been undertaken if called for—
of exchange to French traders with debts abroad.[1] This
formed a temporary substitute for the gold standard. Once
this ceased to exist, there was no objective standard to
which the currency was related. Men tried to anticipate
the future relation of the franc to gold and goods. Purchases and sales of foreign credits were made in accordance
with these forecasts. In this later stage, moreover, when
depreciation was severe, the external decline of money
dominated the internal decline; the exchange rates conditioned price changes.[2]

During the war, a period of relative exchange stability,
pegging, and the abnormal situation of international trade
had prevented the normal interplay of prices and exchange
rates. High prices in France, it is true, contributed to the
increase of imports and may have lessened exports. Since
there was little immediate payment for these goods, however, the reaction was not as quick nor as complete as in
normal times. The increase of imports would normally have
diminished the means of buying more imports, and the
shortage of cash and credit would have worked for a lower
price level and a growing export trade. The intervention of
government credits in this series of events changed the
whole nature of the case. There was little connection between the flow of trade and the means of payment. There
was no sure force which worked to equalize prices between
countries, since the flow of both goods and money was
irregular and disturbed.

Economic and psychological factors were both of importance in the years following the armistice, but, as has been
indicated already, the psychological influences tended to

[1] This was possible because of government borrowings abroad. See
Chapter III.
[2] Charles Rist, *La Déflation en pratique* (Paris, 1924), pp. 113, 129.

become more and more significant. On the basis of these causal factors, one can divide the postwar period into four distinct phases of depreciation.[1] During the first years, 1919-22, the controlling factors were mainly economic. This has been called the cyclical period by Professor Aftalion, because there was a wave-like movement such as is frequently called a business cycle.[2] Confidence was not the decisive factor during these years. The reasons behind credit movements were complex, but they were probably related fairly directly to the flow of commodities between countries, and not to estimates of the ultimate gold value of the currencies concerned.

During the second phase, 1922 and 1923, economic and political factors were more nearly balanced and the estimates of exchange values were based to a considerable extent on the progress of the reparation question. The volume of credits moving against the franc was very large and quite out of proportion with commercial needs. Psychological influences were increasing in strength. This general trend continued with increasing force during the speculative years of the third period, 1924-26, a time of unsettled opinion and wild gambling. These years were characterized by the growing importance of public opinion and capital movements based on the changing value of money. We see this, for instance, in the speculative drive beginning in the last weeks of 1923, called "the battle of the franc," and again in the exchange crisis towards the end of 1925, currently referred to as "the confidence crisis." The former was a deliberate effort to drive the franc down, beginning with the knowledge on the part of a few of the unsound condition of government finance; the latter was a widespread effort on the part of many people to save what they could from what threatened to be the wreck of the French financial system. Following these troubled times, there came

---

[1] See *infra*, Chapter VI.

[2] Albert Aftalion, *Monnaie, prix et change* (Paris, 1927), pp. 18-20.

the final stage of *de facto* stability. This began in the last
quarter of 1926 and continued into 1928.[1] Both the rapid
decline and the ultimate recovery of the franc were conditioned by public opinion. Moreover, opinion frequently
ran counter to many important economic factors in 1926 because of political dangers or hopes. In 1926, for instance,
it carried the franc back to a level scarcely justified by the
financial situation, when a truce between parties gave the
government a chance to work out a consistent program.

The different periods, as given below, are similar to, but
not identical with, those in Aftalion's book.[2]

   I. The war period: 1914-18
  II. The cyclical period: 1919-21
 III. The reparation struggle: 1922-23
 IV. Speculation and realization: 1924-26
  V. Stability: 1926-28

Such a division into periods, though arbitrary in so far
as it sets precise dividing lines, is useful and distinguishes
clearly the actual changes in relationships. The *cyclical
period,* for example, stands out distinctly from the rest of
the postwar period. The erratic up and down movements of
prices and exchange rates in the years 1919 to 1922 were
unlike those at any other time from the outbreak of the
war until 1928.

The Cyclical Period: 1919–1921

Let us turn now to a consideration of the cyclical period.
What were the conditions of economic life at this time?
Wholesale prices were declining slightly; in contrast to
this, the note circulation of the Bank of France was increasing. This was due primarily to the need of the govern-

[1] See *infra,* Chapter X.

[2] A. Aftalion, *op. cit.,* p. 12. These periods were chosen as the basis of
the analysis of the postwar period by the writer in her doctor's thesis,
1926. Confirmation of the choice is now found in Professor Aftalion's book.

ment for funds, and not to the price situation and the requirements of internal trade. Then it is important to note that if there had been any hope on the part of the government that the fall of the franc would check imports,[1] this hope was not justified by events, for imports increased in both quantity and value. This was inevitable in view of the reconstruction needs, which were difficult to estimate. No one could tell how great these needs would be, nor how long the work would take. The uncertainty was further increased by the continued fall of the franc. There was no point of lasting stability, once the exchanges were unpegged, until the government and the Bank of France again intervened in 1926.[2] There was no notable reaction until April, 1920 when exchanges turned in favor of the franc.

During these years, 1919-22, there are four subjects which deserve special consideration. One of these is, obviously, the exchange rates; a second is the budget and various financial programs of the government; a third, the deflationary program instituted in 1920 to take effect in 1921; and a fourth, the course of prices and the relation between the world crisis and French economic conditions. The movement of the various factors, the results of the different programs, are extremely complex. They reflect directly and indirectly the mistakes and losses which occurred during the war, and some of the contradictions and uncertainties were inevitable. It must be remembered that there were no precedents to follow; the adjustment necessary was much more far reaching than that after previous wars, for the changes in money, prices, budgets, and international relations were unusually great. The future course of economic events was unpredictable. Therefore speculation was

---

[1] See *supra*, this chapter.

[2] *Revue d'économie politique* (March-April, 1927), vol. xli, no. 2, p. 374. From August to November, 1926 the treasury bought exchange to mitigate the upward tendency of the franc. In December the Bank of France took over this function. See *infra*, Chapter VI.

rife, forecasts were unreliable, and sudden changes in value became the order of the day.

The movement of the franc on the foreign exchanges during the cyclical period was influenced in the main by three factors. First, there was the technical condition of the market; the lack of credits available at the moment of unpegging was, as has been indicated above, the main cause of the precipitate drop in 1919. Then the second important influence was confidence or lack of confidence, based on the hope of securing foreign credits; the break of the franc after President Wilson's message in December is illustrative of this. It will be remembered that at this time Wilson declared Europe must work out her own salvation, and his attitude lessened considerably the hope of credits from America.[1] Finally, the exchange rates were governed during a part of this time by the movement of prices. At this time, as at no other during these postwar years, prices controlled exchange rates to a considerable extent, directly and through their influence on commerce. Moreover, the movement of prices was mainly independent of exchange rates, though it was accentuated somewhat by this factor.[2]

At the close of the war, it was realized that the monetary units of central Europe might depreciate, but there seemed no clear reason why the victors should suffer in this way. Then, again, the increase in prices was blamed almost entirely on war conditions. A large note circulation was considered to be a temporary abnormality, while the unfavorable balance of trade was a matter which could be righted in a few years. In the meanwhile, credits could undoubtedly fill the gap. These were the thoughts of most of those who gave the matter any consideration. It is interesting to wonder whether or not a wise policy during 1919 and the years that followed could have brought the franc to par. It is possible that if France had shown a clear in-

---

[1] Jules Décamps, *Les Changes étrangers* (Paris, 1922), p. 358.

[2] Aftalion, *op. cit.*, p. 17.

tention to tax and economize, if it had been easier to work out a harmonious reparation policy, and if in some way the United States could have extended credits to help with reconstruction, the franc could have held its own.[1] Such a hypothesis, however, is mere speculation. The views of England, America, and France were in fact divergent. Foreign credits were not put at the disposal of France and money could not be collected from Germany. It must be admitted by the most severe critics of France that her task was extremely difficult; it must be granted by the most lenient that the financial measures of 1919 and 1920 were deplorable.[2]

The return of the franc to par may be considered as still possible at the beginning of 1919. It had become out of the question by the end of the year. The franc was then worth less than half its par value. In view of the heavy burdens within and without the country, no sufficient deflation, export balance, or foreign borrowings could bring it back to its old value. It is rarely possible for a money to double its value—severe depreciation has usually meant a permanent change in value. It is impossible to say precisely at what point the fall, begun in March, 1919, might have been stopped, but it is probable that the value regained after the 1920 price collapse, that is nine cents per franc, might have been retained throughout. It is certain, however, that during all these years many politicians and financial leaders in France expected a return to par and the hope was not entirely abandoned until 1928.

The franc fell steadily throughout the year 1919, with

[1] Germain Calmette, *Recueil de documents sur l'histoire des réparations,* 1919, May 5, 1921 (Paris, 1924), p. 36-61. See the discussion regarding credits for reconstruction.

[2] Rist, *op. cit.,* p. 66. Professor Rist, whose view of French affairs is extremely judicious, said that the year 1919 weighed heavily against France as time went on. See George-Edgar Bonnet, *Les Expériences monétaires contemporaines* (Paris, 1926), p. 96. M. Bonnet says the mistakes of this period had serious consequences.

a few short reactions. The sale of French securities [1] and
some favorable speculation made such reactions. It was
hoped in France that the signing of the treaty would bring
a better state of affairs, but there was disappointment on
this score. [2] The temporary improvements in the franc
alluded to occurred in May, July, August, and September.
The very sharp decline in December, due mainly to disappointment at the American attitude, was followed by
an upward movement, but the fall of the franc continued
after this interruption through the first months of 1920.

Sudden changes in the value of the franc, even more
erratic than in 1919, characterized the year 1920. The peril
inherent in the monetary situation in Europe had finally
been realized. [3] The conflicting currents of opinion and the
uneven adjustment to postwar conditions were reflected in
the sharp up and down movement of foreign exchange rates
and wholesale prices. The net movement of the franc was
decidedly downward, but there were two short periods of
appreciation. The lesser of the two was in February; the
second was in May, and coincided with the fall of prices in
France and other countries. It is interesting to note that
at this time purchasing power parities justified a rise of
the franc, but it is probable that other factors were of
considerable weight. Among these was a slight improvement
in international relations. [4] The plans for the Brussels Conference made foreign speculators more hopeful of concerted action to steady exchanges. The prospect of a good
harvest and import prohibition on some goods lessened the
demand for foreign exchange on the part of the French.
The buying of francs went too far, however, and the decline

---

[1] Jules Décamps, *op. cit.*, p. 350.

[2] *Le Pour et le contre* (Paris, July 6, 1919).

[3] R. G. Hawtrey, *Monetary Reconstruction* (London, 1923), p. 105.
Hawtrey says that American exporters had been misled at first by the
balance of trade fallacy into thinking depreciation a temporary phenomenon. They began to see their mistake by the end of 1919.

[4] *Le Pour et le contre* (May 16, 1920).

which began in July continued with few interruptions throughout the rest of the year.

The Rise of the Franc

The year 1921 was the most favorable one for the franc of the entire postwar period, or, as reflected in the foreign exchange, the cost of the dollar fell from 16.63 francs on January 6 to 12.48 francs on December 29.[1] The highest point for the franc was in May. There were a number of influences which tended to strengthen the French position during this year. For instance, there were the deflationary measures discussed below, which were taken as a favorable sign by many.[2] Moreover, taxes had been increased in 1920. At this time, too, imports declined notably both in value and in weight, so that the balance of trade was favorable during five months of the year.[3] French prices were still low on a gold basis and this, added to other things, helped restore confidence and trade. Meanwhile reconstruction was going forward rapidly and the volume of production increased towards the end of the year, after the short setback due to the general depression. It should be noted that the rise of the franc on the foreign exchanges was greater at the end of the year than was its rise in terms of goods in the domestic markets. It is probable that the judgment of financiers, which was reflected in this, was governed mainly by economic factors such as prices, commerce, and French productive power. Political difficulties over the reparation question were not, as yet, acute. At this time the instability of exchange rates had not been strikingly evidenced by the collapse of the mark. This is one reason why many people were willing to hold credits in France.

Of the three types of influences [4] mentioned above—

---

[1] See appendix.

[2] Rist, *op. cit.*, p. 65. This was not real deflation but was considered to be such by many. See *infra,* Chapter VI.

[3] See appendix.   [4] See *supra,* this chapter.

that is, confidence, the market situation, and prices—prices had more influence on exchange rates during 1921 than at any other time. It is true that confidence was important at all times, but it determined the shorter speculative movements rather than the underlying trends during these three years. The "technical" market situation was not of very great significance except in 1919, when there was a sudden abnormal shortage of means of payment for foreign debts which precipitated the sudden fall of the franc.

The *Crédit National*

Since the financial policy of the government after the war was to a very large extent conditioned by reconstruction, it is well to consider at this point the way in which this matter was handled. It was obvious at once that money would have to be raised in France more quickly than even the most optimistic persons could expect France to collect the bill from Germany. Since the budget was already heavily burdened and deficits had been large during past years, further loans seemed to be the only way of meeting this pressing need. A new institution was created in 1919 for the purpose of managing these loans. This was called the *Crédit national*.[1] It was a *société anonyme* formed for the purpose of making advances to war victims and of floating loans to secure the necessary funds.

It is very difficult to appraise the exact amount of money spent on reconstruction, the original loss through devastation, or the extent of graft and overpayment. One cannot judge accurately the losses sustained by France because of the strong motive for exaggeration which influenced almost

---

[1] *Documents parlementaires, Chambre,* 1924, annexe no. 537, pp. 2109, 2110. The law of October 10, 1919 ratified the convention of July 7. This report of the finance commission discussed the operations of the *Crédit national* and other matters connected with reparations and reconstruction. See also Louis Lamber, *Le Crédit national pour faciliter la réparation* (Paris, 1925).

all the French estimates. Moreover, since the replacement
value was the significant figure, the amount differed with
the changing value of money and with changing costs. It is
equally difficult to estimate the exact cost of reconstruction because of the complex method of payment mentioned
above. A very large part of the payments were made not
in cash but in securities. Both the *Crédit national* and the
government made restitution in the form of credits. *Bons
de la défense nationale, rentes, and obligations* were used
for this purpose.[1] It seems that a very large part of the
payments were made in this way. The total amount spent
under the head of reconstruction up to September 30, 1924
was approximately 129 billion francs. This figure, however,
includes interest charges and pensions as well as principal,
and as to principal, the damage to both private and public
property. This 129 billions is about equivalent to the increase of the internal debt.

The total spent on reconstruction was divided as follows:

Allowances and pensions to war victims.........	36	billion francs
Damages to private property...................	61	" "
Reconstruction of railways and public *domaine*....	13	" "
Interest on loans for reconstruction..............	19	" "
Total	129	" " [2]

The French demands from Germany were set at 180 billion
francs.[3] The justice of this claim, which includes pensions
as well as actual material damage, has frequently been questioned. Moreover, the accuracy of the estimates of dam-

[1] Etienne Clémentel, *Ministre des finances, Inventaire de la situation
financière de la France au début de la treizième législature* (Paris, 1924),
p. 88.

[2] *Documents parlementaires, Chambre*, 1924, annexe no. 537, p. 2109.

[3] E. Michel, *La Situation financière et l'achèvement de reconstitution*
(Paris, 1925), p. 16. See note (1). This figure was that chosen by the Reparation Commission. MM. Millerand and Loucheur had asked as much as
220 billions in 1920. MM. Briand and Loucheur reduced the demand to
171 billions in May, 1921. M. Michel indicates, in his discussion, the figure
40 billion *gold* francs. He adds that the Dawes Plan seems to occasion a
new reduction.

ages has been challenged, notably by Keynes. However important it may be to decide these matters in principle, the sums actually received from Germany were so far below these demands that the original estimates lose much of their significance in retrospect. In one respect they are important, however, amounts paid out by the French for reconstruction were undoubtedly greater because of the hope of collecting from Germany. But as time went on it grew more and more apparent that the problem was one of internal finance and domestic politics. The later repercussions of the reparation question on the franc and international relations were not anticipated.

It is obvious that the expenditure of billions of francs for this special purpose complicated the budget greatly. The expedient of the *Crédit national* and the institution of the "recoverable" budget did little to lessen the difficulties. In fact, they concealed the real situation and postponed the day of adequate effort. The mistakes of these years were serious but they were to a certain extent the inevitable outcome of postwar opinion and needs. The importance of energetic action in reconstruction is recognized by all those who know the spirit of the French peasant. Refugees poured back to their homes with dauntless courage; they were willing to live in ruins, but the government, for the good of the nation, had to see that the means of transportation were restored and food supplies available. By the end of 1921 two million people had returned to the devastated North.[1] The transformation of the countryside was surprising. With astonishing rapidity barbed wire was cleared away, shell holes by the thousands were filled in, roofs were patched, and new crops planted. In fact, the recovery of the countryside was more rapid than anyone aware of the destruction would have believed possible.

It is small wonder that there was much extravagance, waste, and graft in the course of all this rapid reconstruc-

[1] Etienne Clémentel, *op. cit.*, p. 86.

tion. One loophole for corruption was opened by the review of claims by local committees much interested in generous grants to their own *communes*. There was collusion between those who assessed damages and those who contracted to rebuild. Some, even, developed a thriving business by buying claims from peasants outright for cash and then collecting much larger sums at a later time from the government. It must be remembered that there had to be decisions on no less than 3,073,203 claims up to January 1, 1926.[1] As the result of these decisions some people made large profits, while others who were paid in securities instead of cash, or who did not urge their claims at once, lost very heavily.[2] Many war victims were forced to sell government securities when they were greatly depreciated, and to buy goods at prices even higher than those at which their damages had been assessed.

A considerable part of the claims mentioned were paid in the years 1919-22. For instance, about half the sum due for damage to private property, that is more than 37 billion francs, was met during these years.[3] Almost all of this amount was paid in securities, but the interest charge and some cash payments inevitably increased the budget expenditures. The *Crédit national* floated loans amounting to 11 billion francs during this period.[4] Unfortunately, it is impossible to discover the exact amounts spent and the means of payment in any clear fashion. It is significant that the increase in the internal debt was more than 86 billion francs.[5] A large part of this was due to the reconstruction of public and private property. It was not all due to this one cause, however, since the total budget deficits for these years was 108 billion francs,[6] a sum larger than

[1] E. Michel, *op. cit.*, p. 38.
[2] Some accounts were still unsettled in 1927.
[3] E. Clémentel, *op. cit.*, pp. 88, 89.
[4] *Documents parlementaires, Chambre*, 1924, annexe no. 537, p. 2110.
[5] Henry Chéron, *Documents parlementaires, Rapport au Sénat*, February 22, 1926, annexe no. 84, p. 277.   [6] E. Clémentel, *op. cit.*, p. 21.

the amount spent on reconstruction up to this time. There is much confusion as to just what happened, because of the fact that the *Crédit national* did not make all the payments for indemnities, and all the government expenditures were not included in the budget.[1]

The large expenditures which were so necessary to the recovery of France overshadowed financial problems such as the exchange instability. The policy of ever-increasing loans was unfortunate, but up to a certain point it was inevitable. Later difficulties were due both to deceptive methods of handling these complex expenditures and to more serious political problems which made the increase in taxation difficult. There was a notable change in the yield of different forms of revenue at this time,[2] but the increases were not adequate. Two of the more important changes were the increase in the income tax, which had been imposed in 1916 and began to yield considerable revenue after the war, and the business turnover tax, which was imposed in 1920. The yield of the former was almost three billion francs in 1921, as compared with 51 million francs in 1916.[3] The business turnover tax was the most productive of all taxes in later years, although its yield at this particular time was not very high. In 1921, the second year of its operation, it netted slightly less than two billion francs.[4]

Such increases in revenues were considerable, and were the outcome of a dawning realization of the inadequacy of the war taxation. Government receipts were as follows:[5]

1918......................	6.8 billion francs	
1919......................	11.6 "	"
1920......................	20.1 "	"
1921......................	23.1 "	"

[1] H. G. Moulton and C. Lewis, *The French Debt Problem* (New York, 1925), pp. 75–80.

[2] E. Clémentel, *op. cit.*, pp. 112–121.   [3] *Ibid.*, pp. 123, 124.

[4] *Bulletin de la statistique générale de la France*, vol. xii, no. 11, p. 155. This figure given is 1,897 million francs. In 1920 the yield was 942 million francs.   [5] E. Clémentel, *op. cit.*, pp. 14, 21.

The total expenses for the three years equaled 163 billion francs, of which sum 59 billions were included in the "recoverable" budget. The practice of separating these charges from the more permanent ones was abandoned in 1925.[1] Until this was done, no clear understanding of the situation was possible. In fact, during this cyclical period the importance of the budget revision was entirely overlooked by the general public. It was left to the experts to try to devise methods of raising money. But even those most deeply interested in readjustment and sound methods of reconstruction found the problem very much complicated by these separate budgets, the treasury and the *Crédit national,* each included accounts under the head of reconstruction and of loans, and gave each other credits on various counts. Public opinion was not much concerned with this complicated mass of accounts. It was not until later that the deficits stood out so conspicuously that politicians were forced to united and reasonable efforts.

Opposition to Inflation

Even during this first period, however, there was some general concern about inflation. The menace of increasing issues of notes, though vaguely understood, was felt to be a cause of high prices and some of the various industrial ills. There had been considerable objection to the increase in the advances of the Bank of France to the state authorized in February and April, 1919 by virtue of which the limit was set at 27 billion, as compared with 21 billion francs. In order to offset these objections, the state had promised to repay the increase voted in April, 1919 from the proceeds of the next loan. The funds which the government received, however, were immediately absorbed by budget needs, so that there was no surplus remaining with which to carry out this arrangement.[2] Then it was realized

[1] *Documents parlementaires, Chambre, loc. cit.,* annexe no. 537, p. 2059.
[2] *Ibid., Sénat,* 1920, annexe no. 629, p. 1088.

regretfully by those who favored deflation that the government was too heavily burdened with reconstruction and
other expenses to cut down its floating debt at this time.
The importance of the issue was considerable, and the Minister of Finance, François-Marsal, made a convention with
Governor Robineau of the Bank of France which was the
basis of the law of December 31, 1920.

The deflationary measure was to take effect at the end
of 1921. Beginning with that year, the state was to repay
each year two billion francs of its debt to the Bank; [1] thus
it would extinguish the debt in about thirteen years. It is
interesting to observe that this measure aroused little opposition in the Chamber of Deputies. It was passed without
heated debate or long delay, and was expected to exert a
very buoyant influence on the unstable franc. There were
even intimations in the government report of the possibility
of a return to prewar conditions and the former gold par.

Professor Rist has criticized this measure, very justly, as
a mistaken application of principles which had been effective in the more simple circumstances of 1870–76.[2] The law

[1] *Documents parlementaires, Chambre,* 1920, annexe no. 1880, pp. 539,
540. See also *Chambre,* annexe no. 1958, pp. 1660, 1661. The law read in
part as follows:

Le montant des avances fixés provisoirement à 27 milliards par la
convention des 24 avril 1919 et 14 avril 1920, est maintenu à la même
somme jusqu'au 31 décembre 1921.

L'Etat s'engage à effectuer, avant le 1er janvier 1922 le remboursement
nécessaire pour ramener à 25 milliards le montant des sommes prélevées
sur les avances de la Banque de France.

L'Etat poursuivra l'amortissement de sa dette envers la Banque de
France à raison de 2 milliards au moins chaque année et en conséquence,
le montant des avances autorisées sera, chaque 31 décembre, réduit d'une
somme de 2 milliards.

[2] Rist, *op. cit.,* pp. 79–84. He points out that the improvement of the
exchange rate at that time was contemporaneous with but not the consequence of the deflation, which should indeed hardly be called deflation,
since the number of notes in circulation scarcely changed (p. 80), despite
the repayments by the state to the Bank. Moreover, the debt to the
Bank of France was so much smaller as to be quite a different problem
from that of 1919 and 1920.

was executed during the first year and only partially carried
out during the second.[1] This slight reduction of the debt to
the bank was only possible because of the price situation at
the time, and it was not a net reduction of the state debt.
For while these two billions were being paid back to the
Bank, the other portions of the floating debt were increasing. The net change was, in fact, an increase from 81.5
billion francs in 1920, to 88.5 in 1921, and a slight increase to
89 billion francs in 1922.[2] Such figures prove quite conclusively that the effort at deflation was artificial, and ill timed.
Moreover, the long-term debt increased slightly at the same
time and all signs point to the serious embarrassment of the
government in facing its different obligations. It is true that
there was a very slight reduction of the note circulation, but
this followed rather than preceded the decline in prices of
this period.[3] Indeed, there was no significant change for
the better unless we give importance to the psychological
advantage in a resolute opposition toward inflation. There
were decided disadvantages, on the other hand, resulting
from the mistaken attempts of the state to carry out this
convention; one of these was the falsification of the bank
statements which was revealed in 1925.[4] Moreover, this
manner of dealing with the problem led to a false feeling
of security from which the country was rudely shaken after
it had lost the power to recover quickly its former position.
An early search for the deeper causes might have prevented
the piling up of the floating debt and the consequent increasing burden of interest payment.

The fall in prices which came with the world crisis of
1920 made possible the illusions regarding the deflationary
convention. The collapse originated in other causes than
the monetary policy of France. One should remember that

[1] Only one billion francs were repaid in 1922. Repayments in full did
not begin again until 1925. See *infra,* Chapter V.

[2] See table showing internal debt, *infra,* Chapter VI.

[3] See *supra,* Chart V, p. 115.   [4] See *infra,* Chapter V.

the rise of wholesale prices had been practically simultaneous in all countries after the war, whereas the fall of prices
was precipitated in the United States and spread thence
to other countries. There is special interest in this wave-like
movement of the price curves because it was similar in
France, England, and the United States—an evidence of
the degree of economic solidarity between the important industrial countries of the world. It became obvious at this
time that there were more serious problems and maladjustments in the economic world than the volume of paper
money in circulation alone could account for.[1] Inflation
had been an important factor in the price movement but
it cannot be held responsible for all the increase any more
than the very slight deflation can be made accountable for
the subsequent crash.

Postwar Price Increase

There are a number of elements which worked towards
higher prices from the armistice to April, 1920. It is not
possible to make any one of them entirely responsible.
Speculation of various kinds and attempts to readapt production to peace conditions were largely responsible. A
mistaken point of view and unavoidable technical difficulties
combined to bring about the same effect. The optimism at
the close of the war, already discussed, was as evident in the
realm of prices as in that of foreign exchange. It is true
there were conflicting interests of consumers, who hoped
for falling prices, and producers and wholesalers, who flour-
ished with increasing demand; but the most effective influences and forecasts in France and in other countries pointed
to an expansion of industrial activity. There were, moreover, some indications of a rapidly recovering commerce and
a high consumption of goods.

[1] Gaston Jèze, *Les Finances de guerre de la France* (Paris, 1920), pp.
176-192. See discussion of varied influences here outlined.

After the war, various factors conspired to conceal the real loss of purchasing power, which was bound to bring a relapse. In the meanwhile new debts grew and old ones were renewed, so that credit expansion was very great.[1] In addition, the note circulation increased slightly, as has been indicated above.[2] The increase in both cash and credit in France was based in a very general way on anticipation of payments from Germany. The uncertainty of such assets began to be apparent as the liabilities became more and more burdensome. This expansion was not the cause but it was the means by which the price rise continued. The rise would not have gone so far nor continued so long without a ready increase of the means of payment.

It is perhaps more difficult to find the reasons behind all the different price movements occurring in the United States and some other countries than it is in the case of France, for in France the mental attitude, the rehabilitation of the North and the spending of hoarded money were all definite factors which contributed towards the rise. M. Décamps has selected four from a host of possible factors.[3] These are (1) large purchases of land by peasants, (2) the use of *bons de la défense* for money, (3) the eight-hour day, (4) the disorganization of transportation. He stresses especially inflation through bank notes and *bons* and credit.[4] All of these influences undoubtedly had some importance, though the use of the *bons* as money was almost negligible.[5] It is probable that he exaggerates the mechanical impor-

[1] U. S. Senate, *Foreign Currency and Exchange Investigation,* p. 473. Deposits and current accounts of the three large banks increased from about 12 billions in 1919 to 13 billions in 1920. They were only 7 billions in 1918. Moreover, the combined total of clearings for both the Bank of France and the clearing house jumped from 438 to 854 billion francs in 1919 and 1920, respectively. See reports of the U. S. Commercial Attaché in Paris.

[2] See *supra,* this chapter and appendix.

[3] Jules Décamps, *op. cit.,* p. 367.

[4] *Ibid., op. cit.,* p. 369.

[5] See *infra,* Chapter VI.

tance of the means of payment. Only to a slight degree was *creation* of notes and credit an active force; whereas the *desire* to spend and borrow was undoubtedly a very strong influence. The sudden increase of cash in hand did influence the buying attitude of peasants to a certain extent. The mere fact that they had accumulated money without spending much during the war probably encouraged them in some instances to enlarge their holdings of land.[1]

It is usually more important to find the motive than the means of price increase, and in the French experience the psychological elements bulk large. Every evidence indicates a *boom* attitude at the time. Germain Martin is clear on this point.[2]

At this time there developed an optimism without limits, which increased rapidly between 1919 and the month of August, 1920, during which there was a quick and uninterrupted rise in wholesale and retail prices. The collapse was sudden, it lasted until March, 1922. . . .

Speculative factors of the most general sort were very influential. Activity on the stock exchange was less significant than that of wholesale markets, although the value of securities did fluctuate somewhat with prices.[3] The expectation of large expenditures for reconstruction and the sudden increase in the demand for certain commodities led to a fairly general marking up of prices. Such movements have a tendency to be cumulative, particularly when they are accompanied by a policy of readily expansible credit.[4]

[1] Professor Rist agrees with those who give some importance to these land purchases immediately after the war.

[2] Germain Martin, *op. cit.,* p. 228.

[3] Supplément aux *Indices du Mouvement général des affaires,* 4th year, January, 1926, Institute de statistique de Paris, *L'Etude des cycles économiques,* p. 13.

[4] R. G. Hawtrey, *op. cit.,* p. 62. Credit has an inherent tendency to expand, and the problem of controlling it reduces itself in practice to curbing this tendency in time to prevent undue depreciation of the monetary unit. Such an effort was not exerted quickly enough after the conclusion of the war.

Illustrations of the influence of postwar maladjustments on price movements, such as Décamps probably had in mind, were frequent, though rarely referred to in the formal discussions of the period. In the early months of 1919, to mention a trivial but typical instance, there was a sudden shortage of matches in Paris; this sent the price sky high. The reason was that when the peasants began returning to their farms and industrial workers to the textile regions in the North, practically all the matches available were shipped to Lille. Since it was difficult to distribute them from that center to the outlying districts, even in that region they were extremely expensive. Similar incidents occurred in the case of a great many more important commodities. They were due partly to the efforts of the government to help the refugees and partly to the profit-making instincts of private individuals. Such sudden displacements of goods in the hope of large gains led to the accumulation of high-priced stocks of goods and to abnormal shortages in certain sections. Since this was true, it is probable that even without the infectious influence of a general rise in prices in many countries, reconstruction activity would have induced a considerable increase in France.

Perhaps one could generalize these explanations so that they fit other countries than France. For the optimistic attitude after the war was certainly fairly universal. However this may be, in France there was no clear concept of war losses, the deceptive influence of artificial purchasing power was very general, and the hope for a return of "good times" was widespread. The combination of a feverish optimism, and of wasteful habits learned during the war, lead to uneconomic production, speculative buying, and a careless and confused management of affairs. The result was inevitable; the unsound structure was doomed to grow higher and then crash with its own weight. Some measure of deflation was bound to come with this inevitable reaction; this deflation occurred in 1921.

The Crisis

While the rapid rise of wholesale prices [1] and the continued expansion of credit began to cause anxiety, no vigorous action was taken in France in 1919. Other countries considered active measures to check this movement as a feeling of general apprehension began to develop. In England, at this time, the Cunliffe Committee prepared its report, recommending deflation of the note circulation.[2] In the United States, the Federal Reserve Board began to consider seriously the problem of checking credit expansion.[3] In France, on the other hand, deflationary sentiment was at a minimum because of the more obvious needs of reconstruction and the truth was obscured by the temporizing policies of the finance minister. At the same time, it is probable that, though some check on expansion of money and credit in France would have been advisable, it was both more difficult and less necessary to her than it was to the United States and England, who were unembarrassed by actual devastation.

Granted these conditions and ideas, the crisis of 1920 was inevitable. The shock which precipitated or "timed" the fall of prices seems to have been the collapse of silk and the violent economic crisis in Japan.

The ground was well prepared for a crisis, and it needed only to start in one place for it to spread far and wide. The first collapse occurred on the market for material supplied to the clothing industry. . . .[4]

[1] The increase during 1919 in France was from 332 per cent of 1914 in May, to 432 per cent in December. See appendix, p. 510.

[2] Rist, *op. cit.*, pp. 14-22. There had been a first report on August 15, 1918. The second report was dated December 3, 1919. See also Cassel, *Money and the Foreign Exchange After 1914* (New York, 1923), p. 204.

[3] Gustav Cassel, *Money and Foreign Exchange After 1914* (New York, 1923), p. 221, and R. G. Hawtrey, *op. cit.*, p. 103. In October the reserve ratio fell to 48.3 per cent. The rediscount rate was advanced slightly and there was discussion of the advisability of restricting credits and preventing speculation as far as possible.   [4] Cassel, *op. cit.*, p. 232.

Leather, hides, and silk were the first important articles to show marked declines. The banks stopped financing the holdings of large stocks of goods by speculators, particularly the large accumulations of silk, and the price of this commodity dropped 50 per cent in a very short space of time. In this connection, Hawtrey gives importance to the threat of gold exports to Japan and other similar strains on banking reserves in the United States.[1] It would be a mistake to emphasize the importance of any one particular event as a cause of the reaction. It is probable that if there had been no trouble in Japan some other circumstance would have occurred to shake the unsound credit structure. However this may be, the first important change occurred in the United States.[2]

The Federal Reserve rates were raised above six per cent in January, 1920; [3] shortly after this American banks suddenly began curtailing loans to exporters.[4] There followed a slight panic in Paris on the foreign exchanges, when the dollar rose from 11 to 15 francs. This flurry accentuated the distrust both in the United States and abroad which was already considerable. Moreover, there was a growing impression that European budget methods were unsound and that there were difficulties ahead in regard to reparations, which made further extension of credits to foreign countries by the United States seem extremely risky. This change of attitude led to a very sudden change in both physical production and the price of goods. The Federal Reserve Board wholesale index number of prices for the United States, which had increased slightly from January to May, 1920, declined from 269 to 179 in December of the same year.

[1] Hawtrey, *op. cit.*, pp. 106, 107.

[2] Baron Mourré, *Revue d'économie politique* (Paris, 1921), vol. xxxv, no. 2, pp. 545, 567. "La crise actuelle a débuté aux Etats Unis."

[3] Possible parallels between the situation in January, 1920, and in January, 1928, would be interesting to note.

[4] Hawtrey, *op. cit.*, p. 105.

TABLE VII
INDEX NUMBER OF WHOLESALE PRICES [1]
1920
(1914 = 100)

Month	United States	France
Jan	248	447
Feb	248	472
Mar	253	513
Apr	267	562
May	269	575
Jun	262	535
Jul	254	520
Aug	240	536
Sep	232	533
Oct	214	517
Nov	196	489
Dec	179	450

The movements of the price curves of France, England, and America at this time were almost identical; [2] the wholesale indices in all three countries turned downward at practically the same moment. Such close accord between economic phenomena in different countries is surprising. It indicates that there was probably some sudden apprehension, that fear of the further economic expansion and the anticipation of deflation were probably as important as the changes in discount rates which were actually put into effect. Credence is given to such an interpretation by the fact that psychological influences can spread rapidly from place to place, whereas the effect of import and export prices on domestic prices—an alternative explanation for this synchronization [3]—is a much slower affair. The increase in money rates served to hasten the reaction because they indicated bankers' attitudes, and because they made money tighter. In sympathy with this general movement, the Bank

[1] See appendix.

[2] U. S. Senate, *Foreign Currency and Exchange Investigation*, p. 458. Prices in Great Britain declined from May to June.

[3] See curves for the three countries in *Bulletin de la statistique générale de la France*, vol. xiii, no. 3, p. 226.

of France raised its rates from five to six per cent on April 8, 1920.[1]

The fall of prices was as precipitate as the rise. Moreover, the fall of the dollar on the Paris exchange was also sudden, although it did not continue so long. The biggest change in the dollar rate came between May 5 and 12, when it fell from 16.45 to 14.94 francs; then the rate for the dollar turned up again in July.[2] It is not possible to make a detailed comparison of the price and exchange curves, since weekly price figures were not published for this period. The index number represents values at the end of the month. It is quite possible, though not certain, that the exchange rate exerted considerable influence on wholesale prices through the declining cost of imports in francs. The price of cotton, for instance, one of the most important commodities bought abroad, declined notably at this time; [3] wool likewise fell in price; [4] copper, lead, zinc, and tin all showed the same tendency.[5] Food prices which were less affected by exchange rates did not decline so rapidly as did the index number of all the forty-seven commodities.[6] The purely monetary factor, that is to say, the decline of prices registered in paper francs—francs which were worth more on a gold basis—does not account for the whole change between the high points of 1920 and the low point of 1922. In other words, there was a real fall in gold prices in France. Moreover, the franc was worth less than the comparison of prices in the United States and France would justify.[7] In this period of change, the order in which events followed one another was that which is frequently called cyclical; the

---

[1] *Le Pour et le contre* (Paris, December 19, 1927). See *infra,* Chapter VI.

[2] See appendix for exchange figures from *La Cote officielle.*

[3] Lucien March, *op. cit.,* pp. 94, 95.

[4] *Ibid.,* pp. 96, 97.   [5] *Ibid.,* p. 75.   [6] *Ibid.,* p. 300.

[7] U. S. Senate, *Foreign Currency and Exchange Investigation,* pp. 476, 477. See also chart facing page 330. The chart on page 314 indicates that later, by the middle of 1921, subsequent prices on a gold basis had reached a point of relative instability. Later changes in paper prices did little more than reflect changes in the exchange rates until 1926.

reason for the reaction was largely psychological. The sudden collapse of prices in most countries was due both to the changed attitude of speculators and to a shift in the policy of governments and central banks. As always in such cases, those who had large stocks of goods were forced to sell them at a sacrifice, and the movement, once begun, gained impetus through a number of months until low costs and increasing demand turned the tide in the other direction. This further change came eventually in 1922.

The next year, 1921, was the one of great depression and inactivity. Production as measured by the Dessirier index for France fell to forty-nine per cent of prewar in October from seventy per cent in 1920.[1] Then bank clearings, usually a fairly good indication of economic conditions, reflected the depression to a certain extent, though the change from 1920 to 1922 was not very great. In fact, the lowest point was that reached in 1922 after the general production situation had improved; demand liabilities of the four large banks showed a very slight reaction with the depression.[2] In contrast to these indications of slackened activity, the production of iron and steel, the number of car loadings, and the extraction of coal all show a fairly steady progress.[3]

A comparison of these various facts gives fairly clear evidence, therefore, that France did not suffer greatly from this severe reaction in price movements between 1919 and 1922. Her foreign commerce was but slightly affected; it is notable

[1] *Bulletin de la statistique générale de la France*, vol. xiv, no. 1, pp. 106, 108. The textile industry was more adversely affected than were the metal industries. See Louis Pommery, *Revue d'économie politique* (1927), vol. xli, no. 2, pp. 618, 624. The Dessirier index of the *Statistique générale* averages the production of the basic industries, textile, metal, etc.

[2] Morgan Bank, *Statistical Atlas* (unpublished, Paris), p. 13. The four banks are the *Société générale, Crédit Lyonnais, Comptoir d'escompte de Paris, Société générale de credit industriel et commercial*. The figures for December of the different years are: 1920, 13,270 million francs; 1921, 13,319 millions; and 1922, 13,966 millions. The figure for 1926, 22,469 million francs, indicates the rapid later development.

[3] See the *Bulletin de la statistique générale de la France* for these figures.

that exports increased throughout the period and the sharp decline of imports in 1921 probably did not work great hardship.[1] On the whole, the general nature of her productive effort and the abnormal demand caused by the rebuilding of the devastated regions prevented any far-reaching harm. So much for conditions in 1921. In 1922, French economic life was fairly sound, so that the gradual recovery in all countries and partial adjustment to postwar conditions made it possible for her to enter upon a period of activity such that it has been justly called a "brilliant economic revival."[2] During these years and even during the later depression caused in 1926 by the appreciation of the franc, and its subsequent stability in 1927, France has shown an ability to keep on producing which argues well for her future position in the industrial world.

To sum up the events of this period: the rise of prices during 1919 and 1920 had been due to misconceptions. The sudden collapse in 1920 was due to a reversal of opinion, to increased money rates, and to the fall of certain commodities in the world market. The continued decline of prices through 1921 was the natural result of this severe shock to business, and of the forced sale of stocks of goods. The gradual recovery in France and in the world at large from 1922 onward is such as one would expect after a marked recession of a price "wave." It must be observed, however, that this recovery in France was somewhat quicker than elsewhere because of the productive activity stimulated by réconstruction.

The growing difficulties in government finance have already been sufficiently stressed.[3] The energetic start made with the rebuilding of the North had not been accompanied by an equally vigorous effort to meet costs through taxa-

[1] See appendix.
[2] J. R. Cahill, Department of Overseas Trade, Report, *The Economic Conditions in France,* revised to June, 1924 (London, 1924), p. 5.
[3] See *supra,* this chapter.

tion. Increases voted led to small additions to government revenues, but the gap was still wide between receipts and expenditures. A policy of loans was not wise in view of the already heavy government debt, but hardly any other policy was possible at the time. The misunderstanding of the situation is fully brought out by the attempt to cut down government borrowings from the Bank at the time when, paradoxically enough, it was calling for subscribers to its short-term notes. This deflationary effort was costly, not only because of the higher rate of interest on its borrowings from citizens,[1] but even more because it clouded the issue and gave a false sense of security in the value of the franc.[2]

The collapse of the franc in March, 1919, had revealed an alarming financial weakness. The sudden shortage of dollar credits had indicated that the government could not or would not intervene; that private lenders were becoming less eager to hold French credits. Favorable speculation, once so severely shocked, never quite rallied to the support of the franc; the year 1919 was therefore critical. Then it became evident that France was heavily involved in complex problems of international debts, reparations, and the delicate political questions which grew out of them; then it was realized that her borrowings were already crushingly heavy. Moreover, it was apparent for the first time that the previous stability of the franc, based on pegging operations, had been abnormal and temporary, while the attainment of a new and lasting stability was no easy matter. Thus the way was open for large-scale speculation against the franc.

The artificial support of the franc with foreign credits was abandoned, but the new financial expedient of deflation was hardly less artificial in its essence. The convention of 1920 between the Bank and the state gave a false appearance of amortization of the internal debt. Real deflation might pos-

---

[1] Five per cent, as compared with less than three and a half per cent.
[2] It led to the false Bank of France statements of 1924, 1925, for instance. See *infra,* Chapter V.

sibly have resulted in a rising value for the franc, but even this is not certain in view of the difficulties of 1919 and 1920, which had increased the indebtedness of the government to such an extent in many cases that illusory deflation did little or nothing to alter the situation for the better. The net result was a postponement of effective amortization and a dangerous decrease in the margin of advances which the government could secure from the Bank.

This second period of depreciation, 1919-22, has been called *cyclical*. The outstanding fact is the very rapid upward movement of prices followed by a swift collapse. At this time the internal value of the franc seems to be more significant than the external, because the changes in its commodity value are more striking than the changes in its dollar value. This interpretation may lead to an exaggeration of the importance of prices. It should be observed, therefore, that although prices did dominate exchange rates to a considerable extent, it is probable that the depreciation of the exchange value of the franc was only partially interrupted by the fall in commodity prices, and that the exchange rates had a more profound and lasting effect on French life. It is conceivable that had there been a determined budget policy within the country, and capital from American loans or German reparations to lighten the reconstruction burden, monetary recovery might have been possible even in 1919. Government intervention in the exchange markets might under these conditions have prevented the fatal drop of the franc. As it happened, however, at one and the same time the exchanges were upset by the necessity of suddenly adapting themselves to postwar freedom, by the fears and suspicions engendered by international disagreements, and a weak financial program within France. Under such a heavy strain, there is little wonder that the franc broke. The results of these difficulties and delays were disastrous; war losses were converted into new forms of debts, and the day of final reckoning postponed.

CHAPTER V

THE LOSS OF CONFIDENCE, 1922–1927

THE liquidation of war debts and losses could not be indefinitely postponed. Very little of the cost of the war was paid for as it was fought.[1] To a far greater extent the burden was shifted by using up capital resources and by borrowing abroad. The payment in loss of life, in acute suffering and mental hardship, began with the beginning of the war. The financial payment did not begin, to any significant extent, until well after the war; and the total cost will not have been met until all the capital destroyed has burden was shifted by using up capital resources and by new accumulations and constructive effort. [These real changes in French economic life worked themselves out indirectly through two lines of causation: first, through the depreciation of money, which redistributed real values; and second, through the payment of taxes which took from some people and gave to others. These two changes do more than merely reallocate wealth. They bring to light the inevitable, but none the less regrettable, loss in real value. For extreme taxation and extreme depreciation are repressive and destructive forces.]

France began to pay for the war first through the depreciation of the franc; this began in 1919 but became a more serious factor in 1922. She began, second, to pay in taxes with the very marked increase in 1924. It is true that before this date there had been both depreciation and increases in taxation. Both of the facts, however, had been considered to be purely temporary phenomena previous to 1922. The return to a more favorable state of affairs was con-

[1] See *infra,* Chapter III.

fidently expected; the losses inflicted had not gone very deep
and the difficult times ahead were not fully realized. The
years from 1919 to 1922 had so complicated the situation
and burdened the state, however, that there was no longer
any escape. Subsequent events were but the logical sequel of
what had gone before. The acute reparation crises from
1922 to 1924 were followed by serious embarrassment to the
treasury and hostile speculation. Difficulties with the internal obligations of the government led naturally to inflation
and loss of confidence. Moreover, the subsequent increase
in taxation and the revelation of huge budget deficits in
1925 were the preliminaries to the flight of capital and
wild panic in July, 1926. It seems, looking back, that final
recovery on the brink of collapse was the only episode in
the series of events which could not have been predicted.
This was unexpected to many; it certainly was not inevitable. It stands as an impressive and hopeful tribute to the
vigor and eventual understanding and good judgment of
the nation.

The reparation struggle is one of the most unfortunate
connected with the war. It is doubly regrettable because of
a considerable measure of friction and loss which it caused
unnecessarily. In discussions of the indemnity, it was some
time before the emphasis shifted from the rights of the victors to the economic interests of all the nations involved.
It became evident, finally, that the heart of the matter lay,
not in assessing the amount of the bill to be collected, but
in seeing how much could be paid without impairing the
economic welfare of Europe. This change of emphasis did
not finally come until the collapse of the mark and the rapid
fall of the franc gave dramatic evidence of the harm which
was being wrought.

On the outcome of this controversy depended the future
of both the mark and the franc. The turning point downward for both came in 1922, when the serious divergence
of opinions between France and the other countries became

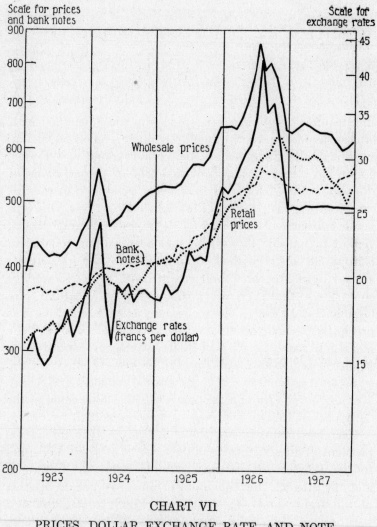

Scale for prices
and bank notes

Scale for
exchange rates

Wholesale prices

Bank
notes

Retail
prices

Exchange rates
(francs per dollar)

1923   1924   1925   1926   1927

CHART VII

PRICES, DOLLAR EXCHANGE RATE, AND NOTE
CIRCULATION, 1923-1927[1]

[1] See appendix for figures.

153

clearly evident. In fact, the matter of reparations was so
important to the franc that it must be given some consideration here. Even now the close connection between the value
of money and the payments from Germany may not be
clearly evident, for the most direct influence was not
through actual payments, but through the attitude of speculators to the general European situation.[1] The wrangles
and disputes discouraged everyone who was concerned with
international finance. So much so that it seemed for a time
as though the disagreement between England and France
might have very serious consequences in the relations of
the two nations. Moreover, it was also possible that the uncompromising attitude of France would prevent the economic recovery of Germany. The future of Europe looked
very dark indeed. Those who had been willing to lend to
Europe, no longer wished to do so; those who had credits
abroad began to shift their investments to gold standard
countries, so that there was a steady outflow of capital from
Germany and France. The movement in the former case was
precipitate, since there were few opposing forces, and the
mark fell with dizzy speed. The exodus of capital from
France was not so rapid, but the depressing effect on the
franc during the next few years was nevertheless very great.
Its value on the foreign exchange fell from nine cents in the
early part of 1922 to five cents at the end of 1923.

Herr Bergmann in his valuable study of the reparation
problem divides it into four periods: [2] (1) from Versailles
to the London ultimatum; (2) the policy of fulfilment
and the struggle for the moratorium; (3) the occupation
of the Ruhr; and (4) the Dawes Plan. During the first
part, as has been said above, the main concern was with
the exact amount to be paid by Germany and the amount
of the resultant yearly payments in kind and in cash. While

[1] Allyn A. Young, *Foreign Affairs* (March, 1924), vol. ii, no. 3, pp. 404, 406.
[2] Karl Bergmann, *The History of Reparations* (London, 1927, translated
from the German edition of 1926).

this was being considered, the tenor of the general discussion was that large payments could be made if Germany would but set herself with a will to accomplish her utmost in this respect. These illusions and hopes were universal despite some difference of opinion as to the precise amount to be paid.

It is the second and third phases of the problem, however, which are most interesting to a student of French conditions. It was during these later years that the divergence of her views from those of other nations brought serious consequences to France. In considering the first postwar years, something has been said already in defense of the French financial policy in so far as it meant a rapid and even extravagant reconstruction program. On the other hand, there is little to be said for the French attitude toward reparations. Even though the subject is controversial, it is impossible to avoid comment on this matter. Although it became increasingly clear in 1922 that Germany must be given a breathing spell and that reparation payments were dependent on her economic recovery, France stood out alone in opposition to measures for her recovery in 1922. Then again France and Belgium were alone in 1923 in insisting, by military occupation, on drastic measures after other attempts to collect seemed to fail. It is true that France had been the main creditor [1] and little sympathy had been shown for her real needs and claims. Despite this misapprehension, it is evident that she must bear considerable blame for the ultimate collapse of the mark and the dark years in Germany that followed. It may be that, in a sense, the occupation of the Ruhr was a necessary forerunner to the Dawes Plan. In so far as this is true, it is an admission of the slow and painful progress of human thought in reaching a solution of a problem which conformed with the general needs of Europe.

Let us turn now more particularly to the year 1922,

[1] See *supra,* Chapter I.

which was one of disillusionment in many quarters. There were hopes both for reparation adjustments and for exchange stability in the conferences of Cannes in January, and of Genoa in April. These hopes were doomed to disappointment. Germany was demanding a moratorium and a temporary setting aside of the payments scheduled under the London agreement. It was finally decided in the Reparation Commission to consider granting a loan to Germany which would ease the situation if it could be made. The Bankers Committee met in May. They considered it feasible to float a large loan in America if Europe would absorb a part [1] and that the whole matter depended on establishing a reasonable schedule of payments. Moreover, in view of this, they secured from the Reparation Commission a decision that the whole question of Germany's capacity to pay should be examined, a decision unanimous except for the dissenting vote of the French member of the commission. From this moment on, France refused absolutely to allow a reconsideration of the total sum to be demanded, claiming that it was in contradiction to the treaty and outside the rights of the Reparation Commission to act in such a matter. Indeed, the statement of Poincaré on this subject was most emphatic [2] and the result was the complete abandonment of the project of a loan. On June 10, the Bankers Committee handed in its report, indicating that its hands had been tied by the French objection to the necessary thorough consideration of the question. It is obvious that no loan such as was contemplated could have been marketed unless the possibility of the payment of interest and capital

---

[1] This was eventually done under the Dawes Plan.

[2] Karl Bergmann, *op. cit.*, pp. 133-138. Poincaré indicated that the reparation debt of Germany was unalterable. He said in the Chamber of Deputies, "Even in the Reparation Commission itself, or in its neighborhood, I can at present perceive the most dangerous machinations directed against us, in order to make the international loan contingent on a new reduction of our claims. This very morning, by virtue of my authority as head of the Government, I notified the French delegation on the Reparation Commission that it could not accept this." (*Ibid.*, p. 135.)

was made certain by the economic recovery of Germany. Hopes of an early settlement, which had been bright at the beginning of 1922, were thus suddenly wiped out.[1]

The effect of the failure of these negotiations on the franc was instantaneous. Previous to this, in 1922, the price of the dollar had been fairly steady around eleven francs. In fact, the condition of the foreign exchange market in general had been better than at any time since 1919. In June the prolonged rise of the dollar in Paris began. The increase at this time was not so sudden as the up and down movements in preceding years, but the turn of the tide was more significant. In fact, the franc never regained the value it lost in 1922 and 1923. From then on it became increasingly sensitive to political events, and the victim of speculation in the widest sense of the word. The later favorable reactions which occurred were powerless to stem the tide that brought about this steady downward trend. Also the fact that the German mark was falling at even greater speed did considerable to add to the dismay and general distrust of the European situation.

From June 10, 1922 to the end of 1926 the exchange movement dominated wholesale and retail prices. The change in relationship between prices and exchange at this time was very marked. A study of the curves shows at a glance that neither the quantity of money in circulation nor the movement of prices was such as to indicate clearly any influence on the exchange rates by either of these factors. It is probable, however, that each exerted some slight influence, though neither one can be considered to be the determinant. Professor Aftalion refers to the change in relationship that took place in 1922 as the growing discordance between

---

[1] *L'Europe nouvelle,* vol. ii, no. 23, pp. 709, 710 and pp. 722-725. This gives some of the documents exchanged by the Bankers Committee and the Reparation Commission.

TABLE VIII

THE RATE OF THE DOLLAR EXCHANGE ON THE PARIS BOURSE [1]

1922

Date	Francs
May 4...............	10.94
11...............	10.93
18...............	10.97
24...............	11.09
Jun 1...............	10.98
8...............	10.97
15...............	11.30
22...............	11.63
29...............	12.04
Jul 6...............	12.26

prices and note issues, due to the dominating influence of the exchange rates.[2] As speculative influences grew more powerful, variations of the exchange rates took place quite irrespective of the general conditions of production. The year 1922 was one of economic recovery [3] but the repercussions of political difficulties on the foreign exchanges led to this fall in the franc, a decline not justified by the economic conditions alone.

M. Maroni, the financial writer for the *Journal des débats* at this time, was one of the first to recognize the importance of psychological factors. In his weekly revue published February 27, 1922 he stressed the political power of speculation. In looking back over the June exchange rates, for instance, he said that foreign opinion had turned against the franc, adding that during these months the rates for the franc were set mainly by New York.[4] His analysis of

[1] See figures in appendix.

[2] Albert Aftalion, *Monnaie, prix et change* (Paris, 1927), pp. 18, 53.

[3] F. Maroni, *Journal des débats*, "Revue financière" (Paris, December 31, 1922).

[4] F. Maroni, *Journal des débats*, "Revue financière" (July 10 and October 29, 1922).

the situation was clear and he himself was free from many of the misconceptions of the time in regard to reparations. It is notable that he traced the influence of the various de-

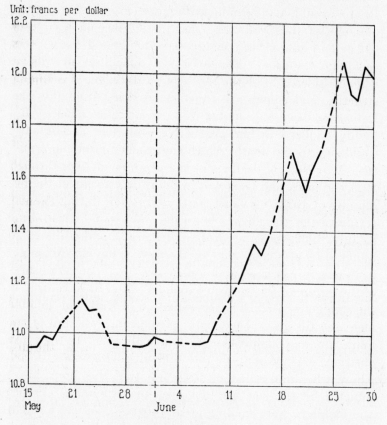

CHART VIII

DOLLAR EXCHANGE, MAY AND JUNE, 1922 [1]

cisions of the Reparation Commission on the value of the franc directly through speculation and indirectly through the fall of the mark.

There is no doubt that the impression created by the vertical drop of the mark was very great. It had not been

[1] See appendix, p. 462, for figures.

realized at first that the difficulties of postwar adjustments could lead to such severe disturbance to economic life as that which actually took place in Germany. The fall of the Russian rouble had been looked upon as a somewhat natural outcome of the profound social disturbance in a country which had never been completely dominated by western economic traditions. Moreover, the difficulties in Austria were considered to be the result of an ill-balanced economic structure and changes in territory resulting from the war. It had not been anticipated that a country as efficient and highly civilized in her productive procedure as Germany could sink to the depths which she reached after the armistice. After several declines in the years from 1919 through 1921 the mark had been worth about half a cent in the beginning of 1922; its value continued to fall during the uncertainties of the allied reparation discussions. From June to July, 1922, its value dropped from 32 hundredths to 20 hundredths of a cent, that is, the cost of foreign exchanges in Germany increased about sixty per cent. The seriousness of the failure of the projected loan had been fully realized in the summer of 1922. The assassination of Rathenau in June increased the general feeling of pessimism; [1] the fall of the mark was more impressive to financial observers than any abstract explanation of the difficulties Germany faced. Those who were still optimistic felt that the direct losses inflicted by the war had not been overwhelming—France and Belgium were making great progress, Germany might conceivably have done the same. Despite this hope, however, the combined effect of war losses, social disorganization, and irresistible pressure from without for the payment of formidable sums was such as to exert a paralyzing effect. It seemed that there was no capital market to which Germany could turn to ease her immediate needs, while there was no definite prospect of release from ultimate burdens calculated to strain every resource. The fall of the mark was

[1] *Journal des débats,* "Revue financière" (July 3 and August 28, 1922).

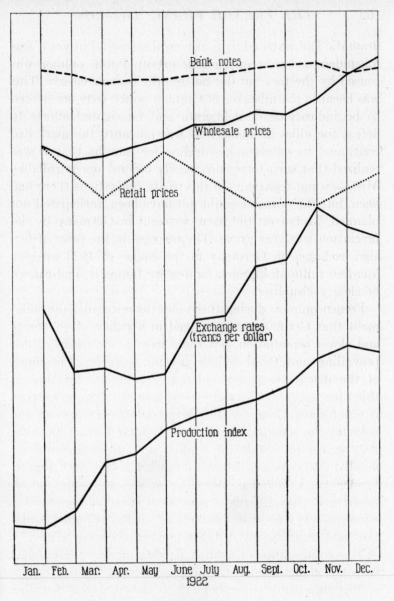

Bank notes

Wholesale prices

Retail prices

Exchange rates
(francs per dollar)

Production index

Jan. Feb. Mar. Apr. May June July Aug. Sept. Oct. Nov. Dec.
1922

CHART IX

VALUE, PRODUCTION, AND NOTE CIRCULATION, 1922 [1]

[1] See appendix for figures.

dramatic and watched with universal interest, but yet it was misunderstood to a considerable extent. Public opinion was roused by the fact but did not see the reasons clearly. This was because the mistakes of German policy were considered to be indications of deliberate and far-sighted efforts to defeat the allies in finance.[1] It was not until the mark had continued its catastrophic decline for months that it was realized that such forces necessarily become uncontrollable. Mistakes and resistance to the treaty obligations there had been, but the outcome could not have been anticipated nor planned. Moreover, the harm wrought in Germany by depreciation was very grave. The increase in the price of foreign exchange in Germany in the course of 1923 was one hundred millionfold. Such figures are fantastic, and cannot be clearly visualized.

French opinion during these months reiterated the judgment that Germany was engaged in a policy of deliberate and clever repudiation, but there were a few critics of this prevailing view. On the whole, it is not surprising that much of the discussion was clouded by prejudice. England at this time judged bitterly the stand taken by France, because it was forcing Germany into industrial disorganization and delaying the economic recovery of Europe. In fact, the year 1922 ended on a note of conflict and misunderstanding; in all matters concerned with foreign policy and finance, France was in a bad position. As far as her production, reconstruction, and foreign commerce were concerned, her situation was reassuring; and even though her budget situation was troublesome, it did not cause any great alarm.

The continuance of budget deficits, however, combined with the difficulties of the treasury, made the convention of 1920 impossible to apply in 1922. The result was a scaling down of the amount to be repaid by the state to the Bank

---

[1] André Fourgeaud, *La Dépréciation et la revalorisation du mark allemand* (Paris, 1926), p. 103. M. Fourgeaud shows that Germany had imposed heavier taxes than France in 1922.

of France. This step was decided upon despite the realization that it would have a bad effect on the speculative attitude to the franc as well as on the resolution of the government as to the future of this deflationary policy.[1] The outcome of the discussion was the nominal repayment of 800 million francs, which reduced the total of such advances outstanding to 24,200 million francs, instead of to 23,000 million francs as was projected under the 1920 convention.[2] The possibility of repayment was limited by budget resources and by the more complex reactions of the *bons de la défense* on the treasury. The government was powerless to control the situation except through a complete and revolutionary revision of her financial policy. Such a revision was hardly possible until the clarification of the reparation situation made its importance obvious to politicians and electors. Meanwhile the floating debt was becoming unmanageable, budget receipts were insufficient,[3] and at the same time all efforts were directed towards collecting from Germany rather than towards settling these internal problems. The year 1922 closed with the prospect of the Ruhr occupation troubling European politics and finance.

THE RUHR OCCUPATION

The occupation of the Ruhr was the inevitable outcome of the preceding disagreement over reparations. Events in 1923 could hardly have been otherwise, granted the widening breach between England and France. Nor could the Dawes Plan have been accepted easily by France and Ger-

[1] *La France économique et financière* (November 18 and December 23, 1922). "Les cascades des changes" due to the rumored suspension of repayments to the Bank of France in the fall was halted by the announcement in November that a part of the agreed amount would be repaid.

[2] *Le Pour et le contre* (Paris, December 24, 1922). See also Charles Rist, *La Déflation en pratique* (Paris, 1924), p. 65.

[3] Etienne Clémentel, *Ministre des finances, Inventaire de la situation financière de la France* (Paris, 1924), p. 21. Budget receipts were 24.2 billion francs, expenditures were 48.9 billion francs, and the deficit was 24.7 billion francs, see appendix.

many without the troubled months of conflict which preceded it. The emphasis of England during this time had
always been on lower demands upon Germany. French opinion was outraged not only by the willingness to scale down
the amount, but even more by the absence of any definite
assurance that this smaller amount would ever be paid. The
suggested moratorium seemed to her to be a preliminary
step towards complete repudiation, and very little was done
to reassure her on this point.[1] It seemed as if the size of
her claims and the power to collect them were melting before her very eyes. There was a desperate feeling throughout
the country that something must be done; the most vigorous
step, military occupation, was decided upon. On January 13,
1923, the French, supported by the Belgians, marched into
the Ruhr.

There were two aspects of the French policy adopted at
this time, neither of which must be forgotten. One aim was
the collection by force of a part of what was due France as
reparations; this aim was doomed to defeat. The desired
commodities, coal, for instance, could be secured only
through work and despite serious opposition on the part of
the Germans. The effort was therefore costly and the material results were most disappointing to the French. The
second aim was probably more important and was to a certain extent attained, though the cost was great. As Mr.
Auld says:

It can scarcely be doubted that the Ruhr was seized primarily
as a pledge and not as a means of getting current reparation
payments.[2]

[1] George Auld, *Foreign Affairs,* supplement (March, 1924), p. xi. "The
fundamental injustice which has been done the French, and which had
its powerful reflex on the French psychology, is that no effective recognition has ever been given to their reconstruction difficulties." Britain,
he adds, was partly responsible for the occupation of the Ruhr because of
her narrow and unsympathetic policy.

[2] George Auld, *Foreign Affairs, loc. cit.,* p. x. See also Karl Bergmann,
op. cit., p. 141.

There is little doubt that the French consider that this
part of their policy was worth the cost; [1] foreign opinion,
on the other hand, is less clear in its verdict. The judgment
of New York and London, which was often most clearly expressed in exchange speculation, indicated the profound distrust with which this move was received.[2]

The fall of the franc in January, 1923, was spectacular.
There was a drop of about ten per cent in the course of
two weeks. Some of this lost ground was later regained when
it was realized that the threatening gesture of France would
not lead to the outbreak of actual warfare. The fall was
resumed, however, as resistance in the occupied zone increased and as it was seen that the measure would yield
little in the way of actual commodity payments to France.
The franc continued during 1923 the decline begun in June,
1922. Moreover, the rate of depreciation was practically the
same. It is surprising, in view of this, that the French did
not realize the extent of hostile opinion in other countries.
They seemed much too absorbed with their own needs to
follow outside criticism. In February, for instance, Maroni
in the *Journal des débats* [3] says there was no reason for the
exchange troubles of the moment. This would seem to ignore any direct connection between the French policy and
foreign apprehension as to the results of this policy. In
March, however, he comments on the unfavorable judgment
of other nations.[4] One must realize that, in the main,
France was isolated and unaware of the general trend of

---

[1] *Documents parlementaires, Chambre,* 1924, annexe no. 537, p. 2140. The
balance of the Ruhr occupation is here given.

[2] There is a confused history behind the occupation of the Ruhr. It
was the result of a plan originally drawn up by M. Seydoux and others,
but the significant part as outlined by Seydoux was the rehabilitation of Germany combined with the exaction of certain guaranties. M.
Poincaré changed the whole tenor of the plan by leaving out the prior
steps to assure Germany recovery. Bergmann, *op. cit.,* pp. 157, 158.

[3] *Journal des débats,* "Revue financière," February 5, 1923.

[4] *Ibid.,* March 19, 1923.

thought in other countries. There was some feeling, certainly, that the fall of the franc was caused by hostile foreign attacks.[1] Such a view was based, in part, on the fact that the fall of the franc was not justified by the general internal economic conditions, since they were, on the whole favorable. If, on the contrary, it had been possible for the French to realize the depressing effect of her Ruhr policy on the franc through the influence of impersonal speculation, it is probable that she would have set the cost of this policy at a higher figure. It seems evident to the outside observer that this one factor alone dominated the fall of the franc in 1923.

As the pressure of speculation on the franc increased, and as the money continued its fall in terms of foreign exchange, the trend of French opinion began to change. There was less assurance as to the success of force, and more worry about the wider effects of the reparation policy. Moreover, it became apparent that the complete reliance of the French on German payments to settle her financial problems had been disastrous to internal finance. Editorial comment in *Le Pour et le contre* changed in tone at this time.

We have permitted too much solidarity to develop between the future of our financial life and the payment of reparations.[2]

Maroni, in the *Journal des débats,* says emphatically:

It can be said without any exaggeration that for several months the movement of the franc on the exchanges has been dominated by no other cause . . . than the occupation of the Ruhr and the reparation question.[3]

The discussions in the Reparation Commission made some progress. Moreover, enlightened French opinion began to tolerate a more lenient view, for the more conservative observers saw that the appropriation of wealth in Germany

[1] *Le Pour et le contre* (April 28, 1923).   [2] *Ibid.* (October 8, 1923).
[3] *Journal des débats* (Paris, October 29, 1923).

by violence was extremely costly.[1] Thus, after two years of acute controversy, violent disagreements, and threats, there developed a milder viewpoint which made possible a *rapprochement* with England, and in the months to come, the Dawes Plan.

Let us look more specifically to the fluctuations of the franc at this time. French soldiers entered the Ruhr in January, 1923. The franc plunged downward. The net depreciation during the year was approximately forty per cent, that is, from 13.55 francs to the dollar on January 2 to 19.61 to the dollar on December 29. The most severe depreciation took place in January, in June, and again in November.[2] The first two instances were quite directly connected with reparations and the Ruhr. The third, though due in part to the new negotiations between the Allies, was also caused in part by the maneuvers of speculators, who began to play the exchanges in a very deliberate way at this time. Variations during the first three months of the year were the most violent which had been experienced in France up to this time.

It is not possible here to trace the movement of the exchange rates in greater detail. If time and space permitted, one could show how each marked change in value was contemporaneous with some new announcement regarding the reparation policy on the part of France or some new move by England. Conditions in Germany were also, to a certain extent, reflected in the value of the franc. The exchange rates were more an indication than a cause of fundamental maladjustment. As an indication, they were not clearly understood; this was a time of illusions and mis-

---

[1] Karl Bergmann, *op. cit.*, pp. 213-215. In late 1923 the *Micum* agreement for deliveries in kind was reached and improved the situation notably. Moreover the new *rentenmark* in Germany led to improved conditions there, and it depended in part on the firm intention to avoid sinking again into the monetary chaos of the preceding months.

[2] See Chart VII, p. 153, and daily exchange rates in statistical appendix.

TABLE IX

FRANCS PER DOLLAR ON THE PARIS BOURSE[1]

1923

Jan	4	14.085
	11	14.475
	18	15.295
	25	15.515
Feb	1	16.845
	8	16.215
	15	16.415
	22	16.450
Mar	1	16.410
	8	16.535
	15	16.275
	22	14.950
	29	15.095

understandings. Certainly, the tendency to blame England [2] and Germany [3] made it more difficult for the French to enter on a constructive and conciliatory policy at this time.

It is regrettable that the improvement in international relations which seemed probable at the end of 1923 was not able to save France from a disastrous exchange crisis. This was because the situation had become highly unstable during these months and speculation had been increased by the collapse of the mark and by the great uncertainty regarding French policy. From the end of 1923 until the middle of 1926 France was destined to undergo repeatedly the painful effects of severe speculative crises. The franc rose and fell on the exchanges in a seemingly irrational and uncontrollable fashion. It offered the most striking instance of extreme variation in value without actual monetary collapse. Similar, though less extreme, movements of the Bel-

---

[1] See appendix, p. 463.

[2] *Le Pour et le contre* (July 15, 1923). ". . . La querelle que nous a fait l'Angleterre au sujet de la Ruhr arrive à son point culminant avec le grand fracas sur tous les marchés de change."

[3] *Ibid.*, April 28, 1923.

gian franc and the lira during much of this time were due,
in part, to the fact that they were conditioned by the same
facts as was France and so were estimated as having approximately the same value. It should be observed that the connection between France and Belgium was particularly close
because of the influence of France over Belgian affairs at
certain times and because of their close financial solidarity.[1]
During most of the postwar period, it was the French franc
which led and the others which followed. There came a time
in 1926 and 1927 when there was a marked divergence of
these three currencies. In 1926 the second attempt to stabilize the Belgian franc succeeded. In 1927 the Italian lira
appreciated rapidly on the exchanges because of government support, and was stabilized early in June. For several
years, however, the French exchange was a fair indication of
the condition of the other currencies. The franc was remarkable because of the extreme range of variation and continued ability which it showed to regain stability and avoid
collapse.

The "battle of the franc" is a descriptive term which
has been applied to the intense struggle in 1924. The drive
of outside speculation against the franc, which finally struck
at the roots of French confidence in their own currency,
brought the franc very near to destruction. It was, indeed, a
hard-fought battle which began towards the end of 1923 and
continued until the complete rout of speculators in March,
1924 left the government in temporary command of the
field. It is best to review the general condition of production
and finance at the end of 1923, in order to understand the
significance of this crisis.

The general economic situation at the end of 1923 was
fairly bright. The production index of the *Bulletin de la
statistique générale de la France* showed increasing activity:
97 per cent of the 1913 level in October, 99 per cent in No-

[1] U. S. Senate, *Foreign Currency and Exchange Investigation*, vol. ii,
pp. 45, 46.

vember, and 102 per cent in December.[1] There was also in
foreign relations, as has been indicated above, a marked
improvement in the relations of England and France; so
great an improvement, in fact, that a committee of experts was to be called to consider Germany's capacity to
pay and other important aspects of the reparation question.[2] It is true that some aspects of the financial situation within France, on the other hand, were less reassuring,
for it was realized as the year drew to a close that the state
would again be unable to carry out the provisions of the
convention of 1920. It was impossible to repay two billion
francs to the Bank of France because of the narrow margin
of resources at the disposal of the treasury.[3] This caused a
wave of pessimism at the very end of the year; it came as a
great surprise because it had not been admitted that the
budget was in deficit.[4] The total of the actual advances to
the state had been very near the legal limit throughout the
entire year but this fact had not been noticed by the general public.

THE ATTACK ON THE FRANC

Hostile speculation began in November, 1923. The movement started in Amsterdam, according to M. Casamajor. In
fact, this speculation has been used as an explanation of
Austrian financial conditions in that year. Pounds were sold
against dollars in that center, and there was a resulting sale
of francs in London as a counter-movement. The fall of the
French exchange thus started in Europe was carried farther
in New York.[5] It was from November 14 on that the franc
was "seriously attacked"; the precipitate rise of the dollar in

[1] *Bulletin de la statistique générale de la France,* vol. xiv, no. 1 (Paris,
1924), pp. 106, 108.
[2] *Journal des débats,* "Revue financière" (December 3, 1923).
[3] *Ibid.,* December 17, 1923.   [4] Rist, *op. cit.,* p. 71.
[5] Jean Casamajor, *Le Marché à terme des changes en France* (Paris,
1924), p. 118.

Paris is indicated by the following quotations taken from the first week of the month.

TABLE X

FRANCS PER DOLLAR ON THE PARIS BOURSE[1]

1923, 1924

(First week of the month)

Oct 4............... 17.165
Nov 8............... 17.405
Dec 6............... 18.430
Jan 3............... 20.535
Feb 7............... 21.460
Mar 6............... 24.760
Apr 3............... 17.300

During the first weeks the decline of the franc was explained variously as due to the reparation negotiations, the usual year-end difficulties, and to budget discussion. As the movement gained impetus, however, it was gradually realized that the origin was speculative and that a very powerful drive against the franc was in progress.

The panic of 1924 was due, more than any other episode of the French experience, to the deliberate efforts of financiers and speculators. The general nervous condition of the French exchange market during 1922 and 1923 has already been referred to, as well as the tremendous impression created by the collapse of the mark. It is obvious that faith in the stability of money had been severely shaken and the possibility of causing extreme changes in value by clever manipulation had been greatly exaggerated. It is not surprising that some adventurers in finance and certain enemies of France seized upon the opportunity which arose in 1923. This opportunity originated in the government's embarrassment in facing its obligations to repay the Bank of France.[2]

[1] These are the quotations for the first week of each month as given by *L'Economiste français*. They do not correspond exactly with those given in the appendix since there was a change in the manner of quoting exchange rates during this period. High and low are given in February, 1924, and after.

[2] *Revue d'économie politique*, vol. xxxviii, no. 4 (Paris, 1924), p. 676.

The margin of the Bank's advances was only one billion
francs; [1] it was therefore obvious that this repayment of
two billions was impossible, for it would have occasioned
an acute shortage of funds in the treasury. It seemed likely,
at the time, that a serious upset to the already precarious
stability would cause the government not only to fail in
respect to its repayment obligations to the Bank but also to
increase its borrowings from this and other sources. The resulting depreciation of the franc would, if carried far
enough, lead to an inevitable decline in subscriptions to the
bons de la défense and so cut off practically every ready
source of government funds. Repudiation of the internal
debt in one guise or another seemed likely, and repudiation,
if it had taken place, would have increased the harm already done to the franc. The fall of the franc would have
gained such impetus that, like the mark, it would rush to destruction. As a result of this interpretation of French affairs
there developed a great deal of short selling in francs. There
was a volume of gambling transactions in francs which has
rarely been precedented.

It proved later that the speculators were wrong and they
paid with heavy financial losses for their miscalculations.
The mistake which they made in 1924 was to underestimate
the resources of the government. It was true that the bungling measures in French finance during much of the postwar period was such as to indicate a general helplessness to
deal with the situation. Nevertheless, this did not mean that
the government was completely ignorant nor completely
lacking in resources. Moreover, the sensitivity of both the
volume of floating debt and the various budget resources to
the fall of the franc was not so great as had been anticipated.[2] The fall was not so fast that it could not be checked
by counter-speculation in the hands of the government. The

---

[1] E. Clémentel, *op. cit.*, pp. 49, 50. The legal limit throughout the year
was 24,000 million francs, see *infra,* Chapter VI.

[2] See *infra,* Chapter IX.

episode was dramatic, the cost was considerable, but the government won out in the end.

During the worst weeks of the crisis of 1924 the franc lost nearly half its value. Whereas it had been worth nearly six cents in October, it touched the low point of three and a half cents on March 11. Various measures were resorted to in the effort to stop the panic. The first notable step, taken in the middle of January when the franc was worth about five cents, was ineffectual; the Bank of France raised the discount rate.[1] Maroni says of this measure that:

The fall of the franc increased its speed as soon as the decision of the Bank of France was announced.

It seems that the psychological effect was extremely bad,[2] whereas the more mechanical influence on the flow of capital was nil.[3] Despite this, a further increase in the discount rate was tried two weeks later and proved equally ineffective as far as the defense of the franc was concerned. On the other hand, it did not disturb the exchange markets as much as the first had done. It was obvious, then, that the government must turn to other weapons. Those tried next were scarcely more helpful than the first. They took the form of further legislation against capital export[4] and in favor of the attempts to strengthen the franc as a means of paying debts. Thus more laws were added to the complex body; the most important of these was the law of February 12, 1924.[5] This second type of measure was likewise unavailing.

In January and February, however, along with these futile

[1] *Le Pour et le contre* (December 19, 1926). The rate was increased from 5 to 5½ per cent on January 10 and to 6 per cent on January 17. See Chapter VI.

[2] *Journal des débats,* "Revue financière" (January 14, 1924).

[3] See *infra,* Chapter VI.

[4] See *supra,* Chapter III. The first law of this kind was that of April 3, 1918.

[5] J. Laurès, *Le Problème des changes et la baisse du franc* (Paris, 1926), p. 64. See also p. 84, and pp. 120, 121 for text of law. *Journal officiel, Chambre,* séance of February 12, 1924, p. 653.

attempts to check the panic, there were the more serious
efforts directed toward the increase in taxation. This third
and successful type of measures by the government culmi-
nated in the voting of the *double décime* and in obtaining a
large foreign loan to fight speculation. The two measures
were very closely allied,[1] for without a tax increase of
twenty per cent it is doubtful whether any help would have
been secured from outside. It is probable that without the
loan of dollars and pounds, the franc would have collapsed
long before the increase of revenues would have come into
effect. On the other hand, neither taxation nor borrowing
was practicable until the extreme need was made manifest
by the vertical drop of the franc in February. This brought
Parliament to its senses and enlisted the sympathy of foreign financiers, when they saw strenuous efforts being
made at last. The collapse from five cents to less than four
in a little more than six weeks may well be called a *sauve
qui-peut*. French capitalists had joined with the others to
sell francs for dollars and pounds. The Chamber of Deputies
struggled with legislative measures, while affairs went from
bad to worse. The "double decimal" tax increase was voted
only after conditions were desperate at the end of February.
It became a law on March 13.

The eventual success of these government efforts became
manifest in the second week of March. Whereas the increase
in the discount rate in January had been futile and legislation against speculation in February had failed, the increase
in taxation [2] voted the end of the same month made it
possible for the Bank of France to negotiate the much-
needed foreign loan and the money thus put at the disposal

---

[1] *Bulletin de statistique et de législation comparée* (March, 1925),
pp. 404-423. Reprint of *Le Compte rendu de la Banque de France, as-
semblée générale,* January 29. See especially pp. 404, 405.

[2] *Journal officiel, Chambre,* séance of March 22, 1924, pp. 1545-1548.
The bill creating new financial resources was originally passed by the
Chamber February 23 and was passed in final form after some amendments
by the Senate March 22.

of France by Morgan of New York and through Lazard Frères of London was sufficient to put speculators to flight. A large part of the loan of 100 million dollars and 4 million pounds was thrown at once into the exchange market for the purchase of francs. Suddenly the short sellers found themselves in great embarrassment; the demand for francs increased by leaps and bounds. So rapid was the reaction that by April 22 the dollar had fallen from the high point of 27.20 francs on March 11 to the low value of 15.32 francs.[1] Meanwhile, the Bank of France was able to begin buying pounds and dollars again as the upward movement of the franc had gained impetus. It was said to have reconstituted the loan entire at this time.[2] The upward movement of the franc was so strong, however, that even such large sales of francs as this implied did not halt the reaction at once.

The close connection between the foreign loan and the increase in taxation was due to the fact that the Bank of France was successful in securing this aid only after a solemn pledge that the budget would be balanced and treasury accounts put in order. Even though it is obvious in retrospect that the government could not accomplish these two aims at this time, the increase in taxation was nevertheless considerable, and marked a real effort on the part of France to put her financial house in order. Without such an effort neither American nor English financial interests would have been willing to come to the support of France. The increase in government revenue from 1923 to 1924 was more than 10 billion francs.[3] The total for the year was 31 billion francs, leaving a deficit, according to official figures, of 9 billions. This budget statement is neither all-inclusive nor accurate, for the gap between ex-

[1] These are official rates. The cost of the dollar outside the *Bourse* rose even higher. The *Revue d'économie politique,* vol. xxxix, no. 2 (Paris, 1925), p. 276, gives the cost of the dollar as 28.74 out of the *Bourse* for March 8, 1924.   [2] *Ibid.,* pp. 276–278.

[3] E. Clémentel, *op. cit.,* p. 21. See appendix, p. 494.

penditures and receipts was considerably greater.[1] However this may be,.the government had succeeded in rousing itself to the emergency. The "battle of the franc" was won and the French currency was relatively stable in the later months of the year.

The importance of the foreign loan, even after the immediate need was past, was very great. It was a weapon which, if used, was sure to frighten away all but the most powerful speculative forces. It assured the franc from the dangers of adventurous attacks of a concentrated nature. It could not, of course, protect it from such general movements of capital as those caused by the almost universal pessimism in July, 1926. Such widespread loss of confidence could not be countered by the use of 100 million dollars. Nevertheless, when speculation was less widespread and had limited sums at its disposal, it could hardly succeed against such a sum in the hands of the Bank of France. The significance of the loans lay, not entirely in the improved technical situation but also in the indication of a more reasonable financial and reparation policy on the part of France. There was not, as was rumored for a time, any direct connection between the granting of the loan and the acceptance by France of the Dawes Plan. There was, however, some connection between the more conciliatory attitude of France and the willingness of English and American banks to come to the aid of the franc. The English loan was repaid almost at once.[2] The American loan was replaced by the seven per cent bonds floated in December in New York.[3]

The later fluctuations of the franc were quite different from this severe crisis. There was no other instance of a vertical drop of the franc followed by a rapid recovery until

[1] The *recoverable budget* was still separate in 1924. See *infra,* Chapter IX.

[2] *Bulletin de statistique et de législation comparée* (March, 1925), p. 405. *Compte rendu de la Banque de France.*

[3] *Revue d'économie politique* (Paris, 1924), p. 1112. The law authorizing this loan was passed November 22, 1924.

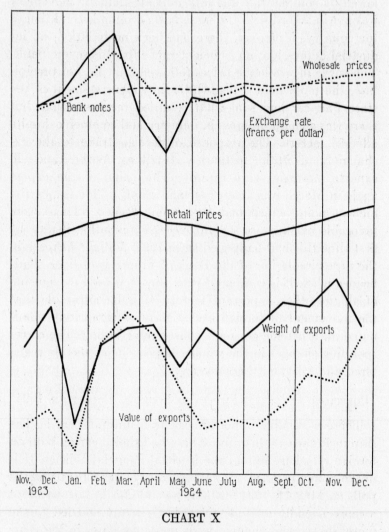

CHART X

VALUE, COMMERCE, AND NOTE CIRCULATION IN 1924[1]

[1] See appendix for figures.

1926. The sharp rise and fall of the cost of the dollar followed by comparative stability indicate that the movement was not in accord with the underlying economic condition of the country. Moreover, there had been no inflation, no industrial depression, no sufficient cause for this severe panic. The curve of wholesale prices followed, but did not precipitate, the movement. Meanwhile, the embarrassment of the state finances had somewhat retarded reconstruction, but there was general progress in industry and commerce despite adverse factors. The response of foreign trade to the exchange bonus in this instance was striking. As the franc fell, exports increased very rapidly. The value of the export trade in March was about four and a half billion francs, the highest point which had ever been reached.[1] There were favorable balances for several successive months; it was the first time this had happened since 1921. A slight increase in the note circulation of the Bank of France is of little significance when it is compared with the very wide movements of all the other important factors. It is incontestable that the movement of foreign exchange rates completely dominated all other factors for a considerable period. The corresponding changes in the wholesale price index merely registered and followed this movement.

POLITICAL CHANGES IMPROVED FOREIGN POLICY IN 1924

There were very important shifts in the political leadership in France at this time. These had their bearing both on foreign relations and on the internal financial policies. It is notable, for instance, that the success of the liberals at the polls on May 11, 1924, made it possible for France to adopt a more friendly attitude towards Germany and led to the many subsequent changes in financial measures in the years that followed. The victory of the *Cartel* on May 11 gave the control to the radical and socialist parties, to MM.

[1] U. S. Senate, *Foreign Currency and Exchange Investigation*, see chart, p. 317.

Herriot, Blum, Briand, Painlevé, and other leaders of the left groups.[1] The *Journal des débats,* in commenting on the election,[2] said that it would mean more change in the internal than in the external policies; the contrary seems to have been the case. Certainly, it was due in large measure to the *Cartel* that the obstinate policy of the *Bloc national* toward Germany was ended. It was through the *Cartel* that the Dawes Plan [3] and the Locarno pact came to be realities. Then again, from this time onward the relation between England and France became more friendly. Feeling against Germany was less bitter and a close coöperation on the part of America in solving certain problems became practicable. In internal affairs, on the other hand, there was less actual progress despite the innovations which were proposed almost at once by the new party. The reason for this was twofold. First, the socialist groups did not have a clear and permanent majority in Parliament, so that it was impossible for them to pursue a strong and consistent policy. Second, the inexperience of these parties in financial leadership led them to propose radical measures which were unacceptable to the nation as a whole. The most striking example of this was the familiar proposal made at various times in different forms, namely the capital levy.[4]

[1] Edouard Herriot, "The Program of Liberal France," *Foreign Affairs* (June, 1924), vol. ii, no. 4. The four main groups which composed the *Cartel* were the radical socialists, the republican socialists, the *Gauche radicale* and the *Groupe socialiste.* The communists were often aligned with the *Cartel.* Outside this combination were the Republican Democratic party, the Democratic Left, the Republican Left, the Right, the Catholics, the Royalists, and certain shifting small groups. For a general discussion of the French political situation in the twentieth century see R. L. Buell, *Contemporary French Politics* (Boston, 1920).

[2] *Journal des débats* (May 11, 1924).

[3] The Report of the Committee of Experts, April 9, 1924, is here referred to as the Dawes Plan, as it is popularly known, to distinguish it from the French Experts Report cited later.

[4] No important financial changes were instituted during 1924. The capital levy was made a definite part of the government financial project in April, 1925. See below, pp. 182, 352.

The accession of the *Cartel* to power caused considerable uncertainty in the foreign exchange markets. There was a period in 1924 after the elections, but while the *Bloc national* was still in control, when the franc was not pegged regularly as it had been in the preceding weeks.[1] In view of this, some maintained that Poincaré had used the funds put at his disposal to discredit the new political leaders by permitting adverse movements of the exchange rates.[2] All that can be confidently stated is that the sharp up and down movements of the exchange rates in May and June were certainly due in large measure to political uncertainty, even if not to deliberate political maneuvers. It was natural that there should be considerable fear of revolutionary measures in finance, which caused uneasiness in France and abroad. When it became apparent, however, that no startling innovations would be made by the *Cartel* during the first year at least, financial markets became more quiet. It was evident from these flurries, however, that the link between politics and finance was becoming constantly more close. The shift in the political lineup made everyone more conscious of the possibility of fundamental changes in taxation and budget. Moreover, the severe shock of the "battle of the franc" in the early months of 1924, made them realize that there was pressing need for fundamental changes of some kind. Then publication and adoption of the Dawes Plan in this year made it obvious that France must work out some way of handling her budget and debt problems without relying entirely on outside resources. Even the exchange crisis, disastrous though it was, was of some service in indicating the need for higher taxes and the great danger of leaving the franc unprotected as it had been since 1919.

[1] *The New York Times* (May 26, 1924). The fact that the old government had practically resigned left the Bank of France without the usual authorization to continue the use of loan funds to support the franc on the exchange.

[2] *Ibid.* (May 17, 1925). The *Quotidien*, organ of the *Cartel*, accused Millerand and Poincaré of rigging the market for election purposes.

Notable progress was made in 1924 towards the understanding of the exchange problem and the realization of its close relation to the whole complex structure of political and economic life.

THE CONFIDENCE CRISIS, 1925

The decline of the franc in the fall of 1925 has been called by some the *confidence crisis*. This term might well be applied to the whole year. Indeed, the pressure which pushed upward the cost of foreign exchanges in Paris was mainly from within the country, and was due to a widespread realization in France, and to a lesser extent in other countries, that the French government was facing an almost insoluble problem. There was at this time a growing realization that the budget must be balanced by increased taxation, that the internal debt was so large that it constituted a menace, that debt maturities for the current year were extremely heavy and that, in addition to all these things, something had to be done about large sums owed to the United States. Thus there was a gradual disappearance of the blind optimism that had been held by many. Moreover, this fear of confiscatory taxation, of repudiation of a part of the internal debt, and of the complete collapse of the franc, led many of the French to buy credits in pounds, dollars, or Swiss francs. There was a steady current of such demands for foreign exchange during most of the year, which has been called the "flight from the franc." A few short periods of calm during the early spring and the late summer were exceptions to this general tendency and were probably due, in part, to a false stability induced by government sales of foreign exchange for francs. The striking characteristic of the exchange situation as compared with 1924 was that it was dominated by a large number of small purchases. In the earlier crisis, especially the first weeks, a few people made large purchases with a concerted aim to destroy the franc. This later decline, on the other hand, was the result of an almost general attempt to gain security and escape the results of the financial difficulties of the government.

The troubled situation in 1925 will be better understood if some of the events of the year are recalled. It must be remembered that at this time France was carrying on a war in Morocco which was a financial drain and alienated a certain part of foreign sympathy which she might otherwise have won. Then troubles in Syria also led to military action and more criticism by other countries. The attempts of the *Cartel* to increase revenues made their position in internal affairs precarious. Proposal after proposal was made and rejected. Six ministers of finance held office during this year.[1] They were MM. Clémentel, de Monzie, Caillaux, Painlevé, Loucheur, and Doumer. The first ministerial crisis was precipitated in April over the question of increasing the note circulation of the Bank of France.[2] Clémentel was followed by de Monzie, whose finance bill included a ten per cent capital levy. Although the opposition to this measure was very intense, the revelation of the false statements of the Bank of France in regard to its advances to the state and the excessive increase in note circulation was the immediate cause of the resignation of the Herriot ministry at that time.[3] Caillaux was the next minister of finance. His appointment occasioned much opposition on the one hand and aroused fantastic hopes of financial revival on the other.[4] The task which he faced was beyond

[1] "La Valse des portefeuilles," see Hon. George Peel, *The French Financial Crisis* (London, 1925), p. 261.

[2] *Journal officiel, Chambre, débats,* séance, April 3, 1925. *Reference Service on International Affairs* (Paris, December 31, 1925), supplement, nos. 4 and 5, p. 2. The discussion of French finance gives a summarized translation of the debates on April 3.

[3] See *infra,* Chapter VI, for discussion of this episode between the Bank of France and the state.

[4] M. Caillaux had been accused of unlawful negotiations with the enemy and of treason during the war. His return to political life was a surprise to some, and he had many enemies in politics and finance. He had, how-

his powers. His defeat was due to a combination of forces. One was the failure of his internal loan, another the check to his negotiations over the external loan in Washington, and a third the hostility of the socialist party. The necessity of his resignation became apparent with the decline of the franc in October, 1925. There is no doubt that hidden maneuvers and speculation of financiers helped to make his position untenable. The subsequent attempts of Painlevé and Loucheur to increase revenues were hardly more successful.[1] The emergency taxation of Loucheur was put into operation, but his more comprehensive measure led to his overthrow. The year closed with the problem unsolved and the franc still hanging in the balance.

The nature of the financial difficulties during 1925 must be examined because of the great importance of this year in the depreciation of the franc. The main difficulty during this year was due to the internal debt, which embarrassed the government in two ways. In the first place, the maturities during this year were especially heavy. In the second place, the floating debt was very large, and was so sensitive to the condition of public confidence that any adverse opinion as to the future led to the failure to reinvest cash received for redemptions, which meant a decline in holdings amounting often to hundreds of million francs a month. The budget of 1925 would not have been unmanageable if the debt maturities had been small. The floating debt could have been handled if the *bons de la défense* had run for longer periods of time. It is true that the external debts loomed on the horizon but immediate payments were not necessary. Moreover, the general economic situation was good, for both production and commerce were active. The internal debt was the troublesome aspect of the situation, closely connected as it was with the loss of confidence and general instability.

ever, the reputation for being a financial wizard, so that much was expected of him in solving the difficulties confronting the government.

[1] See *infra*, Chapter VIII.

The magnitude of the problem can be judged from the fact that the government had to meet a charge of approximately 22 billion francs for maturities on the internal debt during 1925. This was equivalent to about one-half the note circulation and about two-thirds of the budget, which was estimated exclusive of this sum. In addition to these 22 billion francs of maturities, the government had to pay out more than 15 billion francs as interest and amortization on the public debt, and nearly 4 billion francs as pensions and indemnities.[1] Then, a small sum should be added as payment on a part of the external debt. The total of this unproductive expenditure came, therefore, to approximately 41 billion francs during this one year. It was obvious that something had to be done in the way of refunding and new borrowings. One attempt to meet the situation was the Caillaux exchange guarantee loan, which led to disappointing returns. The other obvious way of meeting the situation was by increasing the advances by the Bank of France to the state. This had to be done despite very strong opposition to inflation, in order to avoid the even worse alternative, repudiation of a part of the internal debt. The maturities of the internal debt were as follows:

TABLE XI

MATURITIES OF THE INTERNAL DEBT [2]

1925

		Million Francs
Feb 16	National defense bonds (1915–25)	333
Jul 1	*Crédit national* bonds 6 per cent	3,290
Sep 25	Treasury bonds, 3 to 5 years, 6 per cent	8,237
Dec 8	Treasury bonds, 3, 6, and 10 years, 6 per cent	10,090
	Total	21,950

[1] Henry Chéron, *Rapport au Sénat*, annexe no. 84 (February 22, 1926), pp. 290, 291.

[2] Henry Chéron, *op. cit.*, annexe no. 84, p. 278. See also Clémentel, *Inventaire*, p. 242. See *infra* Chapters VIII, IX. In the summation of the items in the *Inventaire* there is an error of one billion francs.

The government did not have to pay this entire sum in cash. New loans were accepted in payment for a considerable part. These new loans were floated with difficulty, however, and at high interest rates. In fact, the increasing difficulty of the government in placing its securities had already been brought to light by the partial failure of the *Crédit national* loan in 1924. The amount of the loan had been fixed at 3 billion francs, but only 1,552 million francs were taken.[1] For this reason, when the needs of the treasury were great and funds hard to obtain, the government had turned frequently to the subterfuges and occult advances which finally were revealed in April, 1925.[2] The increase in the legal limit of advances of the Bank of France to the state, which took place at this time,[3] merely regularized the indirect advances which had preceded the bill, and did nothing to provide funds for the future needs of the treasury. No provision was made for the impending maturities, and no sufficient margin granted to the treasury to assure redemption of the national defense bonds.

The *Bons* an Index of Confidence

The difficulties caused by the floating debt have been referred to frequently. The short-term *bons de la défense nationale* were through the postwar years the most troublesome elements in the financial situation, but this was never so clearly evident as during this year, when the problem of the internal debt became especially acute. These bonds had been particularly popular during and after the war.[4] They absorbed a large part of the funds which might have accumulated in bank deposits, since the small denominations and short periods—one month, three months, six months,

[1] Georges Lachapelle, *Revue d'économie politique* (March-April, 1925), vol. xxxix, no. 2, p. 210. [2] See *infra*, Chapter VI.

[3] *Journal officiel, Sénat*, séance (April 15, 1925), p. 866. Parliament approved the convention of April 7 between the Bank of France and the minister of finance. Advances were increased from 22 to 26 billion francs, and the note circulation from 41 to 45 billions.

[4] See *supra*, Chapter III.

a year—made them a particularly liquid and convenient investment for idle funds. In times of uncertainty, on the other hand, they were particularly dangerous to the treasury, since the automatic maturity of large numbers of these *bons* meant large payments which might be demanded in cash each month. Normally, when confidence was good, reinvestments about balanced maturities. There was no guarantee, however, that this would be the case. The *bons* came to be a fairly definite indication of the state of public opinion. They led to the cumulative effect of any pessimistic sentiment, since initial government difficulties brought ever-greater demands on the government. It is obvious that a situation very much like that of a run on the bank could develop at any time, and the government could not find a way out of the predicament except through the slow processes of parliamentary action. The figures for the total *bons* outstanding are significant.

TABLE XII

NUMBER OF *BONS DE LA DEFENSE NATIONALE*
OUTSTANDING [1]

(Millions of francs)

	1922	1923	1924	1925	1926	1927
Jan	59,787	58,215	54,889	54,886	46,089	47,224
Feb	60,093	57,317	54,682	54,992	46,068	46,402
Mar	60,840	55,924	54,552	53,945	45,783	47,432
Apr	61,529	53,229	56,194	52,246	46,212	50,251
May	62,891	.....	56,780	51,245	46,384	.....
Jun	63,811	.....	56,343	50,569	46,157	46,970
Jul	62,527	.....	56,287	50,690	44,218	44,804
Aug	62,663	.....	56,598	50,330	45,973	44,274
Sep	63,131	.....	57,180	51,202	46,850	44,106
Oct	60,751	.....	57,181	46,623	45,886	43,825
Nov	57,675	.....	57,045	45,571	48,542	43,349
Dec	59,055	.....	54,538	45,735	49,079	43,464

[1] E. Clémentel, *Inventaire*, p. 44, for parts of 1923 and 1924. *Le Pour et le contre*, November 28, 1926, p. 960, for parts of 1925, 1926 and 1927. The rest of the figures were secured from a reliable source but the name of the source was asked to be withheld. In addition to these *bons,* there was a circulation of about three billion francs of ordinary treasury *bons.* The floating debt was one and a half billion francs in 1923 as contrasted with about 58 billions in January, 1925. See Clémentel, *op. cit.,* p. 9.

Nothing could indicate better than does the chart of *bons* in circulation the growing pessimism of the French. The decline of reinvestments was due in large measure to a widespread desire to place money either in industrial securities

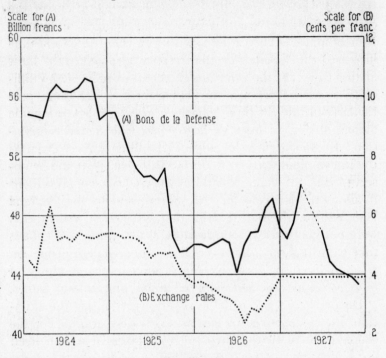

Scale for (A)
Billion francs

Scale for (B)
Cents per franc

(A) Bons de la Defense

(B) Exchange rates

CHART XI

VALUE OF *BONS* OUTSTANDING, 1924 TO 1927 [1]

which rose to a considerable extent with rising prices, or in some kind of security which had a gold or exchange value, such as Suez Canal shares.[2] Then again, a considerable part of the money that had been invested in *bons* was thrown into the exchange market for the purchase of pounds and other gold value credits. This decline in *bons*

[1] Note that exchange rates are cents per franc instead of francs per dollar used in other charts.

[2] The interest on Suez Canal shares was paid in gold or on a gold basis.

outstanding, like the decline in the franc, was the result of a large number of small changes, and so it reflects general opinion even more than it indicates professional forecasts.

The relation of the *bons* to the maturities on the rest of the debt was close. On the one hand, the agitations of the early part of the year, the ministerial changes, and excess issue of notes, led investors to withdraw their funds and thus increased the demands on the treasury, strained to the limit at this time. On the other hand, the discussion of the difficulty of the government in paying off its obligations, particularly in the last three months of the year, led to a panic among holders of *bons de la défense,* who feared repudiation.[1] In considering the sum of 41 billion francs, given as the interest and maturities during this year, it should be observed that this figure should be lowered by several billions if allowance is made for the subscription to the Caillaux loan, and for the fact that all the privileges of redemption were not claimed by bond holders. When the whole debt is taken into account, however, it is observed this deduction is approximately offset by the decline in the holdings of *bons de la défense nationale* of about nine billion francs.

During 1925 various devices were used to ease the situation. For instance, certain advantages were granted for the prepayment of taxes. Then the Caillaux loan was in itself an innovation, for great things were hoped from the clause which made the interest rate vary with the value of the pound sterling.[2] In any case, the difficult position of the treasury, the need for increased resources, and the opposition to this new means of calling out resources, were all

---

[1] For a further discussion of the *bons,* see *infra,* Chapter VI.

[2] Gaston Jèze, *Cours de science des finances* (Paris, 1925), pp. 276-284. There were varying decisions by the French courts, but the general tenor of the decisions had been that gold or exchange payments could not be exacted in France and that nothing could be done to lessen the validity of payments in paper francs. This official recognition of the variation of the franc in comparison with a gold standard currency was therefore a new departure.

brought out clearly in the discussion in the Chamber of
Deputies of June 26, 1925.[1] The emergency was recognized
at that time and new measures were passed despite some
keen opposition. It was argued then by upholders of the bill
that the new loan would bring in some 15 to 30 billion francs
in subscriptions. Moreover, since it was only offered to holders of *bon de la défense,* this would be a conversion loan
and would reduce the interest burden of the government. As
things worked out, however, the results of this new effort
were extremely disappointing; the total secured by the close
in October was approximately 6 billion francs. This was a
very small sum when compared with the hopes and needs of
the government, and the failure may be attributed to two
causes. In the first place, the complex nature of the exchange
clause led to distrust and misunderstanding. That is, the
interest was to vary with the average value of the pound in
francs, the extra being added as the pound went above 95
francs. The possible advantage of this clause as the franc
depreciated was not generally understood, and probably decreased rather than increased the number of purchases.
Then, in the second place, the unfortunate coincidence of
the bank clerks' strike considerably interfered with the distribution and sale of the new securities. This strike had a
peculiarly bad effect because of the custom in France of
selling shares to the depositors in banks by means of personal solicitations made by bank clerks. It is not surprising,
then, that the loan fell short of the government's hope, and
the situation of the treasury was increasingly difficult. There
seemed to be only two ways out of the difficulty; one was
repudiation and the other was inflation. Both were suggested. Inflation was the solution adopted.

The increase in the note circulation during 1925 was
the first of any importance since the close of the war. The
legal limit of the advances of the Bank of France to the

---

[1] *Journal officiel, Chambre,* séance 2, June 26, 1925, pp. 2937-2939. See
also *Sénat,* séance of June 27, 1925, pp. 1203-1215.

state, which had been 21,000 million francs at the time of
the armistice, was increased in April, 1919 to 27,000; this
increase really covered war needs and conditions. Then the
limit was lowered in the following years until it was only
22,000 million francs in 1924.[1] The difficulty entailed in this
reduction has been discussed elsewhere. It is clearly indicated, moreover, by the fact that, despite the repayment
of advances, the notes in circulation *increased* slightly during these years. The effort at deflation was ineffectual, but
at least there was no inflation for several years. This point
must be emphasized here because of the fairly general impression that the depreciation of the franc, as well as the depreciation of other European monetary units, was due
mainly to inflation. In the case of France, although inflation
played its part in deterioration, it cannot be considered as
the prime cause. The difficulties which led to the inflation of
1925, which made increases in borrowings from the Bank of
France imperative, for instance budget deficits, and the internal debt, as well as the various political and commercial
tangles, were causal. There was no free and easy recourse
to the printing presses to meet government bills; when the
new notes were issued, they came after much opposition and
in comparatively small quantities.[2]

The advances of the Bank of France to the government
were 21,800 million francs, according to the weekly statement of January 2, 1925. This is an understatement of
nearly a billion and a half.[3] The actual amount was therefore about 23,000 million francs. The advances equaled 35,-
950 million francs on December 31. The note circulation of
the Bank of France increased from 40,885 million francs to
51,085 in the same period. Inflation may, therefore, be esti-

---

[1] See appendix for figures. See also *infra*, Chapter VI.

[2] André Fourgeaud, *op. cit.*, p. 7. The increase in the note circulation in
France was about 20 per cent during 1925. This must be compared with
the German inflation of 65 per cent during 1921 and 1,027 per cent during
1922. Viewed in this way, the French inflation seems very small.

[3] See *infra*, Chapter VI.

mated as about 14 billion francs. This was approximately the difference between the maturities of the internal debt and the new securities sold by the government. In other words, one form of debt was substituted for another, and the net change was slight. Apparently the net increase in the internal debt was about three billion francs.[1]

The inflation which occurred at this time was not important from a quantitative point of view, as has been pointed out already, but it was of extreme importance in its effect on public opinion. Since it destroyed confidence, it tended to bring about a "run" on the treasury by those who wished cash for their *bons de la défense*. Because it indicated the dire straits of the government, it led to large sales of francs for stable foreign credits. Its effects were, therefore, extremely grave and led eventually to the more serious panic in July, 1926. Four times in 1925 the government had found itself at the end of its resources; in April, June, November, and December advances to the state had to be increased to fill the urgent needs of the treasury, practically empty of all funds.

The December crisis was extremely dramatic.[2] The Minister of Finance, Loucheur, had asked on December 2 for increased advances from the Bank of France and emergency taxation to yield *approximately* three billion francs at once.[3] The debate on this issue became very bitter. Those who opposed the existing government on general principles, and those who opposed inflation in particular, launched a fierce attack, and the menace of a new political crisis caused general dismay. Since a large block of treasury three- to ten-year bonds were to be redeemed on December 8, the seriousness of the situation was obvious.[4] The fall of the government at this moment would probably have brought

---

[1] Henry Chéron, *op. cit.*, annexe no. 84, p. 277.

[2] See *infra*, Chapter VIII.

[3] *Journal officiel, Chambre*, séance of December 2, 1925, p. 3930.

[4] See *supra*, p. 184.

the default on these bonds and the complete discredit of all
government securities. In a stormy all-night session the
issue was fought. The government seemed doomed to defeat
when Briand, who had many times held the position of premier, mounted the tribune and made his famous plea: "For
the first time I cling to power; for if I am overthrown a
grave injury will have been done your country." [1]

His impassioned appeal was not without effect. Although
he insisted he was the enemy of inflation, he asserted that
there was no other way out of the difficulty. "As you vote,"
he said, "think of what will happen if you precipitate a new
political crisis." [2] In staking all on the issue, Briand won
the day, and the government of France was saved from
bankruptcy.[3] The public had finally been roused from its
lethargy by the incident to a fuller knowledge of the uncertainty of the financial situation. This crisis was not to be
the last, however. Confidence had been profoundly shaken
and no real constructive measures had as yet been put in
force.

Politics and economics were so closely entangled with
each other during 1925 that one cannot be considered
without the other. Such political difficulties as have been
discussed especially, and the uncertain majority, made it
impossible for the government to carry to completion any of
its plans for new loans, consolidation, or taxes. The emergency increased as successive ministries met defeat, and the
inevitable approach of the maturities on the debt led to
panic on the exchanges and among holders of government
securities. During a considerable period, the solvency of the
government was in doubt. In 1925 the public learned, for
the first time, the dangers of the floating debt and the impossibility of balancing the budget. This knowledge was

---

[1] *Journal officiel, Chambre,* séance of December 2, 1925, p. 3947.
[2] *Ibid.,* p. 3948.
[3] *Journal officiel, Chambre,* séance of December 2, 1925, p. 3949. The vote
was 298 for and 113 against, the socialists abstaining.

costly, the franc fell from more than five cents to less than four.

THE FINAL CRISIS, 1926

In many respects the year 1926 was but the sequel to the troubles of 1925.[1] The main problem was little altered but the difficulties had become more apparent and the crisis more acute. The internal debt was still the most troublesome feature of the situation. Moreover, the state of public opinion was increasingly sensitive and the sale of francs continued with more or less regularity. The ultimate solution of the problem hinged on the nature and amount of taxation. It had been recognized that France must accept even heavier burdens than she had hitherto borne, but the instability of the prevailing majority made the particular outcome of the conflict of interests very uncertain. The conservatives were fighting for indirect taxation against a determined opposition on the part of the radical left groups. As the struggle grew keener the investing public became more wary. Those who had savings felt that they must seek personal security in foreign investments while politicians waged their uncertain battle over the budget. Confidence, once shaken, did not return; thus the franc sagged from four to three cents during the first half of the year.

It is not possible to follow all the political changes and financial proposals of 1926. Doumer was succeeded by Raoul Péret as minister of finance in March. M. Péret resigned on June 15. The trouble in each case was lack of support for the financial proposals and the adverse attitude of the public as registered in the falling franc. After turning to Poincaré on the right and Herriot on the left, a new ministry was eventually made up on June 25 with Briand premier and Caillaux again minister of finance. From this time on events moved rapidly.

M. Caillaux was known to hold certain daring and untried theories for handling the troublesome floating debt. For

[1] See *infra,* Chapter X.

instance, he was not opposed to inflation to the extent necessary to redeem the *bons de la défense*. This idea, much discussed and generally feared, was called the *plafond unique*.[1]
This theory was not actually a part of M. Caillaux's first
proposals in July. On the other hand, his demands were
extreme in that they included delegation to him of very
wide powers, the permission to make important agreements
with the Bank of France, without the sanction of Parliament, and to use the gold reserve of the Bank to support
the exchange value of the franc.[2] The delegation of the
authority of a financial dictator to a man as little trusted
by the different political groups as was Caillaux was obviously too radical a step for the hesitating Parliament of
the moment. So on July 17 the ministry fell and one of the
worst crises in the history of France threw the financial and
political interests into chaos.

The franc crashed as Herriot was again called to power.
Mobs attacked Americans who had made themselves offensive in certain cases, armed disorders were feared, and a
revolution seemed possible. From July 15 to 20 the franc fell
from two and a half to two cents; that is to say, the dollar
cost more than fifty francs in Paris. It is not surprising in
view of this panic that the Herriot ministry lasted only four
hours in Parliament. On July 21 his budget proposal, presented by Finance Minister de Monzie, was debated in the
Chamber of Deputies. This proposal did little more than reveal the desperate situation of the treasury, and the incapacity of the government to find any adequate solution.[3]

---

[1] See *infra,* Chapter VI. This phrase meaning *single limit* indicates the
assumption that the *bons* were equivalent to cash, and that one limit for
the *bons* plus the note circulations would not lead to any additional inflation. The free exchange of *bons* and notes would ease the treasury and
not make any great difference to the purchasing power of the public.

[2] *Revue de science et de la législation financières* (Paris, October–
December, 1926), pp. 694-696. Very inclusive powers were requested.

[3] *Ibid.,* p. 673. This article (pp. 673-747) gives one of the best discussions of the causes and consequences of the July panic. The Herriot declaration before the Chamber is given, pp. 697, 698.

Although the capital levy was again the core of the program, it was no such specific measure but a general fear of increasing chaos and political hostility that led to complete rejection of his schemes. Feeling ran high as the opposing groups clashed and the ministry went down to defeat on a vote of 290 to 237. The deputies came out of the *Palais Bourbon* to find an angry crowd surging about the doors, hissing and denouncing their destructive political maneuvers.

In this dark hour Poincaré was called to meet the grave emergency. The residue of the Morgan loan was given at once to the treasury to meet its day to day needs. The new ministry obtained a vote of confidence from a chastened Parliament, July 27. It was obvious to close observers that politicians must choose either a truce in their party warfare, the possibility of revolution, or some form of dictatorship. Placed before such a choice, they decided for the least radical possibility, and as a result the new ministry received the support of all but the most extreme members of the legislature. It is notable that, from the start, Poincaré made it obvious that he would accept no compromise. Every measure was made in effect a vote of confidence; in fact, no amendments were acceptable. The sudden recovery of the franc and the political calm after wild excitement were astounding. The franc rose from below two cents to two and a half in five days. Moreover, the run on the treasury stopped and subscriptions to the *bons de la défense* increased more than a billion francs in the next four weeks. The government accepted measures strengthening the power of the ministry and permitting more latitude to the Bank of France in conjunction with the cabinet.

This July panic was to be the final fall of the franc. It led to a complete realization of the difficulties of the government. It brought to the surface the grim determination of the nation to end the meaningless struggles of the deputies and set out on the difficult road of tax payment and debt amortization. The history of the rest of the year really belongs to the account of stability, and will be considered later.[1] It should be noted here, however, that the extreme fluctuations of the franc were over. As the tide turned in favor of French securities and French money, the efforts of the government were exerted to modify the rapid rise of the franc and to prevent the exaggerated swing of speculation in its favor.

The measures passed at this time were fairly simple in their nature. They were remarkable in that they represented a fairly unanimous opinion rather than that they were innovations in the way of financial devices. The striking fact is the immediate confidence in Poincaré. The way by which the Bank of France was able to build up an exchange reserve was the most interesting and most novel feature of the new program. The simple device of allowing unlimited note issues against purchases of exchange made it possible to steady the rates and to build up large foreign credits against future speculation. The workings of this mechanism are described further in Chapter VI.[2] The Bank of France was in fact able to buy the exchange credits sold by Frenchmen who were willing once more to invest in domestic enterprises and confident once more in the value of the franc. This sudden change of attitude was due fundamentally to the new political union. It might have been possible for some of the previous governments to have increased taxation and pegged the exchanges if they had been allowed to put through a consistent and inclusive program, but concessions, compromises, changes, and delays undermined the budget proposals of eight successive ministers of finance. It is possible that there might never have been the necessary unity in Parliament if there had been no signs of disorder and revolt among the people. If a lesson was necessary, the deputies learned it on July 21. The public demonstration of hostility and the vertical drop of the franc brought about

[1] See *infra*, Chapter X.   [2] See *infra*, Chapter VI.

a new state of mind. Then, it must be admitted that the measures of Poincaré, though not strikingly new, were well adapted to meet the new conditions of the moment; there was, in fact, a high degree of wisdom in the very simplicity of the method of the Bank of France in steadying the exchanges and in the way innovations in taxation were avoided. Nevertheless, the important factor in the situation was that the government proposals were quickly adopted, and without amendments. Such vigorous action restored confidence and the technical problems became at once soluble.

The particular means and effects of stability cannot be discussed at this point. The franc gained steadily in value through the last months of 1926. It reached a point of relative stability in December. During 1927 it remained constantly at a value of a little more than 3.90 cents a franc, or about 25 francs to the dollar.[1] There were few purchases on the foreign exchanges compared with the earlier troubled months of 1926. Those that occurred were absorbed by the Bank of France and treasury, so that the rate of exchange was practically unvarying. This stability, as had been predicted,[2] caused some embarrassment to industry and commerce. The loss, however, was not so great as some feared. The sudden disappearance of the exchange bonus continued to depress production for some time. There was, however, no acute crisis and the dislocation to the economic structure was not serious. The production index kept above 100 per cent of 1913.[3] The curves indicate the rapid rise of exchange rates followed by a similar movement of the wholesale price index and the slower response of retail prices. The lesser fluctuation of the production index proves

[1] See appendix.

[2] Committee of Experts, *Report* (décret du 31 mai, 1926, Paris), p. 49.

[3] *Bulletin de la statistique générale de la France,* supplément mensuel (July, 1927), p. 2, and see April–June, 1927, p. 331. The index for May, 1927, was 102 per cent of prewar.

the contention that the trouble was rooted in the financial and political situation, and not in the more general conditions of economic life. The sudden return of confidence, fall in dollar rates, and reaction of prices is evidenced in the precipitate drop of the curves. Stability and calm came quickly upon the heels of the severe panic.

During the span of years from 1922 to 1927 there was a series of crises in external and internal politics. Each one brought with it a more widespread realization of the financial instability of the country, and increased the sensitivity of the franc on the foreign exchanges. The need and the means for acquiring credits and securities which had a sure value in gold became constantly more evident. That is, a larger and larger public sought investments abroad; the flight from the franc became a more and more serious menace. Speculation of an uncontrollable nature became the most serious aspect of the French problem.

CONCLUSIONS

The first series of crises were those growing out of the reparation tangle. The insistence of France, the alienation of foreign opinion, the desperate attempt of the Ruhr occupation, and the final solution of the Dawes Plan all had their effect on the value of the franc and the state of public opinion. In addition to such direct effects, the indirect consequences, inadequate taxation, the growth of the public debt, and the false hopes of these years all paved the way for the later exchange crises and political conflicts. It seems, in reviewing the history of the reparation problem, as if most of the mistakes could have been avoided. A careful reading of the literature of the period, however, indicates that the misconceptions and illusions were deep rooted. Even in the United States, where the interest in reparation payments was infinitely less, the possibility of German indemnities was greatly exaggerated. It is hardly to be wondered at that the education of French opinion was a slow and painful process. No one can deny that mistakes were made, but their cause must be sought in the ideas prevailing at the time. Judgment in retrospect is frequently too harsh. The balance of the reparation struggle shows the heavy losses to France, in prestige, in wealth, and in the burden of debts for which she was in considerable measure responsible.

The later years of this period, that is, 1924 through 1926, were troubled more by internal than by external politics. The *Cartel* with a more liberal foreign policy brought a milder attitude towards Germany. It was not able, however, to command the stable majority necessary to put through its domestic reforms. It is true that some of these reforms were extreme in character and not acceptable to the people as a whole. It is none the less true that the rapid enactment of a consistent and vigorous program, almost regardless of its nature, would have saved the government from the continuing deficits and the distressing exchange crises of 1925 and 1926. Since no such rapid action was possible, the public lost confidence in the government, in its securities and its money. With the realization of the gravity of the situation there came a determination to force Parliament to action. The bitterness of the struggle over taxation had been very real. The desire of the socialists to increase direct taxation was the more intense because of the rising cost of living and the fear of industrial depression. On the other hand, the hostility of the conservatives to what seemed like the confiscation of wealth was grounded on long-standing precedents and on a knowledge of the technical difficulties of carrying out a capital levy. There is something to be said, certainly, for each point of view. Personal interests and the sincere desire to save the country from bankruptcy were strong motives in both camps. The time was not opportune, however, for a thorough reform of taxation; the quickest way out had to be taken. This quick way proved to be to increase existing

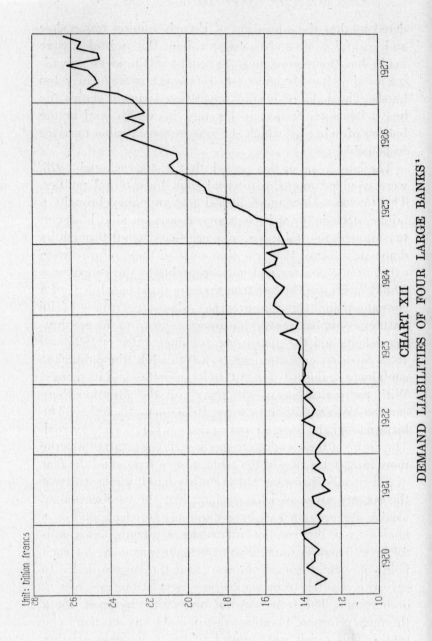

CHART XII

DEMAND LIABILITIES OF FOUR LARGE BANKS[1]

Unit: billion francs

taxes, notably the business turnover tax.[1] This tax brought
into the treasury more than 7 billions of the 40 billion
francs revenue for 1926, and 8 billions for 1927.[2] It and
the other indirect taxes made up considerably more than
half the revenues. This choice made after the emergency of
July, 1926, threw the power suddenly into the hands of Poincaré, made possible the subsequent improvement in the
franc, and justified to a considerable extent the contentions
of the more conservative groups. The contest over taxation
was essentially a fight between classes; the outcome was dictated, not by justice, but by expediency. It is probable that
under other conditions a different ordering of taxes might
have been much better, but at the moment the essential
thing was for the government to escape bankruptcy. Success in this matter saved France from the complete collapse
of the currency.

Through all this period of financial crises, the general
economic condition of France continued to be good. Production was normal or better than normal. The balance of
commodity trade became slightly favorable.[3] The technical improvement of industry continued at a satisfactory
rate, and there were many indications of a healthy condition in almost everything except in finance.[4] It is true
that the depreciation of the franc caused suffering. This
suffering, however, was confined to certain groups and did
not markedly obstruct the current of affairs. The middle
classes, those with fixed income and small salaries, felt the
pinch, but their losses were hidden from general observation

[1] R. Poincaré, *Exposé des motifs du projet du budget,* 1928, *Chambre,*
annexe no. 3248, p. 50. See also *Revue d'économie politique,* vol. xli, no. 2
(Paris, 1927), pp. 340-341. See the discussion of the budget *infra,* Chapter IX.

[2] *Bulletin de la statistique générale* (January-March, 1927), vol. xvi, no.
2, p. 152.

[3] *Statistique mensuelle du commerce extérieur de la France* (Paris,
December, 1926), p. 8.

[4] J. R. Cahill, Department of Overseas Trade, *Report, Economic and
Industrial Conditions in France, 1925-1926,* p. 7.

and were not quantitatively great enough to cut down the consumption of goods to any marked degree. The greatest change was, perhaps, the increased influence of the primarily industrial as compared with the intellectual classes. The further results will undoubtedly be observed as time goes on, rather than in the immediate present.

Throughout the postwar years, the franc has been sensitive not to the conditions in production and in commerce but to the condition of government finance. It has come to vary more and more closely with government credit as reflected in the desirability of government securities, and with the danger from inflation and extremely heavy taxation. Confidence has been the connecting link between the political and financial struggles, and the value of the franc. The cost of the dollar has registered the opinion of the public on government measures. The changes in the level of prices have followed closely the movements of the exchange rates. The widening field of speculation and the growing sensitivity of the franc to psychological forces have been pointed out in a number of instances. This fact, obvious though it may be to those who have studied recent monetary history, gives, nevertheless, a new emphasis to monetary theory. It is not the novelty of the idea that merits attention; it is the lessons which it implies in regard to straightforward, vigorous action in government finance. It is the striking reiteration of the well-known truth, that reserves, if ample, need not be used, that heroic taxation is less disastrous than depreciation, and that determination is more important than technical perfection of method in handling government finance.

CHAPTER VI

THE UNSUCCESSFUL FIGHT AGAINST DEPRECIATION

WAR inflation changed the rôle of money in economic life. It became under the altered conditions an active rather than a passive force. Its new importance was an essential outgrowth of the large increases of the number of notes in circulation, bringing with them changes in the value of money. The usual checks and limits to the value of money were abandoned with inconvertibility. It is obvious that the normal link between the paper notes and gold had to be broken in order to make possible extensive inflation such as the state required. The government, by laws, was able to prevent, to a certain extent, the exportation of gold in payment for imports, and the fact that paper money could no longer be exchanged for gold made it possible to reduce the ratio of gold to paper without a corresponding change in the value of money.

The state's need of funds was the cause of the ensuing trouble and the readiest source of new revenues was the Bank of France, to which the government appealed for loans. The sequence of events is obvious. The marked change in the importance of money is no less clear. When the government made its extraordinary demands on the Bank, it had to take measures to relieve it from excessive pressure. Three important steps were providing for the increase of paper bank notes, the cessation of the exchange of paper money for gold, and the establishment of *cours forcé* for the notes.[1]

[1] See *infra*, Chapter II. Note reference there given to Ribot, *Exposé des motifs du projet du budget, 1919, Bulletin de statistique et de législation comparée* (1920), pp. 452-454. The necessity of inflation and inconvertibility have already been discussed.

They did away with the usual safeguards of monetary value, and new ones had to be found to prevent or modify the severe depreciation that threatened the franc. These new measures were imperfectly adapted to the purpose and were in the main unsuccessful.

The prosecution of the war called for profound changes in economic life. Money was the means by which these changes were brought about. It was the means by which the government altered the habits of production and consumption of the nation. Increased purchasing power in the hands of the government made possible the quick shift of capital and labor from peace-time industries to those important for war. Commerce came to be dominated by the need for steel and shell. Price restrictions and subsidies had a part in these changes, but inflationary money was the main instrument for accomplishing the desired result. This new importance of money is in marked contrast to its usual place in economic life, for, in general, currency is considered to be a passive force. Inasmuch as it facilitates the exchange of goods it assumes significance, but it is not held to be a means for the redistribution of wealth nor a cause of changes in productive effort. It is readily adaptable to such ends, however, when the emergency of war strains the resources of a nation. There can be no hesitation about inflation in such dire need; France did what other nations in a similar position have always done.

It is true that, even under normal conditions over long periods of time, changes in the value of money are likely to favor some classes more than others and so redistribute wealth. For instance, rising prices usually help the industrial classes as compared with those with fixed incomes. Such changes, however, are very different from those which occurred during the recent war. In the first place, because they are gradual they can, to a certain extent, be anticipated and their effects avoided. In the second place, they are not so deliberate as are wartime changes. Thus, a government prosecuting a long and uncertain war makes deliberate efforts to appropriate wealth. It does this by increasing its buying power through inflation, loans, and taxation. It seizes upon purchasing power wherever it can and the bond holders and the salaried classes are, to a great extent, unresisting victims. Those engaged in active production of goods which the government needs are in a position to raise prices and wages and so retrieve a part of the wealth which the government takes from all its citizens. The state, it is true, is apt to make some effort through price control and sumptuary laws to keep prices and the cost of living down. It is not for the public good to advance one class at the expense of another, but yet it is not possible to prevent this effect of inflation for rapid changes in value are unavoidable and take away from the weak to give to the strong.

These profound changes in economic life were not at first realized.[1] Men's minds were distracted by the excitements of defeat and victory. Questions of value seemed academic during the stress of war. They could be postponed, whereas the concrete realities of munitions and war provisions demanded immediate attention. The growing domination of the government over economic life was accepted as a necessary part of the tremendous effort to win the war. As time went on, however, serious changes which had taken place became more and more evident. The instability of the franc on the exchanges was an indication of the fundamental weakness of the currency—a weakness which passed unnoticed as it expressed itself in the rising price level. It became obvious that the franc must depreciate to a certain extent, and it was quoted at a discount of about twelve per cent in terms of dollars during the war. This rate was the one which the government felt most capable of maintain-

---

[1] G. Charbonnet, *La Politique financière de la France pendant la guerre* (thesis, Bordeaux, 1922), p. 45. Note that the early credits were not properly authorized.

ing in the face of the adverse balance of trade, inconvertibility, and inflation. The rise in prices [1] indicated a much greater degree of depreciation, and one which corresponded more closely with the causes affecting the value of money.

The effort to discover new safeguards for the franc increased with the increase of depreciation. The internal change in the franc was represented by the rise of the wholesale price index to 300 per cent during the years 1914-19. External depreciation, which began to take on serious proportions in 1919, was even more alarming to financiers and statesmen.[2] The strict control of the quantity of money of prewar days had been abandoned; the close link between the currency and the value of gold had been broken; the balance of payments became decidedly unfavorable.[3] It was obvious that steps must be taken to protect the franc from the possibility of collapse. It was not an easy matter to substitute new mechanisms once the familiar ones had been abandoned. It was not easy to balance the international payments account with short-term credits and by means of small gold shipments. Moreover, the promise of the state to repay the Bank of France was a poor substitute for the old restrictions on note issues. The fight against depreciation was a difficult one, taxing the ingenuity of bankers and finance ministers.

VARIOUS MEASURES TO FIGHT DEPRECIATION

The most notable support of the franc during the first years of depreciation was pegging; that is to say, the use of gold and foreign credits to prevent the depressing effects, which excessive demands of foreign exchange would otherwise have had, on the franc. This stabilizing effort was ex-

---

[1] The wholesale index number was 355 per cent of 1914 in January, 1919. See appendix.

[2] See *infra,* Chapters VII and VIII for internal and external depreciation.

[3] See *supra,* Chapter I, Chart I, and appendix for figures.

erted with a high degree of success during the war and, under very different conditions, in 1926 and 1927. It was not effective for the long periods, however, in the intervening years. In the second place, legislative measures were relied upon to strengthen the franc, but they were of little avail. Certainly, laws, such as the *cours forcé* and the prohibition of capital export, could not materially affect the situation if the economic and psychological factors were all adverse to the franc; it is even possible, they did more harm than good. In the third place, the discount rate, which can under certain conditions attract capital and improve the exchange rates, was of little use under the changed conditions prevailing during those years. Then, again, loans were of use in the early years of inflation, but they came to be one of the most threatening aspects of the financial problem.[1] Deflation, a fourth attempt to return to prewar ratios of gold and paper, was impracticable and led to deceit and confusion. These efforts to fight depreciation were sincere, but in the main ineffectual. This was not entirely because of faults in conception or execution, but, in part, because the nature and extent of war needs so aggravated conditions that no return to the former situation was possible.

The five ways in which depreciation was fought constitute obviously only a part of the effort to protect the franc. It is not possible to discuss all the steps taken nor all the elements which worked for and against the value of the currency. The discount rate, legislation, loans, deflation, and pegging are particularly interesting because they were used in practically all countries under similar conditions and with varying degrees of success. In France no one of these measures was of great importance until certain other fundamental aspects of the situation were put in order. The one underlying problem—the budget—had to be faced in a vigorous way

[1] G. Charbonnet, *op. cit.*, p. 73. Government loans are not bad unless the proceeds are wasted. They often constitute difficult technical problems, however.

before any efforts to secure stability were effective. Confidence had to be built up on sound government finance and political solidarity before speculation could become favorable. Under the more favorable conditions of late 1926, pegging became a useful thing in the hands of the government; the discount rate became a steadying influence; the loan operations turned to the good rather than the harm of the treasury. During the trying years from 1914 to 1926, however, these spasmodic and ill-coördinated efforts were of little avail.

THE INEFFECTIVENESS OF THE DISCOUNT RATE

The changes in discount rate are one of the most important ways of preventing depreciation when money is relatively stable. The degree to which this is true varies with different countries. There are certain conditions which make the bank rate highly effective in certain places and at certain times. For instance, the four main conditions are worth stressing here because they are all dependent to a certain extent on stable economic life. In the first place, the influence of the bank rate is the more important and powerful as the volume of cash, the basis of the money and credit structure of a country, is limited by law or banking practice in very definite ways. This makes credit steadier than would otherwise be the case. Such a limitation of cash as well as some of the other conditions on which the discount rate depends are most conspicuously realized in England in modern times. To a less extent these conditions are found in other highly developed western countries. Then, in the second place, an extremely centralized banking mechanism, such as that dominated by the Bank of England, is almost essential. Such a system of banking makes possible a consistent and determined policy of reinforcing increases in the rates by other means of limiting the amount of cash and credit. The existence of such a coördinated policy makes small changes influential not only because the increase in the discount rate makes the borrowing of money more expensive by so much, but also because it is an indication of a general tendency to restrict credit, a probable decline in prices, and an increase of caution and conservatism in industry and commerce.

The remaining conditions of the effectiveness of the discount rate, the third and fourth, are aspects of a general stability in economic affairs. The third condition, for example, is that prices and cost should be fairly stable and margins of profits small. If this is the case, as it is during periods of industrial and financial calm, the cost of borrowing influences the amount of capital borrowed to a considerable extent, even though interest is rarely the decisive element in cost. The increase in interest and discount rates leads to less borrowing on the part of marginal producers, and so leads to a contraction of credit, while if prices are rising rapidly, interest is a negligible element in cost. The fourth condition of the effectiveness of the discount rate is the relative stability of exchange rates. When the foreign exchanges are fairly steady, capital moves from country to country in the form of loans in order to secure the higher rate of return which results from difference in interest rates. This was particularly true in the case of England, a country which could change the direction of the flow of short-time credits by small differences in money rates. Such a state of affairs made it possible to strengthen a currency on the foreign exchanges by increasing the discount rate; an increase would lead to an inflow of funds and a higher exchange value for the currencies in demand by other countries. When the foreign exchange value varies greatly, however, interest rates are of small importance as compared with the exchange premium.

The discount rate, therefore, under normal conditions of production and consumption acts both psychologically and mechanically on credit expansion, and so on economic affairs in general. Psychologically, an increase in the rate is taken as a sign of falling prices and credit restriction. Mechanically, an increase in the rate actually increases costs and decreases profits in certain instances and so leads to the contraction of various enterprises. As the reader will have noticed, the preceding statement as to the operation of the discount rate is true particularly of such a country as England. It was less true in the case of France, before the war,[1] than of England. Nevertheless, the discount rate had a certain influence which should not be overlooked, and the changes which came with war conditions deprived France of a tool which was, under some conditions, of considerable use.[2]

The increase in the discount rate at the very beginning of the war was quite natural. It was important to prevent credit expansion when the banks were in a precarious condition, the rate was raised to six per cent on August 1.[3] In this and various other respects, the Bank of France was of assistance to the other banks in the war crisis, according to Germain Martin.[4] It was not advantageous to continue this high rate, however, for the government required easy money, both to facilitate the flotation of loans and to act as a stimulus to production. The decrease in the rate to five per cent which occurred on August 20 held for the duration of the war and continued until April, 1920. The changes in the Bank of France rate for discount of commercial paper and that for advances against securities from

[1] Germain Martin, *Les Finances publiques de la France* (Paris, 1925), p. 107.

[2] Robert Wolff, *Note sur le système monétaire français* (Paris, 1927), pp. 39, 40.

[3] See *supra*, Chapter II. France often used the gold premium policy to prevent the export of gold where other nations might have used a high discount rate. Aug. Arnauné, *La Monnaie, le credit et le change* (Paris, 1926), pp. 191, 192. M. Arnauné gives only slight importance to this mechanism which is given more influence in the comments of English and American writers.

[4] Germain Martin, *op. cit.*, p. 115. The Bank of France was liberal in discounting paper when it was evidently important for commerce and industry.

1914 to 1928 were comparatively few. The dates are given below.

The steadiness of the discount rate during the war was consistent with the French banking policy of the preceding

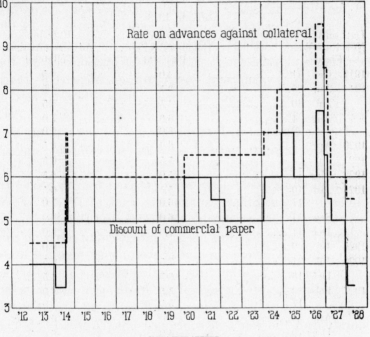

CHART XIII

DISCOUNT RATE OF THE BANK OF FRANCE, AND
RATE ON ADVANCES AGAINST COLLATERAL

years.[1] It took on new significance in that it was maintained despite the internal and external depreciation of the franc.[2] Further than this, the discount rate was decidedly lower

[1] Charles Rist, *La Déflation en pratique* (Paris, 1922), p. 119. Professor Rist here expresses the opinion that the discount rate should be used only in time of crisis and should not be a part of a normal economic policy. *L'Annuaire statistique* (1922), p. 2. The average rate for the previous ten years had been three per cent.

[2] Narcisse Rosenthal, *La Politique d'escompte de la Banque de France depuis 1914* (thesis, Paris, 1926, published in Nice), p. 100: "C'est donc

than the yield on loans floated during the war.[1] Perhaps the
Bank of France should have raised its rate somewhat in
order to limit note issues which are to be attributed to the

TABLE XIII
DISCOUNT RATES OF THE BANK OF FRANCE [2]
1912 to 1928

Date on Which New Rate Was Fixed	Discount of Commercial Paper, Per Cent	Rate for Advances Against Collateral
1912 Oct 31	4.0	4.5
1914 Jan 29	3.5	4.5
Jul 30	4.5	5.5
Aug 1	6.0	7.0
20	5.0	6.0
1920 Apr 8	6.0	6.5
1921 Jul 28	5.5	6.5
1922 Mar 11	5.0	6.5
1924 Jan 10	5.5	6.5
17	6.0	7.0
Sep 11	6.0	8.0
Dec 11	7.0	8.0
1925 Jul 9	6.0	8.0
1926 Jul 31	7.5	9.5
Dec 16	6.5	8.5
1927 Feb 3	5.5	8.0
17	5.5	7.0
Apr 14	5.0	6.0
Dec 29	4.0	6.0
1928 Jan 19	3.5	5.5

large quantity of commercial paper which swelled its portfolio. There is little reason, however, to think that this
would have made much difference. Other factors than the
interest rates dominated economic life during these years.

un fait incontestable et remarquable que la guerre a emmené avec elle
l'abandon de la politique traditionelle de la Banque de France de la hausse
du taux d'escompte en cas du change." See page 22 for the fixity of the
discount rate.

[1] Germain Martin, *op. cit.,* pp. 162, 163.

[2] *Le Pour et le contre* (December 19, 1926; and April 17, 1927; January
22, 1928), p. 309. See also regular issues of the *Bulletin de la statistique
générale de la France.*

Neither at this time nor after the armistice could a fractional change in the cost of money have brought about a marked contraction of credit.

The difference between the prewar and postwar situations must be indicated at this point. The first condition of an effective discount rate has been said above to be that the amount of cash in circulation should be so limited that changes in its volume will not permit rapid and uncontrollable changes in the volume of credit. This condition changed with the war, for the borrowings of the state from the Bank of France meant equivalent increases in inconvertible money. Moreover, since gold was no longer used, this rapidly increasing volume of paper money was the sole basis for the expansion of credit. Thus the increase in the circulation could go on indefinitely once the link with gold was broken. The expansion of credit, therefore, was practically unlimited. The second condition of an effective rate is a centralized banking system with a well-established and clearly understood policy. This condition was also altered by the war, since the Bank of France had never faced so serious an emergency, as that arising out of the recent war, and its policy under such conditions could not be definitely anticipated.

Then again, the price situation after 1914 showed no stability such as was indicated as a third essential element of a successful discount rate policy. In fact, the rapid increase in wholesale and retail prices so far outstripped costs in their upward movement that there were very large profit margins. In such a situation the borrower gained, even if the interest rate was very high. Keynes has illustrated this fact by taking the figures for the English situation in 1919 and the early part of 1920.

It follows from this table [of prices] that a man, who borrowed money from his banker and used the proceeds to purchase raw materials selected at random, stood to make a profit in every single month of this period with the exception of the last, and would have cleared 46 per cent on the average of the year. Yet bankers were not charging at this time above 7 per cent for their advances, leaving a clear profit of between 30 and 40 per cent. . . .[1]

This was even more true in France where wholesale prices rose to 300 per cent of 1914 during the war and as high as 850 per cent in 1928, while in Germany the situation was more extreme than in France; there a loan was practically a gift during the period of collapse. Even the interest rate of 100 per cent a month could not offset depreciation.[2] It is obvious that in such circumstances the change of one or two per cent in the discount rate would be completely negligible. Borrowers with the prospect of large speculative gains could afford to pay the highest rates which the banks demanded. Thus changes in the internal value of the franc quite did away with the influence of the Bank rate.

The fourth condition of effective credit control was the stability of the franc on the exchange. It has been pointed out that, normally, if the franc were depressed, an increase in the discount rate would attract a certain number of investments from abroad and that this growing demand would buoy up the franc. If, however, the franc were depreciating as much as twenty per cent a year, the difference of a few per cent added to the discount rate would not be sufficient to attract capital. The actual situation, as it developed in France, proved that gold currencies were at a premium quite irrespective of the rate which they earned in foreign centers. The loss involved in the purchase of francs, on the contrary, frequently wiped out any interest gain.[3] In other words, the exchange rates were dominated by more subtle influences than the Bank rate, except in so far as the changes influenced public opinion directly in its attitude towards the financial outlook.

[1] J. M. Keynes, *Monetary Reform* (New York, 1924), p. 23. This problem has been considered by others in taking up the matter of the *real* discount rate.   [2] *Ibid.*, p. 27.   [3] A. Arnauné, *op. cit.*, pp. 217, 218.

It was, then, the absence of these four conditions that made possible the erratic psychological effects of increases in the Bank rates. Since this financial instrument could no longer be expected to act as it had in the prewar days, it was the subject of vague speculation and uneasy forecasts. It was realized in a general way that the Bank of France would still use the discount rate to protect itself if the limit of the note circulation authorized by law was being reached. Moreover, the treasury needs were closely linked with the Bank in this matter. A rise in the rate was, therefore, usually a signal that the government and the Bank were alarmed at the situation, that the funds of the treasury were low, and that some desperate effort to check inflation might be made. The result of such surmises was a general distrust of the franc and an attempt to invest money in foreign credits or in goods. These efforts inevitably depressed the value of the currency both at home and abroad. The effect was, thus, contrary to the one desired. The influence of the discount rate was inverted in a number of instances, notably in 1924.[1]

Both Hawtrey and Cassel have argued that ineffectiveness of the discount rate, such as is implied in the preceding discussion, is exaggerated. It is true that they are not thinking primarily of the French case; nevertheless, their arguments seem to be intended to apply to countries such as France and, hence, must be considered here. It is possible that, as they contend, a stricter control of credit might have been exerted during the war when the exchange rates were not varying to a serious degree. Hawtrey discussed the matter critically in 1915. He urged the attempt to contract credit through the Bank rate.

In point of fact it is probable that less than half the production of the country is being carried on for the Government, and the remainder would be as sensitive as ever.[2]

[1] See *supra,* Chapter V.
[2] R. G. Hawtrey, *Monetary Reconstruction* (London, 1923), p. 28.

He says in another place, speaking of England in particular:

The policy of cheap money looked plausible enough. It stimulated trade, and enabled the Government to borrow by means of Treasury bills at small cost. But cheap money stimulates trade because it increases trade borrowing; it increases production because it accelerates consumption.[1]

Part of the consumption which can be attributed to easy money was certainly a disadvantage. It was the consumption of war materials alone which was important to the survival of the nation and had to be increased at the cost of her financial stability.

Hawtrey's contentions have considerable weight though their applicability to France is limited. Cassel, on the other hand, has more clearly in mind conditions in neutral countries. He claims that the influence of discount rate policy on domestic prices remained as before, even though the machinery of international payments had been altered in a marked degree.

The actual conditions of foreign discount policy have, of course, been profoundly affected by the War, even if there is considerable exaggeration in the common assertion that the discount rates no longer have any bearing whatever upon the regulation of international payments. When the managements of the central banks now talk of the discount rate having lost its usual effectiveness, it is probable that they are chiefly thinking of this upsetting of the conditions underlying their foreign discount policy . . . what was really affected was simply the exterior technical machinery of the discount policy, while the essential part of its function, that of maintaining the currency at a stable level of purchasing power at home, still remained, the means to that end being in the main the same as before.[2]

He admits the changed state of affairs in that "we have to regard as normal quite other discount rates than those to

[1] R. G. Hawtrey, *Monetary Reconstruction* (London, 1923), p. 3 (written in 1922).

[2] Gustav Cassel, *Money and Foreign Exchange After 1914* (New York, 1923), p. 108.

which we were formerly accustomed." [1] But he does not
state that even the very high rates prevailing in Germany,
for instance, could not be advanced rapidly enough to keep
pace with depreciation. The disorganization of the money
markets, including that in France, went farther than his
discussion would indicate. He understates the very extreme
changes in economic relationships and the uncertainty
which prevailed in most matters after 1914.

He is probably right in so far as he discusses the changed
influences of the discount rate over international payments,
and undoubtedly there is some truth in these criticisms
made by Hawtrey and Cassel. In a number of instances the
discount policy was weak and vacillating. Special consideration of the French case, however, leads to the opinion that
the increase of the discount rate during the war would have
made comparatively little difference in the situation. When
one passes to the postwar period, moreover, one finds the
situation complicated by the rapid changes in prices, foreign
exchange values, and other elements of economic life. A few
attempts to control the situation will be mentioned below,
—they were, in the main, futile. Their failure may have
been due in part to bungling methods but much more to
difficulties inherent in extreme depreciation.

The policy of the Bank of France was strictly *laissez-
faire*. The discount rate in France was merely a dependent
variable. The Bank of France was guided in its policy by
the desire to further the activities of the government, activities which required currency inflation and industrial expansion. Production was stimulated not only by easy money
and low interest rates, but, to a much greater extent, by government purchases. The increased demand for goods found
its expression in rising prices and this acted necessarily as a
stimulus to economic activity. Thus, the motive force was

[1] Gustave Cassel, *Money and the Foreign Exchange After 1914* (New
York, 1923), p. 109. His book was published in 1923 before the very high
rates in Germany had received much notice.

not low costs, including interest rates, but it was higher profits due to rising prices. War consumption and not monetary policy dominated the situation. The stimulus may have been excessive, but it could have been modified only slightly by the intervention of the Bank of France.

THE DISCOUNT RATE AFTER THE WAR

At the close of the war it is possible that the discount rate might have been increased to advantage, but the five per cent level which had been maintained since August, 1914 was not altered until 1920. It is conceivable that the continued expansion of credit and the rise in prices which occurred after the armistice might have been modified and some excesses avoided if the rate had been increased. In holding to a comparatively low rate, however, France was merely doing what other nations did. The general hopefulness after the armistice, the expectation of a rapid revival of commerce, postponed the increase in discount rates until 1920. This was a natural if unfortunate situation. It is less to be wondered at in France than it was in England, because of the prevailing skepticism among the French regarding the Bank rate.[1]

For various reasons, then, the Bank of France did not interfere in the situation until 1920. The liabilities of the four large banks had nearly doubled during 1919 and continued to grow during January and February of 1920.[2] Bank clearings increased rapidly in the first months of 1920. The figure for January was 10,914 million francs, and for April was 14,705.[3] The growth of the note circulation was less marked, and this fact indicates that the expansion was

[1] Jules Décamps, *Les Changes étrangers* (Paris, 1922), p. 263.

[2] Morgan Bank, *Statistical Atlas* (Paris, unpublished), p. 13. The figures are: 1918, December, 6,747 million francs; 1919, December, 11,968 million francs; and 1920, February, 13,366. The four banks are the Société générale, Crédit Lyonnais, Comptoir d'escompte de Paris, and the Société générale de crédit industriel et commercial. See Chart XII, Chapter V.

[3] See *Bulletin de la statistique générale de la France*, and *infra* appendix.

mainly due to credit and not to cash inflation for government needs. The continuance of such expansion was obviously impossible, but the French were slow to act. It was only after the United States had been forced to protect its gold and the Federal Reserve Board had raised its rates that the French took similar steps.[1] Thus the increase on April 8 did little more than confirm changes which were due to American influences. The downward movement of prices, though probably due partly to the action of the Bank of France, was due also to a considerable extent to the fall in American prices which led to lower cost of imports.[2]

The up and down movements of prices during these years, 1919-22, cannot be attributed mainly to the policy of the Bank. This institution continued its conservative policy. It kept the rate in harmony with changes in prices and industry, once those changes had become fairly evident. The comparison of the wholesale price index and the table of discount rates, as given above, shows that prices seemed to respond in a slight degree to the Bank policy. The increase to six per cent on April 8, 1920 was followed by a price decline. The decrease to five and one-half per cent on July 28, 1921 was followed by an upward movement of the price index number. The same was true after the second decrease to five per cent in March, 1922. The interrelation between the two factors should not be exaggerated, however. French banking measures at this time imitated to a very considerable degree those taken in England and America.[3] Moreover, the foreign exchange rates had a much quicker influence on prices than did the discount rate.[4] The price recession was due, then, to a combination of factors, among which were the foreign exchange rates, public opinion, and the discount rate.

The ineffectualness of the discount rate, not apparent at this time, became more evident after 1921. It was then seen

---

[1] N. Rosenthal, *op. cit.*, pp. 64, 65. [3] N. Rosenthal, *op. cit.*, p. 67.
[2] See *supra*, Chapter IV. [4] See *supra*, Chapter IV, pp. 145-147.

that the attempt to deflate the currency, begun with the convention of 1920,[1] was extremely difficult. The state had been able to repay the Bank two billion francs of its advances even without the help of a high money rate in 1921.[2] Such a repayment was not possible in 1922, however. It was not thought advisable to let the effort to make these repayments dominate completely discount rate policy. There was no further increase in the rate until 1924. It is surprising that there was no strong movement to coördinate this part of the financial system with the deflationary program. The failure to do so was probably because those in control realized the limited influence of the rate and the artificial nature of deflation at this time. The rapid depreciation of the franc during 1922 and the following years would have made any use of high money rates of little value for the reasons indicated above. In any case the effort of the state to repay the Bank of France and deflate the currency amounted to little. The number of notes in circulation remained practically stationary, and the Bank rate was of small importance in economic life, from 1920 to 1924. Deflation in the latter years was impossible because of the price rise, but in neither case was the discount rate paramount. It was called into action after this period of disuse in the emergency of 1924.

On January 10, the government, alarmed by the rapid rise of the dollar and the pound, announced that it would pursue an energetic policy and increased the discount rate from five to five and one-half per cent.[3] The second increase in the discount rate, January 17,[4] to six per cent was little noticed in the general excitement. It is evident that it did

[1] See *supra,* Chapter IV, pp. 136, 137.
[2] Charles Rist, *op. cit.,* pp. 67, 68, 71. This was possible because of the increased purchases of *bons de la défense* which came with the commodity price decline.
[3] *Journal des débats* (January 14, 1924). "La baisse du franc s'est accentuée aussitôt que la décision de la Banque de France a été connue." See *infra,* Chapter VIII.   [4] See *infra.*

little or nothing to improve the franc at this time.[1] In fact, the franc lost about four per cent of its value in the two days following the first change in the rate. It lost about two per cent of its value in the two days following the second increase.[2] The reason for this unexpected result is clear. The attack on the franc had been so effective that general confidence had been shaken. Once panic conditions existed, any slight shock or unexpected event increased the alarm. Then again, with depreciation at the rate of almost one per cent a day, it was impossible to attract foreign credits by offering a slight additional advantage in money rates. To the French speculator, for the same reason, the appreciation of foreign currencies offset any possible difference in the cost of money in the respective countries.

Thus, the effort made to improve the situation did more harm than good. Instead of decreasing speculation, it strengthened the motive for buying foreign exchanges, for the interest cost was negligible in contrast to the risk. The second increase did not aggravate the situation, it passed unnoticed, because the public was already fully aware of the seriousness of the crisis. This inverted influence of the discount rate is a feature of such chaotic conditions as those which prevailed in France during these months and should be considered a psychological as well as an economic phenomenon. In circumstances such as those prevailing in 1924 the recourse to the more mechanical measures was worse than useless. The second expedient, legislation against speculation, was equally unavailing. Like the increase in the discount rate, it affected the ways and means of speculation but made the motive stronger than ever.

There was very little connection between the alterations in the Bank rate and the extent of depreciation. The variations between five, and seven and one-half per cent during the years after 1914 were not followed by similar up and

[1] *Journal des débats* (January 21, 1924), see general comment on financial situation in the *Revue financière*.　　　　[2] See appendix.

down movements of prices or foreign exchange rates. Attempts which were made to use the discount rate as an aid to deflation were frustrated by the tremendous need of the government for funds even after the war was over. This need led inevitably to borrowing both from the Bank of France and from individuals, and prevented the use of the discount rate as a repressive force because of the ever-growing volume of cash and credit. The influence of the bank rate was restricted to a narrow sphere; that is, a slight degree of control over the week to week conditions in the money market, and so over the flotation of government loans, and over the flow of funds from the *bons de la défense* into industrial investment and back.[1]

FUTILITY OF LEGISLATION

Lack of understanding of the reasons for depreciation, evident to a certain extent in discount rate policy, is even more glaringly apparent in the attempt to fortify the franc by restrictive legislation. The use of law in the battle for the franc is the second type of measure which must be considered here. It is neither possible nor advisable to discuss the matter in detail. The complexity and variety of the various regulations precludes an exhaustive account of government action. Nevertheless, they must be mentioned because of the frequency with which such measures have been resorted to both in the recent situation and in other cases of depreciation.

The most obvious and universal legal step is that establishing the *cours forcé* of paper money and disassociating it completely from gold [2] by making it inconvertible. This step was taken during 1914. The further measures [3] taken

[1] See *infra* this Chapter.

[2] Gaston Jèze, *Cours de science des finances* (Paris, 1925), p. 234. Law of August 5, 1914: "La Banque de France et al Banque de l'Algérie sont *dispensées de rembourser leurs billets en espèces.*" See *supra*, Chapter III.

[3] See *supra*, Chapter III. See also Georges Lasch, *De la Répercussion de la valeur monétaire sur la dette publique et privée* (Strasbourg, 1924), p. 68.

at the outbreak of the war which provided for moratoria of payments of various kinds, aimed indirectly to protect the value of the franc. The moratoria which prevented forced sales and bankruptcies tended to safeguard values from the extreme variations which a more severe panic might have occasioned.[1] But the moratoria were of temporary significance only, most of them were abrogated after the first crisis was passed,[2] so measures of this type do not require consideration here. The *cours forcé* was scarcely more interesting, since it was a legal provision which had little or no direct effect on the value of the franc. It was a natural part of the inflationary program of the government, but did not alter the situation in any marked way. The franc would have been used for domestic exchange without such a special insistence on its legal tender quality. It rose and fell in the domestic and foreign markets, regardless of what its value was in the minds of law makers.[3]

Later developments of legal theory as to the right to demand payment in anything other than paper francs are, however, interesting. They indicate the slowness with which depreciation was recognized and the false ideas which were current as to ways of limiting it. For instance, the general tenor of court decisions was that demands for payments in gold were illegal and impaired the credit of the state by casting doubt on the value of its money. It was natural, then, that payments of gold to foreigners under analogous conditions were judged illegal.[4] There were cases, on the other hand, in which the court approved the demands for gold payments which would lead to the entrance of gold into France and therefore increase the national wealth.[5] These

[1] Germain Martin, *op. cit.*, pp. 100-117.
[2] H. E. Fisk, *French Public Finance* (New York, 1922), p. 80, see also *supra*, Chapter III.
[3] Jèze, *op. cit.*, p. 240. Professor Jèze speaks of the need of using some money even if this unit of value depreciates rapidly.
[4] *Ibid.*, p. 280, Cours de Paris, February 22, 1924.
[5] *Ibid.*, pp. 277, 279. 1920 decision of the Cours de cassation, June 7, 1920.

decisions are explainable only on the grounds of "political interests." [1] Some of the decisions which are discussed by Jèze [2] bear evidence of the artificiality of the situation. In spite of the law, there were considerable efforts by individuals to seek protection against inflation either by gold payments or by increases in prices which were practically equivalent. [3]

It is true that payments in actual gold coin were rare. The usual procedure was to have bills drawn up so they varied upward or downward with the ratio of gold or of the gold exchange currencies to paper. Such so-called gold payments were safer from an economic point of view, since they gave the payee assurance of greater stability, but were more difficult from a legal point of view since such contracts could not, in general, be enforced by law. The latter method—that is, price changes—was more widely practiced but often caused friction between individuals who did not clearly understand the extent of depreciation. Conscious attempts to avoid depreciation, such as these, were usually only for large payments and contracts running over a considerable period of time, such as rents. In the case of house rents, for example, there were frequent attempts to alter payments in accord with the gold exchange rates. Where this was difficult, special payments for repairs or exorbitant tips were demanded as a substitute. [4] It was impossible to prevent such transactions by laws when they were clearly to the economic interests of the individual. [5] Such procedure, however, afforded the individual but imperfect security. [6]

[1] Lasch, *op. cit.*, p. 71.   [2] Jèze, *op. cit.*, pp. 270-273.

[3] Lasch, *op. cit.*, p. 63: "Malgré les soi-disant interdictions légales de calculer les créances en monnaies stables, ce procédé est employé de plus en plus fréquemment."

[4] The rent situation was peculiarly complicated because it was affected not only by depreciating value of money but by laws preventing increases in the nominal rents.   [5] Lasch, *op. cit.*, p. 86.

[6] See *supra*, Chapter V, pp. 184, 188. The government policy was somewhat changed with the issue of the Caillaux gold exchange guarantee loan in 1925.

Other laws, aimed to prevent speculation and the exportation of capital, were even more difficult to enforce than those for gold payments. They were more important in the postwar developments than were the gold payment decisions, because of the fairly widespread belief that such laws were effective. This belief did not go unchallenged, and it is impossible even now to give a clear verdict. They may have done some good, perhaps, but it is safe to assert that they did considerable harm.

The most important of this series of restrictions was the law of April 3, 1918.[1] It was reinforced by a number of other laws, decrees, and decisions which continued to be enacted as late as December 19, 1926.[2] The resulting complex mass of regulations led to considerable embarrassment for those who wished to secure foreign credits in an open and legitimate manner, and yet could not prevent efforts to smuggle out capital. The object of this series of laws, generally referred to by mentioning the first one, the law of April 3, 1918 was to prevent the *flight from the franc*. More specifically, it aimed to interfere with transactions which increased the sale of francs and the purchases of foreign exchange. The law is given in abridged form by Professor Jèze.[3]

It is forbidden to any person *residing in France* . . . without written authorization from the Minister of Finance . . . (1) to build up *outside of France* a holding of securities, funds, for deposit or loans, by any method whatsoever of credit or exchange, for his own profit or that of another . . . if the transaction implies . . . *any transfer whatsoever of funds or securities* out of France; (2) to send *out of France* . . . securities if the sale of

[1] J. Laurès, *Le Problème des changes et la baisse du franc* (Paris, 1926), pp. 104-109.

[2] Jacques Lockhart, *Le Marché des changes de Paris* (thesis, Paris, 1927; advanced copy used), pp. 339-365. See especially pp. 339-341, or, see J. Lagneau, *La Législation relative à l'exportation des capitaux* (thesis, Paris, 1925), pp. 51-63.

[3] Gaston Jèze, *op. cit.*, p. 266 (translation mine).

the same does not result in the receipt of francs, or if this sale should not lead to credit in foreign money which would be in harmony with the aim of the present law . . .

It will be seen from a study of the complete texts that the regulations were very inclusive. It is obvious, also, that they attacked the exchange problem from the mechanical side alone, and left the basic reasons for the flight of capital untouched. Such reasons were the fear of the future depreciation, and the desire to escape excessive taxation.

Many stories are told as to the ways and means of getting around these laws. It is certain that there was much exportation of capital even though all the alleged instances may not have occurred.[1] One of the easiest ways of building up foreign credits was to allow the proceeds of commodity sales abroad to accumulate in foreign banks or to reinvest the income from foreign investments. Regulations were framed to prevent this, notably those of October 15, 1925 [2] but they were difficult to enforce. It was usually possible in reporting transactions to understate the proceeds of the sales abroad or to conceal the existence of investments. There was said to be considerable exportation of actual securities, carried out of the country in airplanes, or in various other irregular ways. The securities were bought by foreigners as a speculation and paid for by credits in some stable currency. Tales of the smuggling of gold coin were rife, one even heard of such things as the shipment of coin to Italy in cheeses. In one instance which came to the attention of the writer, a man was thrown into jail because he had brought into the country gilded coins of a base metal under a permit to take out of the country an equivalent amount of gold coin. He then took out full value gold coin which he paid for with depreciated paper. Such a procedure

[1] Anyone who lived in France during the period of depreciation realized the very great number of such occurrences. It is obvious that the effort at concealment prevented traces of them from appearing frequently in print.

[2] J. Laurès, *op. cit.*, pp. 114-118. The extract from the *Journal officiel* is here given.

offered an opportunity for profit as long as the government refused to accept gold for more than its face value in paper money. This fiction ended September 27, 1926 when the Bank of France established rates at which it would buy gold for paper.[1] It is certain that during the months previous to this large deposits were built up by the French in Amsterdam, Switzerland, London, and New York.[2] The French were able to take over from Americans and others residing in France considerable sums in dollars which they allowed to accumulate in deposits abroad. No accurate estimate of these sums is possible. Various statements have been made which would place accumulations in 1926 anywhere between five and thirty billion paper francs. The investigations into the same problem, as found in Germany, made by the MacKenna Committee for the Dawes Commission, brought to light the difficulty of arriving at satisfactory figures. The most that one can say is that the sums were large. This is evidenced by the fact that the operations were admittedly many, by the decline in the value of French securities, and also by statements of bankers in other countries that the sums left with them by French depositors were considerable.[3]

The decline in new capital issues is notable; the figures given by Cahill are:

1923..................	6,772 million francs	
1924..................	5,619 " "
1925..................	3,828 " "
(9 months) 1926..................	3,661 " "

[1] The *New York Times,* October 4, 1926. The rate of 114.70 paper francs for 20.00 gold francs was established at this time. This was lower than the market rate, but considerable gold was brought to the Bank of France as a result of this policy.

[2] J. M. Keynes, "Balance of British Trade," *Economic Journal* (December, 1927), vol. xxxvii, no. 148, p. 556. The increase in credits in London, partly attributable to the "flight from the franc," is £100,000,000 "from the beginning of 1925 to the middle of 1927."

[3] J. Cahill, *Overseas Trade Report,* "Economic and Industrial Conditions in France, 1925-26" (London, 1927), p. 41. See also Chart XXVI and appendix for figures.

In addition to such vague indications of the outflow of capital, the fluctuations of certain gold value securities were striking evidences of the flight from the franc. These securities, with dividends payable in gold standard currencies, varied directly with the value of the foreign exchanges. Some

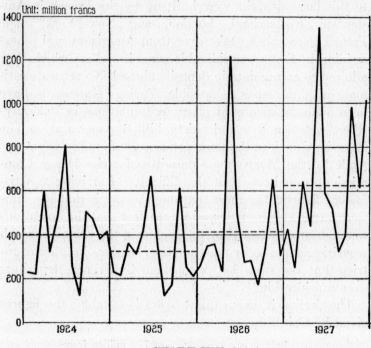

CHART XIV

SECURITIES FLOATED ON THE PARIS BOURSE, 1924 TO 1927 [1]

of them, such as the Suez Canal, de Beers, Rio Tinto, and various English and American bonds, offered safe refuges from depreciation. They were much sought after during the months of greatest depreciation. They varied inversely with the French government issues. No law could prevent the traffic in these shares; thus it was evident that they offered

[1] See appendix for figures. For the first two months of 1924 deduction is made of the very large government flotations which would disturb the curve if not eliminated. The dotted line indicates the average.

one of the easiest means of sheltering French funds from depreciation.

If it had been possible to prevent all purchases of foreign exchanges except those needed to cover the unfavorable balance of commodity trade, there would have been little variation in the value of the franc. But it was not possible to put the money markets of France in a water-tight compartment. Moreover, the attempt to do so led to an exaggerated effort to break through the barriers. Foreign exchanges could not be bought freely on account of such laws. It seemed very important, therefore, to build up foreign credits whenever and wherever this was possible. It may be that the restrictions really accentuated the fluctuations of the franc.[1] It is quite probable that the profits derived from exports would have been invested in France to a greater extent if they could have been moved out of the country for investment more easily when occasion required.

There were many champions of the abolition of these laws.[2] Some of the foremost authorities in the financial world advocated the freedom of capital movements; while some felt that the time for ending restrictions must be carefully chosen, the general drift of the more intelligent sections of public opinion was in favor of putting an end to artificial restraints at an early date.[3] Certainly there is nothing in the history of the franc to indicate that they had been effective. Extreme variations were frequent, and the fact that the franc escaped collapse cannot be attributed to this type of measure. In the case of the 1924 panic, the fall of the franc was not halted by the February legislation against speculation, but, only a few weeks later, by increased

---

[1] J. Casamajor, *Le Marché à terme des changes en France* (Paris, 1924), p. 162.

[2] Germain Martin, *op. cit.*, pp. 388-391.

[3] *Rapport du comité des experts* (décret du 31 mai, 1926), p. 44. "Il ne semble pas en effet que la dite loi ait eu jusqu'ici des résultats vraiment utiles" [laws of April 3, 1918].

taxes and additional foreign loans. Despite the growing appreciation of these facts, however, the laws remained until stability, achieved by other means, was a virtual reality.

THE ATTEMPT TO DEFLATE

It became obvious to French financial leaders after the depreciation of 1919 and 1920 that the measures to protect the value of the franc, which we have just treated, were inadequate. The discount rate had not been an active factor, and there was no reason to suppose that it could fill the need which became greater each month. Laws had been a failure for the most part. A more serious attempt to prevent depreciation was required. According to one reasonable, if somewhat superficial, view of the situation, the prime cause was the increase of the note circulation of the Bank of France. This view was not wrong, but erred in that it was too simple, and too narrow an explanation. It was too simple in that it assumed that deflation was symmetrical with inflation; that is to say, that if a given increase in notes led to a given increase in prices and exchanges, an equivalent decrease in the circulation would lead to equal decrease in prices and exchange rates.[1] This implied a disregard for the fact that the expansion of the note circulation had wrought certain profound changes in economic life which could not be undone. Contraction is a different thing from expansion. The time relationship between prices and costs is different, and the psychological influences are quite distinct. Moreover, the prevailing view on deflation was too narrow in that it did not seek out the real causes of inflation. It argued as if inflation and deflation could be undertaken at will, but the situation was far more complex than this. Inflation was inevitable in the pursuit of war. Deflation could be carried out on a comparable scale only if it, too, were inevitable; that is, if the needs for productive

[1] Charles Rist, *op. cit.*, p. 118.

activity on the part of the state and on the part of private interests were greatly curtailed.[1]

The recourse to deflation to increase the value of the franc was, therefore, a blind and ill-considered attempt. This measure has been discussed to a certain extent in connection with the chronicle of postwar events. The 1920 convention which prescribed the repayment of two billion francs by the state to the Bank of France each year was an indication of healthy tendencies, but was not coördinated with a general financial policy in such a way as to be workable. The reason for the swift passage of such a measure lay in the similarity to the government's policy after the war of 1870.[2] The difference between the recent experience and the earlier one lay primarily in the fact that the quantities involved were much greater and that the time during which artificial conditions had prevailed was much longer. However this may be, subsequent events proved quite clearly that the deflation which was accomplished may have done a little good in some directions but did considerable harm in others. The effort had to be abandoned, and further inflation took place in 1925. The complete rejection of these false hopes and incomplete methods was necessary before the vigorous efforts of the later years brought stability. It was a very long time, however, before the hope of bringing the franc to par was abandoned. The matter was still something of an issue in 1927 and influenced Poincaré in his delay in stabilizing legally.[3] The dates of conventions and decrees and the amount of increase and decrease throw interesting light on the deflationary effort.[4]

[1] The repayment of two billion francs a year over a period of fourteen years, such as prescribed by the convention of François-Marsal, would have been a deliberate effort to depress business, such as has probably never been undertaken anywhere.

[2] See p. 137.

[3] Evidence of this is to be found in the daily press which fought the battle back and forth through 1927.   [4] See the table on p. 232.

The artificiality of the prevailing point of view is brought out in the distinction made by Professor Rist in regard to financial and monetary deflation.[1] This distinction, whether or not it is a valuable one to apply to other monetary experiences, throws considerable light on the French case. Finan-

TABLE XIV

LEGAL LIMITS OF NOTE CIRCULATION AND ADVANCES TO THE TREASURY BY THE BANK OF FRANCE[2]

Fixed by Conventions and Decrees

(in millions of francs)

Advances to the Treasury by the Bank of France			Increase or Decrease	Legal Limit of Note Circulation			Increase
				1911	Dec 29	6,800	....
1914	Sep 21	6,000	3,000	1914	Aug 5	12,000	5,200
1915	May 4	9,000	3,000	1915	May 11	15,000	3,000
				1916	Mar 15	18,000	3,000
1917	Feb 13	12,000	3,000	1917	Feb 15	21,000	3,000
					Sep 10	24,000	3,000
1918	Apr 4	18,000	3,000	1918	Feb 7	27,000	3,000
	Jun 5	21,000	3,000		Mar 3	30,000	3,000
					Sep 5	33,000	3,000
1919	Feb 13	24,000	3,000	1919	Feb 25	36,000	3,000
	Apr 24	27,000	3,000		Jul 17	40,000	4,000
1920	Dec 29	Convention		1920	Sep 28	41,000	1,000
1921	Dec 31	25,000	−2,000		.....	.....	....
1922	Dec 31	24,000	−1,000		.....	.....	....
1923	Dec 27	23,200	− 800		.....	.....	....
1924	Dec 22	22,000	−1,200		.....	.....	....
1925	Apr 15	26,000	4,000	1925	Apr 15	45,000	4,000
	Jun 30	32,000	6,000		Jul 12	51,000	6,000
	Nov 24	33,500	1,500		Dec 3	58,500	7,500
	Dec 3	39,500	6,000		.....	.....	....
1926	Dec 31	37,500	−2,000		.....	.....	....
1927	Dec 31	35,500	−2,000		.....	.....	....

[1] Rist, *op. cit.*, pp. 4, 5, 72.

[2] Germain Martin, *op. cit.*, pp. 142, 143; Aug. Arnauné, *op. cit.*, pp. 294, 295; Etienne Clémentel, *op. cit.*, pp. 49, 50; also *Le Temps* (November 27, 1925); and *Journal officiel, Chambre* (November 23, 1925), p. 3918. *Reference Service on International Affairs* (Paris, November 30, 1925), pp. 1, 2. Notes in excess of 58,500 million francs could be issued after August, 1926, if they were offset by gold value exchange holdings.

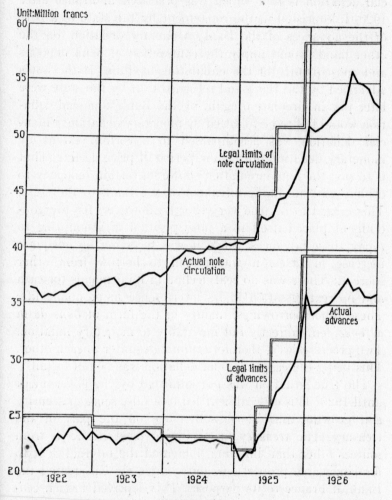

Unit:Million francs

Legal limits of
note circulation

Actual note
circulation

Actual
advances

Legal limits
of advances

1922   1923   1924   1925   1926

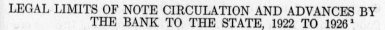

CHART XV

LEGAL LIMITS OF NOTE CIRCULATION AND ADVANCES BY THE BANK TO THE STATE, 1922 TO 1926 [1]

[1] Note the nearness of advances to the limit at times of panic and the curves for advances and notes crossing the limit in 1925.

233

cial deflation is that which was practiced in France after
1920. It consisted in the repayment by the state of a part
of the advances of the Bank. Monetary deflation, on the
other hand, would imply the contraction of bank deposits
and consequently of the circulating medium. If the notes
advanced by the Bank and returned to it by the state were
later put in circulation again by the Bank, financial deflation would fail to be followed by monetary deflation. Financial deflation was accompanied to a certain extent by
monetary deflation during the period of price decline. That
is to say, the note circulation showed a certain tendency to
decline with declining advances of the Bank to the state.
This ceased to be true very shortly, however, for the government placed itself in a false position in attempting to
repay these advances. Since it was receiving no adequate
increase in taxes, it was forced to borrow from other
sources.[1] There was no real decline in its demands for cash
and no real cessation in its interference in economic life.
These other borrowings, mainly in the form of *bons de la
défense,* led indirectly but inevitably to monetary inflation.
Two processes were therefore running counter to each other.
This being the case, financial deflation was bound to fail.

The true situation was not admitted by the government
until 1925. This concealment led to a false sense of security
and growing amount of subterfuge on the part of the
treasury. The treasury, in trying to meet its needs from
sources other than inflation, increased the internal debt to
unmanageable proportions and completely subjugated the
Bank of France to its purposes. This deprived French economic life of the advantages of a powerful independent
check on government and private finance. So, if there were
good results from the 1920 deflation program, they were
negative and consisted almost entirely in the opposition to

[1] Germain Martin, *op. cit.,* pp. 148-160. M. Martin in discussing the *bons*
shows their importance in attracting the peasant and the business man but
points out the dangers inherent in such short-time borrowings.

inflation which was very strong in France and which helped
her avoid some of the excesses of other countries. Its direct
effect on depreciation was, on the whole, very slight, while
its indirect influence on the value of the franc, through the
debt and through financial scandals, was more apparent.
The story of these scandals, growing out of the dominance
of the treasury over the Bank, is worth considering in this
connection.

THE BANK OF FRANCE SUBJECT TO THE STATE

The subjection of the Bank to the state was the direct
result of the needs of the treasury for funds to fulfill the
1920 convention. Back of the falsification of the Bank
statements, publicly admitted in 1925, there lay a history of
successive occult advances through the agency of various
private banks and the central Bank. The beginning of such
practices was in 1920.[1] In October of that year the treasury
borrowed 893 million francs from the various banks.[2] In
the following year, 1921, no hidden advances were obtained
by the treasury; in fact, the state was able to repay 800
million francs to the Bank, the remaining sum which made
up the repayments coming from the amortization account.[3]
In September, 1922, however, the margin of funds in the
treasury was practically wiped out. This meant the danger
of default on the payment of various government obligations; so the state was forced to borrow again from private
banks, receiving 300 million francs from these sources,
which it repaid in a few weeks from the proceeds of treasury
bonds issued at this time. *L'Europe nouvelle* in its issue of

[1] *Journal officiel, Chambre,* séance April 9, 1925, pp. 2144-2154. See
especially p. 2146. In this session Herriot, then prime minister, outlined the
history of the hidden advances. Most of the following discussion is based
on this source.   [2] *Ibid.,* p. 2146.
   [3] See *supra,* Chapter IV, and Germain Martin, *op. cit.,* p. 146. A part of
the interest on advances paid by the state to the Bank went directly to an
amortization account which was applied to reducing the capital sum at the
end of each year.

April 18, 1915, quoting from official documents, has summed
up the advances made during the five years in question.[1]
Such advances continued through 1923 and 1924. They were
made in various ways. Sometimes the treasury discounted
with the Bank various securities of private banks. Sometimes the Bank bought treasury certificates. Generally,
however, the Bank of France borrowed directly from the
private banks, who turned for funds to the Bank of France.
The latter institution was then forced by the government
to discount the treasury certificates which the various banks
had received.[2] The Bank was powerless to resist the government. It is evident from the letter of December 29, 1924,
and again of January, 1925, that M. Robineau, the Governor
of the Bank, did not at first advocate the increase in the
legal limit of advances.[3] A little later, however, he pleaded
in vain to have the situation regularized by the increase in
the legal limit for advances to the state. He insisted, moreover, that it would be impossible to avoid indicating in the
next Bank statement a note circulation decidedly in excess
of the legal limit of 41 billion francs.[4]

The amount of money involved in these loans was not at
first very large. Since in most cases repayment was made
after a few weeks, the amounts did not accumulate. Nevertheless, the situation became increasingly difficult with the
passage of time. The embarrassment of the treasury, which
had begun in 1920 under the *Bloc national,* led to the sub-

---

[1] *L'Europe nouvelle* (eighth year), no. 374, pp. 519–527. Extracts from the
parliamentary debates and from the important letters exchanged on this
subject are here given. The citations here made cover the episode in an
adequate way and give in an abridged and readily accessible form the
essence of the original debates.

[2] *Ibid.,* pp. 524, 525. See the letter of Clémentel to the Governor of the
Bank of France on March 5, 1925. In it he outlines this procedure and
mentions the nine banks which participated in a loan of 955 million francs
to the treasury.

[3] *Documents parlementaires, Chambre* (April 9, 1925), p. 2152.

[4] *L'Europe nouvelle, loc. cit.* (April 6, 1926), p. 526, letter of Governor
Robineau to Herriot.

terfuge described above, which continued under the *Cartel*. The reduction of the legal limit of the Bank's advances to the state at the end of 1923 had aggravated the difficulties. As a result of this proceeding the occult advances increased in amount during 1924. Despite this fact, the state again repaid a considerable sum, 1,200 million francs, to the Bank in partial fulfillment of the 1920 convention. The repayments amounted to nothing more than the paper transfers of certain sums, an appearance of amortization offset by new and less advantageous loans. The public was deceived, and the Bank of France placed in a false position, while official admission of the embarrassment of the government and its intense need of funds could not be indefinitely postponed.

As the borrowings of the treasury increased during 1925, the situation become more acute. The discrepancy between the actual advances and the authorized advances reached 3,130 million francs on April 2, 1925.[1] This was not an enormous sum, but it offset almost exactly the specious repayments to the Bank in the preceding three years; it did not indicate any marked increase in inflation, but merely a continuance of the previous situation. The significance of the whole episode was to a considerable extent political. It indicated the difficulty of the government, deprived under the 1920 convention of a working margin of funds, when it needed a breathing space of some months to work out adequate reforms in government finance. The fact that the *Cartel* felt forced to continue the false situation which existed when it came into power in the spring of 1924 is a sign of the weakness of its political position in Parliament. It feared that, in view of the existing sentiment against inflation, no government could propose the increase actually needed to tide it over the existing emergency. Herriot preferred to continue the fiction of deflation rather than risk the storm of public opposition.

[1] *L'Europe nouvelle, loc. cit.,* p. 521.

The deflationary program [1] was the basis of the troubles of the treasury and was therefore, in part, responsible for the confidence crisis of 1925. The extent of the difficulty may be indicated in a schematic way by contrasting the actual total of advances to the state with those which would have been made if the 1920 program had been carried out in full.

TABLE XV

ADVANCES OF THE BANK OF FRANCE TO THE STATE [2]

(in millions of francs)

Legal Limit of Advances

	As Scheduled in 1920 Convention	As Actually Established at End of Each Year	Reduction Accomplished Each Year
1920............	27,000	27,000	....
1921............	25,000	25,000	2,000
1922............	23,000	24,000	1,000
1923............	21,000	23,200	800
1924............	19,000	22,000	1,200
1925............	17,000	39,500	(2,000) [3]
1926............	15,000	37,500	2,000

The difference between the plan and the accomplishment is very striking; it amounted to more than 22 billion francs in 1925 and 1926. The effort made to reduce the advances was even more unsuccessful than is at once apparent from this comparison because the amounts actually repaid were made up, to a considerable extent, of the sums which accumulated automatically with the Bank as the result of the interest payments of the treasury. A part of such interest payments had to be applied by the Bank each year to the reduction of the capital.[4]

[1] See *supra,* Chapter IV, pp. 136-139.

[2] Germain Martin, *op. cit.,* p. 141, and Aug. Arnauné, *op. cit.,* pp. 294, 295. See also appendix; for more detailed statements as to the legal limit of advances, see *supra,* this chapter.

[3] This figure is not a net reduction. It was merely the sum paid by the state to the bank at the end of the year as amortization. In 1925 the net change was an increase of 15,500 million francs. In 1926 the repayment was followed by further repayments to the Bank.

[4] *Le Pour et le contre* (December 16, 1923), and *supra,* p. 173.

· The revelation of 1925 brought out the fact that the true situation was reflected not by the sum of admitted advances of the Bank after repayments, but by the size of the port- folio of the Bank of France, which was swelled by the loans to private banks [1] and by the increase in the *bons de la défense*.[2] It was these two factors in the financial system which made it impossible for "financial deflation" to be fol- lowed by "monetary deflation." On the one hand, the dis- counts of the Bank led to an increase in the note circulation, either directly by the payment of cash or indirectly through the growth of deposits which were later drawn out in cash.[3] On the other hand, the *bons de la défense* occasioned an increase in the note circulation, either through loans for which they served as collateral or because they had to be paid in cash when they matured.

The distinction between monetary and financial deflation, though somewhat arbitrary, is seen therefore to be appli- cable to the French efforts from 1920 to 1925. The govern- ment was able to cut down the advances which had been the main cause of inflation but did not bring about a net deduction in the note circulation. Because the effort was at variance with the true situation of government finance, because other treasury borrowings led to the drawing these notes into circulation again, there was no significant and lasting deflation. It is surprising that the one-sided effort should have continued as long as it did. There is reason to believe that the subterfuges were fairly widely known be- fore the public revelations in 1925; too many ministries had

[1] *Revue d'économie politique,* vol. xl, no. 2 (1926), p. 306. The portfolio of the Bank of France which had increased to a monthly average of 5,854 million francs in January, 1925, fell to 4,132 in May; see also appendix, bills discounted.

[2] See *supra,* Chapter V, pp. 186, 187, for table and curve of *bons de la défense*. This shows an increase in the *bons* during 1924 and a decrease in 1925 when the advances of the Bank to the state were increased by law. The subsequent fluctuations of the *bons* were due mainly to other causes than the needs of the treasury. Note a similar state of affairs in the last week of July, 1926.   [3] Charles Rist, *op. cit.,* p. 75.

been involved in the proceeding to make possible any real secrecy. Since there had been no indication in the public press, foreign opinion was greatly shocked when the truth came out.

The turning point in the situation was indicated, perhaps, by the change in attitude on the part of the Governor of the Bank of France indicated above.[1] He maintained at first that the legal limit of advances should be kept as it was, with the expectation that the situation could soon be righted. But the difficulties of the treasury increased and led to larger borrowings and a more rapid expansion of the note circulation. The Bank protested on February 5 that the expedients of the government were futile.

. . . there is no ground for hoping for an end to the increase of the circulation unless the increase in prices and wages comes to a halt under the influence of a rigorous policy of decreasing all expenditures, of security for savings, and of the resulting decline in the foreign exchanges.[2]

An even more urgent protest and an appeal for an increase in the legal limit of advances followed on February 26. The government replied that additional funds from taxation would ease the situation. Meanwhile, occult advances continued, and there was no real change. On April 6 the Bank sent a solemn warning to the government, indicating that the weekly Bank statement must reveal the truth. This statement, as actually published on April 9, showed a note circulation of more than 43 billion francs, 2 billions in excess of the limit which had been set on September 28, 1920, and left unchanged since that date.[3] This irregular situation was rectified by the law of April 15, 1925.[4] The new legal limit of the note circulation was set at 45 billion

[1] Cf. *supra*, this chapter. *Journal officiel, Chambre*, séance, April 9, 1925, p. 2152.   [2] *L'Europe nouvelle, loc. cit.*, p. 523.

[3] See *supra*, this chapter, table of conventions, laws, and decrees.

[4] *Journal officiel, Chambre, débats*, 2nd séance, April 15, 1925, pp. 2203-2208.

francs, and the advances which the Bank could supply the treasury at 26 billions. Thus the measure was passed and the situation regularized, but the Herriot government was forced to resign, partly in consequence of these disclosures.[1]

Blame for this unfortunate series of episodes in French finance cannot be placed on any one man or on one political party. It is obvious from the above outline of irregular dealings, beginning in 1920 and continuing for almost five years, that many people were concerned, that both the *bloc national* and the *Cartel* shared the responsibility. In fact, French statesmen for several years had been robbing Peter to pay Paul. The results of their actions were threefold: (1) to lessen the margin of resources available to the treasury and thus weaken the government credit; (2) to enhance a strong, almost fanatical, sentiment against inflation, and (3) to postpone other and more useful measures in defense of the franc. These results worked against the franc in almost every instance. There is little good to be said of such one-sided deflation. In fact, many of the troubles of France can be traced back to the François-Marsal convention of 1920 which led to concealed inflation.

Loans as a Substitute for Inflation

The fourth general method of lessening depreciation was government loans, more sound in theory than deflation, even though they led to great difficulties in the end. The use of short-time loans was very important to the government during the war, for they made it possible to supply the treasury with funds without relying wholly on those which were directly inflationary.[2] That is to say, the advances of the Bank to the state, which consisted mainly of newly printed

---

[1] *Journal officiel, Sénat,* 2nd séance, April 10, 1925, pp. 859, 860. See *supra,* Chapter V, p. 182.

[2] Germain Martin, *op. cit.,* p. 433. The 1924 loan, a ten-year loan, obviated inflation during that year.

notes, were supplemented by cash subscribed by individuals who bought government paper partly paid for with savings. To the extent that these represented actual savings on the part of individuals, they meant the avoidance of inflation. But this process of absorbing savings could not go on indefinitely. It soon ceased to represent a real reduction of consumption by individuals and led almost as directly as did the advances of the Bank to the issue of new currency which the Bank was forced to print. Loans, when they are issued on as large a scale as in France since 1914, result in inflation because they lead to deposit credits in many instances and eventually to the drawing of cash into general usage. Government securities become collateral for commercial loans or lead to deposit credits when they are paid off at maturity.[1]

It must be remembered that the French internal debt was already large at the outbreak of the war. Large additions, therefore, were possible only with the aid of inflation, which increased the nominal value of cash in the hands of individuals and caused them to respond more generously to the offer of government securities. Thus, the amounts which the government received as the result of its loan operations soon ceased to represent saving or sacrifice on the part of citizens and became merely a small deduction from the larger additions to the note circulation. In so far as this was true, loans ceased to be an alternative to inflation and became instead a roundabout means of inflation.

The connection between such loans and the inflation which they brought varied according to whether such loans were for a long or short time.[2] That part of the French debt, for instance, which was to run for ten years or more did not greatly increase the danger of depreciation.[3] Since the problem of the value of the franc was a short-time problem, as economists measure short time, there was a reason-

---

[1] See *supra*, Chapter III.   [2] Charles Rist, *op. cit.*, p. 78. See footnote.
[3] See appendix for detailed statement of French internal debt.

able expectation that the government would be able to pay
or refund the loans which did not come due till after the
liquidation of the reconstruction obligations. This expectation was stronger in view of the fact that the French had
always favored government loans and that the material
wealth of the nation had not been permanently impaired
by the war.[1] The short-time debt, on the contrary, was
urgent and menacing. Three- and five-year bonds brought
maturities at just the time when budget deficits were exceedingly large. Even more serious was the problem created
by the floating debt, which consisted mainly of the much
discussed *bons de la défense nationale*. It is interesting to
consider a statement of the composition of the public debt
at this point.

An analysis of Table XVI indicates that the floating
debt was by far the most dangerous element in the situation. This was true not only because of the fact that it
matured early, but also because of its size. It is obvious that
the perpetual and long-term debt was not a cause of worry
to finance ministers. Even when it was equal to 156 billion
paper francs in 1926, it was worth only about the same as
before the war on the basis of gold values or of commodity
prices. There was, therefore, no reason to suppose that the
burden was unbearable. The short-term debt of about 39
billion francs was slightly more troublesome. There had
been no such debt in 1913. The issues of the portion of the
internal debt which came to maturity soon after the war
led to great embarrassment on the part of the treasury. It
is probable, however, that even the troubles resulting from
such maturities as occurred in 1925 could have been faced
with calm if the floating debt had been manageable.

The floating debt consisted in part of the advances to the
state by the Bank of France, which have been already discussed,[2] but the greater part consisted of the *bons de la*

---

[1] Moulton and Lewis, *The French Debt Problem* (New York, 1925), pp.
424-429.   [2] See *supra*, Chapter V.

TABLE XVI

FRENCH PUBLIC DEBT [1]

1913–1927

(In millions of francs)

Date Dec. 31	Internal Debt				External Debt			Grand Total
	Perpetual Long Term	Short Term	Floating	Total	Po- litical	Commer- cial	Total	
1913	31,162	—	1,432	32,594	—	—	—	32,594
1914	31,966	—	7,462	39,428	—	510	510	39,988
1915	46,367	632	11,912	58,911	726	1,245	1,971	60,882
1916	57,756	427	20,214	78,397	3,355	4,098	7,453	85,850
1917	69,904	516	33,476	103,896	14,479	5,559	20,038	123,934
1918	97,248	531	43,015	140,794	23,074	6,208	29,282	170,076
1919	101,722	914	79,236	181,872	25,892	7,674	33,566	215,438
1920	133,176	423	81,593	215,192	29,192	6,767	35,959	251,151
1921	138,392	10,309	88,583	237,284	29,564	6,091	35,655	272,939
1922	134,042	26,835	89,207	250,084	29,996	5,448	35,444	285,528
1923	143,775	39,975	86,958	270,708	30,470	5,255	35,725	306,433
1924	146,511	46,636	87,490	280,637	31,048	5,431	36,479	317,116
1925	153,144	41,803	88,864	283,811	31,100	5,285	36,385	320,196
1926	156,856	38,796	93,545	289,198	31,764	4,782	36,743	325,941
1927	—	—	—	281,000			36,743	317,743

défense nationale. These reached the high point of nearly 64 billion francs in June, 1922. There is no doubt of the fact that they served a useful purpose when they were first introduced by Minister of Finance Ribot.[2] Since they were in small denominations and matured after short intervals—one month, three months, six months, or a year—they formed a convenient investment for funds temporarily idle; but for the same reason they formed a very uncertain element in the French financial structure.[3] Since much of the money invested in *bons* was not needed in industry merely because of seasonal fluctuations, or was money put aside temporarily awaiting more permanent investment, they were sub-

[1] Henry Chéron, *Rapport, Sénat, No. 84* annexe au procès-verbal de la séance du 22 fevrier 1926. This report gives figures for the years 1913-1925. The 1926 figures were received through the courtesy of the finance ministry. The figures for 1927 are based on statements found in *L'Europe nouville* (December 24, 1927 .

[2] See *supra*, Chapter III.

[3] Rist, *op. cit.*, p. 75. *"Toute nouvelle émission de bons constitue donc une émission potentielle de billets."*

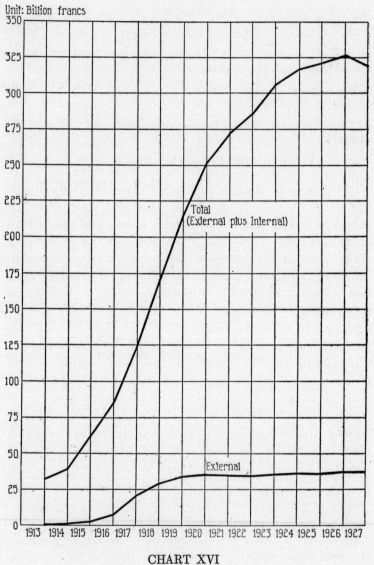

Unit: Billion francs

Total
(External plus Internal)

External

CHART XVI

FRENCH PUBLIC DEBT, 1913 TO 1927

ject to sudden fluctuations over which the government had little control. They were dominated sometimes by the needs of industry, again by the state of public confidence, or by money rates and price changes. Various influences had borne upon them, and there are a number of theories which account for their changes. The two most interesting of such theories are the theory of the *circuit fermé* and the *plafond unique*.

The Plafond Unique

The theory of the *plafond unique*—or the single limit—was fairly widely held but was not discussed at great length in theoretical writings of the time.[1] This is perhaps because it was generally discredited by economists. Nevertheless it must be taken into account here because of its bearing on the general attitude towards the solution of the debt question, inflation, and various budget projects. It was one of the reasons for the opposition to granting Caillaux extreme authority in 1926.[2] He was said to favor this view and was judged by many to be for this and other reasons too adventurous in finance. The essence of the theory was as follows. It was considered by some that the *bons de la défense,* because they were issued in small denominations of 100 francs—or even less at certain times—were used in paying debts as if they were cash. The further conclusion was then made that if the *bons* were equivalent to money, it would save the treasury considerable embarrassment if they were considered as such and freely exchangeable.[3] The term "single limit" was based on the plan of adding the amount of the *bons* to the legal limit of the note circulation and allowing the increase of paper notes up to that single limit. It was thought that the new total for Bank of France notes would not be reached because some would prefer to hold

---

[1] Bertrand Nogaro, *Finances et politique* (Paris, 1927), pp. 170–175. See also *Journal officiel, Chambre,* séance November 22, 1925, p. 3901.

[2] See *supra,* Chapter V, p. 194.   [3] Germain Martin, *op. cit.,* p. 376.

bons instead of notes. This was a matter of small importance, however, in the view of the holders of this theory. They did not fear any increase in prices from such additions to the note circulation since they thought that the *bons* were already pushing up the price level as much as would cash.

This theory is not one which has to be considered purely in the abstract. Observation and investigation throw some light on its validity. There are two reasons for rejecting the idea that the *bons* were used as money. The first is that when at any time, such as in January, 1924, or December, 1925, the idea got abroad that the government might not be able to repay the *bons* in cash, the result was a rush to the banks in the attempt to secure cash before such an event should take place. A state of mind such as this would indicate that the public did not consider the *bons* as good as cash in any sense. Then, a second reason for rejecting the above hypothesis is that based on the general observation of the extent to which *bons* circulated. This did not indicate any extensive use of the *bons* as money.[1] It is true that certain department stores, such as the *Printemps,* advertised that they would receive the *bons,* but the fact that they took pains to do so is evidence that such a practice was not usual.

In order to get a clearer understanding of the situation the writer made an experiment in January, 1926. She bought a *bon* worth a hundred francs running for one month. Before its maturity she tried to use it as payment in a number of stores. Her request was regarded as unusual, and she was refused in every case. Moreover, the post office where it was bought refused to buy it or discount it. A branch of the *Comptoir d'escompte* refused to take it at any price, even when asked to do so as a favor. It was finally accepted by a *Bureau de change* at a discount of one franc

[1] George-Edgar Bonnet, *Les Expériences monétaires contemporaines* (Paris, 1926), p. 94. "The *bon* is neither legally nor practically money."

and minus the interest of 25 centimes which was received when it was bought. It was disposed of only after proof of identity had been given, and a form signed with name and address. Such red tape for a sum equivalent to about four dollars seems to indicate that the *bons* do not pass readily in payment of debts.

The truth of the matter seems to have been that the *bons* were occasionally used in certain transactions, such as the transfer of real estate. Where the sums involved were fairly large, this was a natural procedure. It is also true that other securities were occasionally so used and even other forms of property, such as cattle. There is nothing very significant in such exchanges which approximate barter. There is no justification for assuming that the *bons* were like money.[1] The proposal to treat them as if they were equivalent to cash never entered seriously into any government proposal but did disturb public opinion occasionally. It brought with it the fears of unlimited inflation.

The Theory of the Closed Circuit

This theory, the *plafond unique,* brings us to a consideration of another related doctrine, the *circuit fermé.* This latter was more widely held, however, and had a greater degree of plausibility. Its general purport was a denial that the *bons* were a danger.[2] It emphasized not so much the need for getting rid of the *bons* through consolidation or liquidation but the comforting theory that the flow of money in and out of the investment in *bons* was a natural phenomenon and one which entailed no danger. It was like the *plafond unique* in that it scouted the extreme fears of inflation, but it differed in that it fixed attention on more fundamental matters at the base of the financial difficulties. It minimized the danger in allowing the circulation to respond to what were considered natural economic needs.

[1] Moulton and Lewis, *op. cit.,* pp. 137-138.
[2] See *supra,* Chart XI and Table XII.

The theory of the *circuit fermé,* or the closed circle, is one which rests upon the concept of the need of a definite amount of note circulation as an objective reality determined by independent economic conditions. It is suggestive in some ways of the ideas held by the Banking School in England; like this earlier theory, it stressed the needs of trade as the important factor in determining the volume of note circulation, rather than the importance of a definite numerical limit. The closed circle theory is, however, one especially applicable to the French case and not generalized for other countries. Even though its significance is thus limited, it throws interesting light on some of the broader problems of the relation of money to prices. For instance, it assigns to the debt and to the paper currency a subordinate position. M. Bonnet discussed the theory at some length in speaking of the short-term loans; he says:

By the very nature of these loans to the treasury, their renewal should be assured in a manner which is almost automatic. It is on this observation that the celebrated "theory of the *circuit*" rests: the sums of money drawn from the treasury are rediffused among the public who reinvest them and so on. Thus subscriptions should normally compensate for the maturities; and a large scale demand for repayments is not to be feared. The theory is exact if one takes care to specify that certain conditions are necessary for its operations.[1]

The conditions are so important, however, that if they are accepted the theory becomes a truism.

It is essential that the general level of prices shall not be so high as to call out a larger volume of monetary instruments; that confidence in the treasury be absolute; and that the fear of a rapid depreciation of the monetary unit be avoided.[2]

It is obvious that these conditions are so inclusive that they allow little room for change of any kind. In fact, the

[1] George-Edgar Bonnet, *op. cit.,* p. 106.
[2] *Ibid.,* pp. 106, 107.

acceptance of the conditions removes the need of any explanation of the stability of financial affairs which would be inevitable.

The theory of the *circuit fermé,* as much other abstract discussion, is best understood when considered in the light of the practical measures advocated in its name. One such measure was the plan of the reducing of the rate of interest paid on the *bons.* It was claimed by those who put forward this scheme that, since renewals were automatic in the very nature of the case, the state could well cut down the burden resulting from a high rate of interest. Since it was said that the money which the public withdrew from the *bons* accumulated in bank deposits, it was considered certain that the banks in their turn, looking for a short-time employment of these idle funds, invested a large part of them in *bons.* In this way the government quickly received the money again even when individuals withdrew it temporarily. Thus the yield on these investments was said to be a minor consideration. M. Loucheur, one of the first to put forward these ideas, was joined in his contention by M. Maroni, the very able financial writer of the *Journal des débats.*[1] The theory was criticized, on the other hand, by M. Décamps, head of the *Service des études* of the Bank of France.[2] He criticized the theory because it assumed that the price level was a factor determined independently of the amount of currency in circulation. He maintained, on the contrary, that the temporary increases in the circulation which came from the withdrawals of money from the *bons* might buoy up the level of prices so that the need for a larger circulation would become a permanent reality.

There seems to be considerable justice in M. Décamp's criticisms of the *circuit fermé.* Even if it is granted that the notes withdrawn from the *bons* return in one way or

---

[1] Germain Martin, *op. cit.,* p. 344. M. Loucheur in 1922 advocated the reduction of the interest on the *bons* on this ground.

[2] *Ibid.,* p. 347.

another to the treasury, it is a matter of great concern to
the government whether they return to it slowly or quickly,
and this matter is not covered by the theory in an adequate
way. It is a familiar fact that at certain times the money
withdrawn from government securities was turned over
very rapidly in commerce and as its velocity of circulation
increased, permitted more rapid changes in the level of
prices. Even if it be argued that the need for a larger circulation was responsible for this phenomenon, the fact
remained nevertheless that indirectly the *bons* increased
the amount of cash and allowed this need to be filled too
easily. The frequently maturing treasury *bons* were not a
cause, but they certainly were a responsive mechanism in a
time of increasing costs for foreign exchange and commodities. It is not possible to discuss here the relation of the
note circulation to prices, that is to say, the quantity theory.
It is sufficient to say that the money taken from *bons* was
used to buy goods and that when people generally distrusted *bons* they preferred goods. Thus, their demand for
goods increased and the price level rose, lessening considerably the possibility of investing large sums in government
loans at a later date. The interrelation between notes, *bons,*
and prices was certainly close, though the causality did
not run directly nor exclusively from the *bons* to prices.

M. Décamps, in opposing the reduction of the interest on
the *bons,* pointed out the two weakest points of the theory.
M. Germain Martin, who summed up this controversy
which had been carried on in the main in the public press,
joined Décamps in his conclusion that the renewals were
not automatic. He said:

In 1923 the increase in prices had the same result; it increased
the needs of the public and decreased the subscriptions to the
bons. But it is impossible to affirm that on the other hand the
decline in prices must inevitably bring about a return of this
capital to the treasury.[1]

[1] Germain Martin, *op. cit.,* p. 353.

He adds farther on:

If prices are permitted to rise under the influence of the exchanges, or for other causes, the purchasing power of the public, put aside in the form of *bons,* as the *bons* fail to be renewed, becomes an instrument not only for making permanent such a price increase but also for accentuating it in calling out inflation.[1]

The very great fluctuation in the *bons* in 1925,[2] which occurred after the publication of this discussion, seems to verify the conclusions drawn. The renewals were not automatic. The sums varied widely and this variation caused great difficulty to the treasury.

Such fluctuations could not have been lessened by the rate of interest paid. In fact, the unimportance of the rate became more and more apparent. This was true not so much for the reasons originally advanced by M. Maroni and others in the *circuit fermé* but because of the predominating influence of confidence in the government. The *bons* had been at the outset an alternative to inflation, since for a number of years they were a means of bringing back to the government many of the new notes issued. They had formed a less volatile element in the financial situation than either bank deposits or hoards, but they were never considered permanent investments. They resembled, rather, time deposits with banks which might be withdrawn on short notice. Furthermore, as the amount of the *bons* increased, the value of those which might be withdrawn each month increased proportionately. So, as time went on, the inflation, always potential in these *bons,* tended to become a reality. The public was able to call out large increases in the note circulation, if it judged that the various alternative uses were more productive than short-time investment with the government.

The *bons de la défense* offered no sure escape from infla-

---

[1] Germain Martin, *op. cit.,* p. 353.   [2] See *supra,* Chapter V, pp. 185–188.

tion despite the contentions of the advocates of the *circuit*. They absorbed idle cash, it is true, but they also yielded up such cash very readily when the public wished to use it for some other purpose. Official pressure made the *bons* a method of attracting to the treasury the funds of banks, insurance companies, and individuals, but their usefulness diminished as the emergency of war time passed. In fact, it is probable that a certain amount of inflation in 1923 and 1924 would have done less harm than did this uncertain mass of floating debt which was equivalent to coagulated circulation, since the money put into the *bons* did not represent savings. Long-time loans would have held a different place in economic life. They were fed, in part, at least, by savings, and were accompanied by a restriction of present consumption on the part of those who wished more wealth in the future. Such investments would have reduced the number of exchanges and might have made a real difference in total inflation and the value of the franc.

Pegging the Franc

The four main lines of protection for the franc—the use of the discount rate, legislation, deflation, and government loans—were of little avail. It is true that each served in a limited way to improve the situation for short periods, but none was able to check the downward course of the franc for any considerable time. There was a fifth means of control which was more efficacious, but it depended, as did the others, on favorable conditions; it was broader in scope and bore more directly on the value of money. This fifth method was pegging; it consisted of the use of foreign loans or deposits in such a way as to lessen or eliminate fluctuations in the value of the franc on the exchanges.[1] It meant that foreign credits were supplied to all comers at fixed rates,

[1] F. W. Taussig, *International Trade* (New York, 1927), pp. 378-380; and Edgar S. Furniss, *Foreign Exchange* (Boston, 1922), pp. 126-129.

and tended to lessen speculation and limit the demands for foreign money to the small volume growing out of trade and investment needs.

The success of pegging was closely linked with government finance; the favoring conditions varied, in 1917 American aid, in 1926 new political and financial effort. The objects also varied. In the first instance, during the war, the French government wished to prevent the fall of the franc. In the second important instance, in 1924, the government wished to rout speculators and to prevent the collapse of the franc, which threatened at that time. In the third instance, in 1926, the object was to prevent the sudden rise in the value of the franc. The two essentials in each case were a large supply of funds and confidence in the government's ability and determination. In these three cases cited, the government's efforts were rewarded by success. In a fourth instance, however, in the early summer of 1926, efforts to peg the franc were futile. The circumstances and significance of these various episodes must be considered briefly.

War-time pegging of the franc was natural and almost inevitable. It was for the good of belligerent and of neutral nations alike, that there should be as much stability as possible in monetary values and thus a ready interchange of goods. It is obvious that the franc would have fallen much more than twelve per cent [1] in the face of her heavy adverse balance of payments if no efforts had been made to supply the growing demand for foreign exchange. The unfavorable balance of visible trade during the war years amounted to more than 62 billion francs. A large part of this uncovered balance was met by borrowings abroad.[2] During 1914, about one hundred million dollars in loans

[1] See *supra*, Chapter III, pp. 99, 103.
[2] Moulton and Lewis, *op. cit.*, pp. 24-26 and 345-353. Professor Moulton estimates that about one billion francs was offset by export of specie. Loans made by France to her allies should be taken into account, for they in-

TABLE XVII
EXCESS OF IMPORTS OVER EXPORTS[1]
(in millions of francs)

1914	1,533
1915	7,098
1916	14,426
1917	21,541
1918	17,584
	62,182

was secured.[2] Further dollar credits amounting to 250 millions were secured in October, 1915.[3] Other loans increased the figure and made it possible for the French government to supply her merchants with exchange from 1914 to April, 1917.[4]

After the entrance of the United States into the war, the difficulty of pegging, which had increased with the rapidly growing volume of imports, was greatly lessened. In Germany the mark lost about sixteen per cent of its par value in 1916 and declined further in 1917 and 1918.[5] Although the depreciation of the mark was due to a number of factors, one of these was undoubtedly the absence of such loans as those which France enjoyed. The importance of these credits can hardly be exaggerated; they amounted to approximately three billion dollars and would have been larger if need had required. They made possible the stability of the franc during the war, and the very great increase of imports.

War-time pegging was natural, and so was the cessation of this unusual procedure when the hostilities were over.

---

creased the amount of the unfavorable balance. They are here given as amounting to ten billion francs.

[1] See appendix, and also Chapter I, *supra*.

[2] E. L. Bogart, *Direct and Indirect Costs of the Great World War* (London, 1919), p. 82. This netted only 240 million dollars, though the nominal sum was 250 millions. See *supra*, Chapter III.

[3] U. S. Senate, *Foreign Currency and Exchange Investigation*, p. 309.

[4] See *supra*, Chapter III, pp. 98, 103.

[5] U. S. Senate, *Foreign Currency and Exchange Investigation*, p. 531.

It is true that the transition was unnecessarily abrupt,[1] but pegging could not have continued indefinitely. It was too costly and difficult an undertaking to carry on except in case of urgent necessity. The sudden drop of the franc in March, 1919 is an indication of what might have happened during the war if there had been no government intervention. The extreme fluctuations of the succeeding months indicate that the government was unwilling or unable to exert this form of control.

It was not until 1924 that government intervention on the exchange markets occurred again on a large scale. This second use of foreign credits to support the franc was quite different from that during the war. The occasion was the deliberate attack of speculators who sought by repeated sales of francs to force the value of the franc to zero. Defensive methods called for the use of the speculator's weapons; it was clearly a case of fighting fire with fire. Fortunately, the government was able to secure funds abroad to match the flood of sales with purchases, and the speculators covered hurriedly; some even suffered bankruptcy in their inability to supply the francs they had sold short. Pegging in this instance, as during the war, would not have been possible if the government had been in a vulnerable position. During the war it was strengthened by United States support, and in the later crisis by increased taxation and the backing of certain banking houses.[2]

Pegging proved to be an effective means of fighting depreciation in 1924. It proved to be equally good in preventing appreciation in 1926 and 1927. Here again artificial control of values was possible to a certain extent because the more important economic or political considerations led to a renewal of confidence. This fact is brought out by a study of the fall of the franc in May, June, and July, 1926, despite attempts to support it on the exchange. The difficulty was due to the prevailing political distrust. Al-

[1] See *supra,* Chapter IV, pp. 127, 128.   [2] See *supra,* Chapter V, pp. 173-176.

though the government used considerable sums to buy francs, it could not prevent the rapid decline.[1] Then, the sharp reaction in favor of the franc at the end of July was due, not to the use of foreign credits, but to the return of confidence with the beginning of the Poincaré ministry.[2] It appears that pegging succeeded only when the credits at the disposal of the government were approximately equal to those used by others to buy or sell, and that the size of funds used by individuals to buy foreign exchanges was dependent on the state of public confidence.

Confidence returned with almost unbelievable suddenness when the union ministry under Poincaré was constituted. With the return of confidence the strongest motive for selling francs disappeared. The changed situation brought with it a new opportunity and a new danger. The opportunity was the ease with which the state could accumulate large holdings of foreign credits, disposed of by those who preferred domestic investment once more. Such holdings stood as a wall of defense against later possible speculative attacks on the franc. They took the place of the exhausted Morgan loan fund.[3] The danger was the possibility of industrial dislocation and depression in case of a sudden increase in the value of the franc. The opportunity and the dangers were met with one simple and yet extremely clever device. This proceeding resulted from the laws of August 3 and 7, which permitted the Bank of France to issue paper notes against exchanges in unlimited quantities.[4]

These laws, passed by the Poincaré government,[5] did not call for any great changes in economic life, nor any startling readjustment of public or private finance. They

---

[1] *Le Pour et le contre* (July 18, pp. 593, 594, and July 25, 1926, p. 670).
[2] See *supra,* Chapter V, p. 195.   [3] See *supra,* Chapter V, p. 197.
[4] J. Lockhart, *op. cit.,* pp. 27-29, see note 1; *Le Pour et le contre* (August 15, 1926), *Revue de science et législation financières* (October-December, 1926), vol. xxiv, no. 4, pp. 673, 674.
[5] See *infra,* Chapter X.

depended for their success on simple principles and on the force of political unity. Although it is true, for instance, that the government was empowered to adjust taxes by decree according to the changed value of the franc,[1] and that this was a new and extremely important provision, it did not involve a radical change in tax policy. Again, the establishment of the *caisse de gestion des bons de la défense nationale* did not alter the situation in a marked way. It was a step in advance, in that it established a procedure and an organization for handling the floating debt, but it was neither revolutionary nor novel in its essential outline. In the third place, the law which permitted the increase in the note circulation, in order to peg the franc, was merely an extension of its existing functions and was based on well-known principles of banking.

It was natural, for instance, to permit the Bank to increase issues of paper money when it was increasing its gold assets franc for franc. It was natural, moreover, that the privilege of increasing note issues made the actual increase unnecessary. The legal limit of the note circulation in August, 1926 was 58,500 million francs, at which point it had been fixed on December 4, 1925.[2] The number of notes in circulation touched its high point, 57,258, on August 5. It did not pass the limit set on December 4, 1925, during 1926 and 1927, despite the privilege of the law of August 7. There is every reason to believe that the number of notes in circulation was correctly revealed in the regular statements of the Bank of France. This seems obvious in view of the fact that there would be no strong motive for falsification with a considerable margin between the notes issued and the notes authorized under this provision. The circulation was, in fact, little more than 52 billion francs in Decem-

---

[1] *Revue de science et législation financières* (1926), vol. xxiv, no. 4, pp. 675, 676.

[2] *Journal officiel, Sénat,* séance of December 4, 1925, p. 1684. See discussion on pp. 1657–1684. See *supra,* Chapter V.

ber, 1926 as compared with a minimum of authorized circulation of more than 58 billions.[1]

Nevertheless, the importance of the new legal provision should not be underestimated. It was thanks to the increased margin that the Bank was able to carry on its extensive pegging operations. The purchases of foreign exchange were considerable; they amounted to approximately 20 billion francs in June, 1927.[2] These accumulations caused the Bank no embarrassment. The government had arranged in agreements, not made public, but generally known, to make good any loss due to the fluctuation in the value of exchange. Moreover, the immediate expense of the purchases was met by the creation of new notes and deposits.

The result of this pegging was the stability of the franc. Since the Bank of France absorbed all offers of foreign credits for francs at a fixed price, it was impossible for the franc to rise even though the sentiment was decidedly bullish. During the latter part of 1926 and 1927, the rates fluctuated within very narrow limits. The net change from day to day was comparable with that of the pound sterling which was then on a gold basis. All that was lacking at this time to make stability complete was an official announcement of a permanent rate of redemption for francs in gold or gold exchange. The postponement of such an announcement was probably due more to political than to economic causes.

The results of this *de facto* stability will be considered later in more detail.[3] They are seen in the slowing down of industry and commerce, as well as in the increased value

[1] See *infra,* appendix.

[2] The item *divers* in the Bank of France statement is the best indication of the varying size of these transactions. Smaller amounts of gold and gold credits were also included in other items under assets. *Divers* equaled more than 22 billion francs in the statement of June 30, 1927. See *divers* in appendix; see also *Le Pour et le contre* (July 3, 1927), p. 591.

[3] See *infra,* Chapter X, pp. 429-437.

of French securities and in other important factors. Some
of the more technical aspects of pegging the franc in 1926
and 1927 will be considered here. They illustrate the surprising importance of the nominal transfer of funds in
building up confidence, and in clarifying the financial situation. Some of these operations of the Bank of France and

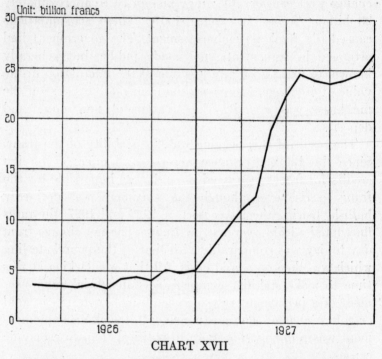

CHART XVII

MISCELLANEOUS ASSETS OF THE BANK OF FRANCE,
1926 AND 1927 [1]

the treasury seem, in fact, to amount to little more than
paper transfer of funds. Nevertheless, they made all the
difference between control of the financial situation and
extreme uncertainty.

The secret of the success of pegging the franc at this time
lay in the unlimited resources at the disposal of the Bank

[1] See appendix, p. 491, for figures.

of France under the new arrangement. These potential
resources, in the form of new notes, cost nothing unless they
were actually needed. Since they were not needed, the new
procedure was easy and painless. When the tendency of the
franc was upward, the purchase by the Bank of all the foreign exchange offered and the sale of francs prevented this
tendency from exerting any strong pressure on the exchange
rates; there was no logical limit to this procedure. The
actual limit, however, was set by the amount of credits
which the French had abroad in excess of their normal
credits, and by the funds with which foreigners wished to
speculate or invest in France. The results as indicated in
the Bank of France statements show that the funds were
large but not so great as to bring about any serious inflationary danger. The fears which some felt proved, in the
main, to be unwarranted, as is evidenced by the relative
stability of the note circulation of the Bank of France
throughout the period of pegging.[1]

It is interesting to trace the flow of funds from the Bank
to private individuals, to the treasury, and back to the
Bank. In this case, and for the period under consideration,
the circle seems to have been very nearly complete.[2] Although neither the government nor the Bank published a
full statement of its operations, one can follow them with
a certain degree of accuracy.

The following table based on the weekly statements of
the Bank of France shows how it was possible for the Bank
to accumulate its large holdings of foreign exchange without increasing the actual number of notes in circulation.
This table is not complete nor does it give actual figures,
in fact, it is greatly simplified in order to show as clearly as
possible the flow of funds. It is based on the statements
made to the writer at the ministry of finance, and cannot
be verified in any printed sources. The assets in the hands

[1] See *infra,* appendix.
[2] See *supra,* this chapter, the *circuit fermé.*

of the public are merely the counterpart of the liabilities
so listed.

TABLE XVIII
THE FLOW OF FUNDS

JUNE, 1926

	BANK OF FRANCE		PUBLIC	TREASURY
	Assets	Liabilities	Assets	Liabilities
Advances	36	..	..	36
Exchange holdings..	0	..	30	..
Deposits	..	..	..	..
Notes	..	52	52	..
Bons 1 year (or less)	..	..	49	49
" longer	..	..	40	40

JANUARY, 1927

	BANK OF FRANCE		PUBLIC	TREASURY
	Assets	Liabilities	Assets	Liabilities
Advances	26(—10)	....	....	26(—10)
Exchange holdings..	20(+20)	....	10(—20)	....
Deposits	....	10(+10)	20(+20)	10(+10)
Notes	....	52(— 0)	52(— 0)	....
Bons 1 year (or less)	....	....	44(— 5)	44(— 5)
" longer	....	....	45(+ 5)	45(+ 5)

The public surrendered:

Exchange	20 billion francs to the Bank
Notes, no net change	" " to Treasury back to Bank
Short term *bons*..........	5 " " to the Treasury
Total	25 " "

The public received in return:

Long term *bons*...........	5 billion francs
Deposits with Treasury and Bank	20 " "
Total	25 " "

The steps taken were as follows: the Bank offered paper
notes to Frenchmen who wished to sell exchange credits—
mostly dollars or pounds. This the bank was free to do
because of its unlimited right to expand the note circula-

tion to buy exchanges. The public then, with an unusual
amount of cash in hand, did one of several things. It either
deposited cash with the Bank of France, in which case the
note circulation was immediately reduced, or more probably accepted deposit credit instead of cash. If this were
not done, however, individuals holding cash either deposited
it with the treasury, which had granted new privileges in
the way of interest on deposits, or bought long-time (or
short-time) *bons* with the cash. One way or another, therefore, the treasury found large amounts accumulating in
cash. These it used, as is shown in the above table, to reduce
its debt to the Bank of France. The Bank thus found large
sums coming in cash from the treasury department, which
it devoted either to the purchase of exchange or to the
reduction of the note circulation.

In effect, then, the exchange was paid for by deposits.
The treasury department substituted private deposits for
its debt to the Bank, the Bank held exchange reserves offset
in part by deposits, and by the decrease in its advances.
The system worked beautifully, several very important
results were attained without any considerable cost. In the
first place, the franc was kept stable. In the second place,
the Bank accumulated large gold credits with which it could
combat any possible speculative movement against the
Bank, and in the third place, the treasury repaid a considerable part of its borrowings from the Bank, which increased
confidence in the government position.

There were, of course, certain dangers, but these never
materialized. It is obvious, for instance, that if private depositors had suddenly withdrawn their money from the
Bank or the treasury, the treasury would have had to secure
further advances from the Bank, and the Bank would have
been forced to increase the note circulation. There was no
such general demand, however, because of the prevailing
optimism and because prices were relatively stable. Moreover, if there had been such a tendency to withdraw funds,

it is probable that the Bank could have sold exchange and the treasury could have sold securities either to the individuals or to banks in which individuals left their cash. To this simple yet effective mechanism, therefore, must be attributed both the ease with which France entered on a period of stability and the growing assets which fortified the position of the franc. This whole process is a form of pegging and one peculiarly well adapted to French financial life. It was not new in principle, but it was original in this particular form and operation.

The fight against depreciation passed through many discouraging phases. It was finally won by means of a political unity and of simple yet ingenious financial schemes. The novelty of the French situation was one of the difficulties in the way of constructive finance. The discount rate, tried in some instances, was found to be an erratic and uncertain instrument because of the unusual psychological and price situation. Laws against speculation were tried and found wanting because they ran counter to very strong economic interests. Deflation, a natural procedure to adopt to strengthen the value of money, was too violent a remedy and merely led to later inflation. Loans, used when possible, to avoid large note issues, led indirectly to further increases in the circulation. Pegging was partly successful, but it proved ineffectual, until the political truce had been won and a strong policy restored public confidence. The conclusion to be drawn from this series of efforts and failures is that the value of money is a delicate thing, that none of the usual forces bearing upon it can be counted to act in the expected and normal way if public opinion has been reduced to panic by severe depreciation. The remedy must strike first at the heart of the disease, must show that determination and force are united to one end, and that a coördinated policy of some sort has been begun. The nature of the policy is often of less importance than the resolute manner in which it is undertaken.

CHAPTER VII

Price Changes

INTERNAL depreciation is a very different thing from external depreciation.[1] The rise of commodity prices in any country has a wider immediate significance than the rise of the price of foreign exchange. Everyone regrets the addition of a few centimes to the cost of a loaf of bread or a pair of shoes, but very few care if the pound sterling gains a few francs in value. It is true that the exchange rate comes to have a very important influence on economic life both directly and as a determinant of public opinion and economic forecasts, but this is true only after commodity price changes have been keenly felt during months or years.

Nevertheless, discussions of depreciation usually focus on the exchange rates rather than on prices. This dates from the very early debates on currency problems.[2] There are a number of reasons why this has been the case. In the first place, the difficulty of measuring and expressing price change is very great. The exchange rate, on the other hand, expresses clearly and incontrovertibly the value of money in terms of another money in a highly specialized market.[3] There is no question of the validity of figures based on the

---

[1] League of Nations, *Memorandum on Currency and Central Banks*, 1913-25 (Geneva, 1926), vol. ii, p. 125.

[2] J. W. Angell, *The Theory of International Prices* (Cambridge, Mass., 1926), p. 58. "Ricardo seems to come close to the purchasing-power-parity doctrine." Ricardo generally discussed the gold premium rather than the price rise when considering depreciation. He is not always consistent in this, for in his chapter on international trade, and at some points in his essays and letters, he uses the notion of a general change in prices.

[3] External depreciation will be discussed in Chapter VIII.

exchange quotations,[1] whereas index numbers which attempt to express in simple form the changes of a fluctuating mass of values are subject to uncertainty and doubt. The index number of wholesale prices, for instance, is not the obvious measurement of a concrete reality, but it is a sophistication which varies as different mathematical formulæ are used and different articles chosen. The index number is useful and sufficiently exact to show general changes of monetary values from year to year. It cannot, as does the exchange rate, show even the general fluctuations from week to week and day to day.

Then, in addition to this, the forces which bear on the internal value of a money are complex and varied. It is impossible to get a mathematical expression which includes all value changes. Such an inclusive expression, even if it could be found, would mean nothing.[2] The measure of price change therefore depends on the choices alluded to above, that is, the mathematical formula and the commodities to be included. Under the best of circumstances one cannot make allowances for altered costs of production, changes in grades and qualities, sudden freaks of demand, and other varied influences which lie behind an upward or downward movement of prices. They can neither be disregarded nor taken completely into account. Moreover, there can be no par in the case of prices. One cannot say that there is a normal price for a pair of shoes or a loaf of bread. It is impossible to take into consideration all the elements of cost, all conditions of demand, and extract from them a clear and definite result. The most one can say is that shoes cost so much at a given date, or that bread should not vary by a wide margin from the cost of wheat. Recent statistical studies have tended to invest the year 1913 with a special

[1] The quotations represent actual transactions.
[2] A. A. Young, "Fisher's 'The Making of Index Numbers,'" *Economic Problems New and Old* (Boston, 1927), pp. 296, 297. Professor Young states that as a matter of pure theory the problem of index numbers "cannot be completely solved."

significance and "normality" merely because it was the year before the war.[1] It is obvious as time goes on that a prewar basis of comparison becomes less and less significant. There is no reason to hope or expect a return to prewar conditions. New inventions, new desires, new balances of class interests, and new standards of living have made a profound and lasting difference. It may be that some prices will return to a 1913 level, but if so it will be largely a matter of chance; the prewar level is in no sense a standard of what should or will recur.

On the other hand, the value of the franc in terms of gold is a definite fact. At any given time the relationship of the franc to gold standard currencies is simple and fairly exact; it is possible to talk of a percentage decrease in terms of gold with mathematical precision. It is true that gold in its turn may vary in terms of goods, but the simple ratio of gold to paper money none the less persists.

In the second place, we find a reason for the emphasis of the exchange rates as a measure of depreciation in the characteristic traits of popular opinion. It is obvious, for instance, that people in general consider the rise of prices as a phenomenon quite apart from changes in currency value. This fact was strikingly evident during the war when almost all the increase in the cost of living was blamed on profiteers. Even after years of depreciation and after the general development of an exchange consciousness in France, there was talk about a disproportionate increase in costs. When a good four course dinner could still be bought for five gold francs, people complained because it cost twenty-five paper francs.

There is, of course, constant interaction between external and internal depreciation, between prices and exchange

---

[1] The Bureau of Labor Statistics and Irving Fisher changed the base for the index numbers of wholesale prices from 1913 to 1926 in January, 1928, a change which is an expression of the relative character of the "base year" here indicated.

rates, but there is less parallelism than has sometimes been assumed.[1] Katzenellenbaum says

> At any given moment *the degree* of depreciation of money with regard to commodities need in no way correspond with the degree of depreciation of money with regard to the foreign exchange.[2]

Those who hold the purchasing power parities doctrine do not admit that a sharp distinction in the treatment of the two aspects of depreciation is necessary. Those who, on the contrary, think that the rise of prices and the rise of the exchanges are two different results of a common disturbance to financial life consider the distinction important.[3] The frequent divergence of the two effects and the wide differences which can persist for considerable periods make a separate treatment not only possible but imperative.

War-time Price Increases Not Surprising

Various causes have conspired to raise the cost of living and price levels the world over in the past fifteen years. At first, probably, scarcity and the fear of scarcity; then, later, monetary disorders helped to accentuate the upward movement. Great changes were experienced—speculation became a conscious element in action, and dealers held goods for expected rises.

The situation in 1914 and 1915 was comparatively simple. From the very outbreak of the war prices rose, because of interruptions to transportation, risks, actual scarcity, and other reasons. Inflation was an important factor in the situation, but at the very beginning it was hardly more than a passive factor. It seems probable, for instance, that if there had not been an increase in the number of bank notes either

[1] S. S. Katzenellenbaum, *Russian Currency and Banking, 1914–1921,* p. 16. "This parallelism, which attracts many economists, has, however, no real existence.   [2] *Ibid.,* p. 16.

[3] Bertrand Nogaro, *La Monnaie et les phénomènes monétaires contemporaines* (Paris, 1924), p. 178.

a change in the velocity of circulation, or an expansion of book credits would have served the same purpose. A continued price increase from various causes, to an extent greater than the increase in currency, has occurred in most countries in the last fifteen years.

During the early period of depreciation, 1914-19, as has been already noted, the divergence between internal and external depreciation was very great. At the close of the war, with the sudden release of control, the exchange began to register a depreciation almost as great as that indicated by the wholesale price index. After many sharp fluctuations, prices and foreign exchange rates came into fairly close agreement in 1926. The two measures of depreciation both registered a loss of value of more than 500 per cent as compared with 1913.[1] This harmony helped to furnish a basis for stabilization. From the beginning of 1927 exchanges for several months were nearly stable, while the price indices recorded some fluctuations. This was a natural aftermath of the times of erratic exchange movements.

Through all the troubled years after 1919 the exchange was the most delicate barometer of impending events in the economic and financial world as it affected France. Its significance comes in large measure from its indication of the future purchasing power of money in goods. The value of one money in terms of another has a definite significance both for the speculator and the investor, but the value of money in goods affects more people and to a greater degree.

It should not be inferred from the above comment on price fluctuations that absolute stability is to be expected or desired. It is even too much to expect perfectly compensating increases and decreases of prices such as would lead to stability as expressed by an index number. A degree of

---

[1] If account is taken of the influence of the exchange on prices, the range of price increase for 1926 was between 108 and 132 per cent of 1914; that is, internal depreciation was greater by so much. (*Service des études de la Banque de France.*)

stability,[1] however, such that wholesale prices do not vary
more than five or ten per cent a year, is of the utmost importance to the economic world. The net change in prices
which occurred in England in the hundred years after the
Napoleonic wars amounted to about forty per cent.[2] This
was equivalent to an average of about one-half of one per
cent a year. It is true that it was not spread evenly over the
century. There were several sharp rises and declines, notably
the one which took place after 1848, but if allowance is made
for several sudden breaks one may say that for the larger
part of the period this change was fairly even and regular.
The situation in England was typical of that in other countries. In general, one may say that the change did not make
a very great difference to consumers, with the exception of
certain periods, for small increases spread over time do not
in actual fact make as much trouble as theorists often claim.
The investor, for example, is constantly shifting and adapting himself to new conditions; the consumer rearranges his
budget; the wage earner is apt to receive higher wages with
promotion and a growing experience and so can absorb some
of the difference this way. The man who has retired on his
savings suffers, it is true, but his loss is not so great as to
make a profound impression on economic life. If financial
panics can be avoided and if unemployment does not take
place on any large scale, these gradual trends of prices do
not make a very great difference. Escape from rising prices
is possible through the choice between commodities, between investments, and the ability of the wage earner to
fight for some slight increase in wages. And slowly rising
prices, if output expands sufficiently, may be accompanied

[1] Gustav Cassel, *Money and Foreign Exchange After 1914* (New York,
1923), p. 254. Cassel, Keynes, Hawtrey, and all the more important writers
on monetary theory seek the same goal but different means of attaining it.

[2] J. M. Keynes, *Monetary Reform* (New York, 1924), p. 18. The low
point of purchasing power 61 in 1815 contrasts with the high point of 104
in 1883. Compare Richard T. Ely, *Outlines of Economics*, fourth edition
(New York, 1923), p. 320.

by stable or even by rising real wages. The figures of price differences as one adds and substracts them on paper make no allowance for these choices and adjustments. Finally, it is notable that the monetary changes of the past have often been accompanied by an increase in general prosperity.[1]

Quite other than this is the effect of great price increases, such as the war brought. Then the differences were twenty and thirty per cent a year; there was no way of adjusting one's manner of living without serious loss. Certain classes of the population, of course, reaped benefits where others lost, but the net result was seen in grave economic dislocation and harm. Where differences are great, unusual gains going into the pockets of some individuals do not offset the losses which fall on the mass of the population. The high profits to which rapidly rising prices lead often bring about an increase of middlemen and of useless speculation. Then, the investor can find no way out except by buying speculative shares, which leads the ignorant into many disastrous ventures. The consumer attempts to anticipate further increases in prices by stocking up with goods, or submits to it by lowering his standard of living to the point of real privation. The wage earner, as a matter of fact, has stood the recent price changes comparatively well; the effects have fallen mainly on the middle classes. Even though in France these effects work themselves out slowly and sometimes inconspicuously, they can be traced in the changes in education and professional life, the loss of some aspects of moral and financial stability, and in a lessening of the economic independence which has been characteristic for a considerable period. It is probable that France has not lost more than have some other countries where depreciation was met in different ways, as for instance, Germany or Italy. Even if this be true, however, it should be remembered that the in-

---

[1] During the last part of the nineteenth and the beginning of the twentieth century in France, as well as in England, the United States, and pretty generally, a rising price level was accompanied by unusual prosperity.

dustrial situation of France in the decade just before the
outbreak of the war was unusually propitious. In addition
to positive losses, therefore, one must count the progress
foregone.

Price fluctuations that come from changes in industrial
technique and changes in demand are inevitable, and not
necessarily harmful; those which come from sudden changes
in the volume of money and credit are apt to be disrupting
and harmful. It is interesting to try to show the difference
between the two sets of phenomena. Of course, it is not
always possible to prove conclusively that one or the other
is operative, but the study of the relative movement of different commodities shows something as to this. For instance,
when prices are tending in different directions—that is,
about as many falling as rising, even though the increases
may be greater in extent than the decreases—it is *probable*
that the cause is primarily not inflation. In order to cast
light on such an inference, a study of the frequency distributions of price relatives and a summary of the gains and losses
will be given later in this chapter.[1] A study of the curves
gives credence to the view that when the preponderance of
the movements, though slight, is all in one direction, the
cause has probably been an expansion of money and credit.
There is need for much further analysis than has been attempted here in order to understand fully the part played by
inflation.

The general nature of recent price increases is familiar;
they are similar to prewar changes except for the influence
of the very great variations of the exchange rates. As was
usually the case, there was a stimulus to production, the increase of paper profits despite high interest rates, the lag of
retail prices behind wholesale, and a tendency for the gap
between the two to close each time wholesale prices reacted
downward. The cause of price increases has been more complex than has been generally admitted, however. At certain

[1] See *infra,* this chapter, pp. 314, 315.

times it was mainly the government demand for goods, at others, internal inflation and rising incomes, then again the exchanges gave an upward push through the cost of imports, and risk and speculation increased costs in various ways.

The theoretical implications of the French experience are not always clear. For the war, the facts seem to justify a simple application of the quantity theory. For the later years one needs a more complex explanation, putting more stress on the psychological factors. It is well to recall that the struggle over the quantity theory divides opinion into two main groups—those who feel it wise to qualify the theory to such an extent that it fits any possible situation, and those who reject it entirely because they cannot find in it either a means of prediction or a guide for control. There are others, a group which is becoming more numerous as attention is increasingly focused on monetary affairs, who admit a certain general relationship but deny that the theory can really *explain* either the causal sequence of events in the past or the short-time fluctuations of more recent years. Modifications and qualifications are dependent upon placing a great importance on velocity of circulation. This last is an interesting aspect of the monetary problem, but it must occupy the place of x in the equation and take up the slack not accounted for by changes in the volume of currency and credit. Velocity of circulation is the outward manifestation of confidence, of estimates of the future value of money. It is as flexible as the very opinions of the people, once they have been shocked from their normal habits. It has not been profoundly altered in the case of France [1] as it was in the case of Germany, Austria, and Russia, but the fact that it might have become so at any moment is an element of weakness in the quantitative method of approach for those seeking a guide for policy or prophecy.

In the years immediately after the war, the lessons which

[1] Exception should be made for a few weeks in July, 1926.

the quantity theory offered to statesmen were not at once
realized. The efforts at deflation,[1] while based on consciousness of the menace of the large volume of notes in circulation, showed a complete misunderstanding of the more
remote implications of the theory. It was assumed that the
government could bring about a return to normal economic
life by a series of mechanical contractions in the circulating
medium. As the difficulties in such a policy became more apparent, the conflicting interests of those who wished prices
to rise and those who wished them to fall expressed themselves in the keen political battle of 1924-26. This battle
was focused around programs for tax increases as directly
bearing on the monetary situation.[2] Experience during
these years taught the French that the quantity theory must
be applied to practical affairs, with a due consideration of
all the influences. In 1924, for instance, it was not actual inflation that broke the franc; again, in 1925, fear of inflation
exaggerated the effect of the actual increases made.[3] Moreover, it was the exchange value of the franc which led to
internal depreciation, and the quantity theory cannot account directly for this aspect of money value. Behind this
depressing influence lay the budget situation, and still further back in the line of causation lay the political conflicts
which made vigorous action difficult. Looking then to stability which succeeded depreciation, we see that it was based
on an improved political situation and a cessation of party
warfare. Prices became steady as well as exchange rates,
as soon as a constructive government policy became possible.

The relation of prices, exchange rates, and note issues differed during the successive phases of depreciation which
have already been indicated.[4] Five such phases can be distinguished both from the changing nature of the curve
of prices and a general analysis of economic relationships. It
is well to repeat these divisions here.

---

[1] See *supra*, Chapters V and VI.   [3] See *supra*, Chapter VIII.
[2] See *supra*, Chapter V.   [4] See *supra*, Chapter IV.

I. The war period: 1914–18
II. Cyclical period: 1919–21 [1]
III. The reparation struggle: 1922–23
IV. Speculation and realization: 1924–26
V. Stability: 1926–28

While there is some room for question as to where the lines of demarcation should be drawn, there is no reasonable doubt as to the changing character of the relationships and the growing dominance of exchange rates over prices. The first period is obviously distinguished by war measures. The second is marked by the influence of the world price movement on France. The two subsequent divisions are notable because of the growing importance of exchange rates in determining the course of prices and the increase of speculation. During the years from 1922 to 1926 the cost of the dollar came to be the main indicator of, and reason for, price changes. This came about, on the one hand, because of the various effects of the flight of capital on internal production and finance, and on the other hand, because of the increasing consciousness of depreciation and the deliberate attempt to adjust internal prices to gold prices.

Professor Aftalion, in his book *Monnaie, prix et change,*[2] bases his analysis on the changing relation of prices and note circulation. Although his treatment differs slightly from that given here, it agrees on the most important points of the interpretation. The war period, he says, was characterized by the general agreement of the price changes with the increasing note circulation.[3] In the years 1919 and 1920 there was a partial agreement between the two factors;[4] in 1920 and 1921[5] there was an almost complete disagreement between prices and the note circulation, due to the cyclical movement alluded to above. In the years 1922–24, on the other hand, the divergence of the two was at-

---

[1] The use of the word *cyclical* should not be taken to imply the acceptance of any theory of business cycles.

[2] Albert Aftalion, *Monnaie, prix et change* (Paris, 1927).

[3] *Ibid.*, p. 10.   [4] *Ibid.*, p. 13.   [5] *Ibid.*, p. 21.

tributable to the foreign exchange values.[1] The final period, which Professor Aftalion distinguishes, 1925 and 1926,[2] was marked by increasing harmony between the note circulation and prices. This study is based on a careful quantitative study of the actual facts and has been made the starting point of a searching criticism of the quantity theory. It differs in emphasis from the analysis made here in that it takes as a starting point the changing volume of the note circulation, whereas we stress prices in the first instance. It should be noted in particular that the agreement claimed for 1925 and 1926 really exists only in regard to the net changes during those years, and not the week to week or month to month fluctuations.

The General Upward Trend

The span of years from 1914 to 1927 was one of unprecedented change. During that period the index number of wholesale prices moved from 100 to a high point of 854 in July, 1926, and settled to relative stability at about 650. If a straight line curve were drawn from 100 in 1914 to 650 in 1928 many of the points of actual price indices would fall on or about such a line. The notable exceptions are that already mentioned for 1926 and an earlier high point of 600 in 1920, and a third sharp fluctuation in 1924. These three sharp rises, followed by reactions, broke the otherwise steady trend. The various other measures of internal price changes, the retail index, and the cost of living figures, are in partial agreement with the wholesale index, showing the lag which one is accustomed to expect. The figures for the fourteen years under consideration are given on page 510.

The close agreement of the price increases with the changes in the note circulation during the war years was commented on in Chapter III.[3] To a certain extent the

[1] Albert Aftalion, *op. cit.*, p. 18.   [2] *Ibid.*, p. 54.
[3] See *supra*, Chapter III and Charts I and IV.

changes in the quantity of money in circulation may be properly considered the cause of the price movement. There was, on the other hand, a complete lack of agreement between the internal and external values of the franc. While the franc was losing its command over goods in France, it was maintaining a large part of its purchasing power of goods in other countries. This is evidenced by the cost of the dollar in francs, which was approximately 116 per cent of par,[1] due, in large measure, to the pegging operations of the government.[2] But the fact that it could be maintained in spite of internal depreciation is interesting and instructive. Emphasis is frequently placed on the necessary harmony between different aspects of the value of money; it is not always realized that there can be serious lack of harmony persisting through a number of years. Recent events have made it plain, however, that the forces dominating the interior and the exterior value of money are frequently different, even though the two may come into agreement at the end of a considerable period, as they did in France in 1927.

There were four main factors which conditioned price increases during the war.[3] The first and most obvious was the inelastic demand of the government for certain commodities. The second was the redistribution of income and the consequent change in consumption and demand due to the government interference in production and to the various sudden changes resulting from the war. The third was scarcity, enhanced by invasion, submarine warfare, and other such events. The fourth, which operated in the contrary direction, was the attempt at price control.[4] The first three influences were jointly responsible for the increase in prices, but it is impossible to assign to each its respective

---

[1] Aftalion, *op. cit.*, p. 11. See also exchange figures in appendix.

[2] See *supra*, Chapter III.

[3] Compare these factors with the earlier discussion of war conditions, Chapter III.   [4] See *supra*, Chapter III.

importance; they were all, at the same time, the result and the cause of the inflation of the note circulation. Price control, on the other hand, tended to moderate the upward movement of commodity prices, though it probably served mainly to delay changes which eventually took place.

The factors behind price increases have been characterized as quasi-monopolistic by Lucien March in his detailed study of the war price situation.[1] He distinguishes the effects of war conditions from the interference of the government through taxation, price fixing, and other means. For instance, one might suggest the closing of certain markets, notably in international trade, the limitation of the supply of certain commodities, and the artificial power to raise prices which war conditions gave to some manufacturers and sellers. These would come under our third heading, scarcity. His comparison of the conditions during war and those under monopoly is valuable in that it indicates the importance of the demand side of value, which we have already stressed. It is obvious that during these years normal considerations based on cost of production ceased to have their accustomed weight.

The concrete expression of this imperative demand, we have said, was the expansion of the note circulation. Since new bank notes were spent, and since the velocity of circulation appears to have been normal, the increases in the price level approximately corresponded to the growth of the means of payment.

The Cyclical Price Movement

The end of the war brought fundamental changes in the factors governing the value of the franc. The second period

---

[1] Lucien March, Honorary director of the *Statistique générale, Mouvement des prix et des salaires pendant la guerre* (Carnegie Foundation Study, Paris, 1922), pp. 9, 10. He gives a detailed and thoroughly documented history of prices during the war years.

of depreciation was marked by very sharp and sudden price reactions, which corresponded neither with the changes in the note circulation nor with changes in the rates paid for foreign money. These were "cyclical" movements, corresponding to price movements in other countries and taking on the characteristic sequences and wavelike form which have long been familiar, though in this case it should be noted that the span of the "cycle" was shorter than the seven to eleven years which economists have considered typical.[1]

The causes behind the price movement were various, although it is not easy to point to any one predominant cause. In regard to the first upward swing of prices, it should be noted, in the first place, that the relaxation of war regulations was the natural preliminary to some adjustment of prices to the changed conditions in various lines of production. Thus, other readjustments probably took place, such as the spending of money by those who had deprived themselves of necessities for a number of years, but who felt such privation could not continue indefinitely and bought what they needed, hoping somehow they could find the money to pay.[2] Speculation, in the broad sense of the word, had much to do with the price increase.[3] In so far as the movement originated in the United States, it was due in part at least to the overestimate in that country of Europe's power to buy. The need for reconstruction goods was obvious, the ability to pay was assumed. In the face of these influences, the cessation of the government's pressure for goods had surprisingly little effect; certainly the influence of this factor was ignored, and so its effect was delayed for almost

---

[1] See *supra*, Chapter IV.

[2] Professor Rist (interview, May, 1927) said that many people who had been living on reduced incomes during the war spent a part of their capital at the close of the war, thinking they could replace it during the expected years of prosperity.

[3] See *supra*, Chapter IV. Reference is here made to the boom attitude of mind which existed in 1919.

a year. Nor was the rapid upward rush of prices halted by the relative lack of inflation in 1919. Some of these aspects of the economic happenings of 1919 have never been completely explained.

Four factors, which were in the main peculiar to France, may well be mentioned again. These were those given as explanations by M. Décamps, namely, large purchases of land, the use of *bons de la défense* as money, the eight-hour day, and reorganization due to peace conditions and reconstruction. These have been discussed in Chapter IV;[1] it is probable that the use of the *bons* and the eight-hour day had less effect than the other two influences. Certainly, there is no clear evidence that the *bons* were a frequent substitute for money, or that the shorter work day led to higher labor costs.[2] However this may be, explanations of the price rise are numerous, and no *one* cause is to be found.

The actual course of price indices should be noted at this point. Immediately after the armistice the wholesale index fell slightly, until it was ten per cent lower in May, 1919 than it had been in November, 1918.[3] Immediately thereafter began the steady rise which has been discussed above, and which reached its peak in April, 1920. The upward movement in the preceding few months had been very rapid. The retail index, which had lagged behind the wholesale index during the war, did not show the same rapid climb. On the other hand, it continued its upward movement longer than the wholesale index, and did not reach its high point until November, 1920, when it stood at 426. The wholesale index was only a small fraction above this value when the retail index turned downward. It is interesting to note that the index number for food products alone paralleled closely the retail index during the postwar months. March brings

[1] See *supra,* Chapter IV.

[2] It should be noted in this connection that there were many exceptions to the eight hour law, which made it inoperative in a majority of cases at this time.   [3] See table, p. 507.

out this fact but it is of limited significance, since the retail index is composed mainly of food products.[1] The index number for wages followed the movement of both, but at a slower pace. The cost of living index moved steadily upward throughout the postwar years, even after wholesale prices fell in 1920, indicating a certain artificiality in the downward movement of commodity indices.

The fall of prices from April, 1920 on was as rapid as the rise had been. The situation had the earmarks of a panic, even though it must be admitted that the disrupting effect on production was much less than might have been expected from such dramatic changes of values. Both banking conditions and the production of basic materials showed surprising stability in the face of the crisis.[2] Economic conditions at this time have been discussed in Chapter IV. It is sufficient to add here that prices were not the guide to enterprise, to the usual extent, they were rather a contradictory and interfering force which did not entirely prevail over other factors, though they had an undoubted influence.

The sudden reaction downward has been partially explained in the discussion of general conditions in 1920.[3] The cause was directly or indirectly the determination to deflate credit and currency which was evidenced in all countries, but it was "timed" by the collapse of the Japanese silk market and prices of clothing materials in the United States. The channels through which prices were affected were mainly speculative. Interpretations, fears, forecasts, led to sudden selling movements and the bottom seemed to drop out of the commodity markets. In other words, it is necessary to turn to the psychological line of influence to explain the very close synchronization of price

[1] L. March, *op. cit.*, pp. 233, 234, and also pp. 300, 301.
[2] The Dessirier Index shows a slight increase in production through 1919-21. *Bulletin de la statistique générale* (October, 1924), pp. 73, 84.
[3] See *supra*, Chapter IV.

movements in different countries which took place at this
time.

The downward movement continued into 1921. One result was the tendency to bring together the wholesale and
retail indices, which stood at 385 and 382 on a 1914 base in
February, 1921. Then they moved together in the first
months of recovery until the rapid rise in the wholesale index again opened up a gap, which was not closed until 1926.
The lag between the two indices, judging by the turning
points, seems to have been about seven months, though no
exact statement in this regard is warranted by the study of
this short period of fourteen years.

THE RELATION OF PRICES AND COMMERCE

It has been said above that the harmony of world price
movements was due to the force of speculation. Let us
consider briefly the alternative channel of influence, international trade. If we examine the changing volumes of
commerce,we see that there was indeed a marked reaction of
trade, but that this reaction was not so much a cause as
an accompaniment of other changes in economic life. That
is, the swing of the price level occurred more quickly and
went farther than did the change in trade, though the movements of the latter were generally in the direction which
one is led to expect. In the first place, the rather erratic
movement of the figures for excess of imports over exports
indicates that various factors were influential at this time,
and that no close relationship between the price movement
and trade can be posited. Then, secondly, the sharp decline
of the franc would lead one to expect an increasingly favorable balance of trade for France, but no such marked tendency is obvious. The increase in both exports and imports
was notable in February, but the excess of imports changed
only slightly. Thus one does not find the steadily increasing
volume of exports which the simplest application of foreign

trade theories might lead one to expect. Then, in the third place, if one is to assume that a price movement originating in the United States spread to France, one would expect for one reason or another a large volume of cheap imports into France, depressing the French price level. But, on the contrary, if one notes the value per ton in foreign commerce it is evident that although imports became slightly cheaper in francs, they were more costly in dollars. But even so the volume did not decline as fast as one might expect. More-

TABLE XIX

FRENCH FOREIGN TRADE [1]

1920

(000 omitted)

	IMPORTS		EXPORTS		EXCESS OF IMPORTS	
	Quantity, Metric Quintals	Value, Francs	Quantity, Metric Quintals	Value, Francs	Quantity, Metric Quintals	Value, Francs
1919 Dec ...	93,434	5,589,838	28,577	3,217,600	64,857	2,372,238
1920 Jan	26,622	3,577,085	4,492	1,245,400	22,130	2,331,685
Feb	34,387	4,454,448	10,259	2,150,784	24,128	2,303,664
Mar ...	42,084	5,225,921	8,989	2,100,869	33,095	3,125,061
Apr ...	39,003	4,865,959	10,364	2,110,093	28,639	2,755,066
May ...	39,102	4,005,824	7,578	1,842,674	31,524	2,163,150
Jun	43,908	4,417,561	13,553	2,805,512	30,355	1,612,049
Jul	50,276	4,102,825	10,567	2,097,415	39,709	2,005,410

over, although the value of exports per ton, on a gold basis, declined, there was no steady decrease. In other words, foreign trade seemed to be to a certain extent independent both of the exchange rates and of the price movements in the two countries. Certainly there was no powerful influence on French prices through commerce at this time. This is understandable in view of the fact that the revision of prices for international commodities is not necessarily immediate, and that goods might often sell in some markets above or below their general value. Certainly the changes which took place were not great enough to bring on the

[1] U. S. Senate, *Foreign Currency and Exchange Investigation*, p. 484.

reversal of prices. There is no indication that the gold value of imports changed more markedly than the gold value of exports, and therefore no hint that commerce with the United States depressed French prices.

Considering the flow of commerce for the year 1920 as a whole, the notable fact is that for the first time since 1914 the combined values of the franc in terms of dollars and of commodities in terms of francs gave a bonus to export trade; in other words, the franc was worth less than purchasing power parities justified, and gold prices in France were falling. Nevertheless, the excess of imports in weight for the year was higher than in 1919. The difference was certainly not great, but was enough to indicate that commerce was not responding to foreign exchange rates in the way one would have expected, and did not in its turn affect prices to any great degree. On the contrary, one sees that after the price decline in terms of paper francs had got well under way, it began to exercise an influence on commerce and brought about an excess of exports in 1921.

It is well to note in this connection that a satisfactory analysis of the relation of international commerce to price levels is not possible because the figures available are not always complete nor comparable. There are, moreover, certain changes in the character of French foreign trade which make the matter exceedingly complex. There has been, for instance, an increase in the industrial exports of France as compared to raw materials, which tends to increase the value per ton of the total exports. This change has been particularly noticeable since 1920, when a very real increase of large scale and highly specialized production began along with reconstruction.

During the year 1921 the French balance of trade was more favorable and the franc rose in terms of dollars.[1] This might have led to a slight increase in prices, but no such effect is observable until late in 1922, when the ex-

[1] See *supra,* Chapter IV.

change rates began their rapid rise and became without doubt the determining factor. It is apparent, therefore, that commerce was, from every point of view at this time as well as during all the other years of severe depreciation, a negligible factor in determining price currents. It was not even influenced by prices to the extent which one might expect; demands were too inelastic, speculation often overlooked existing profit margins with an eye to changes in the future. Production and foreign trade expanded despite the crisis and erratic price movement. This relatively great independence of some of the basic factors such as note circulation, exchange rates, prices, production, and commerce, is in sharp contrast to the close synchronization of price curves for France, the United States, and England during 1921 to 1924.

The Exchange Rates Dominate Prices

The third period of depreciation,[1] 1922 and 1923, is characterized by the increasing influence of exchange rates over all other economic factors. From 1922 to 1924 the dollar led prices in their upward course. During these two years, however, exchange rates did not cause an immediate and almost equivalent change in the price level as they did in the following years. The steady upward pull is shown in the indices for wholesale and retail prices as well as in the cost of living. The wholesale index, which was 320 in January, 1922, was 395 in January, 1923, and 505 in 1924. The retail index number did not gain during 1922 but rose from 309 in January, 1923, to 376 in January, 1924. The cost of living index rose five per cent in 1922 and about thirteen per cent more in 1923.[2] It was made very sluggish, however, by the inclusion of rents which were fixed by law.

[1] See *supra*, Chapter V.
[2] In January of the respective years the cost of living index was: in 1922, 291; in 1923, 324; and in 1924, 365; see appendix.

During this period of depreciation, price changes did not seem to have a very detrimental effect on economic life. Production increased by leaps and bounds, rising above 100 per cent of 1913 in the course of 1923; it reached 105 per cent in March, 1924.[1] The following figures show interesting progress.

TABLE XX

INDEX OF PRODUCTION IN JANUARY OF EACH YEAR

(1913 = 100)

1921	64
1922	68
1923	90
1924	105
1925	110

The movements of prices and the power of speculation were not apparently disturbing to those who directed this notable expansion of manufacturing. Paper prices seem to have had little influence on underlying conditions in 1922, though they were of growing importance in 1923; nor did gold prices, which varied within fairly narrow limits during these two years.[2] The injustices and maladjustments were less during this time than in the stormy time to come. It was during this period, however, that the exchange rates definitely preceded price movements for the first time and began to exert a causal influence which was to grow with increasing uncertainty and speculation.

CLOSE HARMONY BETWEEN EXCHANGE AND PRICES

The fourth period, as we have divided depreciation,[3] was the time when the influence of the exchange rates over wholesale prices was most complete. There was, during this time, a close correspondence from month to month, some-

[1] See appendix.
[2] U. S. Senate, *Foreign Currency and Exchange Investigation*, pp. 314, 474.
[3] See *supra*, this chapter.

times from week to week, so that the curves could be very
nearly superimposed. There was, it is true, a tendency on
the part of prices to rise more slowly than the cost of exchanges, but if we judge this by examining gold prices we
find the difference was very slight. This was due in no small
measure to the increasing money consciousness which is one
of the interesting features of severe depreciation. There was
a growing realization of the need of an adjustment of prices
to exchange rates, which tended to bring the two into a very
close relationship.

The year of panic, 1924, is striking for the almost simultaneous fluctuations of prices and exchange rates. It is obvious that this must have been the product of conscious
speculation and price changing. The wholesaler, dealing in a
somewhat specialized market and having business mainly
with professionals, was of course much better able to do
this than was the retailer, who cannot protect himself so
well. A comparison of the indices for wholesale and retail
prices is sufficient evidence of this fact. This gap which
opened up between the two classes of prices led to the extraordinary advantage of the foreign residents in low exchange countries during the early years of depreciation.[1]
The reason for it lies partly, as has been suggested, in the
nature of the two markets, which make frequent changes
less difficult in the more specialized dealings of wholesalers.
Then, the tradition in retailing has been to allow a certain
margin above the purchase price for the new selling price,
irrespective of replacement costs. In the case of the small
shopkeeper, this practice was almost ironclad, and held for
the up as well as the down swing of prices. Indeed, it was
the basis for sure and conservative profits in normal times,
and the peril involved during times of very rapid change
was not clearly evident; so for several years retailers failed

[1] One result of the increasing understanding of depreciation was the creation of taxes and special prices for foreigners. The advantage of foreigners
disappeared in most cases of prolonged depreciation.

to protect themselves, and their savings bore the brunt of
the first shock. A further reason for the sluggishness of retail prices is to be found in the relations between the
buyer and the seller. The consumer was the last of the various economic agents to sense the meaning of depreciation;
he was, moreover, indignant when any price increase was
made which he did not anticipate or understand. In a country like France, in particular, where the small neighborhood
shop played a very important part, the force of public opinion was a real power in keeping prices down. The contacts
in retail trade were personal, and it was important for the
shopkeeper not to alienate his patrons, since he could not
easily move his center of operations. Merchants knew that
buyers counted their *sous* and preferred to risk financial
losses rather than drive them away by inexplainable
increases in prices, at least during the early years of depreciation. Then as they began to see the rapid increase of
replacement costs, they were shocked into action.

It is therefore evident that retail prices could not follow
exchange rates as closely as did wholesale prices, though
the general upward trend in both came definitely from the
rise in the cost of foreign money. The agreement between
wholesale prices and exchange rates was increasingly evident, so also, the retail price curve tended in the later
months of depreciation to reflect the short-time fluctuations of the franc in the exchange markets. There is here
another case of speculation leaping over the usual steps in
causation, to make for almost contemporaneous fluctuations
of related phenomena. Whereas, in the early period of
depreciation there was a lag of wholesale prices behind
exchange rates determined by the influence of import and
export prices on commodity prices in general, and then a
lag of about seven months between wholesale and retail
prices, which was conditioned in part by the period of
replacement of stock by shopkeepers, in the later period
both types of merchant looked to exchange rates to deter-

Unit: per cent

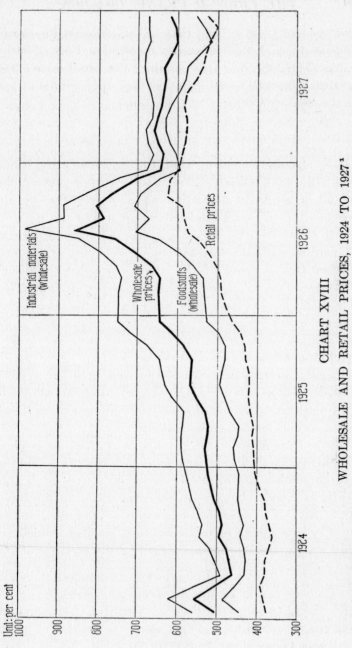

CHART XVIII

WHOLESALE AND RETAIL PRICES, 1924 TO 1927 [1]

[1] See appendix for figures.

mine some of their selling prices and anticipated the slower influence through the cost of raw material and prices set by dealers nearer the source of supplies. The retail price curve for 1926 [1] has the same slope as the other curves except for the sharp movement in the summer.

THE QUANTITY OF MONEY AND PRICES

It is strikingly evident that the exchange rates came eventually to dominate prices. To a certain extent the amount of money in circulation was a cause of the upward movement of prices. A study of the figures of the Bank of France shows that the increase in the note circulation was not parallel with the fluctuations of the value of money.[2] The first fact to observe is that there was a slow but decidedly upward trend in the volume of money in circulation from 1922 on. The second notable fact is the month-end increase which breaks the smooth progression. The third fact which stands out is that there are some very slight wavelike movements which occur at the time of the major exchange and price movements, but that these are neither as sudden nor as extensive.[3] A comparison of the wholesale price index and the month-end note circulation for three years will indicate this state of affairs.

If one considers the three years here given, it is clear that there is no close correspondence between prices and the note circulation during 1924, if one is interested in the month to month changes. In the year 1925, on the other hand, there is a measure of agreement between the two variables, due perhaps to the political situation which focused attention on proposals regarding the increase of the note circulation and so influencing prices not directly but through the exchange rates.[4] In 1926, the note circulation

[1] See Chart No. VII.
[2] League of Nations, *Memorandum, op. cit.,* vol. i, p. 19.
[3] See comment on Aftalion, *infra,* this chapter.
[4] See *supra,* Chapter V and Charts V and VII.

TABLE XXI

NOTE CIRCULATION AND INDEX OF WHOLESALE PRICES [1]
1924–1926

	1924		1925		1926	
	Prices 1914= 100	Note Cir- culation (million francs)	Prices 1914= 100	Note Cir- culation (million francs)	Prices 1914= 100	Note Cir- culation (million francs)
Jan	505	38,834	525	40,515	647	50,617
Feb	555	39,344	526	40,791	649	50,991
Mar	510	39,949	524	40,892	645	51,491
Apr	459	39,824	523	43,049	664	52,208
May	468	39,556	531	42,702	702	52,734
Jun	475	39,664	554	43,000	754	53,073
Jul	491	40,324	569	44,220	854	56,021
Aug	487	40,034	569	44,701	785	55,146
Sep	496	40,338	567	46,353	804	55,010
Oct	507	40,528	584	46,678	767	54,578
Nov	514	40,447	618	48,085	700	53,262
Dec	518	40,603	646	51,085	641	52,907

does not follow the upward sweep of prices at the middle of the year. Prices in their turn have come into partial agreement with the note circulation after the speculative fever is over. In fact, the chart shows in dramatic relief the way in which the peaks and troughs of the value of the dollar and of internal commodities are cut across by the rising line of the note circulation, which appears almost straight in comparison with the sharp fluctuations of the other phenomena. There seems to have been considerable bank resistance to the upward pressure on the note circula-tion exerted by the rising price level. Once again we must conclude that inflation was not a cause but to some extent a concomitant of price changes.[2]

In the first six months of 1924, the period of greatest price fluctuation, the net change in the note circulation was a

[1] Price figures from *Bulletin de la statistique générale*. Note circulation figures from the statement of the last week in each month, of the Bank of France, see appendix.

[2] A. Aftalion, *op. cit.*, pp. 18, 36. Aftalion states that the quantity of money merely adjusted itself to the shifting price level after the war.

little more than one billion francs, or about three per cent. Moreover, the range of fluctuation was not much greater. The Bank of France statements give the figures 39 billion francs for the first week in January and 40 billion francs for the first week in July. We have observed elsewhere, however, that these statements are not completely accurate for this time.[1] The margin of error was probably about one billion francs. The fluctuations of the wholesale price level, during this time, amounted to twenty per cent and the change in the value of the dollar was approximately sixty per cent.[2] It is true that if one considers the changes in credit they show a greater sensitivity to the changes in prices than does the note circulation. This is not because the means of payment was a cause of the price fluctuation, but rather because there was less resistance to the expansion of credit when prices changed than there was in the case of the more sluggish note circulation. The figures for bank clearings follow closely the fluctuations of the foreign exchange rates.[3]

TABLE XXII

BANK CLEARINGS

1923	Oct	23,674
	Nov	22,980
	Dec	21,515
1924	Jan	36,847
	Feb	37,252
	Mar	46,651
	Apr	34,643
	May	33,705

It must be remembered in considering the curve of money that the significant aspect of the economic situation during severe depreciation was the month to month and week to week change, and not the net change over a year or two.

---

[1] See *supra,* Chapters V and VI.

[2] The maximum change in the wholesale price index was from 555 in February, 1924, to 459 in April. The change in the dollar was from 24.76 francs in March to 15.50 in May. [3] See appendix and Chart XXXII, p. 432.

It was the sudden up and down swing of values in 1924 that caused the high degree of sensitivity of various economic factors to the exchange rates, that brought about shifts in wealth and other changes in fundamental relationships.

The comparison of data in the year 1924 is particularly impressive because the dents in the curve are very clear cut and the time relationship is therefore easily demonstrated. Moreover, the short-time movements were so marked that they obliterate almost entirely the general trend with which we are less concerned. Let us review the situation briefly at this point.[1] There was first the sharp upward movement of the cost of foreign exchange, beginning in November and continuing until March. There was a rapid acceleration of price increase following this and almost identical in its rate of change. This is attributable in part to the previous exchange rise and in part to the simultaneous movement of the cost of gold currencies. The downward turn of prices was almost contemporaneous with the downward turn of exchange rates in March; the nature of the data does not permit of an exact statement of the lag.[2] The note circulation rose perceptibly at the beginning of the year and declined slightly after the recovery of the franc in March. The agreement of prices and exchange rates is the most striking thing that is to be observed. Unfortunately, weekly data for prices are not available at this time to indicate the exact degree of correspondence, but the wider range of fluctuation of the cost of foreign exchange seems to give it quite clearly the dominant rôle. Certainly public opinion of the moment would concur in this interpretation.

The careful study made by Professor Aftalion brings out interesting aspects of the situation. He insists on the necessity of looking for a common cause in a situation where the movement in time is in such close agreement.

[1] See Chart No. X.
[2] The price indices are given for the last of the month.

During the second period, from 1922 to 1924 . . . the comparison of the two curves gives a clearer, more uniform impression [than in 1920-21]. . . . The movements are frequently simultaneous. There is certainly a slight lag of prices after exchanges. . . . It is evident that the foreign exchanges have dominated prices more than in the preceding period . . . almost exclusive of other factors, to a certain extent.[1]

There are, in fact, two ways of looking at the matter. One may say either that the exchange movement, influenced by speculation, caused the price movement; or one may say the common cause was speculation. Then again, behind the force of speculation one finds the disturbing influence of government finance and the political troubles of the times.

The detailed analysis by Professor Aftalion is very interesting in that he attempts to apply the methods of analyzing business cycle data,[2] frequently known as the Persons' method, to the French case. He proceeds to calculate the seasonal changes and the trends for the years 1920-24 [3] and then presents the figures for prices, exchange rates, and the note circulation in the form of standard deviations from the trend. The result of this work is to indicate a closer harmony between the three factors considered than is evident in the crude data. This treatment is very interesting as a method of throwing into relief the month to month changes. It eliminates two of the obscuring factors and so makes the general conclusions arrived at all the more striking. On the other hand, the validity of casting the data into the form of standard deviations in order to indicate that quantitatively the changes in note circulation are almost equivalent to changes in prices is open to question. Division by the standard deviation eliminates the very fact most significant in the study of depreciation, that is, short-time deviations. The percentage deviation is the fact on which

[1] A. Aftalion, *op. cit.*, pp. 40, 41.   [2] *Ibid.*, pp. 22-64.

[3] The seasonal high point for the note circulation is found to be October, the low point June.

one wishes to focus attention. The year 1924 was characterized by the size of its deviations. The impressive fact is that
the deviations of the note circulation could be so much less
than the deviations of prices, i.e. for prices, 18.7 per cent,
for circulation, 3.5 per cent.[1] One can say that the intensity
of variations is five times greater in the case of prices than
of the note circulation. This fact then presents a reason for
saying that prices influenced note issues more than the note
issues did prices, and the fact should be indicated rather
than eliminated. For the purpose of demonstrating the time
relationship, Professor Aftalion's method of treatment is
much clearer than is the comparison of the basic material
without these adjustments.

The gradual upward trend of both prices and note circulation is in sharp contrast to the more erratic short-time
movements. The net increase of prices, for instance, is 13
added to 411.1, whereas the note circulation is 18 points
added to 369 (i.e. 36.9 billion francs).[2] The increase in
neither case is very great if viewed in these terms: it is not
wise to segregate such a short period from the other years.
It is clearly a matter of chance that the increase in the note
circulation appears larger in this instance. If the period
were advanced by six months the opposite situation would
be apparent; the change in note circulation would be much
smaller than the change in prices. This can be seen by a
glance at the curves which are given on a logarithmic scale,
and so show proportionate changes throughout.[3] If the
price changes and note changes are both expressed in terms
of the increase since 1913, the change in prices is very much
greater. These comments are made, not as a criticism of the
methods used by Professor Aftalion, but merely to warn
the reader against reaching superficial conclusions from considering short-time comparisons. In fact, the slope of the
trend is comparatively unimportant in this case.

[1] A. Aftalion, *op. cit.,* p. 26.   [3] See *supra,* this chapter.
[2] *Ibid.,* p. 23, note 6.

THE TIME RELATIONSHIP IN 1926

The second most significant episode in the study of price relationships is in 1926, and for this time more data are available than in 1924. It is possible to compare the week to week changes and so make a more accurate study of the significant curves. The results bear out the conclusions already made, except for the fact that the influence of speculation is even greater in bringing the various factors into almost instantaneous accord.

The increasing harmony between different economic factors, even in times of rapid change, is strikingly evident during the crisis of 1926. At the end of July the exchange rate turned down first by a very few days, followed by a rapid decline in wholesale prices. In September the slight rise in both exchange rates and prices was practically simultaneous. The reaction of both, which began on October 23, was led by the fall of the dollar on the exchange. The stability of the exchange rates which characterized the end of the year was accompanied by a slight rise in the index of wholesale prices. It is notable at this time that many prophecies pointed to a fall in prices which did not take place, and many stores tried to capitalize these forecasts and create the impression through advertising bargain sales that prices had actually dropped. But in spite of such early impressions, there was no significant decline in retail prices, any more than there was in wholesale prices. Those who were aware of the lag of retail prices probably discounted such hasty prophecies from the outset.

It is difficult to see why the expectation of a price decline was so persistent. There seems to have been no basis for it except the possible inference that because the stability of the exchange rates was a desirable state it must lead to many benefits and the public might imagine that a decline of prices would serve its interests, if it did not analyze closely the relation of price movements to productive activity in general. Those who were aware of the experience in Germany and in other countries which had stabilized knew that stability brought with it higher rather than lower prices in almost every case. Certainly high taxes, high interest rates, the need for general readjustment, and the influence of stability on foreign commerce would lead one to expect higher prices, at least for a short period after stability became a fact.

STABILITY, COMMERCE, AND PRICES

In regard to foreign commerce, public opinion went wrong again in anticipating a violent and unfavorable change in the flow of trade. It must be remembered that from December, 1926 on, the franc was approximately stable at one-fifth of its prewar value. There was from then on a period of almost two years of virtual stability, unenforced by any legal provision or any official announcement. As the exchange rates became steady and prices adjusted themselves to new conditions, the exchange premium which arose from the difference between French paper prices and international gold prices disappeared and the advantage which it had conferred on French exports competing in a world market likewise disappeared. Nevertheless, there was no sudden and sharp decline in French commerce. The new stability brought advantages, which offset at least in part the former gain due to price differentials, and so a real decline in the risks and uncertainties which must have aggravated costs in foreign trade. It is true that exports declined somewhat, but despite this the figures for exports in February, 1927, for instance, were still higher than for any previous February, and imports declined slightly. The figures for a few months are given in Table XXIII.

The inference to be drawn from the figures is that the expansion of French commerce had been to a considerable extent in spite of, and not due to, the monetary situation.

TABLE XXIII

FRENCH FOREIGN COMMERCE[1]

1926, 1927

(in millions of francs)

		Imports	Exports
1926	Nov	4,994	5,329
	Dec	5,123	5,395
1927	Jan	4,079	4,709
	Feb	4,780	4,597
	Mar	4,414	4,694
	Apr	4,298	4,255

It is true that some industries had gained very markedly in exporting to countries where they could not normally compete, but on the whole the development of such unusual opportunities was undoubtedly retarded by the knowledge that the advantage was temporary. The bulk of French commerce followed the lines laid down for it in the past. Since a very large part consists of specialties and is not met by as keen competition as is the case with raw materials and standardized manufactured products, one would hardly expect to see very great short-time changes due to sudden price differentials. The expansion of commerce after the war was due probably to an increase of mass production in France, which marked a more or less permanent change, and was due only in a very small degree to depreciation. The fact to remark in studying the influence of depreciation or stability on commerce is that a change in the value of money seems to affect commerce in the first instance by increasing exports and imports together or by decreasing both, instead of at once increasing the difference between the two sides of the commercial balance.

It is true that there was a notable depression in 1927, the result in part of the slowing down of commerce. The effect on the textile and metal industries was conspicuous,[2] but the adjustments which occurred were less extensive

[1] See Chart XXXIV, p. 443.   [2] See appendix.

than had been anticipated. The production index on a 1913 base was as follows:

1926	Nov	129
	Dec	123
1927	Jan	117
	Feb	113
	Mar	108

In contrast to this it should be noted that bank clearings and car loadings showed a slight increase:

1926	Dec	60,775 cars loaded daily
1927	Jan	56,663 " " "
	Feb	61,967 " " "

The external signs of city and country life indicated that the hardship which undoubtedly existed was not as severe as had been feared. There were few striking evidences of misery, perhaps because workers in France, like those in America during the war, had been buying a better quality of clothes and household goods, and so were better equipped to meet the period of temporary unemployment. It was common knowledge, though not evidenced in printed reports, that many industries had been putting aside enormous profits, which allowed them to run at a loss during the first months of stability.[1]

PRICES COULD NOT FALL

The expectation of price declines was doomed to disappointment, as has been said above. This is obvious when one realizes that internal depreciation from 1922 to 1927 was merely a partial reflection of profound monetary changes. It was an outward sign of the exchange movements which were the outcome of budget and banking con-

[1] Professor Rist called this fact to the attention of the writer in an interview in May, 1927. For obvious reasons profits were often concealed from the tax collector and the public as far as was possible.

ditions, of political discord, and public hysteria. Since it
merely registered changes in underlying facts, there was no
reason to expect a sudden reaction such as would have
occurred if prices had been the causal factor, or if, on the
other hand, they had been in conflict with other important
factors. Once the uncertainties of political life and exchange
depreciation were over, prices came to reveal the more
normal relationships of production and consumption. These
relationships did not call for any considerable increase in
prices after the adjustments of 1926, which brought the
various values into fairly close harmony.

There was, on the other hand, no sufficient force to turn
prices downward. Costs of production were fairly high, and
it was hardly to be expected that wages could be forced
downward after their steady upward movement. The burden of taxation limited to a certain extent any downward
movement of prices. It is true that the risks due to sudden
large changes in values were no longer to be feared but, on
the other hand, with stability there came a realization that
a considerable amount of physical depreciation had occurred
which producers and merchants had not taken into account
during the time of rapid fluctuations. This depreciation had
to be allowed for in the new scale of prices and was an
element which tended to prevent any marked decline.

The increase in nominal incomes which had been a natural accompaniment of rising prices had led to freer spending habits which helped keep prices up. It is true that with
stability the demand for goods fell off considerably, but this
was a temporary phenomenon and did not lead to a collapse
of prices as it might have done if the cause had been less
clearly understood. Prices came to adapt themselves to the
gold value of the means of payment, and, as this did not
decline but increased slightly through the years 1927 and
1928, prices were very nearly stable throughout those years.
Certain lines of goods, such as shoes and textiles, which had
been bought more freely than was normal, showed signs of

severe depression. It was realized that business policy would have to be formulated with a view to narrow profit margins and efficient management.

To a certain extent, this relative stability of the price level after 1926 was due to conscious attempts to get away from the wild speculation which had preceded it. During the years 1925 and 1926, there had been tremendous paper profits but the losses which offset them had wrought serious harm; even those who had reaped large profits realized that such conditions were dangerous and could not last. Public opinion came to be united in the desire to avoid all those financial disturbances which had come through budget controversies, note inflation, ministerial crises, and wild commercial ventures. Although it was urged by many that stabilization at a lower level than four cents would help many industries and would not lead to a severe panic, the general tenor of opinion was so strong that the franc was not allowed to depreciate further on the exchanges, and so kept its value in the internal markets as well.

THE ILL EFFECTS OF A RISING PRICE LEVEL

Those who have experienced severe depreciation cannot question its ill effects. It strikes at the basis of sound production in that it prevents forecasts, and because it undermines savings which should build up new capital equipment. Wild price movements bring confusion to investment markets and make speculation an essential part of the very simplest market transactions. In the years of uncertainty which we have described, notably 1925 and 1926, the French had just begun to experience the economic disorders from which Germany and the other central European countries suffered. They were sufficient to warn her away from the precipice. This did not happen until many changes in the distribution of wealth had taken place, some of them bringing real suffering and loss to the nation, most of them due to chance rather than merit, to the sudden shifting of opportunities which were seized by the weak as well as the strong. These sudden profits and losses are one of the most conspicuous features of depreciation.

Another aspect of this same matter is the dispersion of prices which occurs when the change of values is very sudden. It is a reason for the shifts in the distribution of wealth, and the difficulties under which manufacturers were laboring. When we look at the dispersion of price relatives on a certain base we are seeing a cross-section of economic life which offers one of the clearest revelations of maladjustment. We are emphasizing not so much the lag of one thing after another in time as the differentials which exist at a given moment of time. The slow adjustment of retail prices to wholesale prices has been referred to repeatedly. It is possible to carry the analysis farther and show that in the case of both wholesale and retail prices some advanced rapidly while others remained at low levels. The possible losses due to such discrepancies are immediately obvious. When it is realized, for instance, that the range of price relatives in 1922 was between 100 and 600 per cent of the base, 1901–10, and that in 1926 the scatter of price relatives was between 200 and 1,800 per cent of the same base, it is evident that there arose grave difficulties for the sellers of the more sluggish commodities. If it were possible to assume constant differentials between different price groups, the losses involved would not be great, but when, on the other hand, at certain times textile products were soaring and at other times agricultural commodities, it is obvious that dealers were very much at sea as to how to carry on their business in a safe way.

The ills of depreciation come largely through the dispersion of the movements of different prices. A study of the scattering of price relatives around their means at different times opens up a wide range of problems. If we consider those of prices in France during 1923 through 1926, we see

CHART XIX

FREQUENCY DISTRIBUTION OF PRICE RELATIVES
(Base 1901-1910)

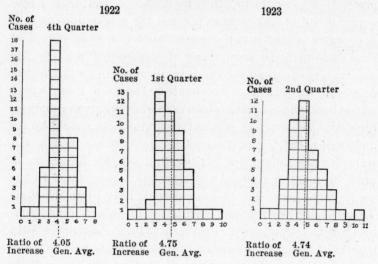

1922

No. of Cases — 4th Quarter

Ratio of Increase   4.05   Gen. Avg.

No. of Cases — 1st Quarter

Ratio of Increase   4.75   Gen. Avg.

1923

No. of Cases — 2nd Quarter

Ratio of Increase   4.74   Gen. Avg.

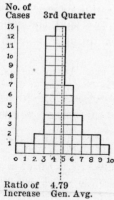

No. of Cases — 3rd Quarter

Ratio of Increase   4.79   Gen. Avg.

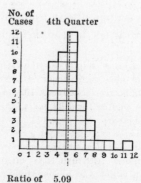

No. of Cases — 4th Quarter

Ratio of Increase   5.09   Gen. Avg.

that very marked changes in relations between prices took place. It is possible to infer, for instance, that sound economic development is best favored by a situation such as is revealed by the highly concentrated frequency curves of 1923 as contrasted with those of the later years.[1] As the uncertainty of values increased there came conflicting movements in the prices of commodities, so that there was a wider dispersion of price relatives, and in practical economic life a slowing down of productive activity. It should be remembered that the position of the price relatives does not stand for the differences in prices but for the differences in the movement of prices with respect to a given base. In the study made here, the ten-year period, 1901-10, is the base. This was first used for the calculation of French index numbers but has been superseded recently by the use of the 1914 base, which makes the index numbers comparable to those used by other countries.[2] The use of the earlier base, however, does not affect in any significant way the range or concentration of the dispersion.[3]

Oliver's study of price indices and the dispersion of the different values about their mean shows that the selection of commodities in the ·French index number is well bal-

[1] See *infra,* this chapter for the frequency curves. The production index shows rapid development during this year. The low point of 50 in July, 1921, should be contrasted with 102 for December, 1923.

[2] See the figures for 1914 on a 1901-10 base, *Bulletin de la statistique générale* (January, 1924), p. 123.

[3] The general principle guiding the use of figures and statistical measures in this study has been to keep as close as possible to the figures given in the original sources. Although these might be adjusted and refined in certain instances, it is not wise to undertake such changes in a study not primarily statistical in character. It is better to keep the material simple and easy to verify than to reduce slightly the margin of error. The material available in the French case is frequently not sufficiently accurate to justify exact measurement and certainty of precision. There is, however, no reason to think that the errors are large enough to invalidate the general conclusions drawn. Nonquantitative judgments based on opinions of experienced observers have served to verify conclusions based in the first instance on the figures themselves.

CHART XX

1924

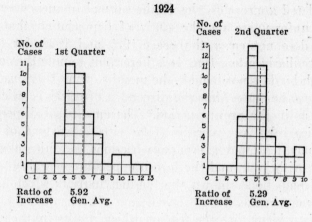

No. of Cases   1st Quarter

Ratio of   5.92
Increase   Gen. Avg.

No. of Cases   2nd Quarter

Ratio of   5.29
Increase   Gen. Avg.

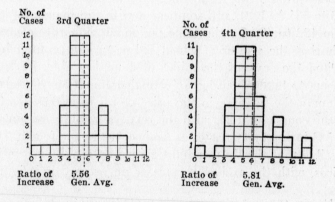

No. of Cases   3rd Quarter

Ratio of   5.56
Increase   Gen. Avg.

No. of Cases   4th Quarter

Ratio of   5.81
Increase   Gen. Avg.

anced, and that the average is such as to represent them fairly accurately.[1] The distribution of all items for the years considered approaches closely the normal frequency curve. It is unfortunate for the study of depreciation that his work does not cover the years 1925 and 1926, for they are peculiarly interesting. It is important to note that even though he does not include the months of most serious disturbance he states that the dispersion of prices is twice as great as in the prewar period.[2] The amount of dispersion of price relatives varies directly with the extent of the movement. Moreover, economic frictions and injustices increase with both, and the feverish speculation which tends to develop breaks down the familiar barriers which limit economic change.

It is evident that the friction which results from changing price differentials is both technical and mental. There is a disturbance immediately felt in production and a feeling of unfairness and injustice which affects later economic relationships. Take, for instance, the increase of wheat from 433 to 531 in 1924, and compare it with the change in flour from 422 to 498 for the same period.[3] It is hardly conceivable that the grower of wheat did not make profits which excited the envy of the miller of flour, less able, for some reason, to take advantage of changing conditions. Or again, compare the increase in the price of tin from 667 to 1,028 in the course of 1925, with the relative stability of mutton at 583 in the first quarter as against 599 in the fourth. It is possible that the tin merchant gained by rapidly advancing prices, with the exchange rates as an excuse, or it is pos-

---

[1] Maurice Olivier, *Les Nombres indices de la variation des prix* (thèse pour de doctorat, Paris, 1926). He presents the arguments for the geometric average but his data do not cast serious doubt on the validity of the French index number which is based on the arithmetic average. See the later study by M. L. Dugé de Bernonville, "Essaie d'un indice pondéré des prix de gros en France," *Bulletin de la statistique générale* (January-March, 1928), pp. 201–224. See especially page 218.

[2] Olivier, *op. cit.*, p. 86.   [3] See appendix.

CHART XXI

1925

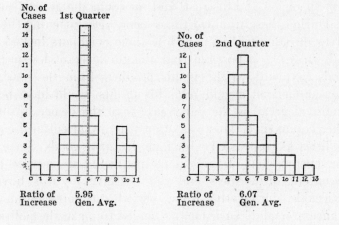

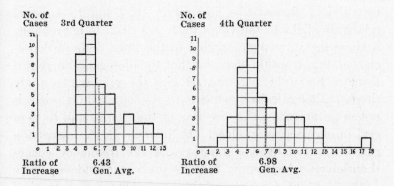

sible that he lost by putting his prices too high for the consumer of his wares. In either case it is certain that the man who sold mutton would look on the tinner's policy with suspicion and distrust, and so would the general public. During these troubled times some were fattening themselves on abnormal gains, while their neighbors looked on with envy. It is possible that the producer of low-priced goods frequently withheld his products from the market, even though on a gold basis his profits would have been almost as great as the paper profits of the dealer in some other commodity. This was often true of agricultural commodities as contrasted with manufactured goods. Some of the repercussions of these maladjustments are seen in the discontent of retailers and the hostility towards buyers noticeable during the worst periods of depreciation in France. Certainly such factors tended to make the political situation more chaotic and to interfere with reconstruction and the sound development of the nation's resources.

To return to the more objective aspects of the matter, one finds that Olivier's measures of dispersion and dissymmetry show them to be greatest in 1920 and 1924, being relatively slight in the years 1921 and 1922. It is probable, if these measures were applied to the later years of depreciation, that it would be found that the divergence increased three or four fold as compared with the prewar. To apply these mathematical refinements to the material on prices is not necessary when the direction of the change and its general implication is so clear. The increase in the dispersion can be judged by a comparison of the frequency curves themselves, which show that as the range widened from 1,000 to 1,900 per cent of the base there was a marked change in the shape of the curves.

In the frequency distributions for the four quarters of 1923, the concentration in the value from 300 to 600 per cent is very marked. There is a distinct mode which is close to the general average for the group. In the case of the later

CHART XXII

1926

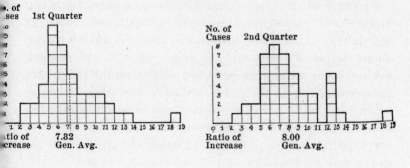

No. of Cases — 1st Quarter

Ratio of Increase — 7.32 — Gen. Avg.

No. of Cases — 2nd Quarter

Ratio of Increase — 8.00 — Gen. Avg.

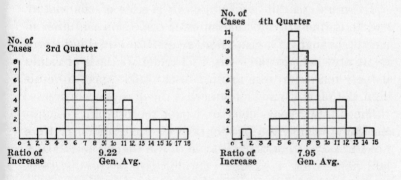

No. of Cases — 3rd Quarter

Ratio of Increase — 9.22 — Gen. Avg.

No. of Cases — 4th Quarter

Ratio of Increase — 7.95 — Gen. Avg.

three quarters it practically coincides with the average. Granted that the sample is fairly small, 45 commodities, it would be hard to find a better instance of the normal curve.[1]

In 1924, on the other hand, there is a decided tendency to skewness, almost to bimodality.[2] This is due, without any doubt, to the direct influence of the exchange crisis on certain prices, whereas others were not immediately affected. For instance, the average for the group of textile raw materials changed from 721 to 875 during the year,[3] whereas cotton was 1,187 per cent of the base in the first quarter. Food products of domestic production were for the most part still in the four and five hundreds, whereas imported metals had risen sharply.

In 1925 the spread of price relatives became even greater. The symmetry was less marked than in 1923, but the concentration of values about the mean was still notable. The further scattering of the prices which are most affected by exchange rates in the upper end of the scale is balanced by a better adjustment of the domestic prices to each other in the lower range. It is clear, however, that unusual influences are at work, as compared with 1923. The grouping of values above 800 per cent is not such as one would expect to result from the play of random forces.

The disorganizing effect of monetary instability is dramatically represented by the skewed curves of 1926. Here

[1] See figures in appendix. The relatives on the 1901-10 base for the 45 commodities included in the general index number are given in the regular issues of the *Bulletin de la statistique générale*. This is the best readily available material for the study of the detail of price movements. (The other wholesale price index of the Statistique générale is based on 47 commodities.)

[2] The distribution of the relatives would normally be skewed but not bimodal. The distribution of the logarithms of the relative would be normal if there were a large sample and no great price movement. In these cases the skewness is so great that the distribution of the logarithms would also be skewed. See A. A. Young, *Economic Problems New and Old* (Boston, 1927), p. 293, footnote.

[3] The general averages for the period ranged from 509 to 623.

the mode and the mean are no longer in close accord. The spread of relatives through the wide range of values from 100 to 1,900 per cent is far from normal. The first quarter of the year comes closest to the normal curve; the second shows the disrupting forces at work in the price system, forces growing out of the uncertainty of all economic life and cumulating in the crisis of July, 1926. A comparison of this curve with those for 1923, which represent the fairly normal grouping of the constituents of a price index, shows that the economic system was seriously strained. The efforts to adjust prices to exchange rates led to great inequalities which could not persist. The commodities which stood at the upper end of the scale in the second quarter of 1926 were almost without exception directly affected by the exchange rates.[1]

The third quarter of 1926, which followed the rapid improvement of the financial situation, shows a tendency towards adjustment by way of the general progression of the undervalued products towards the upper end of the scale. This led to a much greater concentration as stability increased in the last three months of the year. The narrow range, the approximation of the mean and the mode, are indicative of a more normal exchange and price situation. There was a tendency for prices to become adjusted to costs of production and for the gaps between various classes of products to close.[2] The last curve of the series given is not normal as were those of 1923 before the extreme monetary disturbance, but it is symmetrical when compared to the second quarter of the same year. The increased concentration and the narrowing of the effective range to about 1,000

[1] A list of price relatives which were more than 1,000 per cent of the base is significant because it shows the influence of the international price level through the exchanges: rice, tin, cotton, hemp, lead, jute, wool, silk, colza oil, linseed oil, benzol. Raw sugar, zinc, were in the 900's. The lowest relatives are in the group of meats and dairy products.

[2] The gap between retail and wholesale prices, which had been 127 points in January, was reduced to 50 points in December. See chart.

per cent, as compared with 1,400 per cent in the previous quarter, show a normality which augured well for a return to reasonable price relationships.

It is possible that the index number containing the selection of commodities made in 1901-10 would fail to give a normal dispersion for years as far removed as 1926 and 1927. Certain allowances should be made for this fact. It is even possible that some revision of the composition of the index number may prove advisable after a return to more stable conditions has taken place. The relative for rubber, 342, as compared with a general average of 695, is obviously affected by special conditions which made its price in the base year out of line with other prices. If such artificial elements are few, as they seem to be, they are eliminated to a sufficient degree by the averaging of all the items. It should be remembered, however, that profound changes have occurred and that the use of an average based on prewar conditions should be subject to a measure of critical analysis. Changes in the technique of production, in qualities used, in the demand for goods should influence the index number to a certain extent but it should not be assumed that the year 1914 was normal in these respects, whereas the year 1927 was abnormal.[1] Such assumptions overstep the bounds set for scientific treatment. It is difficult for the person who is seeking knowledge, without prejudice and without favor, to be sure of a norm. If the sampling of data is sufficiently large, the normal frequency curve is the surest test. It is possible that the abnormality of distribution is due to an unrepresentative sample or that it is due to some temporary abnormality inherent in the economic situation, such as the monetary troubles of the second quarter of 1926. It is too soon to judge the French index number from the point of view of postwar adjustments. The conclusions which may be made tentatively are that the sampling is sufficiently representative and that dissymmetry

---

[1] See *supra*, Chapter I, many indices have been changed to a 1926 base.

brings out the interference of monetary factors, notably through the exchange rates, in economic life.

MONETARY DISTURBANCE MOVED PRICES TOGETHER

It is interesting to add to this analysis of the situation a comparison of the upward and downward movement of price relatives in the different periods. During those quarterly periods when exchange influences were less important, the up and down movements tended to offset each other, as would naturally result from the changing play of supply and demand. The index number moved up, however, because the commodities which were increasing in price tended to move farther than those which were declining. This is what *a priori* reasoning would lead one to expect— the upward pressure of prices is almost always more effective than the downward pressure.[1] In contrast to this situation, during those times when the economic life was dominated by the powerful and artificial influence of confidence and the flight of capital and an increased velocity of circulation due to these causes, the large majority of the prices moved in the same direction. In evidence of this the quick reaction in 1924, which has already been indicated in another connection, should be noted here. (See Table XXIV on following page.)

It is possible, then, to use the direction of movement of price relatives as a rough indication of the nature of the causes behind such changes. If one disregards both the direction and the extent of movements but considers merely the degree to which prices move in the same direction or in different directions one has a *measure of agreement* which varies in units from 0 to 45 because of the number of relatives. This measure may then be plotted to test whether the times of most general agreement of movement are the

[1] A. A. Young, *op. cit.*, p. 291, see footnote. This is not simply because there is "more room" upward.

TABLE XXIV

PRICE RELATIVES CLASSIFIED BY DIRECTION OF MOVEMENT

By Quarters

Fourth Quarter, 1922, to Fourth Quarter, 1926 [1]

		DIRECTION OF CHANGE			Net Movement in Any One Direction
		Up (1)	Down (2)	No Change (3)	(4) (column (1) minus (2))
1922	4th to				
1923	1st	42	3	0	39
	1st–2nd	24	20	1	4
	2nd–3rd	21	21	3	0
	3rd–4th	33	10	2	23
1924	1st	42	2	1	40
	1st–2nd	9	35	1	26
	2nd–3rd	32	9	4	23
	3rd–4th	29	14	2	15
1925	1st	25	19	1	6
	1st–2nd	31	13	1	18
	2nd–3rd	32	9	4	23
	3rd–4th	29	14	2	15
1926	1st	38	7	0	31
	1st–2nd	38	7	0 (sic)	31
	2nd–3rd	40	4	1	36
	3rd–4th	13	32	0	19

times when monetary forces seem to have been paramount. The result is as complete a corroboration of the assumptions as one could hope with the data at hand. The main limitation of this comparison is that the individual price relatives are available for quarterly periods only, and that during a span of three months many differences are ironed out and disappear. Nevertheless the rough test here made shows that the high points of our measure, the last quarters of 1922 and 1924, and the second quarter of 1926, were admittedly times of great financial, particularly foreign exchange, disturbance. In contrast to this the second two quarters of 1923 and the end of 1924, which are low points

[1] See appendix, price relatives from the *Bulletin de la statistique générale.*

for the *measure of agreement,* were in fact times of relative financial calm. The net movement of the wholesale index does not indicate the existence of different causality because the various factors behind price increases unite in one swiftly moving, upward tendency during these years. In times of greatest monetary and financial upset, however, the average movements of price relatives are smaller, but the agreement of movements is actually greater. Moreover, it is possible that the test here applied to the French case might be used in analyzing price movements during more

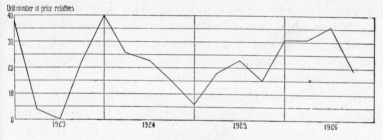

CHART XXIII

MEASURE OF AGREEMENT, 1923 TO 1926

normal times, in order to cast some light on the nature of the causes at work.

In 1923, the cause of price increases is to be sought in *real* factors of economic life, that is, notably in production and consumption conditions rather than in changes of income, and gold values. But at the end of 1922, early 1924, and again in 1926, extraneous and abnormal factors, such as changes in the gold value of incomes evidenced in foreign exchange rates, were the forces behind a very concentrated price movement.

In the study of price movements we are dealing with a complex mass of varying elements. There can, therefore, be no such focus of influences as in the case of the foreign exchange markets. Commodity price movements are normally due to diverse factors and the movements are, therefore, various, as has been indicated above. At certain times, however, the more simple concentrated forces which drove exchange rates to extremes acted through speculation and through import prices on the level of wholesale prices to dominate all other price tendencies. In such circumstances, the causes behind price increases are simple and easily understood; in other circumstances, they are complex and deserving of more detailed analysis than is possible here. These later periods have been pointed out as those when the *index of agreement* was low and when the movements of price relatives were conflicting. The difficulties which result from such movements are felt by those who suffer from price lags and abnormal price dispersions. They are evidenced by abnormal profits and the loss of real wealth by certain classes of the population.

In the study of the complex material the truth is often more clearly brought out by the charts themselves than it can be through the more cumbersome medium of words. It is obvious from the charts that the maladjustments became less as time went on, and the gaps and lags were closed by the anticipation of future movements through speculation. Once this adjustment of rates of change between the wholesale, retail, and cost of living values had taken place, conditions in France became stable. From that time onward depreciation became once more the concern of bankers and financiers and not, as during the more troubled times, the concern of the general public. It then mattered little whether the franc was worth two cents, or six cents, so long as the new adjustment of different price groups to each other was maintained.

CHANGES GROWING OUT OF PRICE INCREASES

Among the more obvious results of the varied and extreme price changes, we have pointed out the shifts in financial power between different elements of French economic life. These have been so great that it is probable that different men and different intellectual influences are' now guiding the productive power of the country as compared to the years before the war. It is notable, for instance, that the conservative, saving, middle-class producer and merchant is no longer the dominant force in economic life. He has been, to a considerable extent, superseded by the man who believes in risk and new ventures, who struggles for the control of markets and works toward the organization of trust and price rings. Such changes should not be exaggerated, but none the less they exist. In appraising them, one must set the new spirit of organization and innovation against the loss of stability and small economies. If the worker has become spendthrift, economic life is less stagnant. The bond owner has lowered his standard of living, but a more aggressive type of industrial leader has increased his power and has given to the French public more standardized goods at a lower cost. Such changes as these are impossible to measure, but they are nevertheless extremely significant and must be taken into account.[1]

Even though the attention of financiers has been focused to a large extent on exchange rates rather than on price levels, in recent years, it must be realized that the changes in economic, social, and political life come about through the interaction of exchange rates on the internal price level. A part of the importance of the exchange rate is due to sensitivity of the quotations to all the important underlying factors of economic life. It has been the barometer, the warning signal, the test of government policies and the

[1] The traveler in France notices with interest the general introduction of running hot and cold water into hotel rooms, even in small towns. The spread of electricity to the small communities, the gradual increase in electrification of the railroads, the numbers of automobiles, the extensive improvement of buildings and fresh paint are noticeable everywhere. Some of this outlay of money is motivated by the desire to put into equipment money which might otherwise be taken by taxes. Some of it is due to a new spirit of enterprise and more adventurous business endeavor.

expression of approval or condemnation on the part of the French people. It is well to observe at once that the sums of money lost and won in exchange speculation would have been quantitatively of little importance if there had been no effect on internal prices. The important influence, then, has been that of price changes on production and distribution bringing about new conditions in French life.

The comparison of the fluctuations of exchange rates, prices, and the means of payment has made it quite clear that the quantity theory has not served as a sufficient explanation of recent events in France. It may be well to say again at this point that although the quantity theory was applied in the first instance to long-run phenomena there has been a tendency in recent years to apply it in the short-run. This would extend too far the influence of currency on prices. It is better to admit the general tendency of the various factors to adjust themselves to each other than it is to look on the volume of currency as the causal factor and try then to work out some formula which will cover the apparent discrepancies of the data. Truth lies in the quantity theory only if it is realized that there are several different ways in which prices, exchange rates, and currency and credit are adapted to each other. The control of the flux of economic life can lie only in lessening the arbitrary influence of extra-economic agencies, chief among which is the influence of the government working through printed notes and excessive borrowings.

Summary

The changing relation of prices to exchanges has been traced in the preceding pages. During the first postwar period (for the war period has little significance in this connection), prices fell, not because the exchange rates dictated such a fall, but because confidence collapsed, prices in other countries fell, demand lessened, and a price fall once begun for these reasons was accentuated somewhat by an improvement of the franc on the exchanges. It was prices which led and the foreign exchanges which followed, but subsequent to this period, the reverse was true. Prices were drawn steadily away from the low point of 1922 by the climbing value of foreign currencies.

As prices rose and instability and distrust increased, the time lags between the various factors decreased. Conscious calculations anticipated events in place of the slower repercussions of world prices on internal prices and the rising cost on retail prices. At this time social injustice increased, frictions and discontent multiplied. The evils became so great that ingenuity finally had to come to the rescue, prices became dependent on exchange rates, retail dealers began to mark up their wares with the least signs of further depreciation. The use of gold values became more widespread, even though limited by law. In fact, it is probable that if matters had become worse in 1926, sliding scales would have been introduced for wages and prices as they were in central Europe. Luckily for France, she escaped the worst stages of collapse.

The turn of events in 1926 led to exchange stability, and, within six months, to comparative price stability. Price stability was protected from further price fall by the falling off of demand due to the decrease in paper incomes and to unemployment, and also to high taxes and costs. So from this time on through 1927 and 1928 wholesale prices fluctuated within certain narrow limits instead of falling sharply, as had been expected by many. Meanwhile the reordering of the relationships between different price categories increased as the continuance of the *status quo* became more likely.

An appraisal of the maladjustments and their evil effects has here been based partly on lags, partly on dispersion, and partly on the general external effects which may be seen by any observer who is familiar with French life.

These three forms of manifestations are merely different aspects of the same thing. The discussion of dispersion adds something which cannot be derived from a study of lags alone. It is somewhat more dramatic in its revelations, for it takes a cross-section in time and shows the gaps and discrepancies caught at particular moments. It posits nothing as to an ultimate readjustment; it simply photographs the inequalities and leaves the student to reconstruct the social and economic effects. Hints have been thrown out that the index number means different things at different times, and that it should be supplemented by a measure of dispersion. During times of quiescence, for instance, the average eliminates the effect of compensating changes; during times of fluctuation, it is a partial measure of the extent of the influence of artificial financial factors, money, or exchange. The shape of the curves and the diversity of the movement sustains the adequacy of the French index; they bring out the same difference in the movement of prices which is seen in other studies of the detail of economic life. As regards the French index number, it is possible that later readjustment of the base year or a reselection of commodities may have to be made, but it is not clearly indicated by the distribution of items up to 1927.

Economists of the English classical school and their followers in America have sometimes been accused of emphasizing too much the price-money relationship. The criticism may be justified if it refers to narrow interpretations and the assumptions of exact and measurable mechanisms. It is not justified if it refers to the larger interpretations of the relations of prices to production, distribution, and the financial structures of nations. Prices are the means of rationing goods which exist and of determining the direction of further production and the nature of capital equipment as well. Changes in prices, moreover, lead to realignments of social forces, the strengthening of certain classes, and the power of the producer as against consumer and investor.

Once instability has attacked the economic fabric of a country, familiar relationships cease, speculation is unavoidable, and consumption becomes unbalanced and misleading. Such a situation cannot long exist. It is essential to build up consciously some price framework based on gold, exchanges, or goods, so that the differentials may be steady as expressed in some element of intrinsic value. This process of achieving stability has come in some countries through sliding scales, in others through the introduction of the gold standard, or through the introduction of new currency units. In one way or another it must come. The new stability, however achieved, is the outgrowth of the development of a money consciousness. It results because internal depreciation cannot continue indefinitely on a large scale; the public realizes that prices must be kept within certain narrow zones of fluctuation.

CHAPTER VIII

The Rising Exchange

EVERY age has its adventures in finance. With the gradual evolution of economic institutions there come new opportunities for combination, investment, and creative effort which are seized by the more imaginative with gain to themselves and progress for society. With the more rapid changes—wars, revolutions and discoveries—there come more sensational rearrangements of economic life. The few who are first aware of the new ordering of forces take the leadership in industrial and financial affairs, gaining large profits and a new ability to control. The gains of the more acute incite the rest to new endeavors and unfamiliar speculation. Keynes says:

No man of spirit will consent to remain poor if he believes his betters to have gained their goods by lucky gambling.[1]

The financial adventures of the postwar period have generally originated in the exchange markets. Whereas, in earlier times power and fortunes were built on the enterprise of the merchant prince in distant lands, on the development of a new industrial technique, railroad expansion, or combinations, postwar fortunes were built on monetary depreciation.

The financial prizes of the years after 1919 fell to those who saw the significance of monetary instability and were quick to act on it. In all countries where depreciation was marked great opportunities were open to those who understood what was going on.[2] These opportunities resulted, in

[1] J. M. Keynes, *Monetary Reform* (New York, 1924), p. 29.
[2] Richard Lewinsohn, *Histoire de l'inflation,* traduit de l'Allemand par H. Simondet (Paris, 1926). See especially pp. 361-378.

part, from the obvious gains to be made by selling one currency for another when differentials in value were observed; that is, a purchase of pounds in the beginning of 1925 by a person holding francs led to a later gain when the appreciated pounds were sold for francs. There were chances for both time and place arbitrage.[1] Then there were the less conspicuous opportunities which resulted from different price levels in different countries, and the advantage of borrowing when debts could be repaid in money of a lower value. In addition to this, the various changes in industry offered unprecedented possibilities for the adventurer.

These gains were not necessarily based on a contribution to real wealth. They were sometimes built on the losses of the less speculative and sometimes on the mistakes of those who guessed wrong. It is recognized that there was much injustice and suffering, a ruthless redistribution of wealth which did not necessarily lead to future well being. The changes in depreciation were more dramatic and uncertain than were those of changing industrial technique, though not so arbitrary as those which came with violent class conflicts. Certainly events were capricious and many profits undeserved. Depreciation was a destructive, and not a constructive, force, though it brought some few gains with it.

Of course, France did not experience the catastrophic declines which occurred in Germany, Austria, and Russia. Her troubles were primarily financial and never disrupted completely the structure of her productive institutions. Moreover, the speculative gains in France went to a certain extent to those with a real understanding, at the expense of the ignorant, and so were based on a rough kind of economic justice. The French had learned something from the collapse of currencies in central Europe and began to

[1] Swiss francs and dollars were probably most sought after until 1925 when the pound sterling became a third important gold value currency. These arbitrage dealings became less desirable to banks because of the increased uncertainty of fluctuation, but the more speculative individuals took advantage of the chance for large gambling profits.

understand the meaning of depreciation. This understanding led to a growing fear of inflation and a willingness to accept taxation as a painful alternative. While some individuals were piling up profits as a result of depreciation, the general public was learning slowly the importance of clinging to simple remedies, and of saving the franc through budget adjustment just as it was slipping to the verge of the precipice.

Changes in external depreciation were more violent than those of internal depreciation. In fact, the rise of prices was similar in many ways to the cyclical movements which had been frequent before the war, although they became more extreme as the exchange movements came to dominate them. As this close connection became established between the two aspects of depreciation, the familiar relationships of consumer and producer were threatened and economic life became abnormal in many ways. The early price movement which had occurred while exchanges were relatively stable had not disturbed the usual currents of business as did later exchange fluctuations; but they were more difficult to control. The control of exchange rates led to a differential between the two values and a very abnormal situation in commerce; it is probable that pegging, while necessary to the carrying on of the war, made future adjustments more difficult.

While it is not possible to separate entirely these two aspects of depreciation, it is important to note that from a short-run point of view their characteristics and effects are distinct. So important is this fact that one must expect that when the two values of the currency draw together, after a period of profound disturbance, an approach to stability is inevitable. It is well to contrast the early years of extreme depreciation, when the two curves are different and the social effects entirely distinct, with the stages of collapse or of newly achieved stability, when the two come to fluctuate together. There are some surprising similarities between the period of collapse and that of newly gained stability. This results from the fact that the trader and business man who have suffered all disturbing ups and downs of depreciation seek by various devices to escape uncertainty. If stabilization is possible, they try to bring it about in a normal way. If this seems unattainable, they attempt to vary prices with exchange rates and so avoid unexpected differentials by keeping the *rates of change* of prices and exchange rates the same. This leads to a growing stability in gold values at times when currency values are changing most rapidly. So at the limit of depreciation, as at the very beginning, prices and exchange rates come into a measure of harmony.

Such changes in the attitude towards money as those leading to the conscious discounting of future depreciation spread gradually from a very few people to those who are least familiar with financial problems. There is an increase in the number of nonprofessional dealers in exchange, and this, as always, leads to wider fluctuations. Finally the general public becomes aware of the spread of the monetary disease and the pressure of demand for foreign exchange becomes tremendous; the full force of speculation bears down on the currency. In France the culmination of this tendency was the crisis of 1926. The vertical drop of the franc at this time must be explained on psychological grounds, for the basic reason was the desertion of the franc by the public, and the swelling of the stream of capital exports which carried the franc toward collapse.[1]

SEVERE DEPRECIATION SUGGESTS MODIFICATION OF THEORIES

Before things reached extremes, there was no conscious need for a theory of depreciated currency. Familiar formulations of the quantity theory and the relation of the bal-

[1] Unofficial estimates of capital exports in 1926 vary from about 5 billion francs to 20 billions. No exact figure can be given. See *supra*, Chapter I.

ance of payments to exchange values seemed to many to furnish adequate explanations of the fall of the franc. The large accumulation of foreign debts, in particular, was taken to explain the decline of 1919, and later inflation was given as a reason for postwar depreciation. But although at first glance exchange movements conformed to existing theories, a closer examination of what happened after the war shows that no such easy explanation is possible. The order of events was changing and complicated; in the spring of 1920 prices turned down, followed by a lesser fall in exchange rates. This decline made possible deflation, which was not comparable in amount to the price change. Moreover, after the first decline, exchange rates turned up again and eventually prices also rose, followed by some expansion of the note circulation. It is obvious that such a changing sequence casts doubt on the applicability of the quantity theory and that the mere existence of large foreign debts could not explain these erratic fluctuations of exchange rates. Those who tried to understand the significant causes had to study the reasons behind the shifting of capital balances and speculative movements. The increasing proportion of the floating debts which had no relation to commercial dealings made this task very difficult.

The rapid increase of speculative balances was the fundamental reason for the sudden, violent movements of exchange rates.[1] The situation was markedly different from that of prewar years. During normal times the tangible items of the balance of payments [2] had been the more im-

---

[1] Jules Décamps. *La Situation monétaire et l'avenir du franc* (speech made to *l'Union Republicaine,* December 19, 1924 (Paris, 1925), p. 8. M. Décamps emphasized in a number of speeches and articles the importance of the *flottante,* the mass of short-time commercial credits. He did not consider these credits completely liquidated in 1926 (interview with the writer).

[2] The distinction usually made is between visible and invisible items, but it seems well to make a somewhat different distinction here. Some of the invisible items, such as tourist trade, were regular and calculable, whereas capital movements were rapidly expansible and immeasurable.

portant ones and floating credits had been used mainly to balance temporary excesses of exports or imports, or to take advantage of short-time changes in money rates. Such credits were not under normal conditions very large, nor were they related very closely to the steady streams of investments which flowed from countries with much capital to those where new opportunities offered. There were, then, few sudden changes aside from the seasonal and cyclical swings, and these did not often affect the exchange rates to any notable extent. Gold exports, gold premiums, and various banking policies brought about quick reactions after any unusual movement. All this changed with the war. The credits extended by some countries to others were so large that the time and manner of repayments or refunding became urgent matters. The problem of paying for future imports when debts were already large [1] suggested many dangers to the keen observer. The elasticity of the foreign credit markets had been destroyed and future strains were bound to bring serious results.

In considering the various factors which govern the flow of short-time credits, one observes that there is a considerable volume which results from very real needs and which is independent of speculation. Then there is a residual or marginal sum which is not so easily obtained and which is responsible for fluctuations of the exchange rates. During the war the state was willing to cover the residual demand for foreign exchange and because of this readiness the demand never became very large in amount. The willingness of the state to supply any need reassured private financiers to such an extent that they took on this task themselves to a considerable degree, and the exchange rate was pegged without very great expense. Once the state

---

[1] See *supra,* Chapter III, p. 23. From the figures available it would seem that there were approximately two hundred million dollars' worth of credits extended to French merchants by private traders during the war period. It is not possible to give an exact figure, for some French foreign security holdings were liquidated to meet external debts.

withdrew, however, the amount of this marginal need became very great, for the attitude of private financiers changed with the new situation. Private credits were used not for investment but for speculation, and could not be shifted without influencing very markedly the demand and supply of foreign credit.

The reasons for holding balances in foreign countries are various. First, it is at certain times desirable to have funds in other centers to facilitate commercial dealings; and second, there are advantages growing out of differences in money rates. In the third place, with depreciation there appears the additional motive, the speculative opportunities of gaining from changes in relative values; and, in the fourth place, as the values become more unstable, the desire for security at all costs leads to a large demand for foreign exchange.[1] With each successive phase the controlling motive is less the result of commerce and more a product of speculation. Short-time capital movements become more than a balancing item, they become a tremendous force which modifies the most important elements of economic life.[2]

Even during the war, when the franc was pegged, the supply of balances by private financiers was extremely important. The fact that the government stood ready to fill any notable discrepancy between supply and demand led to confidence, and this confidence led to the ready supply of capital by individuals. These private funds approximately equaled those supplied through government negotiations.[3] It is even doubtful whether the government could have pegged the franc if the pegging had not brought in its train the support of many bankers. Whether public opinion

[1] This attitude is comparable to the desire of people to save even at a cost, represented by the cost curve of interest falling below zero.

[2] There has been a gradual shift of opinion in respect to the balancing item. Whereas, gold was traditionally given that rôle, it is now fairly generally considered that the more mobile forms of credit really perform this function.   [3] See *supra,* Chapter III, p. 102.

would have continued to support the franc in this way if the United States had not entered the war and put its funds at the disposal of the French government, is a matter for conjecture. Certainly the resources of France were becoming depleted in 1917, and it is generally the case that when reserves become low speculation withdraws its support. If the government had been embarrassed in its pegging operations, it is likely that bankers would have refused funds on private accounts. Thus confidence was the keystone of the arch supporting French finance.

The two notable war-time changes in the conditions affecting the franc, inconvertibility and the increased importance of capital items, both increased the likelihood of rapid fluctuations and enhanced the rôle of speculation. But because both were the natural result of war and because of the relative stability of the franc on the New York market, the significance of confidence during the war has sometimes been overlooked. Then, after the war there was a further change in the exchange situation. There was the further abandonment of fixed values when the artificial connection between the franc, the dollar, and the pound was suddenly broken. This was comparable in importance to the breaking of the link between the franc and gold in 1914. Then in addition to this, the motives governing the desire for credit changed with the increasing uncertainty in all phases of economic life. Thus the exchange problem became more and more abnormal, the future of the rates more incalculable. From a technical point of view, there were different limits and signs of future changes. From the broader social point of view, there were prospects of large gains and losses and an element of gambling in almost every economic endeavor.

Variety and surprise have characterized the years since the armistice. From 1919 to 1921 there was a sharp up and down movement of prices. This was accompanied in France by erratic exchange movements. The first break in the ex-

change value of the franc has been ascribed to technical
conditions. The second sharp break following the favorable
movement in the spring of 1920 was due partly to political
worries and partly to commercial needs. A similar break
occurred in 1921 but it was not quite so severe.[1] Then, in
1922, the reparation conflict came to dominate the whole
exchange situation for France, and the result was the decided upward swing of the cost of the dollar. This was accelerated by the collapse of the mark, which influenced those
speculators already very sensitive to unfavorable influences.
From this time on the drift of speculation was against the
franc and interest began to focus more and more on the
question of how the government was going to pay its bills
if it could not collect from Germany; thus the political situation both external and internal became increasingly important. Very naturally such a precarious state of affairs opened
the way for another kind of speculation, namely a deliberate
attack on the franc such as that which took place in 1924.
This year was marked by the most violent exchange variation of the whole period, but the permanent harm was not
so great as was that of the slow but cumulative force of
public opinion which forced the franc down through 1925
and the early part of 1926. As we note these influences, it is
apparent that though their nature differs somewhat at different times, they are alike in that they are the results of
estimates and the manifestation of opinion. In fact, no
theoretical explanation of the franc is complete without
emphasis on the intangible psychological forces. The older
theories have to be modified and adjusted if they are to fit
these striking postwar changes in value.

The discussion of the French exchange problem has emphasized the broader influences rather than the technical
aspects of exchange dealings. This is because the reasons
for the decline of the franc, as well as for its ultimate stability, are rooted far back in French political and economic

[1] See *supra*, Chapter IV.

life. It is, therefore, essential to emphasize the broader aspects of the case and to keep from the confusion of detail and matters not of primary significance to the larger movements of the franc value. The significant turning points were, as has been seen, in 1919, 1920, 1922, and 1926. Even the severe crisis of 1924 can be given a subordinate place, since it was to a considerable extent merely an interruption in the steady upward trend of the cost of foreign exchange which was characteristic of those years.

Four Aspects of Exchange Problem

It is possible, however, to distinguish four main aspects of the exchange problem. These are questions of *measurement*, of *prediction*, of *control*, and of *stability*.[1] All of these problems are basic in financial life and are closely connected with production, investment, government finance, and matters of distribution and exchange. They take on different meanings, however, as depreciation becomes extreme. It is obvious that in using the foreign exchange problem as a starting point one might carry one's investigation in almost any direction to advantage. In times of severe monetary dislocations the exchanges constitute the core of most of the larger economic difficulties to a peculiar degree. Thus these four matters become of the utmost concern to the statesmen and the general public. The different significance of these four things under more static conditions is worth noting.

Measurement, the first of the four aspects of the exchange problem, is a simple process under normal conditions. When the gold standard is working in the usual way and exchange dealings are confined to the narrow and highly specialized markets of professionals, there is no difficulty involved. The

---

[1] *Control* refers to the ability to limit the zone of variation in money value. *Stability* is here used as meaning the selection and maintenance of a new and permanent value as for instance, four cents, for the franc.

simple ratio of the franc to the dollar or the pound, based
on relative amounts of gold content, is tied to certain known
quantities. Even the slight variations which occur are clear
and precise in their meaning. Since all dollars are equivalent, and all pounds, the variety seen in the exchange quotations is mainly the specious one arising out of the different
gold content of the units and the additional complication
introduced by the time element in transferring funds from
one center to another. The variation in the relation of the
unit is precisely measured in quantities of gold.

Prediction, in the second place, is fairly easy under normal exchange conditions. Since the specie export points set
limits beyond which quotations for foreign money cannot
go, and since these points are determined by such definite
things as the cost of transportation and insurance for risk,
there is no very great uncertainty as to the point where a
reaction in value is apt to set in, though there is considerable uncertainty as to when this reaction will take place.
In any case, the fluctuations are kept to a narrow zone
within which professional dealers take their profits. Those
who deal in the exchanges know with a reasonable degree
of accuracy the conditions which govern the gold export
points. Moreover, since the market is in the hands of the
insiders fluctuations are more regular and of shorter duration than is the case when more people are speculating.
This situation changed completely after 1914.

Then, in the third place, control was a different problem
before the war from what it has been since. Although methods of control have differed considerably in different countries, central banks have exercised a considerable influence
in most cases. The technique was probably most efficient in
England, where the discount rate was the main instrument.
Because of the financial experience and traditions of England, funds flowed quickly to London with a slight increase
of money rates. France, on the other hand, used different
methods and exerted a less powerful influence on the ex-

change rates; through her gold premium policy she steadied the rates to a certain extent.[1] This method made it impossible for Paris to be a financial center comparable to London, but it seems to have been fairly well adapted to French needs. The exchange rates varied little and were not a disturbing influence in economic life. It is true that one is accustomed to consider the exchange rates as subordinate and dependent factors, and so they were to a considerable degree, but this was due in part to the gradual development of the financial methods alluded to above. In fact, stability, the fourth aspect of the exchange problem, was in no sense an urgent one in the more important European countries.[2] Granted the gold mechanisms, professional dealings, central bank control, and a normal economic life, monetary units, kept within a narrow zone of value, did not need any definite stabilizing forces such as those to be considered in connection with depreciated currencies. Thus it is only in considering the postwar situation, that one can understand the full significance and complexity of the exchange problem.

Depreciated money is a particular case in the general field of monetary theory. Each one of the four points just mentioned will be found to act differently in depreciation as compared with situations generally considered normal. Nevertheless, the particular case throws light on the general problems, and so merits careful consideration. Even though the conclusion reached might be compared to those based on the study of a diseased or deformed human body, it is evident that from the study of the serious ailment one can learn to control the lesser. Thus analyses of postwar fluctuations make it easier to understand those which are less violent, even though many of the relationships are quite different. For instance, one can learn methods of control by

[1] See *supra*, Chapter II.

[2] Countries on a gold exchange standard such as India were constantly working at the problems of stability and control.

studying the points at which attempts to control have failed.[1] Moreover, stability may become at any moment instability, the normal the abnormal—change and revolution are constantly imminent.

Once depreciation sets in, the four phases of the exchange problem become troublesome matters. Difficulties in measurement, which were not existent before, throw many stumbling blocks in the way of constructive policy. There was, in the first place, the conflicting evidence offered by internal as compared with external depreciation [2] and it was not always possible to say which indicated the true situation in regard to money values. It became difficult to express the changes of value on the exchanges in terms of goods, so that the meaning of the quotations was narrowly limited. Then again, the franc often rose in one market while it fell in others, which made it almost impossible to know whether the franc was falling or whether some other currencies were rising. Exchange quotations became a mass of contradictory indications of values changing in apparently arbitrary fashion, whose real meaning could not be understood. These difficulties became much greater as depreciation passed beyond the incipient phase of the war to the severe phase of post-war years.

PREDICTION BECAME IMPOSSIBLE

The possibility of predicting a reaction in exchange values under normal conditions has been explained; no such possibility existed once depreciation went to any length. Of the many who engaged in exchange transactions since the war, those who gained as well as those who lost will agree that no safe forecasts were possible. The gains and losses were the results of sheer gambling in most cases. As Keynes said in 1923:

No one can have complete confidence whether they [the exchanges] are to be a great deal better or very much worse.[3]

[1] See *supra,* Chapter VI.
[2] See *supra,* Chapter VII.
[3] Keynes, *op. cit.,* p. 124.

While it is true that under certain conditions all the more important influences—prices, commerce, revenues, and so on—indicated a rise, yet at that very time, perhaps, public opinion, the most uncontrollable element, caused a contrary movement. Such was the case in 1926.

The consideration of the more important fluctuations of the franc value during these years makes it plain that at no time was an economic factor, or even a group of economic factors, as immediately important to the franc as was the tide of public confidence. Moreover, the attitudes of the French were governed by different forces at different times. During the early years of depreciation they were dominated by a blind optimism which was more tenacious than the wiser speculators could have expected. Then, after the continuous sag of the value of the franc, the French began to watch various economic signs, to have vague ideas of what was behind money value, and to govern their actions by such things. Such indications were both financial and political. They were found in the security market, in budget speeches, in announcements regarding commerce. This attempt to understand the situation was an indication of progress, but it was not always a manifestation of a clear and balanced insight into conditions. It made the position of the professional hardly less precarious since he could not anticipate what economic doctrine, only half understood, might become prevalent at any time. This state of affairs existed from 1922 to 1925.[1] Then, as the dangers and difficulties became patent and a less experienced group was added to those who had already puzzled over the exchanges, public opinion fastened its attention with frantic determination on the note circulation and the budget. This was the condition with which Briand, Caillaux, and Herriot tried to deal in the spring of 1926. It was a time of hysteria, when terror expressed in economic language drove capital abroad. No one could have predicted such a wild outbreak, though many

[1] See *supra,* Chapter V.

knew that it was a possibility. Then, in addition to these changing influences on public opinion, tax programs, particularly those which approached the capital levy in form, sometimes excited tremendous disapproval, though occasionally they had been considered without creating a very great stir.

It is apparent that to predict the major exchange fluctuations under such conditions was as hazardous as to prophesy the weather a year in advance. Of course, it was possible during some stages of depreciation to make forecasts which were more often right than wrong. This was particularly true during the very early and the very late stages. For instance, in the beginning, exchanges did approximate the values indicated by real economic factors, and again in the later stages of decline, as in Germany, cumulative forces came into action which made it certain that the fall once commenced would continue. In fact, in the stage called collapse it may be assumed that the line of descent in logarithms is a straight line. During most of the years of French depreciation, however, within the broad limits set by stability and collapse, no prediction was possible.

The very short-time exchange fluctuations, on the other hand, assume more regularity than do the major movements. It has frequently been possible for those who knew the nature of the market and followed regularly its minor variations to know at what time it was best to take profits and so to predict in a general way the day to day movements. It was necessary, of course, to realize the considerable margin of error, because various catastrophic events upset conditions. A study of the detail of the exchange rates indicates that the speculator who liquidated his holdings on the fourth day of an up or down movement would on the average make a profit. Moreover, the down movements are, as one might expect, of shorter duration than the up movements. In the majority of cases in which foreign exchanges dropped, values turned in the other direction within a two-day period, whereas on the upward trend the wave would often last four or five days. This frequent profit taking, while an evidence of the uncertainty of the situation as a whole, is at the same time an indication that there was no universal expectation of a continued long decline.

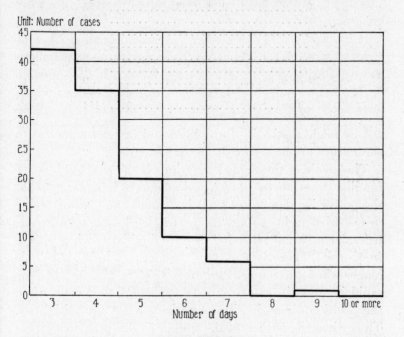

CHART XXIV

NUMBER OF EXCHANGE VARIATIONS, ACCORDING TO
DURATION

In order to classify in a rough way the fluctuations of the exchange rates, the daily quotations given in the appendix have been considered in respect to the direction and duration of change. The result of a chance sampling of these data gives the following frequency table. (See Table XXV.) This sampling includes about one-third of the changes in direction of exchange quotations, exclusive of the one- and two-day changes. Since, however, it is incomplete, it must

TABLE XXV

FREQUENCY OF EXCHANGE FLUCTUATIONS OF VARIOUS DURATIONS[1]

Number of Days	Number of Instances
3	42
4	35
5	20
6	10
7	6
8	0
9	1
10 or more	0
Total	114

not be made the basis of any hard and fast statement as to the nature of these short-time movements.

The result of these quick reactions is the saw-tooth curve familiar to students of the exchanges. It is apparent that the professionals felt out their instrument and, while trying to consider each case on its merits, tended to take a conservative attitude which led them to liquidate their positions frequently. There is a natural tendency to hold on a little longer when the momentum appears to be greater, and the rapid increase in rates suggests to dealers that even when the reaction occurs it will not entirely offset the initial rise. Thus when the decline of the franc was sharpest, most speculators did not liquidate as soon as was their custom. Such a state of affairs as is indicated in these fluctuations was both the result of and the opportunity for short selling in francs. To the extent that the insiders controlled the market, the curve is characteristic of such conditions. However, since after 1919, the general public began to take part in such transactions, it is probable that professionals followed as well as led in such up and down swings. The times when the public was most active are indicated on the curves by a breaking away from this seesaw motion with a noticeable rise or fall, only slightly dented by the contrary movements.

[1] See appendix. Fluctuations of less than three days are excluded.

This new influence can be seen in the exchange curves of 1925 and part of 1926.

One expects to find a certain regularity in the fluctuations of the exchange rates arising from seasonal changes in commodity trade, but this ceased to be true once depreciation gained headway in France. Keynes, writing in October, 1923,[1] says that the franc was at its best in April and May and at its worst in October and December. It does not seem wise to look for a seasonal swing in the postwar period; eight years is too short a time to make this useful, particularly when several of the years are conspicuous exceptions to any rule. For instance, the improvement of the franc in the late spring of 1924 was obviously not seasonal, and if the sharp break of the first months of the year is passed over with a smoother line, there was no net improvement at that time.[2] Then again, May and June were bad times for the franc in both 1925 and 1926, whereas August and September were times of marked improvement in those two years, in large measure because Parliament was no longer in session. It is true that December was a black period for French finance in 1919, 1922, 1923, and 1925, but this was definitely due to the year-end settlement on the one hand and to the bitter budget debates on the other. In general, in the years 1922, 1923, and 1925, the seasonal movement which might be expected is entirely obliterated by the more marked upward trend of the cost of the foreign exchanges.

It is probable, then, that there were two types of fairly predictable movements which were observed by the most clearsighted: in the first place, the very short-time fluctuations which were the result, to a considerable extent, of technical conditions; and in the second, the slower trend which can be represented after the fact by the straight line drawn from the 1918 value of eighteen cents a franc to the

[1] Keynes, *op. cit.*, p. 122. Compare Albert Aftalion, *Monnaie, prix et change* (Paris, 1927), p. 24. He gives a seasonal curve for notes in circulation.   [2] See *supra,* Chapter V.

1927 value of four cents a franc. This latter line could have been forecast to a certain extent by a consideration of the adjustment necessary to bring the franc into harmony with the price level, the volume of notes in circulation, the value of the budget, and other factors with which customary relations may be observed. It is this kind of change which the quantity theorists can most successfully explain. As for the intermediate changes, those characterized as week to week and month to month, they were unpredictable in the extreme. The slight tendency to rhythm found in day to day changes is one which does not obtain in all cases, while the ultimate value of the franc would have been a very risky subject of prophecy because of the wild uncertainty of political conditions.

The Difficulty of Control

Prediction is of importance primarily to those seeking individual profit, though of course the sum of individual profits goes to make up the gains of a nation. Certainly, however, control is of much greater significance to social welfare, and at the same time more difficult to accomplish. By control we mean the attempt to steady or limit the fluctuations of exchange rates without trying to keep them at a fixed value or without deliberate choice of a permanent level of value. Pegging, for instance, is such an effort; it often aims to keep currency in a precise relation with some other money, but sometimes merely to steady and modulate it. The difficulties of pegging under conditions of severe depreciation have been pointed out. It is possible only when reinforced by confidence, and when economic conditions are fairly favorable.

The complexity of the problem derives from the fact that control of any kind depends on the support of public opinion, and public opinion sometimes depends on attempts to control. This was illustrated by the readiness of bankers to furnish private credits during the war, because the government met the additional needs. Certainly any steadying influence was more difficult when financial habits became disordered and the possibility of variation increased. Those capital exports which are due to the action of a large number of people are much harder to stop than those which are occasioned by a very few financiers. When many are speculating, intervention in the exchange markets must be backed by larger sums of money. Thus the Morgan loan of 100 million dollars was effective in 1924, but was not sufficient to stand the steady pressure of small selling orders in 1926. One may take the billion dollars of foreign exchange accumulated by the Bank of France in 1927 as an indication of what would have been necessary to meet the 1926 emergency.[1]

Moreover, the control of the exchange through pegging is, in the last analysis, a temporary and artificial procedure. There can be no lasting certainty until all aspects of the value of money have become adjusted to each other. And this cannot be permanent unless there is reason to suppose that the government will order financial affairs so that the new equilibrium shall not be upset. Attempts to steady the exchanges have been considered in Chapter VI, "The Unsuccessful Fight Against Depreciation." These have been in the main technical and financial measures; for example, deflation, the increase of the discount rate, the attempt to limit inflation by issuing loans, and various restrictive laws. Any of these measures might have been effective if depreciation had not passed beyond the incipient stage. As it was, they were worse than useless, they were taken as indications of the desperate condition of finance and so influenced public opinion adversely. Often in this paradoxical situation well-tried financial expedients failed, and the arrival of a new personality on the political stage steadied the exchanges even if no constructive financial policy was presented to the people. In the face of such erratic forces, it is hard

[1] See *supra,* Chapter VI. Chart XVII.

to see how the franc could have been subject to much control. It is probable that the support given the franc in the worst crises, notably in 1924 and during a part of 1925, was the best effort that could have been put forth from the technical point of view.

Such control, therefore, as was effective was that which aimed, through general political and financial improvements, to free the exchanges from the abnormal influence of speculation. The close relation of the budget to the exchange rate, certainly not a normal phenomenon, was one of the most delicate features of the situation. As Rist stated,

The most effective methods of lowering prices and raising the value of the franc on the exchanges are to increase production and to achieve a balanced budget. This last, in particular, exerts on the exchanges a powerful influence in inducing speculation to take positions only in the direction of a rise and in assuring, therefore, a large inflow of foreign capital, the most responsive element in the balance of account and the best guarantee of favorable exchanges.[1]

It is true, of course, that all measures which steadied the exchanges had some direct or indirect connection with the future volume of the note circulation. But this connection loses some of its immediate significance when one realizes that everything which bore on the government's financial situation had an influence on the note circulation. Looked at in this light, it seems as if fluctuations of the exchanges and the rise and fall of the note circulation, each acting on the other constantly, were essentially joint results of a common cause. The removal of this cause was contingent on the solution of political and financial difficulties in which France became involved. The abnormal expenditures and the disordered income of the government had to be put to rights before the ordinary monetary mechanisms, which acted on the note circulation and on capital movements, could have their usual, quieting effect. Since monetary dif-

[1] Charles Rist, *La Déflation en pratique* (Paris, 1924), p. 129.

ficulties had a broad basis, remedial measures had to be very comprehensive. Production in the devastated area. international commerce, and taxation all had to be readjusted to changed conditions; and, above all, there had to be a reasonable certainty of government stability before the fears of radical finance were set at rest.

The problem of steadying the exchanges had to be met in different countries in different ways, since the original difficulties developed from different disorders. There were, of course, marked differences between countries, for example, England never experienced severe depreciation, and so could use the usual financial expedients of deflation and discount rates. There were also marked differences between countries in similar stages of depreciation, such as Germany before 1921 and France until 1926, for in Germany the external debt was the disturbing element and foreign relations the field on which the struggle was fought. In France, on the other hand, the immediate dangers were internal and a part of the disturbance was due to the unmanageability of the internal debt.

It is also important to distinguish the effects in one country of various means of control during successive phases of depreciation. Once the early stage, best exemplified by England, is passed, the ordinary instruments of finance tend to have a perverse effect. Since the gesture to restrict the circulation or to circumscribe financial activities is taken as a sign of weakness by the more cautious observers, it is also taken as an indication of further ill-judged expedients and emergency measures, such as the issuance of further loans, more note issues, and sudden and untried tax programs. The natural consequence is the attempt to shift balances abroad and the rapid fluctuation of exchange rates. It was not until the second stage of depreciation that this was true of France, nor until that time that government finance came definitely to dominate other economic elements.

Control of runaway money is never easy. Once the public

is thoroughly alarmed, all kinds of absurd and unimportant events may influence the ideas of capital holders. The newspapers have tremendous power and the casual remarks of officials are taken as the basis for purchases and sales of exchange. Since opinion comes to exercise a real influence and is more than the anticipation or expression of economic facts, the responsibility of the government in clarifying opinion is very great. It is probable, for this reason, that the *Experts' Report* in 1926 had more influence than is generally recognized.[1]

The main limiting factors seem then to have been these: first, the economic needs of France resulting from the war; second, budget disorders closely related to the debt problems; third, the changing note circulation and excessive increases in the debt; and fourth, and paralleling all these concrete causes, public opinion, interpreting and exaggerating the difficulties. The result was the uneven up and down swings of the franc value with a serious net loss to the nation's well-being.

STABILIZATION CALLS FOR THE CHOICE OF A NEW PAR

Once a reasonable degree of control has been attained, the problem of final stabilization looms on the horizon. This necessitates the deliberate choice of a new par value, and is a delicate matter unless virtual stability has been of such long standing that the new value has been universally accepted as a permanent basis of economic transactions. The time element is of great importance in easing the tension and simplifying the work of the statesmen. A period of six to nine months seems to be needed to bring the different aspects of economic life into harmony.[2] If, as was the case in France, stabilization takes place after such an interval of calm, the final step is of comparatively little consequence.

[1] *Rapport du Comité des Experts*, (Décret du 31 mai, 1926, Paris).
[2] Note the drawing together of the curves at the end of 1927, Chart I.

Nevertheless, until the new value is an accomplished fact, there is always some speculation as to possible values which causes uncertainty and variation in exchange dealings.

The choice of the new norm may be made within a fairly wide zone, because political factors compete with economic interests in determining possible values. For instance, no government can easily afford to take on itself the recriminations of those who lose more because the value is arbitrarily increased—or, on the other hand, who lose because it is decreased. Any definite legislative action arouses at once all forms of complaint, and the new monetary value is made the scapegoat for all ills. It is interesting to see how in some circumstances an unstable exchange becomes a powerful force in politics. After the turmoil of July, 1926, Poincaré was able to put the question of confidence on almost any measure and win the day. He made it quite clear that he would accept no compromises and that his defeat on any important measure would mean the collapse of the currency. Thus, the potential instability of the franc made it easier to put through a consistent program, the danger of instability made actual stability more desired and, in a sense, easier to obtain. Politics and finance influenced each other in such a way that the stage was prepared for stabilization.

To the politician, the value chosen is apt to signify the balance of power between different social groups, the producer and the consumer, the capitalist and the wage earner, those who live on profits and those who have fixed income. The interests of these groups are normally different and it is only after a threat of catastrophe that they become temporarily harmonized in the desire for stability. Even at such a time they do not subordinate their narrower interests completely, and tend to disagree when the problem of the final value is under discussion. For this reason it is regrettable that the value of the franc could not have been fixed definitely in September or October of 1926, when the general wish was for calm and security. It is only in view of the

very close connections between political and economic life
that the delay seems justified. For it is probable that the
period of tentative stability allowed Poincaré a longer interval and stronger support for the passage of his budget
proposals.

The economist, in contrast to the politician, views the
value chosen in respect to its purchasing power relations
with other countries, the future of international commerce,
the gold value of the budget burden and the quantity of
paper money. It is never possible to harmonize all these
factors completely, though a reasonable adjustment may
be reached. There are some, Keynes, Cassel and Gregory,
for instance, who chose for special emphasis the purchasing
power aspect of the new value of the currency. They advise,
in particular cases, keeping any slight advantage for commerce by setting the exchange value of the money low,
rather than high, to encourage production. Keynes has
stressed also the significance of the ratio of the debt service
to the total budget, which must ultimately approach normal
on a gold basis. In the case of France in particular, Keynes,
in 1926, urged further depreciation in order that the internal
debt might ultimately sink to a value equivalent in gold to
that of prewar days. Professor Moulton, on the other hand,
also with the debt in mind, in 1925, urged appreciation and
chose the figure 6.43 cents a franc.[1] This would have made
it difficult to export to most countries. It would, however,
have helped creditors as compared with debtors. Still others,
viewing the matter from different angles, looked mainly to
the advances of the Bank of France to the state and the note
circulation. These latter urged the difficulty of increasing taxation and favored holding the franc at a value

[1] H. G. Moulton and Cleona Lewis, *The French Debt Problem* (New
York, 1925), pp. 207, 208. He also urged the forced consolidation of the
internal debt. This project was, however, entirely unfeasible politically, as
was quite evident later; the mere suggestion led to violent panic. Professor
Moulton later qualified this view in an interview with the writer in April,
1926.

consistent with the amount of advances actually outstanding.

The problems of stability will be discussed further in a later chapter.[1] They are mentioned here in order to complete the subdivision of the exchange problems into its four main aspects, that is, measurement, prediction, control, and stability. Although there comes a time in the history of depreciation when stabilization is very much desired, the manner, time, and value of carrying it through arouse great antagonisms. The difficulties involved are illustrated in the case of the first unsuccessful attempt to stabilize the Belgian franc. It seems that this effort in 1925 might well have been successful if another value had been chosen and larger external loans had been secured.[2] It is obvious that the choice of the new value is a delicate technical matter which is unfortunately obscured by political problems. It is probable that those who advocated the lower values of the franc with a view to stimulating production exaggerated the influence of such a choice. Events in various countries indicate that stabilization at any value was apt to cause depression for a short time. This is true because it is not the differentials between prices which are stimulating so much as it is the increase of such differentials.

The Peculiar Importance of Exchange Rates

The foreign exchange rates, in the case of France, came to have a marked influence on the whole economic life. While it is true that they were primarily indications of underlying conditions, they were for short periods more powerful than this fact would imply. It is just here that there is a point of difference between those who emphasize price levels

[1] See *infra,* Chapter X.

[2] *Le Pour et le contre* (October, 1926), pp. 854, 855. The later attempt in 1926, which succeeded, was supported by an external loan and internal consolidation of the short-term debt. Moreover, the franc was set at a lower value, 35 to the dollar.

and note circulation and those who give great importance
to exchange rates. If it is true that exchange rates merely
anticipate future changes in the note circulation, then the
man who is directing affairs of state can put his mind
on the problem of preventing excessive note issues and
let things take their course. This is undoubtedly the case
when depreciation is in the first stages. As instability becomes greater, the desirability of government securities, and
of property within a nation, becomes less, so tax receipts
and the proceeds of loans diminish, and the statesman who
is working to limit note issues finds the treasury already
being emptied of funds. It is at such times as this, when a
strong tide of opinion often makes funds flow away from the
state, that the minister of finance may have to turn to his
only sure resource, the central Bank, and secure notes. This
additional currency, moreover, though issued as a temporary
expedient, may not easily be withdrawn, and in this way a
short-time speculative wave may leave a lasting impression.

It is for this reason that at certain times the control of the
exchange rates was more important than the control of
any one single factor. If there were no wild fluctuations in
the value of the franc in terms of foreign money, the public
left their investments in government securities alone, and
the minister of finance was able to keep things going without any inflationary measures. The increases in taxation
voted in 1920, 1924, and 1925, were sufficient to meet the
normal demands of the state if there were no unusual withdrawals of money from the *bons de la défense nationale.*[1]
Thus any successful effort to steady the exchanges had a
very great effect on the whole financial situation. Moreover, experience has demonstrated that it is possible for the
government to exert a considerable influence on foreign exchange rates, while direct price and credit control are diffi-

---

[1] The peculiar nature of the *bons de la défense* must be remembered.
See *supra,* Chapter III. They were not traded between individuals to any
extent, but repayment from the government was guaranteed.

cult to achieve. Hawtrey and others have pointed out,[1] that
one cannot well stabilize both; and since there must be an
adjustment between the exchanges and the price level, one
point must be fixed and the other allowed to come into
harmony with it.

Exchange speculation was based on a scrutiny of real factors; but these were more general and complex in their nature than some of the narrower expressions of the quantity
theory would account for. In France the main problem was
the condition of government finance. The mechanism
through which this affected the franc has already been described. The first excessive need for funds led to borrowings
from the Bank of France by the state, then to short-time
loans, and still later to some long-time loans. All of these
forms of borrowing caused additions to the note circulation.
This increase in notes affected the government in three
ways. First, there was the direct effect through the influence
of the price level on government expenditures; this we have
considered the least important. Second, there was the indirect influence through the maturing *bons;* this latter
charge on the state made a net addition to expenses, with no
offsetting increase in receipts. Then, there were, in the
third instance, the complex effects of speculation and the
flight of capital, which interacted in such a way as to lessen
government receipts from all sources and make the passage
of an adequate tax program extremely difficult. It will be
evident, when these three matters have been considered,
that the contemporaneous flow of commerce, gold reserves,
the discount policy, and attempts at price control were of
little importance in comparison with them.

THE BUDGET BASIS OF SPECULATIVE INFLUENCES

French inflation was due to the existence of large budget
deficits. This was not the case in every country. In the

[1] R. G. Hawtrey, *Monetary Reconstruction* (London, 1923), p. 143.

United States, for instance, what inflation there was came
through the expansion of industrial activity and through the
increase of government borrowings. The increase in securities as well as in industrial and commercial values which
could be used as collateral for loans led almost inevitably
to growing bank deposits for the use of manufacturers and
merchants and the drawing of currency from banks into
circulation. In France, on the other hand, the order of
events was more simple and obvious; the state being in
need of funds, borrowed from the Bank to pay its bills. As
the quantities of notes so pumped into the circulation
pushed upward an already rising price level, there was a
secondary effect such as the one described as taking place
in America. The need for means of payment increased and
the pressure on banks for cash was at times great. The following comparison shows that the note circulation increased faster than the liabilities of the banks.

TABLE XXVI

CREDIT AND THE NOTE CIRCULATION [1]

Condition of three large banks, 1913-1918

(in millions of francs)

	Cash	Bills Discounted	Deposits and Current Accounts	Bank of France Note Circulation
1913	471	3,494	5,435	5,714 plus gold
1914	1,209	1,309	3,888	10,043
1915	999	1,912	3,715	13,310
1916	1,052	2,531	6,401	16,679
1917	1,287	3,805	6,083	22,337
1918	906	4,626	6,858	30,250

The slight expansion of discounts and deposits contrasts
strongly with the increase in the note circulation. Thus it

[1] U. S. Senate, *Foreign Currency and Exchange Investigation*, pp. 470,
473. The three banks given are the *Comptoir national d'escompte de Paris*,
the *Crédit Lyonnais*, and the *Société générale*. For a detailed study of the
credit situation of the large banks, see Jean Lorin, *Les Banques françaises
de dépôt pendant la guerre* (thesis, Paris, 1923), bank statements are given,
pp. 359-392.

seems evident that the inflationary influence came through the government as a buyer of war supplies, in the first instance.[1] Even in the later years the exchanges, dominated by the budget, and not the expansion of bank credits, were the impelling force which kept prices up.

The origin of the deficits was, in the first instance, the need for supplies; second, large expenditures of the government on reconstruction; third, bad management of the budgetary mechanism, the failure to collect taxes, the misuse of credit. The size of the budget deficits cannot be measured at this point. In fact, it is probable that no accurate figures for budget deficits will be available for several years.

It is important to note, however, that the political influence on the exchanges is due to the fundamental importance of budget deficits. Granted the definite influence of exchange rates on prices in the French case, we come inevitably to a psychological theory of the short-run value of depreciated money. Any reasonable objection to such a theory must be based not on a doubt as to its validity but rather on questions as to the way in which to make such a theory serve the ends of practical economic life. Such conclusions are not new, but they open up new lines of analysis not so far employed by those who follow exclusively the older body of doctrines associated with the English classical school.[2]

In addition to the purely statistical data bearing out these contentions, the study of public opinion and of financial judgments during the latter periods of depression has been extremely enlightening. A careful survey of the day to day and week to week expressions of opinion in comparison with the movements of the exchange rates is a help in understanding the depreciation of the franc at those periods.

It is obviously impossible to reproduce here such a de-

---

[1] See *supra*, Chapters III and IV.

[2] The emphasis on the psychological factor in continental economics has been greater than in England.

tailed study, but it is worth while to consider a few weeks
of the years 1925 and 1926 in this manner. Such an exposition will serve both as demonstration of the correctness
of the general conclusions made, and as a sample of the in-
tricacy and unexpectedness of the variation of exchange
rates. So strange were these variations that a chronological
study of French finance has its humorous as well as its
serious aspects. One minister scarcely had time to install
himself in the formidable building at the *Place de Louvre*
before the desk was cleared for his successor. It is obvious
that financial projects worked out under such conditions
would be full of flaws, while their rejection was based partly
on their novelty and partly on political antagonisms. The
press featured these proposals in a dramatic way. Almost
every Frenchman paid some attention to the various projects and according to his approval changed the investment
of his savings or rolling capital. The result was the extreme
fluidity of all funds and a growing distrust of the government on the part of the people.

The Situation in 1925

There is little wonder that in 1925 the French people began to think something was wrong. The direction of the
ministry of finance was in the course of the year in the
hands of six different men [1] advocating as many different
programs.[2] The difficulties of the Herriot ministry in April,
after the attempt to put into effect a capital levy, led
to the year's first sharp fall of the franc in the spring. The
stability which lasted through August and September was
based in part on the hope that Caillaux had some new formula for handling the pressing difficulties. His internal loan,

[1] They were MM. Clémentel, de Monzie, Caillaux, Painlevé, Loucheur,
and Doumer. See also *supra* Chapters V and VI.
[2] *Reference Service on International Affairs,* Survey No. 5 (November 15,
1925); Special supplement, Nos. 4, 5. December 31, 1925.

the first to be tied up with gold,[1] aimed to bring the government 15 billion francs, but it was a flat failure. Only about six billion francs were brought in; about half of this was in cash and the rest was the result of the conversion of other loans.[2] Meanwhile the heavy maturities of the year 1925, 22 billion francs, made the treasury situation very grave,[3] but few people realized it until later. A feeling of false security had developed after Caillaux started to work. The adjournment of Parliament always gave a breathing space, and summer tourists notably increased the temporary demand for credits; the franc was worth almost five cents in September. While it is fairly certain the French unit was being pegged through the summer, it is also probable that this did not necessitate any large volume of purchases. In the autumn, however, the situation was far from sound, and the news of the failure of the Caillaux debt negotiations in Washington was sufficient to precipitate the crisis which was due on many counts. Nevertheless, the government was making a desperate effort to hold on to a precarious stability.

The fall of the franc in October might be attributed to the failure of the United States debt negotiations, but, except for the initial disappointment, such hardly seems to be the true explanation. There were other things happening in France which made a greater impression. In fact, there was considerable feeling of relief in some quarters that the negotiations had fallen through, while the failure of the internal loan was a serious setback. The government's half-successful measures to conceal the insufficiency of the yield did not tend to restore confidence. Tax receipts were

[1] The relation of the franc to the pound sterling was made the basis for changes in the interest rate on these bonds. It therefore developed that the interest rate was practically constant on a gold basis. The loan was supposed to be bought only by holders of *bons de la défense*. But the stipulation was not strictly enforced.   [2] See *Le Temps* (October 22, 1925).
[3] See *supra,* Chapter V, and *infra,* Chapter IX. Etienne Clémentel, *Inventaire,* p. 242.

less than estimated for September; trade was unfavorable, and autumn buying called for fairly large purchases of foreign exchange in Paris. It is probable that there was a considerable amount of speculation of two kinds. First, there were those who felt that there were possibilities for large gains from manipulating the exchange values, despite the rout of speculators in 1924. Second, there were investors of a different type who began to look to the foreign bank deposits and shares for stability of value. This was the time when the French tried to discover how to save their capital from annihilation as the Germans had tried before them.

The situation was, therefore, far from simple in the autumn of 1925. A number of factors tended to pull the franc to a lower level and many disturbing political currents existed under the surface of affairs. Certain powerful bankers opposed Caillaux for personal as well as for business reasons. There were financial interests which still hoped that a capital levy would be imposed that would place them in a strategic position. The selling of the franc was said [1] to originate in Paris rather than in New York, which is an additional reason for supposing that it was determined by the internal more than by the external situation. The Caillaux ministry fell in October. The difficulties described above were enhanced by the increasing menace of the socialist party, which had been holding a conference at Nice. The resignation of Caillaux did not affect the franc adversely at the moment. As the *New York Times* explained:

The event had, however, been already so fully discounted by speculators in exchange that it was comparatively easy to support the franc in a market so full of uncovered bear positions.

The same journal continues: [2]

There was, however, a species of intervention in the franc market last week, but it was carried out by private banks apparently desirous of obliging the new premier. . . .

[1] *New York Herald,* Paris edition (November 23, 1925).
[2] *The New York Times* (November 2, 1925).

Painlevé took over the finance portfolio after the resignation of Caillaux and elaborated a plan along new lines. The striking, outstanding feature which led to his downfall was the forced consolidation of the 3-, 6- and 10-year treasury bonds.[1] During these troubled weeks the cost of exchange continued to rise and the effect on industry was marked. Factories received such large orders that they were alarmed and hesitated to accept them as dependable, while at the same time the trends of foreign commerce became confused.

The second Painlevé ministry did not last long.[2] The proposals had been so entirely unpalatable to the general public, the effort to compromise the capital levy issue had been such a failure, and the effect on the exchanges was so unfortunate that his position became untenable. Speculation followed these events very closely. The Paris Herald said:

> On the assumption that the fall of the Painlevé government would be favorably received abroad operators in Paris began selling foreign currencies in the early morning so the pound opened lower at 123 and the dollar at 25.38. But the first foreign advice showed that the opinion of Paris was far from being shared abroad and consequently sellers had to cover rapidly.[3]

It was true in this case, as so often, that the foreign centers —London and New York—did not analyze closely the different projects, but were upset rather by the frequency of the change of policy. They argued on the reasonable principle that almost any active measure was better than hesitation and delay. Owing in part to this outside opinion and in part to the difficulties in France over trying to form a ministry, the fall of the franc was rapid at the end of the month.

---

[1] Exception was made for those maturing in 1925, but the public did not rely on this provision since it was not obvious where the money was coming from to meet these obligations.

[2] The Painlevé cabinet with the premier as minister of finance lasted only from November 10 to November 21.

[3] *New York Herald,* Paris edition (November 23, 1925).

Briand, called on for the second time in the week of the end of November, finally consented to form a ministry. The condition of public sentiment by this time had become almost hysterical. The fear of the repudiation of the maturing treasury *bons,* together with an exaggerated objection to inevitable inflation of the note circulation, led to large withdrawals of money from the *bons,* which went in part to swell the deposits in banks.[1] This reduction in the sums in *bons* embarrassed the government still farther and the circular interaction, which has been so often referred to, is instanced at this time. The situation was extremely critical at the beginning of December.

It was at this time that the Chamber of Deputies was most unruly. Moreover, the Finance Commission was unreasonable.[2] Premier Briand found it necessary to stake everything on the emergency bills of December 3. The galleries of Parliament were crowded, the public and press waited in suspense, when in a fiery speech the Premier called for united effort to save the country from financial ruin. The dangers of the moment could hardly be exaggerated, and the need for immediate action was imperative. The bill which was finally passed despite tremendous opposition, to the great relief of those who understood the emergency, provided for an immediate increase in the note circulation and Bank advances to the state, as well as special taxes which were to bring in approximately three billion francs in the near future. As a piece of legislation designed to meet a special and urgent need, it was in the main successful. It is probable that nothing less drastic could have been of any service at that time. Public opinion was ready to desert the franc, and the budget and treasury situations were in an even worse condition than they were later in July, 1926.

[1] *Journal des débats* (November 30, 1925). See regular article, "Revue financière."

[2] *Revue de science et de législation financières* (October-December, 1926), vol. xxiv, no. 4, p. 678. "The power of the finance commission had become a veritable scandal."

The hasty legislation initiated by the new minister of finance, Loucheur, was followed by a more studied budget proposal. It was, however, like the other, very drastic in its provisions.[1] Politicians who had yielded to stress of persuasion and fact in the first heat of emotion were unwilling to make further concessions immediately. Moreover, M. Loucheur had many personal enemies. The result was that he was forced to resign after having been in office only a few days, and the difficult post was again vacant on December 15. It is interesting to trace the day to day fluctuations of the franc at this time. The sharp changes in direction are clearly dictated by political events.

TABLE XXVII

FRANCS PER DOLLAR ON THE PARIS BOURSE[2]

December, 1925

(high—low)

	First Week		Second Week		Third Week	
	High	Low	High	Low	High	Low
Mon	25.74	25.59	26.02	25.86	27.88	27.59
Tue	25.46	25.35	26.16	25.97	27.88	27.72
Wed	26.20	25.80	26.71	26.65	27.49	27.18
Thu	26.35	26.10	26.48	26.42	27.65	27.55
Fri	26.21	25.93	26.99	26.58	26.96	26.65

	Fourth Week		Fifth Week	
	High	Low	High	Low
Mon	26.87	26.72	27.50	27.41
Tue	27.32	27.11	27.03	26.94
Wed	27.10	26.85	26.42	26.34
Thu	27.19	27.00	26.86	26.73
Fri	....	....	....	....

Let us compare the curve with contemporaneous events. The dollar moved upward the first few days of December. The confusion and conflict in Parliament made it extremely unlikely that funds would be raised before the eighth of the

---

[1] *Documents parlementaires, Chambre, Exposé des motifs du projet du budget,* no. 2180. See especially pp. 296-306.

[2] *La Cote officielle.* See *infra,* appendix. Monday of the first week is November 30. Friday was a holiday in the last two weeks.

month to pay off the treasury bills. The night of the second or third was the time of Briand's eloquent appeal, which succeeded in improving a desperate situation. The new taxes were voted with an increase in the limits of Bank advances and note issues to tide the treasury over this particular emergency. This measure was passed on the third, and on the fourth and seventh the franc improved markedly. Moreover, the dreaded inflation did not have an adverse effect.[1]

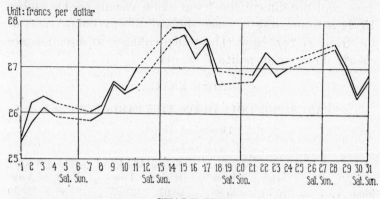

Unit: francs per dollar

CHART XXV

DOLLAR QUOTATIONS ON THE PARIS BOURSE, DECEMBER, 1925

As is frequently the case, however, speculation exaggerated the good effects of the temporary measure, and a contrary movement set in on the eighth. This was the day on which M. Loucheur presented his budget project.[2] In it he discussed the deficit for the year[3] with considerable frank-

[1] *Le Matin*, December 5, 1925. The effect of the new inflation had been discounted during November, since it seemed inevitable.

[2] *L'Homme libre* (December 17, 1925) comments thus humorously on the new sense of security: "On a voulu s'installer sur 7 milliards et demi d'inflation comme sur un édredon et pour un long sommeil. Le mauvais coup à peine accompli, l'on était saisi à la gorge. Pour justifier 7 milliards et demi d'inflation il fallait proposer 8 milliards d'impôts."

[3] Loucheur, *op. cit.*, pp. 7-9. The deficit for 1926 given is 5,600 million francs. It was the first official statement of such a large insufficiency and came as a shock to those who had not followed the financial discussion

ness, and proposed new and heavy taxation. Meanwhile the maturing *bons* were successfully paid off, and the operation was spread over several weeks with the coöperation of the banks, so that the full effect did not appear in the advances of the Bank to the state during this week.[1] The exchange in Paris reacted favorably after this second flurry, but, as New York was not happily impressed by the increase in note circulation, it took a bear attitude, and the movement turned against the franc a third time. This was both cause and effect of the approaching government crisis.

On the fourteenth, the price of exchanges in francs touched its high point for the month. Opposition to the Loucheur bill had become very bitter. The amount of speculative dealing was reported to be great. It cannot of course be measured. That it was partly the result of the political struggle, and designed to shake the ministry, can hardly be doubted. Nevertheless, the general public had lost patience and some of the speculation represented capital movement by individuals who feared collapse. The rise of a franc and a half in the price of the dollar within two days was very rapid. On the fifteenth the budget proposal was rejected by the Finance Commission. On the same day Loucheur resigned. This brought a change in speculative pressure and a reaction in the exchange.[2] There was, moreover, an exaggerated sense of relief at the refusal of the Loucheur tax proposal. The talk of a Socialist *coup d'état* which had been very rife in the past weeks was less alarming. The lessening of speculative activity was noticeable, and the appointment of Doumer as minister of finance was received favorably by the press and by the exchange market. It is

closely. It may be added that the estimate was not all-inclusive. See Chapter IX.

[1] Advances increased only 200 million francs. Maturities were about 2,500 million francs. See appendix for advances.

[2] *New York Herald,* Paris edition (December 15, 1925). "From a general point of view the financial situation of France remains as difficult as ever and the market has no reason to modify its tendency."

interesting to note that these fluctuations were thought to be controlled by Paris, and not by New York or London. The *Paris Midi* stated:

The exchange curve has reached a level at which it seems disposed to remain. In fact, with the market, completely lacking in speculative position because of the absorption of funds . . . foreign centers for some time past have done nothing but confirm the fluctuations of Paris. We find in our own conditions, particularly in the political situation, the most important influences which govern the franc.[1]

The appointment of Doumer [2] brought a temporary political truce. It was realized that the budget discussion would not be completed until after January 1, 1926, and the intensity of feeling was lessened temporarily.

One of the most interesting events was that which occurred on December 18. It was at this time that the industrialists made their proposal to raise funds voluntarily to help take care of the internal debt. They were to give their factories as security in the raising of a loan of consolidation. They promised to furnish three billion francs and had various schemes for increasing this sum later.[3] The result of

[1] *Paris Midi,* December 16, 1925. "La courbe des changes a atteint un niveau où elle semble vouloir se consolider. En effet le marché dépourvu de positions speculatives par suite de l'absorption préalable du disponible . . . l'étranger ne fait depuis quelque temps que confirmer les mouvements de Paris . . . c'est chez nous et particulièrement dans notre situation politique que nous trouvons les grands facteurs de la tendance du franc."

[2] *Paris Midi* (December 16, 1925).

[3] *L'Echo de Paris; Le Matin* (December 19, 1925); *L'Intransigeant,* January 1, 1926. The striking thing to observe is that the proposal to stabilize the franc was made by producers who ordinarily gain by rising prices despite rising cost. The northern manufacturers, however, found the disorganization due to the wild changes in the prices of raw cotton, for instance, more upsetting than was the stimulus of rising prices. They offered, therefore, to undertake this considerable sacrifice to save the franc. Fear of enhancing the political power of one region or group led to the pigeonholing of the scheme. Nevertheless, in spite of its rejection, it had a powerful psychological effect.

this generous proposal was immediately felt on the exchanges. The dollar fell below twenty-six francs on the nineteenth. This figure has not been included in the table of daily quotations since it occurred on Saturday when the Bourse was closed. The effect was very striking, and there is no doubt that this plan, though not carried to a conclusion, was in considerable measure responsible for the improvement of the franc in the latter part of December.[1] There was a quick contrary movement of the exchange, due partly to profit taking. The exchanges went to higher levels again on the twenty-first. Movements as sudden as those of the nineteenth are, in part, due to uncovered purchases and so invite a reaction. The net effect is only visible by smoothing the curve. The rise of foreign exchange rates was very rapid.

The announcement on December 23 of the plans for a socialist conference to be held early in January was a signal for a new fall of the franc. The movement continued until the twenty-eighth. The effect of the Socialist announcement was due to the fact that their action constituted a menace to the government majority. The Socialists formed a well-disciplined group and commanded about a hundred votes in the Chamber of Deputies. If they refused participation, the result would be an inability on the part of the ministry to put through a budget measure. Their hostile tone at this time was disturbing, in particular, their opposition to the existing turnover tax and their refusal to consider its increase was one of the outstanding difficulties.[2] This tax had proved and was to prove in the future one of the best

[1] This is the first of those events which indicate that the French, as a nation, were resolved to save the franc despite the delays and mistakes of politicians. A study of the press, in this and subsequent months, is impressive. The tide of opinion was most irresistible in the demonstration of July, 1926. The common sense of the people made itself felt in the end.

[2] In the elections of May 11, 1924, when the Cartel was victorious at the polls, they had pledged themselves to abolish this tax and to lighten indirect taxes generally.

sources of revenue, and had a special importance because
its yield increased with rising prices.

The new financial proposals, including a doubling of the
turnover tax, were announced on the twenty-fourth. The
Cartel was offering a counter proposal. The exchanges became unfavorable to the franc as sentiment appeared to
oppose the ministerial plan. The technical situation of the
market also made considerable purchases of foreign exchange in Paris necessary. Briand, fully aware of the deli-
cacy of the situation on the twenty-ninth, with the dollar
at 27.50 francs, walked about in the corridors of the Chamber of Deputies expressing his opinion in such a way that
there was no doubt as to his intentions:

> "If anyone wishes my skin," M. Briand remarked to one of his
> friends the other day, "he'll have to come and get it in the
> Chamber of Deputies, and I shall be ready to defend it. The
> results will be obvious when I have proclaimed from the tribune
> where the blame lies." [1]

He let it be overheard that he would throw all his prestige
into the balance and would not be overthrown without pro-
claiming the responsibility of the crisis to the nation. The
result was a moderation of the attacks on the government.
When Parliament adjourned for two weeks, feeling was
somewhat improved, and Briand seemed to have won considerable ground. The result is reflected in the fall of the
dollar to twenty-six francs in the beginning of January.
The government and the Bank had managed to handle the
year-end settlements with sufficient skill to prevent extreme
pressure, and there was a short period of calm again.

The erratic series of ups and downs during December,
which at first seemed without reason, proved to reflect very
justly the prevailing opinion of financiers. The public was
discounting constantly the possibility of an improvement
of the budget problem. The peak of the difficulty occurred

[1] *Le Matin* (December 29, 1925).

just before the resignation of Loucheur. It was due partly
to the shock of realization caused by his frank statement
of the difficulties and partly to political hostility to his
measures. The improvement at the month-end was due to
the industrialists' proposal and the vigorous point of view
it indicated, and also to some slight progress on the part of
the government in working out a plan. The efforts of Briand
at this time are notable. He stood the country in good stead
during this trying period.

Exchange rates are not always so sensitive to political
events as they were in December, 1925. It is true none the
less that the connection between the two became closer with
the continuance of depreciation. The tendency was for the
automatic links in the chain of causality—increased note
circulation, price changes, and so on—to become relatively
less important. The slow reactions between a monetary
policy, prices, commerce, and capital flows was accelerated.
The final outcome was a direct and immediate influence of
political events and maneuvers on exchanges, followed by
an inevitable effect on monetary policy, prices, and so on,
and the movement of funds abroad. Experience had taught
that certain acts on the part of the government would lessen
the value of money; people did not wait to feel the pinch,
but sought escape in gold value investments. The synchronization of the quotations of the dollar and the pound with
those securities on the Paris *Bourse* whose value was tied to
gold, such as the Suez Canal, Rio Tinto, de Beers, and so
on, was notable.[1] The purchase of such securities was one
of the easiest legal ways of refuge from depreciation. The
public became highly sensitive to budget policies and monetary details. They had undergone an intensive education,
and the result showed in the quick value changes.

What conclusions can be drawn from the study of this
varied mass of material, what lessons are there for the

[1] See charts, as for instance those of the *Agence économique et financière*
(26 Boulevard Poissonière, Paris) for 1925.

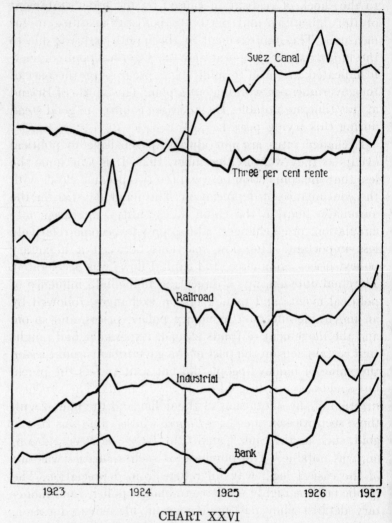

CHART XXVI

VALUE OF FOUR FRENCH SECURITIES, 1923 TO 1927 [1]

[1] See appendix for figures.

government which seeks to build sound economic life on the ground cleared by the destructive forces of depreciation? There are some things to be observed which are new, some things to be reaffirmed which are old. Confidence was long ago recognized as the foundation of any monetary policy. A restatement of this truth indicates that such laws, for instance, as limit the amount of the note circulation or the credit policy of central banks are important only in as much as they secure confidence and prevent distrust of political maneuvers. The changing sequence of events in different stages of depreciation indicates that one cannot rely only on economic repercussions. Public opinion, rational or irrational, mental valuations, may outweigh all other factors and bring about events which are surprising. Inflation may lead to *lower* prices if accompanied by constructive measures. A lowering of the discount rate may *attract* capital if it points to sounder conditions, even though a high rate is supposed normally to have this effect. Government borrowings may be larger when the amount of *authorized* borrowings is lowered. Such facts, in a measure paradoxical, argue in favor of a more flexible economic theory. They point to the need of developing a scientific economic psychology, difficult to achieve with exactness but none the less important.

The variety of exchange movements and the different configurations of the factors which determine the value of the franc made it difficult to trace any unified principle, to find any one outstanding fact to give meaning to the situation. With the study of the importance of capital flows and of the influences which guide judgments on the value of money, it becomes obvious that the day of unconscious economic life has passed. It is then increasingly important to find the main conscious methods of control. In an era built on credit rather than money [1] the relation between

[1] R. G. Hawtrey, *Currency and Credit* (second edition, London, 1923), pp. 1-17, argues from credit to money rather than from money to credit, the

bank deposits and gold becomes very slight; the discount mechanism is called in to act as a control on bank deposits which, if left alone, would be subject to dangerous expansion. Moreover, production is less and less designed to meet immediate needs and, more and more, through roundabout processes of capital construction, aimed to meet future as well as present demand. The influence of price and money changes on the distribution of wealth makes it evident that this very delicate part of the machinery of economic life must be regulated with care; the volume of production is artificially restricted in almost every field. A certain measure of conscious price fixing is a result of the growth of large-scale industry. There is a marked tendency for every phase of economic life to be controlled by design.

This is not a new development, for the mercantilist system was based on a definite aim and carried out according to carefully evolved programs. The situation is none the less different. The new self-consciousness is not based on a singleness of purpose nor on a consciousness of racial destiny, but rather on the nature of the mechanisms by which the economic processes are carried out. The sensitivity of credit is the basis for the attempts at artificial guidance of production and distribution. The growing importance of central credit institutions and of small groups of financial experts and bankers is one of the outward signs.

The new self-consciousness, the outgrowth of a practical, psychological age, as opposed to a philosophic age concerned with the problems of the race and of the nation, presents new problems. The growth of deliberate control is taken by some to point to the advisability of completely abandoning the more automatic checks on economic action and reaction, such as the gold standard. There is no reason for passing from one conclusion to the other. Human analysis is bound to err. It is all the more important now to

---

traditional order of consideration. His treatment is appropriate as applied to actual conditions in which credit bulks very large.

cling to those reliable mechanical checks which work for the relative stability of economic phenomena. Any simple and understandable mechanism helps to limit the zone of uncertainty and adds so much to the possibility of control.

It is only when the mechanical elements become incompatible with rational control that they should be rejected. For example, it may be well to discourage the common use of gold as a means of payment and use it only as one of the basic elements of monetary structure. Certainly, the general use of gold allows the public to draw large quantities of the precious metal into hoards where it lies idle and from which it may emerge suddenly and bring about gold inflation or change the ratio of gold to credit. But gold in the hands of the government can be economized and used mainly for the purpose of international payments. Moreover, it is still true that there are nations whose credit control is so primitive and whose finances are so unstable that gold, with its intrinsic value, is of obvious service as a balancing item.

It is best, then, to retain all the reasonable and familiar mechanisms within nations and between nations, adapting them to a more harmonious control. It is well to confine artificial intervention of bankers and economists to those fields in which the elements are, to a great extent, artificial creations. In the first place, credit is, at times, a controlable force.[1] In the second place, taxation, the product of laws, is subject to adjustment and change. It is these two series of problems, particularly taxation, that have been at the base of the French difficulties and of France's recovery. Every crisis may be interpreted in terms of one or the other type of interference. It was increasingly realized just before the war that price fluctuations, mainly due to credit changes, were the result of artificial developments of economic life and were subject to a measure of control. It was not so widely understood that taxation was one of the very impor-

[1] Credit is here used in the widest sense.

tant means of guiding production and consumption. In
America, where the state has absorbed a relatively small
amount of public wealth, problems of taxation have been to
a large degree ignored by the general public. The war, which
has increased taxation even in the United States, has
brought forward this problem, along with the problem of
credit control, as one of the most pressing. The struggle of
different classes to gain strategic advantages in the economic world, which has been in its turn intensified by
recent political conflicts, has made the matter of taxation
one which can no longer be ignored.

Monetary depreciation has thrown the searchlight of
public opinion on these two problems. Taxation and credit
control are the two most potent forces in economic life.
The dramatic struggle over the capital levy *versus* inflation, over direct *versus* indirect taxation, has had many a
startling result. In France the problem of taxation has been
more vital than the problem of bank credit. This was realized to an increasing extent and led to the unification of
public opinion after the dark hours of panic. The political
truce made possible a coherent policy of increased taxation as the different crises brought out the growing importance of government finance. Thus, a clearer understanding
of the points at issue and the conflict of interests finally
made possible a consistent policy. The vigorous and successful efforts to reduce the floating debt in 1927 were the
outgrowth of a general appreciation both of the difficulties
and of the effectiveness of a sound government policy. The
final *dénouement* in the case of France is a hopeful indication of the possibilities of control of economic forces. There
is something impressive in the fact that the French were
able to check the fall of the franc under difficult conditions
and after a precipitate drop. The efforts of August, 1926
were surprisingly successful, and the calm was almost as
sudden and unanticipated as the storm had been.

CHAPTER IX

THE BUDGET

EVERY Frenchman now knows that there is a budget. It is doubtful whether one in twenty, before the war, knew or cared that there was such a thing behind the payment of taxes and execution of government works. Financial education has been the result of experience and loss. The distribution of yellow tax slips in 1926, taking away the salary of one or two months' work, brought a new appreciation of the importance of public finance. It began to be realized at this time, moreover, that the changing power of money as a buying instrument brought even greater hardship. Men in cafés turned to examine the statements of the Bank of France and grew accustomed to reading the intricate budget proposals. They became aware of the connection between shrinking revenues and a growing note circulation. During the postwar years economics became indeed the language of the man in the street. A sensitive, close contact grew up between the parliamentary discussions of government ways and means and the wild variations of value in the banks and the *Bourse*.

The government had turned in time of need to three successive reservoirs—notes, loans, and taxes. The first seemed to offer unlimited resources. The government could count on the Bank of France as a source of easy loans in the form of new notes; for the Bank, authorized by the government, could create money to lend by the use of the printing press. The interest payable was low and the necessity of repayment vague and distant. Nothing could have been easier than this source of revenue, until two limits began to appear. The first limit came as a direct result of putting such a large mass of purchasing power in the hands of the government. It is evident in the maladjustment of prices. The second limit was political and psychological, and led to bitter opposition to further inflation after the war. The two, working together, curbed the postwar use of these Bank loans.

After the first Bank loans to the state, the first public loans were issued. Short-time loans, *bons de la défense*,[1] and, later, four consolidation loans, drew into the treasury the spare funds of individuals and industries.[2] The government managed to absorb most of the slack in the circulation. The money which accumulated in bank deposits with rising industrial profits was invested by the banks in government bonds. This was due, in part, to the attractiveness of short-time securities easily liquidated and, in part, to government pressure on the banks to fall in line with the financial program of the state. The efforts of the government were successful as far as the emergency of the moment was concerned.[3] The large increase of the public debt is evidence of this fact. Nevertheless, the methods used were not such as to obviate future difficulties. Heavy accumulation of maturities in the year 1925 have been noted as one instance of these short-sighted methods. The high rate of interest on the loans issued was another.[4] The refusal of the public to subscribe to loans in 1924 and after was a third.[5]

[1] See *supra,* Chapter III, p. 94.

[2] See *supra,* Chapter III, p. 97; and also Germain Martin, *Les Finances publiques de la France* (Paris, 1925), p. 161. Germain Martin says there was an impression that the government feared failure each time a loan was floated.

[3] H. G. Moulton and Cleona Lewis, *The French Debt Problem* (New York, 1925), pp. 67, 98.

[4] See *supra,* Chapter III, p. 111. If the government was to subsist on loans it had to pay enough to attract capital, but such a policy was aimed to meet an immediate emergency, irrespective of future difficulties. See Germain Martin, *op. cit.,* pp. 165, 166.

[5] It is surprising that the government thought that loans could continue indefinitely without any clear policy of amortization or of monetary stabilization.

The pyramiding of the internal debt was more ominous than the actual additions would lead one to expect. Each increment weighed more heavily on the nation than its mere size warranted. The end came in 1924, when this second source of revenue seemed to dry up rather suddenly.[1] Moreover, the dangers of the floating debt to the franc were just beginning to be evident at this time. The government had to adopt a more far-sighted policy. Taxation was the inevitable means of meeting the large budget needs. It was to taxation, then, the third source of revenue, that the government was forced to turn.

Budget Reform Came Late

It was through these three factors, then, that the budget influenced depreciation—note inflation, debt increases, taxation—and, one should add, the lack of taxation. The starting point of the trouble was obviously the budget deficits. The matter of deficits, technical, and relatively unimportant in normal times, became a stumbling block in the way of sound progress.

This effect came about in the following way. In general, the significance of a budget lies partly in the orderliness which it introduces into government expenditures and receipts, and so in the restrictive influence it has on waste, as well as the possibility of planning government undertakings with some degree of exactitude.[2] It has been stated already that French methods before the war were not entirely satisfactory.[3] Frequent deficits, confused practices, and the carrying forward of accounts through a period of years were in part responsible for the traditional uncertainty, which the war made much worse.[4]

[1] The failure of the *Crédit national* loan has been referred to in Chapter V.

[2] Robert Buty, *Le Vote du budget et l'amélioration des méthodes du travail parlementaire* (thesis, Paris, 1926), pp. 16, 17, 20.

[3] See *supra*, Chapter II, pp. 56-59.

[4] One difficulty in a budget study consists in the fact that the total budget figures as given by the government do not include the same things in

The year 1924 was the first year in which there was any real attempt to balance the budget. The severe exchange crisis and the passage of the *double décime* tax were both of great significance in this connection. The struggle over alternative sources of revenue became more intense. It was during this year that the business turnover tax became a definite political issue, and the most serious agitation for the capital levy began. So intense was the struggle over these proposals that programs of heavy taxation came to menace the franc through their tendency to accelerate the flight of capital. But taxation was destined to be an important aid to the franc in 1926, at the crucial moment.

In 1925, as the result of the publicity given to government difficulties, there was a focusing of attention on finance and a step forward in the inclusion of most expenditures in one budget. This was first done by Finance Minister Caillaux in 1925. Even the so-called unified budget, however, did not include all government expenditures—railroad subsidies, post, telephone and telegraph, and the treasury being the main categories omitted. Even now, after these steps toward unification, the budget is not easy to understand. Very few outside a limited official circle know how large the deficits have been.[1]

For the most part, these were irregular and ill-coördinated efforts to do away with deficits and to improve the tax situ-

---

different years. There was a tendency to cut down the number of budgets by including the outside items in the main budget. This ended in the doing away with the recoverable budget and an almost complete unification in 1925. In 1926 the institution of the *caisse de gestion des bons* again changed what was included in the "budget."

[1] An extensive study of the budget is now in process. Professor R. M. Haig, a recognized authority on taxation, is making a thorough study of the question in order to build up a complete and accurate statement of expenditures and revenues. The results of this work will soon be available to the reader and will carry him much farther than can the present general study, which aims primarily to bring out the monetary side of the problem. The work referred to will be a part of the research undertaken by the Columbia University Council for Research.

ation. The first proposals of the income tax, finally put into effect in 1916, have been alluded to in Chapters II and III. It seems reasonable to excuse some of the delay in increasing taxes on the ground of the difficulties arising from the war; but such extenuating circumstances should not be made the explanation for all mistakes. There was a considerable measure of political chicanery in the delay in raising taxes after 1918. Political leaders attempted to postpone and shift responsibility. The result was the makeshifts and the confusion of postwar years. The crashing of franc values of the year 1924 had given the first healthy shock to public opinion. Parliament pulled itself together and passed with sensational speed the law of March instituting the *double décime,* or the twenty per cent increase of taxes.[1] It was after this that the taxpayer first began to feel the pinch. The nation was not at the end of its difficulties, however, in assuming this new burden, for the gap between receipts and expenditures was not closed. Deficits continued and the public was soon to become aware of this fact. The increases in taxation voted in 1925 and again in 1926 reached crushing rates [2] before the government could hope to "buckle the budget."

Conclusions regarding the budget must be qualified. As has been indicated, the subject offers serious difficulties even to experts on government finance and to persons long familiar with the French method of handling the government accounts. It is extremely doubtful whether there were more than a dozen people in France who knew in 1925 and 1926 with any degree of accuracy, say within five per cent, what the deficits were. It is certain that this small group found it necessary for political reasons to withhold most of their knowledge from the public. Whether later studies will be able to dig up all the facts is much to be doubted; cer-

[1] See *supra,* Chapter V, pp. 173, 174.
[2] Henry Bérenger, *L'Europe nouvelle,* "L'Accord franco-américain sur les dettes de guerre" (Paris, May 8, 1926), p. 658.

tainly contemporary investigations were greatly handi-
capped by secrecy.[1]

It is fortunate for the student of monetary theory that
there are only two things which he must know about the
budget. In the first place, he must be able to tell in a general way whether large deficits existed, that is, ten, twenty,
or thirty billion francs. In the second place, he must then
try to understand the attitude of public opinion toward
the budget and why it rejected inflation, turned away from
loans, and finally accepted taxation. A general understanding of these two aspects of the situation, however incomplete, is not inadequate for an analysis of the variations in
the value of the franc. The purpose in this case is not to
explain in its entirety any one of the multitudinous factors
in the economic situation, but to bring out the relation
between those factors—namely, between the budget, exchanges, and prices. The importance of budget deficits must
be admitted at the outset. It is true that small deficits can
be absorbed in the general financial systems, that is, by the
Bank, the treasury and the credit institutions, who can
handle them without serious shock to the price-trade-pro-
duction situation. Small deficits existed before the war and
will probably recur unnoticed. Large deficits, however, cannot be tolerated in a healthy condition of affairs.

It is clear that deficits of this kind existed. In working
over the various estimates in government and private
reports one arrives at conclusions which are illuminating, if
not accurate, as to precise amounts. Government figures for
deficits were, until the end of 1925, billions of francs below
what might be called the effective deficit. Secondly public
opinion was very confused and gradual progression towards
adequate taxation was possible only after the situation of
public finance became obviously alarming.

A study of the size of the deficits is essential, despite all

[1] G. Charbonnet, *La Politique financière de la Banque de France* (Bordeaux, 1922), pp. 21-25.

these difficulties. The figures are large even if we reduce the paper franc values to gold dollars. Fifty billion francs, the highest official figure given for the year 1918,[1] amounted to almost ten billion dollars at that time, or about the equivalent of the total gold value of the French and English debt to America. It is probable that the addition of treasury deficits to those of the budget would have made the sum larger. Granted this, it is probable that, in the following years, deficits as indicated by government figures declined. The yearly average to 1926 was probably about 25 billion francs, if one can judge by the increase in the public debt.[2] Deficits declined to about 10 billion francs in 1926. The improvement was due not to any considerable decline in expenses, but to the gradual increase of taxation.[3]

Contemporary opinion indicates a vague realization of what was going on. It is interesting to note to what extent, either because of direct economic relations or because of conscious discounting, facts conformed to theory. It appears that neither speculation nor the changing price levels were influenced by the finer shades of change in the budget deficits which were of extreme interest to those in the ministry of finance. It was the larger changes that brought about marked fluctuations in the franc. No close correspondence existed. This was true because of the lingering ignorance of the French as to the budget. Part of this may be explained by the publication in 1924 of figures showing a decreasing deficit in the *Inventaire* of the Minister of Finance, Clémentel. These figures were so incomplete as to

[1] See *infra,* this chapter.

[2] Henry Chéron, *Rapport au Sénat,* no. 84 (Paris, February 22, 1926), p. 277. The increase in the debt was from 33 billions to approximately 300 billion at the end of 1925. See Chéron report for the internal debt until October; it increased until the official figure given for March 31 was 297 billions. See *Projet du budget* for 1927.

[3] J. R. Cahill, *British Overseas Trade Report, Economic and Industrial Conditions in France,* 1925-26 (London, 1927), p. 37. Indication is given here of the increase in certain of the taxes, the greatest being that of the business turnover.

give a false impression of the situation. It is not possible
here to analyze in detail the reasons and nature of this
incompleteness. The presentation of the subject in Professor Moulton's book [1] gives much light on the subject
for the student who wishes to make further critical study
of the budget figures. The deficits are given by Clémentel
as follows:

TABLE XXVIII

BUDGET,[2] 1914-1924

(in billions of francs)

	Expenditures	Receipts	Deficit
1914	10.4	4.2	6.2
1915	22.1	4.1	18.0
1916	36.8	4.9	31.9
1917	44.7	6.2	38.5
1918	56.7	6.8	49.9
1919	54.2	11.6	42.6
1920	58.1	20.1	38.0
1921	51.1	23.1	28.0
1922	48.9	24.2	24.7
1923	45.8	27.7	18.1
1924	40.2	31.1	9.1 (provisional)

THE SITUATION IN 1924

These figures, published in 1924, were staggering to the
Frenchmen who had just begun to suspect the existence of
deficits. The document received some attention even though
it was highly technical and concealed almost as much as it
revealed. Observers noted that there was less cheerful ignorance after its appearance, and that the political struggle
over possible tax expedients roused more general interest.
No one among the more enlightened leaders found it to his
advantage at this time to admit the full extent of the difficulties. Many probably did not really know them. In fact,
the possibility that the franc might never return to par
was hardly suspected and had not yet been admitted in

[1] Moulton and Lewis, *op. cit.*, pp. 69-95.
[2] Etienne Clémentel, *Inventaire de la situation financière de la France
au début de la treizième législature* (Paris, 1924), pp. 14, 21.

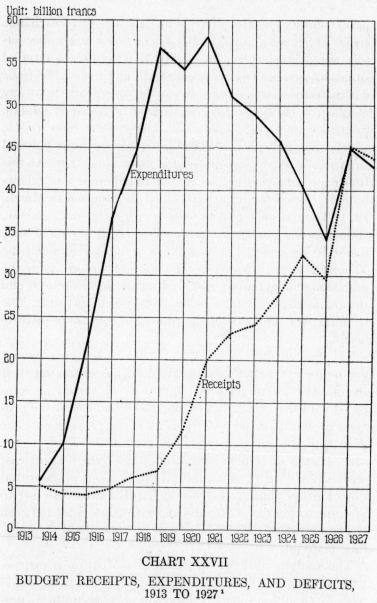

Unit: billion francs

Expenditures

Receipts

CHART XXVII

BUDGET RECEIPTS, EXPENDITURES, AND DEFICITS,
1913 TO 1927 [1]

[1] See Appendix for figure.

377

parliamentary debates. The blame for the 1924 exchange
crisis, which may properly be put on the foreign speculators, may be placed to a lesser extent on the French internal
situation as well. The sensational fall and rise of the franc
did more to arouse the public to the emergency than any
number of parliamentary discussions or financial studies.
Confusion of thought continued, but at least more people
were thinking. With this change, the bearing of the political
situation on the economic became more immediate. At this
time capital movements became more ominous. Two factors
brought to pass the improvement of the situation in March,
1924. The passage of the twenty per cent tax increase,
known as the *double décime* [1] was a hopeful sign of sane
methods. As a sequel to this the government obtained the
Morgan loan with which to fight the speculators. Thus the
immediate budget and treasury situation was improved and
the panic abated with a firmer government attitude. The
troubles over the value of the franc, however, were scarcely
begun.

The precise amount of the deficit in this year cannot
yet be ascertained. Professor Moulton has estimated it at
16 billions.[2] There are other figures which should be compared with this. For instance, one should note that the provisional figure given by Clémentel was 9 billions. The
growth of the internal debt was 10 billions. There is not
such a wide discrepancy between these figures as to cast
serious doubt on them as accurate indications of the situation. Farther than this it would hardly be wise to go; to
attempt to place the amount at some exact point between
the two estimates would be unwise in view of the fragmen-
tary material.

The analysis made of the budget by Moulton is instructive. It is probable that at this date he himself would
wish to modify statements which were as accurate as possible at the time of publication. His estimate has been criti-

[1] See *supra*, Chapter V.   [2] Moulton and Lewis, *op. cit.*, p. 92.

cized by M. Meynial, who sets a lower figure. The discussion between them brings to light some of the mooted points. Professor Moulton, in his study, shows clearly the contrast between the American and the French points of view on budget procedure. He also states plainly for the first time the significance and the extent of extra-budgetary government expenses. His statement probably places the deficit too high. He reaches the total of 16 billion francs by adding the following items:

TABLE XXIX
THE 1924 DEFICIT [1]
(in millions of francs)

General budget	27,730
Recoverable	12,344
Special account:	
Maintenance of troops of occupation	818
Total	40,892
Total less cancellations	40,091

TABLE XXX
EXTRA-BUDGETARY EXPENDITURES
(in millions of francs)

Crédit national	2,064
Securities turned over to *sinistrés*	790
Amortization of external debt	1,200
Advances to railways	667
Interest to the Bank of France	696
Total, extra-budgetary expenses	5,417
Total expenses (less cancellations)	45,508.6
Revenues	28,980.1
Deficit	16,528.5

One or two modifications leading to a somewhat lower estimate of the deficit should be made in these figures. For instance, M. Meynial [2] criticized this estimate, saying that

[1] Moulton and Lewis, *op. cit.*, pp. 93, 94.

[2] Pierre Meynial, *Revue d'économie politique* (Paris, November-December, 1925), p. 178. This first criticism is not justified as Professor Moulton apparently made due allowance for the usual inclusion of this item in both budgets.

Moulton, by adding the recoverable and the ordinary budgets, has counted twice a sum of about three and a half billion francs, and that, in addition to this, receipts to the extent of 819 million francs from Germany have been omitted.

Sums spent for amortization should logically be deducted from budget expenses if all borrowings are likewise to be deducted from receipts. Amortization is not easy to compute exactly from available figures. It seems probable that if all such payments, including those on the external debt, repayment to the Bank of France, and budgetary payments on the *rentes amortissables,* are added together the sum would be four or five billion francs; in Professor Moulton's statement of extra-budgetary expenses there are nearly two billion francs.

The many factors which obscure the situation make it hardly worth while to continue the effort to arrive at a precise figure for the deficit. A consideration of the available facts leads to the conclusion that the deficit of 1924 was not much over 10 billion francs. This is approximately Meynial's estimate. If such a conclusion as a 16 billion franc deficit is set against changes in the debt, it is apparent that Moulton has over- rather than under-estimated the amount. Money spent must have come from some source, either from revenues or from borrowing. Since government securities did not increase more than 10 billion francs, according to the official statement, the deficit can hardly have exceeded this figure by a large sum. The official provisional statement of the deficit, in the Clémentel *Inventaire,* is nine billion francs, certainly a minimum figure.[1]

The 1925 Deficit

The amount of the 1925 deficit is even more uncertain in some respects than that of 1924. Official estimates, such as those given by Caillaux and the succeeding ministers of

[1] Hon. George Peel, *The Financial Crisis of France* (London, 1925), p. 299.

finance, are obviously conservative figures. The real deficit was, for the most part, concealed. In the search for the forces behind inflation and behind the changes in the floating debt one must get nearer the real needs of the government and go beyond the changes which were merely paper transfers from one kind of debt to another. Official figures, though various, seemed to favor an estimate somewhere between four and six billion francs. A critical study of these estimates and some of the facts lying behind them increases the impression made by the above study of 1924. Although progress had been made toward frankness, there was no general, clear knowledge of the situation. Even the officials most concerned differed honestly as to the amounts to be secured.

The whole question of how to treat amortization is uncertain. There are a number of items in the budget to cover the payments on the *rentes amortissables*. There are, moreover, small sums to meet certain payments on foreign debts. In addition to this, the treasury paid out in 1925 large amounts for the purpose of meeting debt maturities. The question naturally arises as to whether the deficit should include these items, not normally dependent on the ordinary receipts and expenditures. Moreover, a considerable part of this amortization was offset by an increase in another form of the debt, that is, the advances of the Bank of France to the state. It is not clear whether this should be made to offset the reduction of other categories of the debt or whether the advances by the Bank should be considered as an indication of the amount of the deficit. The total maturities for the year 1925 were about 22 billion francs.[1]

This strain on public resources led to an increase of certain parts of the debt, notably the advances of the Bank to the state, which was almost precisely equivalent to the reductions of the *bons du trésor* and parts of the debt. If these are taken as offsetting items, the remaining deficit is

[1] See *supra,* Chapter V.

indeed small. Such a procedure would hardly indicate the real difficulties in the situation, nor the fact that the advances meant inflation of the note circulation. That is, the most unstable and menacing part of the debt was increased, the part which affected prices most directly and led to panic on the exchanges. Just such a shift from one form of debt to another, through the deficits of budget and treasury, brought the two crises of 1925 and eventually the acceptance of a new tax program. It is necessary, therefore, to consider further the matter of this deficit.

We can examine the matter from either of two angles. The first is the question of the changes in the internal debt; the second is the difference between revenues and expenditures. The apparently different results of this approach are substantially consistent, and can be reconciled to each other. By both methods one arrives at a deficit of ten billion francs for 1925. This statement is made with the knowledge that it is not completely accurate. Those who are most familiar with the French situation realize most clearly how important these qualifications must be. Debt statements were not issued frequently by the treasury; they appeared only once or twice a year. Moreover, figures regarding the *bons de la défense* were admittedly unreliable because of the shifting nature of these investments, which led to large day to day fluctuations simultaneously all over France.[1]

The official statement of the internal debt for the year is found in the Chéron report:

TABLE XXXI

The Internal Debt, 1924 and 1925 [2]

Dec 31, 1924	280,637,000,000 francs
Oct 31, 1925	283,811,000,000 francs
Increase	3,471,000,000 francs

[1] It should be remembered that any post office could issue these and the amounts could not be regulated. This caused considerable anxiety in 1926 and 1927, when demands for these *bons* increased very greatly with increasing confidence.

[2] Henry Chéron, *Rapport au Sénat,* no. 84 (February 22, 1926), p. 277.

A careful analysis of the changes in different parts of the debt reveals the fact that this statement of the increase is to be depended on as the real increase of the formally acknowledged debt. Moreover, the discussion in the Chamber of Deputies for February 16, 1926 shows the following situation.

TABLE XXXII

CHANGES IN THE INTERNAL DEBT DURING 1925 [1]

Increase

	(Million francs)
Perpetual and long-term debt..................	5,942
Advances by the Bank........................	12,900
Total increase..............................	18,842

Decrease

Short-term debt	6,736
National defense bills........................	9,031
Total decrease	15,767
Net increase	3,075

This figure—three billions for the increase in the internal debt—may be taken as a starting point in calculating the budget deficits. This does not serve our purpose, however, as has been said above, for it is the shift from treasury *bons* to notes that caused the main difficulty.[2] We must consider to what extent and under what conditions the increase in the note circulation was synonymous with the deficit. It is important to attack the problem from the other side, to recognize the importance of changes in the form, as well as the size of the debt, for instance, the substitution of advances by the Bank for *bons*.

Let us turn now to a calculation of the deficit based on the differences between receipts and expenditures. As the

[1] *Journal officiel, Chambre,* February 16; See also *Chambre,* annexe No. 2316, Cartel Budget Proposal.
[2] See *supra,* Chapters V and VI.

budget was originally drawn up, a surplus was forecast for the year 1925. This hope was based on the idea that the 1924 deficit would be very small. However this may be, the surplus for 1925, anticipated at the time of passing the budget bill, was estimated at only a few million francs, a negligible sum when added to 30 or 40 billions for the total budget. The budget project met with repeated delays. In fact, the government lived on provisional credits until July.[1] For various reasons tax receipts fell below expectations by about two billion francs. This made some deficit inevitable, but its actual size was not realized for months.

Calculations of the increase of expenses over estimates in 1925 are entirely provisional at this time. They are generally considered to amount to more than four billion francs. They fall under the following headings.

TABLE XXXIII

EXPENSES IN EXCESS OF ESTIMATES[2]

(In millions of francs)

Payments on the external debts (included in the budget)	1,000
Post, telegraph, and telephone	300
Railroad subsidies	700
War in Syria and Morocco	800
Pensions	1,600
Total	4,400
Taxes less than estimates	2,000
	6,400[3]

[1] Special reprint of law, *Projet du budget 1925, Chambre,* annexe No. 88 (Paris, July 14-17, 1925), *Journal officiel.*

[2] Louis Loucheur, *Exposé des motifs du projet du budget, Chambre,* No. 2180 (Paris, 1925), pp. 296-306. This is based on Loucheur's statements and various discussions in the public press.

[3] In an interview, Loucheur said that the deficit was only three billions, a statement which must be based on a deduction of three billions due to the

There is a second budget estimate that is worth considering. Louis Dausset, a recognized authority on French
finance, reaches a figure of about nine billion for the deficit
on the budget proper. There is no reason to think that his
figures are as accurate as those given by Loucheur a few
weeks later, but they should be taken as a confirmation of
the opinion that the Loucheur statement has not in any
case overestimated the expenditures. Dausset's figures given
in the *Information* are as follows.[1]

TABLE XXXIV
ESTIMATE OF DEFICIT

	(Millions of francs)
Failure of revenue as compared with estimate....	5,000
Post, telegraph, and telephone.................	1,000
Syria and Morocco...........................	1,000
Miscellaneous	1,000
Total......................................	8,000

Sifting carefully the known from the unknown, the important from the unimportant, one arrives at certain useful
results. In the first place, budget deficits were large enough
to throw the whole monetary mechanism out of gear from
the beginning of the war until the end of 1925. In the second
place, these deficits were offset by loans, and notes, which
were in a sense loans from the Bank to the state, and which
added to the permanent burden of the state. In the third
place, in the year 1926 and after, the gap was so nearly
closed that we can leave the further estimates of the possible small deficits to those who can devote themselves to
the intricacies of French public finance. And finally, the
difficulty which the expert finds in arriving at any definite
figure must stand as a sign of the uncertainty and ignorance

---

hoped-for increase in taxation voted December 4. This hardly seems to be
a justifiable modification, however, since the taxes had not been completely
collected by March, 1926, and will not necessarily be applied to the expenses
of 1925 exclusively.

[1] Louis Dausset, *L'Information, midi* edition (Paris, November 28, 1925).

of people at large, who had less time and experience to apply to such matters. They did not learn until almost too late how to protect themselves. Loucheur,[1] finance minister in December, 1925, made revelations for which he deserves considerable credit, since they turned people's minds towards two possible ways of escape. For the individual, escape lay in securing gold value securities and bank deposits. For the nation, rescue lay in a rigorous tax program. The subsequent turn of affairs in 1926 hinged on the question as to whether the people of France, acting individually to depress the francs, would overwhelm the efforts of the people as a state to bring about a new budget régime. It was the collective force, rather than individual interests, that won in the crisis of July, 1926.[2]

The clearest indication of the improved budget situation in the years 1926 and 1927 is the relative stability of the total internal debt. Notable also is the sharp decline in the total of advances made by the Bank to the state. These were less than 24 billions in January, 1928.[3]

From 1926 on, inflation, if it occurred in France, was due to pressure of commercial needs rather than to direct demands from the state. It is true that the large sums invested in the internal debt tended to have an inflationary effect on economic life and that some of this effect might work itself out slowly after the direct demands of the treasury had ceased. It is possible that this was actually the case in France in 1928, when there was an increase in the note cir-

[1] Louis Loucheur went out of office under a cloud of criticism. There were two main reasons: one was condemnation aroused by a large personal fortune and the other lay in the fact that he had imposed heavy taxes. See *supra*, Chapter V.

[2] One must grant due credit to M. Poincaré, but it is important to realize that the general willingness to turn over control to him was the important factor in his success. He was not a man of many schemes, as was Caillaux; he was, however, a statesman who called forth the universal comment, "J'ai confiance."

[3] *Le Pour et le contre* (January 8, 1928), p. 42. The exact figure given in the Bank of France statement of December 29 was 23,900 millions.

culation of approximately five billion francs. It has been pointed out, for instance, that government security as collateral could serve as the basis for loans. Moreover, as the government tended to cut down its floating debt, a certain amount of cash was forced into circulation, which might have an inflationary effect on business greater even than the amount of cash actually originating this movement. The possible relationships are interesting but they are merely effects of the general situation under consideration here, namely the disappearance of the budget deficits as an influence for inflation and the tendency of the government to cut down the public debt, even though the change was very small in amount.

DEPRECIATION NOT THE CAUSE OF DEFICITS

There is one line of theory which has a very real bearing on the practical handling of a disturbed budget and currency situation. This is the supposed relationship of prices and exchange rates to budget deficits. It has been stated by some that budgets cannot well be balanced while the value of money is changing.[1] Looking at the matter from a purely theoretical point of view, there is much to be said for this reasoning. This does not mean, however, that it can be applied to every practical situation. It is apparent, for instance, that in the case of France the budget was more urgently in need of attention as a cause of exchange disturbance than the exchange as a cause of budget deficits. This question goes beyond the limits of purely abstract theory in its importance. It is a matter of practical statesmanship whether it is wise to stabilize a currency first or to attempt to wipe out large budget deficits before holding the currency to a fixed value.

[1] J. M. Keynes, *The Nation*, "Some Facts and Later Reflections about the Franc" (London, January 30, 1926), p. 604. Mr. Keynes here discusses practical measures to improve the French situation, which was so very uncertain at the time of writing. He says, "I maintain therefore that the first step is to prevent further exchange depreciation."

There was some doubt in 1925 and 1926 as to which policy should be pursued. The uncertainty was, to a large extent, dissipated by the report of the Experts' Committee. They indicated that, since the first cause of depreciation had been budget disorder, the first remedy must be the balancing of the budget.[1] The report was submitted on July 3, 1926. Immediately after this, occurred the alarming panic on the exchange and the rapid change of ministers, ending in the Poincaré régime.[2] The Experts' Report was not definitely acknowledged by Poincaré as an influence on his subsequent measures for the reordering of finance, but its effects are seen in the nature of the remedies chosen. In many important respects the steps resemble the simple but forceful suggestions outlined in the report. However this may be, the government did take steps to prevent budget deficits before the franc was pegged and before stabilization became either an actual or a legal fact. One such step was to lessen the pressure of the floating debt on government resources, and another, to make provisions for taxation. After such measures, the franc tended to rest at a point slightly below four cents and there the government finally pegged it from December, 1926, until 1928.

There are a number of reasons why, in the French case, the budget balance had to precede stabilization. One of the main reasons lies in the fact that the taxation was so evenly balanced between direct taxes that did not vary with prices, and indirect which did change with price movements. A second explanation is that a large part of the expenditures were fixed irrespective of prices.[3] Another major reason was that those who were speculating, both professionals and outsiders, had learned to look to the budget as one of the main signs of the financial condition of the country. In any case, a careful analysis of budget items, both as to expenditures and as to receipts, shows that the government was

[1] *Rapport du comité des experts* (décret du 31 mai, 1926), p. 53.
[2] See *supra,* Chapter V.   [3] See *infra,* this chapter.

wise in handling the various problems in the sequence which was actually adopted. It must be added at this point that the conclusions here reached are pertinent only to the French case. If depreciation had been greater, it is possible that the German method of stabilizing the mark first would have been more appropriate; if depreciation had been less, it is possible that the English method of budget balancing by heroic taxation would have been applicable sooner.

The analysis of the budget items which bear on this question, given below, was made in 1925, before the question of policy was actually decided upon. There is no need, however, for modifications at the present time, since events have corroborated the general conclusions drawn. The problem naturally divides itself into a consideration, first, of the influence of internal prices on the budget, and second, the effect of exchange rates on the budget.

First, then, it is important to note that, regarding price changes, increases have been less than twenty per cent in the years of severe depreciation between 1920 and 1927. The following table gives the approximate differences, judged by a comparison of the figures for January of each year:

TABLE XXXV

WHOLESALE PRICES IN FRANCE [1]

Yearly changes

1920-1927

(1914 = 100)

January of	Index Number	Net Change	Percentage Increase or Decrease
1920	415	— 82	— 20
1922	320	— 95	— 30
1923	395	75	19
1924	505	110	20
1925	525	20	4
1926	647	122	20
1927	635	— 12	— 2

[1] See figures in appendix.

The changes here given are wholesale prices, but the case would be even stronger if retail prices were chosen, for, despite the unusual situation which prevailed, the changes of the retail prices each year were less than those of the wholesale. The index of wholesale prices is the more serviceable, however, because it represents more commodities.[1]

The next step in the analysis is to see what sums may be taken to vary with varying prices, that is to say, what part of the government expenditures move in sympathy with prices. It has been recognized that the total of all government expenses has not been easy to determine. The reason for this lies partly in the outlays of the treasury and partly in the various items grouped under supplementary budgets. It is possible, however, to arrive at a fairly accurate figure, and then to allow a reasonable margin for error. The figures given below are taken from the Chéron report and will serve our present purpose.

TABLE XXXVI

FRENCH BUDGET [2]

(Millions of francs)

Year	Debt Service	Total Budget	Amount of Budget Exclusive of Debt Service
1920	11,269	40,209	28,940
1921	11,410	37,178	25,768
1922	14,144	37,428	23,284
1923	14,676	37,944	23,268
1924	15,622	35,837	20,215
1925	15,484	34,220	19,246
1926	15,881	36,646	20,865

[1] The wholesale index is made up of forty-seven commodities, whereas the retail index is based on only thirteen. There is a less used wholesale index based on forty-five commodities.

[2] Henry Chéron, *Rapport au Sénat,* no. 84 (February 22, 1926), pp. 290, 291. The *dette viagère,* that is, fixed charges on account of pensions, relief, and other similar obligations of the state, is not included in the service of the debt in this statement, since it might well be argued that pensions should have increased with prices. This did not take place to any marked degree. See also *Journal officiel, Chambre débats,* January 27, 1928, p. 335.

If this table is compared with the one which precedes it, it will be noted that in the years of greatest price increase, 1923 and 1925, budget expenditures exclusive of interest on the debt—but including pensions—amounted to 23 and 20 billion francs, respectively. A further calculation will show that, without making allowance for hidden appropriations which could hardly have been large at this time, the maximum possible increase in budget expenditures due to increasing prices must have been less than five billion francs during these years; that is, twenty per cent of 23 billion francs should serve as an outside estimate for the years 1920 through 1926. Moreover, it is hardly reasonable to assume that this maximum increase ever became a fact for a number of reasons. In the first place, retail prices lag behind wholesale and a part of the budget expenditures would be more influenced by the retail price situation. In the second place, one can see from a study of the actual budget outlays, exclusive of interest, that increases were throughout the period less than five billion francs a year; in most years expenditures declined.

It is well to look more closely, however, into the nature of budget expenditures. The budget law considered most carefully in arriving at the above conclusions was the *Projet du budget* for 1925,[1] a year of marked depreciation. A study of the various appropriations reveals the fact that they were, to a considerable extent, for wages and salaries. Other items were for cost of material for the equipment of government offices or employees and for construction undertakings in which the state was engaged; some of these items would naturally be those arranged for by contracts months in advance, and so would be insensitive to uncalculable changes in prices. In view of these well-known facts, it seems reasonable to set the increase in expenditure attrib-

[1] *Loi des finances de 1925* (Paris, printed but not published by the Bureau de statistique et de législation comparée). See especially pages 37-79 and pages 418-496.

utable to rising prices at three billion francs. Even if it is higher than this, however, and attained the maximum of five billion indicated above, this would amount to only fourteen per cent of the total budget, including interest items— a figure which was large but still less than the changes in revenue which occurred at this time. The analysis indicates, therefore, that the deficits were not to any large extent caused by this aspect of the situation.

The estimate here given is confirmed in a general way by an unpublished study of the statistical department of the Morgan Bank of Paris.[1] The effect of price increases upon material expenditure is here said to be approximately twenty per cent. If this is adjusted as a percentage of the total budget expenditures, it amounts to approximately three billion francs, as stated above.

A careful study of the individual items is the basis for choosing the lower of the two limiting figures. If an examination is made of innumerable separate appropriations which make the budget very complex, one finds, for instance, that the Ministry of Finance paid out about two billion francs in salaries and indemnities, neither of which was a category affected immediately by changing prices.[2] In fact, in 1925 a large part of the 22 billion francs allotted to this ministry could not very well change during the course of any one year.[3] Turning then to expenditures of the Departments of the Army and Navy, which totaled five billion francs,[4] a considerable part was used for the payment of salaries and wages, and the support of military colleges—institutions which were not able to increase their appropriations as prices rose. Taking a third instance, the Department of Justice, an examination of the separate items shows that few were apt to be influenced by price

---

[1] The Morgan Bank, *Report* of January 28, 1927. Confirmation in this report is interesting for the figures were reached independently.

[2] Very few changes would be made in these without the passage of laws which were hotly contested and suffered long delays.

[3] *Loi des finances de 1925*, pp. 423-432.   [4] *Ibid.*, pp. 442-452.

movements over a period of months. It is not possible to
give here a detailed list of such separate items and the
reasons in each case for thinking that they would not be
altered with the rising price level. It is sufficient, perhaps,
to refer the reader to the original material for a confirmation of the conclusions made here. Such an examination
will show that the department most apt to be affected is
the Ministry of Public Works. Appropriations to this department, however, amounted to merely one and a half
billion francs in 1925. Then, the Ministry of Foreign Affairs
would also be affected by changes in prices and exchange
rates, but the sums assigned to it came to less than a billion
francs, and so would not occasion any considerable change
in the total expenses of the state.[1]

One must carry the analysis further to include the influence of the rising exchange rates on the budget, as well as
the influence of prices on the budget. The study which has
been made shows that it is much like that exerted by the
price level; it is probably less in extent, since there are
comparatively few of the requirements of the state which
must be met by goods purchased abroad. It is not possible
to estimate exactly to what extent the exchanges would
accentuate or lessen the effect of prices on the budget, since
it is impossible to ascertain at what dates the government
bought commodities abroad, or what arrangements were
made in regard to payment. It is probable, however, that
by means of provisioning the treasury in advance with exchange credits and, in some cases, with the help of foreign
loans, the state avoided paying at the extremely high rates
which the pound and the dollar reached during certain
weeks. There was, for example, a maximum net change in
the cost of the dollar in 1926 which amounted to thirty
per cent. It is reasonable to assume that the difference
between the budgetary estimates of government expenditures for foreign exchange in 1925 was on the average well

[1] *Loi des finances de 1925*, pp. 495, 496.

under this increase of thirty per cent. This effect would be felt on a much smaller number of items than those already said to have been influenced by price movements. It should be noted that payments on the external debt were not large. In the year 1927 total payments exclusive of those to the United States equaled 305 million gold francs, and the actual cost of these payments was calculated at a high rate of exchange, namely 150 paper francs to the pound sterling.[1] An examination of the exchange rates during the year shows that the government would have gained by a considerable margin on this appropriation.[2] It is fair to assume that the government handled this situation with a reasonable degree of foresight, and the above cited conservative provision for 1927 payments confirms such a view. There is no indication that the government lost on this score. Certainly those who handled the treasury accounts were in a position to know the coming fluctuations of the exchange rates before the man in the street could be aware of them.

Although these estimates are in no sense exact, they are far from being the result of mere guess work. The figures here given have been compared with comments on the budget in financial reviews and with those in reports of various organizations which have not, in most cases, been published. The conclusions were almost invariably the same; that the trouble with the budget arose, in the first place with the growing debt charge and, in the second place from large unpredictable drains on the treasury for repayments of maturing national defense *bons,* both of which facts led to increases in the advances by the Bank of France to the state. This was the one source of funds which did not dry up after the government had turned to it repeatedly.

[1] *Le Pour et le contre* (October 17, 1926). The payments for 1926 had been 350 million gold francs. See also the *Revue d'économie politique* (Paris, March-April, 1926), p. 258.

[2] The actual exchange rate was about 125 francs to the pound during most of the year.

The reason for its unique responsiveness lay, of course, in the ability of the Bank to print notes for the government on request. The more general factors which lay behind the inability of the state to float new loans or pay the interest on old loans was, in the last analysis, confidence, which varied sharply from day to day.

Further, it must be observed that price changes affect not only the expenditures but the income of the government, and in the case of France a rise in price meant a considerable rise in taxes. It is best to confine the present discussion to a statement of the increase in the business turnover tax. This came to be one of the very important sources of revenue after the war. It was put into effect in 1920 and began to return more revenue than the income tax almost at once. The yield increased with the activity of French business. The figures taken from the budget are somewhat ambiguous because the rate of the tax, as well as the productivity due to price conditions, was altered. The change is due to this cause as well as to rising prices.[1]

TABLE XXXVII

YIELD OF THE BUSINESS TURNOVER TAX [2]

(In million francs)

1920	942
1921	1,911
1922	2,281
1923	3,015
1924	4,090
1925	4,535
1926	7,468
1927	8,000

The increase in 1925 was about five hundred million francs and in 1926 about three billion francs. In the latter case, a fraction of the increase must be attributed to the increase

[1] The original rate of the tax was one and one-tenth of one per cent; this was increased to one and three-tenths of one per cent after voting the *double décime* in 1924. In 1926 the tax was increased to two per cent.

[2] See appendix.

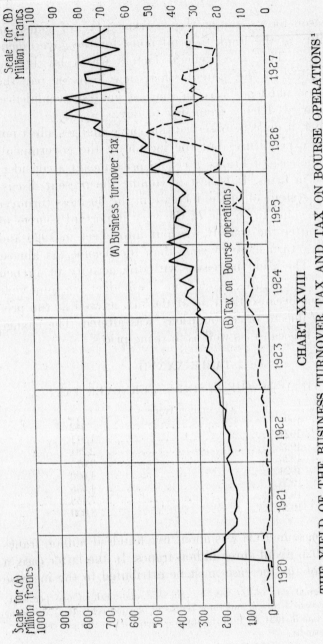

Scale for (A)
Million francs
1000
900
800
700
600
500
400
300
200
100
0

Scale for (B)
Million francs
100
90
80
70
60
50
40
30
20
10
0

(A) Business turnover tax

(B) Tax on Bourse operations

1920 1921 1922 1923 1924 1925 1926 1927

CHART XXVIII

THE YIELD OF THE BUSINESS TURNOVER TAX AND TAX ON BOURSE OPERATIONS [1]

[1] See appendix for figures.

in the rate. This tax, and other indirect taxes, helped to fortify the French budget against sudden price changes, and is one reason for the advocacy of such taxes in the Experts' Report.[1] Among the other taxes of this general nature may be mentioned the *régistration* tax, which increased about one billion francs in 1925. The total of all increases in 1926, as compared with 1925, was 10 billion francs.[2] The increase of 1925, as compared with 1924, was three billion francs. In the light of these facts, it seems reasonable to assume that the increase was directly attributable to the increase in prices to the extent of more than two billion francs; this figure might well be accounted for by receipts from the business turnover tax alone. If this is correct, the deficiency caused by increased expenditures was very nearly met by receipts increasing automatically with rising prices. Budget deficits from this cause might occur, but they could not be very large.

French experience has borne out this line of reasoning. Once deficits were eliminated by serious efforts to increase taxation, the value of money tended to become stable. The fluctuation of the currency had been an effect more than a cause.

KEYNES' SOLUTION

There has been another and contrasting theory with regard to the budget, which has been most clearly expressed by Keynes. He has seen in the effect of price changes on the budget an active force to relieve the government of the large burden of the debt charge.[3] So he reasoned that if, with a budget of 40 billion francs, the debt service were more than 20 billions, there would be a heavier real sacrifice to the nation than if the total budget were 60 billion

---

[1] *Rapport du comité des experts* (décret du 31 mai, 1926), pp. 22-29, see especially page 27.

[2] J. R. Cahill, *op. cit.*, p. 36. The figure for 1925 is here given as 32,957 million francs; 1926, 42,457 million francs. See appendix.

[3] J. M. Keynes, *The Nation, loc. cit.*, pp. 515-517.

francs while the interest on the debt remained at about 20 billion francs. Such a change in relationships might come about with inflation and rapidly rising prices; so he urged the French minister of finance, "whoever he is or may be," to take steps in this direction. He says that the trouble in the past had been that ministers of finance "have failed in spite of all their efforts to depreciate adequately *the internal purchasing power* of the franc." This suggestion is most interesting, because it runs counter to the accepted ideas of what a country should do. Certainly the French had achieved, in their own minds, a great moral victory when they resolved to stop depreciation. In Keynes' suggestion we find a startling challenge to such newly won principles.

There is surely a fallacy hidden in the apparent simplicity of this solution. In the first place, violent changes are almost always harmful to productive life, and if such changes were to take place it must be on a large enough scale to alter materially the relation of the debt to the whole budget. In the second place, Mr. Keynes does not mention in this connection the very real political and economic difficulties in the way of increasing revenues to meet such a new situation. As has been said above, some revenues increase with rising prices, and thus with inflation, this holds true only with relatively slow changes such as we have indicated—less than twenty per cent a year—whereas more violent changes might lead to taxation of industry that would be repressive, and to a net decline of tax receipts. It is not possible that the whole increase could come automatically; there would have to be new laws to increase direct taxation as well as indirect. Legislation, moreover, is slow and controversial, deficits become cumulative waiting on parliamentary action, and the danger of a complete collapse of the currency may well threaten.

It is probable that amortization of the debt such as France began in 1927 was an easier solution than further inflation, which would have continued the period of chaotic uncertainty. Amortization was at least an orderly and predictable process.[1] Here again we are on doubtful ground if we attempt to give quantitative statements of the amount of debt reduction undertaken in these years. In 1925, it has been pointed out,[2] the supposed reduction was 22 billion francs, but this was actually offset by new debts. In 1926, there was probably a slight reduction in the debt, but it was barely noticeable. In 1927, on the other hand, the net change was probably about nine billion francs—a really considerable sum.[3] This included 2,033 millions for the amortization of *rentes* and parts of the small payments on external debt, which are provided for in the budget proper, and 2,500 millions for the *caisse de gestion d'amortissement,* and 1,500 millions for the external debt—for instance, payments on the debt to England. The total thus reached is large. It is even possible that it would necessitate an unbearable amount of taxation. None the less, the French preferred to try this in 1926, rather than consider either partial repudiation or further inflation.

The serious dangers to social and economic life which had become apparent in 1926 made the French accept this very painful alternative. Mr. Keynes, in his advice to the minister of finance, does not take account of the uncontrollable, cumulative action often characteristic of inflation, even if undertaken with a deliberate plan. He does not anticipate such a collapse as the mark suffered and yet, with the uncertainty already characteristic of the French situation in 1926, it is probable that any further tampering with the currency would have brought about this result. Moreover, as a further objection to inflation as a solution of the debt

[1] Henry Chéron, *Rapport au Sénat,* no. 225, April 4, 1926, vol. ii, p. 113. It should be noted that there was a slow but dependable decline in the debt charge due to cessation of pensions and relief payments; for instance, military pensions were, in 1925, 68 million francs; in 1926, 60 millions.

[2] See *supra,* Chapter V.

[3] Poincaré, *Projet du budget 1927, Chambre,* annexe no. 3248, vol. i, p. 23 Amortization for 1927 is here stated as 8,950 million francs.

question, it should be noted that depreciating currency puts
the main burden on debtors whose incomes and salaries are
fixed; that is, it penalizes just the group of French citizens
who had already suffered most severely. Taxation, on the
other hand, strikes hardest usually on the manufacturer
and therefore tends to readjust the balance to some slight
degree. Legislation with this in mind could, perhaps,
arrange a tax program such as to bring about a greater
degree of justice whereas inflation is indiscriminate and
unmanageable.

FUTURE BUDGETS

After the war, the size of the budgets at first declined
with the falling off of military expenditures; then there
came a turn in the other direction in 1926.[1] This was the
inevitable result of the attempt to meet amortization with
taxation, rather than inflation. The budgets for the years
1926-28 were as follows.[2]

TABLE XXXVIII

Budgets, 1925 to 1928

(in millions of francs)

Year	Expenditures	Receipts	Excess or Deficit
1925............	34,220	33,528	— 792
1926............	36,646	32,306	—4,340
1927 [3]	39,541	39,959	699
1928 [4]	42,441	42,496	55

The increase here indicated for 1927 is less than that which
actually occurred because of the separation of the *caisse
de gestion* of the floating debt from the general budget

[1] See appendix.

[2] *Bulletin de la statistique générale de la France* (January-March, 1928),
p. 152. See appendix.

[3] Poincaré, *Exposé des motifs du projet du budget 1928* (Paris, April 7,
1927), annexe no. 4310, pp. 65, 122; see also pp. XVI, XIX. Compare with
table in appendix.

[4] *The New York Times* (December 26, 1927), p. 6 M. Poincaré gives the
figures as 42.1 billion francs for 1928 as compared with 39.7 for 1927; the
credits granted are 41.5 billions for 1928 as compared with 39.5 billions for
1927.

and the allocation of special revenues to cover this charge. The addition of this sum and local taxes would raise the effective budget to more than 50 billion francs.[1] This very large amount, a heavy charge even if reduced to gold values, represents probably the limit of possible payments.[2] Those who have considered the French situation closely agree that in the future a revision of the budgets downward is to be expected.

There are a number of possible developments in future budgets, but further increases in the total wealth absorbed by the state is not one of these. It is true that as far as taxation is concerned, it is probable that there are still groups in France who are undertaxed; the farmers, for instance, have not paid as much as city dwellers, and the tax receipts from incomes are much lower than one might expect. Nevertheless, adjustment of these difficult problems is a matter of time and legislative maneuvering. The more simple and rapid methods such as those adopted in 1920, 1924, and 1926,—the increasing of existing rates, can go no farther. *Le Pour et le contre* states, in 1927, that twenty per cent of the very heavy budget charge is upon "wealth, in formation," and adds that this is a very dangerous situation for a country which has been subjected to heavy capital losses during the war. The analysis of tax receipts as presented in Table **XXXIX** on following page is worth noting.

Various estimates of relative burdens in France and other countries have been made. None of these can be taken as exact, but they come fairly near to the true situation. On the basis adopted here, a comparison of the total govern-

[1] Henry Chéron, *Rapport au Sénat* (1926), no. 656, pp. 9, 10. The *Caisse d'amortissement* was to have been between four and five billion francs. The treasury receipts to be compared with this figure were 4,450. See also *Le Pour et le contre* (January 1, 1928), p. 1. This includes departmental taxes to the extent of about six billion francs.

[2] F. François-Marsal, "French Finance and the Franc," *Foreign Affairs* (New York, January, 1927), pp. 201, 202.

TABLE XXXIX

DISTRIBUTION OF TAXES,[1] 1928

(in millions of francs)

Direct taxes on incomes..............	12,005
Taxes on capital and transfer taxes....	8,514
Sumptuary taxes	783
Consumption taxes	8,655
Tax on alcohol	1,963
Business turnover tax...............	8,562
Total...........................	40,482

ment receipts with the national income, it is claimed that the government absorbs nearly thirty per cent. The following estimates come from responsible official sources.

TABLE XL

PART OF NATIONAL WEALTH ABSORBED BY TAXES[2]

Country	Chéron Report	Bérenger Report
France	33.2 per cent	28.2 per cent
Germany	18.0 " "	(not given)
Great Britain	24.9 " "	22.3 per cent
United States	14.8 " "	11.7 " "

It is better to accept such estimates as approximately correct than to attempt an exact statement, since the precise amount of French national wealth cannot be determined during this period of transition.

If, then, taxes cannot be increased, can expenditures be reduced? Here there is little immediate hope of improvement. Thorough discussion of this matter in 1926 indicated that at that time a possible cut of about 3 out of 36 billion francs might be made in expenses.[3] This was the largest estimate of reduction made at that time. Since then the situation has been altered by the attempt to make con-

[1] *Le Pour et le contre* (Paris, September 11, 1927), pp. 761, 762.

[2] Henry Chéron, *Rapport au Sénat*, annexe no. 225, vol. i, 1926, p. 10. Henry Bérenger, L'Europe nouvelle, *loc. cit.*, p. 659. The figures are for 1925. See also *Journal officiel, Chambre, débats* (January 24, 1928), p. 253.

[3] Olivier Duchemin, *Le Journal des débats* (January 5, 1926).

siderable reductions of the internal debt and by payments to England on the external debt. It is probable that little or no reduction is now possible. If extravagance and waste are cut down at a few points, they will be more than offset by increases in salaries which are very much below pre-war scales. In order to see the difficulty in tax reduction, it is well to recall that fifty-four per cent of the budget goes to pay for the public debt, and that the military and civil expenditures have become already lower than prewar on a gold basis.[1] Reduction, if it is to take place, must therefore come through a decrease in the debt.

The future of the budget depends, to a considerable extent, on the future of the Dawes annuities and on the payment of the debt to America. If sums due from Germany should exceed the amounts payable to England and America, this could be used to reduce the internal debt; but such a situation is hardly to be anticipated. In fact, there is as much possibility of a reduction in German payments to France as there is of a cut in French external debts. The most that France can reasonably hope at the present time is that the Dawes annuities will approximately cover her external debt charge, and that she will be able gradually, through taxation, to reduce the internal debt. She can, of course, in the meantime readjust her tax rates so that they will not fall so unjustly as they do at the present time. It is also possible that she can increase her revenues slightly from her monopolies, *domaines,* and colonies.[2] This development is necessarily slow and fluctuating however.

The budget situation is immeasurably better than it was two years ago. The French have wiped out the tremendous

[1] Morgan Bank, *Statistical Atlas,* Paris (unpublished), p. 5. An estimate is here given of the division of the budget into 54 per cent for the debt service, 17.4 per cent for military expenses, and 27.7 for civil expenses.

[2] The sale of the match monopoly to the Swedish International Match in the summer of 1927 was an interesting step. No very large sums can be gained by such dealings, however.

deficits and have shouldered their burden of taxation. There is, therefore, no real danger of further inflation, and no serious menace to the stability of the franc. Granted a reasonable attitude on the part of the creditors of France, the franc should maintain a value at approximately four cents. The price of the stability of the franc from 1926 was steady production, efficient management, and the payment into the hands of the state of a very large share of the product of labor and capital. Progress is essentially slow, but even the enormous internal debt will eventually become manageable with regular amortization payments.

CHAPTER X

STABILIZATION

DURING a period of seven years the value of the French franc was as uncertain as the weather. In terms of other currencies it sometimes varied four or five per cent a day.[1] Such unpredictable and disconcerting changes gave the impression to some that its value was a matter of chance and that the gains based on its fluctuations were so great as to make efforts to secure normal profits of comparatively little use. As cynicism grew, uncertainty increased, and the normal relations between production and consumption, wealth and saving were seriously threatened by the new state of mind. Instability became a disease which attacked the very heart of French economic life.

Fortunately for France, however, instability is an ill which tends eventually to bring its own cure, unless the different stages succeed each other very rapidly. Thus, although France passed from mild to severe depreciation with great rapidity in 1919, this phase did not develop rapidly into collapse as it did in some countries. Thanks to this fact, certain financial measures were passed in the years 1924-26 which were a help toward later stability; the most notable of these measures were tax increases. The steps taken in the second phase of depreciation were not adequate, however, and France slipped toward collapse in 1926. It was at this time that the French began to see the harm of instability, the need for a constant unit of measurement,[2] the dangers to production of uncertain profit margins and

---

[1] See *supra*, Chapter VIII.

[2] R. G. Hawtrey, *Currency and Credit* (London, second edition, 1923), p. 2. "A *unit* for the measurement of debts is indispensable."

prices, the loss to wage earners under certain conditions, and the dissipation of savings which might hamper later development. This consciousness of the effects of instability was an important factor in the ultimate recovery. Without an almost unanimous desire to secure peace, the political unity of August, 1926 would have been impossible. Out of the ills of depreciation came the general desire to steady financial conditions, and the panic was followed by a sudden calm. From the end of 1926 until the moment of legal stabilization the franc was as steady as any other European currency.

Once public opinion is sufficiently unified to support a sound financial policy, stabilization becomes an easy matter. This implies, of course, that there is no strong reason for the government to interfere with the normal workings of economic life through inflation or radical tax programs. It is impossible to overlook the economic prerequisites to stability but, in general, it is true that economic forces, if not interfered with by political and psychological influences, tend to establish rather than to break down stability. In the case of France, certainly, the lack of support given the government brought with it the vacillating policy and budget deficits which meant a continual threat of inflation, but once this situation was cleared up the natural tendency to an equilibrium of economic factors was manifest in monetary stability.

Stabilization is not easy, however, if the value chosen is to be considerably above or considerably below the point at which the value of money has come to rest in a natural way. The effort to increase or decrease its value leads to both economic and political complications. It sets one class against the other, and is apt to cost the government considerable sums either in the form of heavy fixed charges on a gold basis or of money spent in pegging operations. If, on the other hand, the value chosen is the same or slightly lower than that prevailing in the exchange markets, and if

the threat of government interference in economic life has
been permanently removed, the final step in stabilization is
comparatively easy.

The difficulties which have arisen in a number of countries have been due to the fact that general economic conditions were not sound, or to the fact that the government
was still in such a weak condition that the possibility of
balancing the budget in a normal way was still somewhat
in doubt. There have been a number of cases of premature
stabilization, where the value of the new unit was set so
high that the government could not give it the necessary
support during the period of price and trade adjustment. It
is interesting to note in passing the difference between the
problem in certain other countries and the problem in
France.

STABILIZATION IN OTHER COUNTRIES

The various countries can be divided into two groups in
regard to stabilization.[1] There are, in the first place, those
whose currencies were not seriously depreciated and who
could therefore return to par. There are, in the second place,
those currencies which fell so low that the return of the
original unit to its former par was practically impossible.
It should be remembered, in this connection, that the introduction of a new monetary unit, even if called by the same
name as the old one, as happened in Germany, was not the
same thing as bringing the money back to par. It meant,
rather, a very drastic measure of repudiation, none the less
regrettable because it was in a sense unavoidable.

In the first group of countries whose currencies were
brought back to par may be noted: [2] Denmark, Great

[1] *Bulletin de la statistique générale de la France* (April-June, 1927), p. 321.
A list of countries and various facts regarding their stabilization are here
given.

[2] U. S. Senate, *Foreign Currency and Exchange Investigation,* Vol. ii.
See following pages for the respective countries, Denmark, p. 97; Great
Britain not given here; Netherlands, p. 138; Norway, p. 159; Spain, p. 240;
Sweden, p. 262; Switzerland, p. 289.

Britain, Netherlands, Norway, Spain, Sweden, Switzerland, United States. Some of these countries found it necessary to take definite steps to assure the usual relations with other currencies, and to return to a full gold standard. Others simply allowed events to take their course, since they had not suffered either severe depreciation or marked appreciation, and did not need any artificial support.

Great Britain alone of this group had a serious problem to face. It is interesting to compare her difficulties with those of France, for both were troubled by internal maladjustments which made the return to par difficult. In the case of Great Britain, however, the justification of restoring the currencies is now generally admitted. The British problem was the outgrowth of her position in foreign trade and unemployment, and was made more complicated by the theory that a lower value for the pound would have solved her industrial problem temporarily. Since she was not weakened, however, as was France, by a poor tax apparatus, large budget deficits, and an unstable political system, the outcome was very different. The announcement of the prospective return to the gold standard in 1925 led to a gradual return to par by April. Although there were some difficulties during the next few years, there was never any serious question as to the steadiness of the pound sterling and no need for extensive artificial support. Thus Great Britain stands practically alone in respect to the complete restoration of the currency.

The second group of countries presents problems of stabilization which are more intricate and various. The important countries are noted in the table presented on following page, with the date of stabilization.[1] The striking thing to note about this list is that the countries which suffered complete collapse attained stability more quickly

---

[1] U. S. Senate, *Foreign Currency and Exchange Investigation,* vol. ii. See following pages: Austria, pp. 19, 22; Belgium, p. 49; Czechoslovakia, p. 70; Hungary, p. 119; Poland, p. 177; Russia, pp. 199, 218.

Austria 1922
Belgium 1925, 1926
Czechoslovakia 1926
France 1928
Germany 1924
Hungary 1924
Italy 1927
Poland 1925, 1927
Russia 1924

than did those which maintained a large fraction of their original value. Austria, for instance, noted for the very rapid decline of the crown and for chaotic financial conditions, reordered her finances in 1922 and 1923.[1] This was due, in part, to two facts: in certain cases those countries most disturbed by depreciation received outside support from the League of Nations, to hasten recovery; and the ills which depreciation brought taught the public certain lessons which made sane financial policies politically possible.

It is important to note in particular how much Belgium and Italy differed from France in regard to stabilization. It is particularly surprising that Belgium, though closely linked with France in exchange value fluctuations for six years, was able to stabilize two years before France. There are a number of reasons which made this possible.[2] One important factor of the situation was the government ownership of the railroads. This made it possible for the government to work out a plan whereby the internal debt was consolidated, and the government used the railroads as the basis for a sale of long-time securities.[3] This lessened considerably the objection to forced consolidation, and strengthened the financial situation of the government. Moreover, the political struggle had not been as intense in

---

[1] J. Van Walré de Bordes, *The Austrian Crown* (London, 1924), pp. 205, 206.

[2] The earlier attempt to stabilize the Belgian franc, in 1925, failed because of insufficient outside support and internal budget difficulties.

[3] *Le Pour et le contre* (Paris, October 31, 1926), pp. 854, 855.

Belgium as in France, so that it was possible for the government to risk the hostility involved in a reduction of the value of the unit. The fact that the charge on Belgium for reconstruction, and therefore the internal debt, was lighter, was a part of this general situation which made it possible to stabilize the Belgian franc at a time when French conditions were still uncertain.

The success of Italian stabilization was based on other factors, but here, too, conditions were very different from those in France. Because of the political dictatorship, it was possible to restrict foreign commerce in an unusual way, and to put certain impositions on banks and large enterprises which would have been impossible in France. It is true that the Italians handled the debt agreement with the United States in such a way as to make a very favorable impression on public opinion in the world at large. The prompt acceptance of the terms and the payment of the first instalment on the debt helped the position of Italy in international markets. In comparing her situation with that of France, however, it should be noted that the terms of the debt agreement were very lenient.[1] Moreover, the internal conditions noted above made it possible to put through a forced consolidation of the internal debt such as France could not contemplate. Despite these considerations, however, it is remarkable that the Italian government could increase the value of the lira and keep it stable without any break from 1927 onwards.[2]

Belgium, then, attained stability by further depreciation, and forced consolidation of the internal debt. Italy gained a higher value for the lira by means of restrictive measures, a lenient debt settlement, and a firm attitude toward financial problems. Both made use of foreign credits and both

[1] W. R. Batsell, *The Debt Settlements and the Future* (Paris, 1927), pp. 89-91.

[2] *The New York Times*, June 3, 1927. Italy announced the stabilization of the lira on June 2.

came through the time of depression without very great hardship. France was forced to postpone this inevitable step until the severe crisis of 1926, and the prolonged calm, stabilization *de facto,* of 1927 and 1928, which made possible financial changes.

It is not possible to discuss the various measures behind the other cases of stabilization, all of which differed from those of France in their essential features. It is well to note in passing, however, that Germany reached stability through complete collapse, and that her early success was consolidated by the Dawes Plan and the establishment of the Transfer Committee, which was to prevent the adverse effect of reparation payments on the exchange.[1] Thus she was protected from further exchange instability by the interests of all those nations who were receiving payments. In addition to this, large government and private loans flowed into the country once the reparation difficulty was temporarily adjusted. In this respect, her situation was like that of Austria, Poland, Hungary, and Czechoslovakia.[2] Foreign financiers studied the problem and foreign agencies supplied temporary credits. Pegging arrangements were made which were technically adequate and the programs of financial reconstruction adopted were based on sane budget procedures and heavy taxation. In these instances

[1] The Dawes Report, *Reparation,* Part V (see World Peace Foundation, vol. vi, 1923, no. 5), p. 368. "Treaty funds collected in Germany are all to be deposited in the new bank to the credit of a special account and are only to be withdrawable by the creditor nations *under conditions and safeguards which will adequately protect the German exchange market* and the interests of the creditor nations and the German economy." (Italics ours.)

[2] For studies of these cases see the following reports: Austria, W. T. Layton, C. Rist, *The Economic Situation of Austria,* Report for the Council of the League of Nations (Geneva, 1925); Poland, E. W. Kemmerer, *Poland,* Report of Commission of the American Financial Experts (Warsaw, 1926); *Poland,* J. F. Dulles (printed by Sullivan and Cromwell, New York, 1928); Hungary, A. A. Young, *Economic Problems New and Old* (Boston, 1927), pp. 37-62; Czechoslovakia, C. Rist, *La Deflation en Pratique,* Paris (1924), pp. 87-112.

international supervision lent a support which was neither
possible nor desirable for France.

THE PECULIARITIES OF THE FRENCH CASE

The French problem of stabilization was, therefore, different from that of any other nation. This was true, first,
because of her economic situation, and second, because of
her political conditions. The instability of political life, as
contrasted with that of England, Belgium, and Italy, has
been indicated. Based partly on the composition of the
Chamber of Deputies, it was aggravated in matters of
finance by the strong influence of the *rentier* class. It was
natural that the large number of government bond holders
formed a serious obstacle to early stabilization. Since they
had pocketed a very considerable loss in the value of their
securities, they felt that their interests should be given some
weight in the choice of the new value of the franc. It was,
therefore, not possible to come quickly to the final decision
because of strong public sentiment favoring a higher gold
value. The extent of the losses which the bond holder faced
can be indicated by the figures which show the real values
in 1926 as compared with those in 1913.

DEPRECIATION OF GOLD VALUE OF THREE SECURITIES [1]

	Three Per Cent *Rente*		Bank of France		Thomson Houston	
	Bourse Quotation	Gold Value	Bourse Quotation	Gold Value	Bourse Quotation	Gold Value
1913 av.	87.12	87.12	4,665	4,665	761.00	761.00
1919 av.	62.25	43.31	5,685	3,955	856.00	595.50
1925 av.	47.15	11.50	10,050	2,452	386.50	94.50
1926 (June 30).	47.20	6.88	12,400	1,809	370.00	54.00

This table, which gives three typical French securities
before and after depreciation, shows strikingly the loss
which was sustained, and reveals the fact that in the case
of the *rente* it was due to the combined action of the fall in

[1] *Rapport du comité des experts* (*décret du 31 mai, 1926*, Paris, 1926),
p. 66.

the *nominal value* in francs and the decline in the *purchasing power* of the franc. The *three per cents* fell to less than a tenth of their worth in 1913. The decline of other government securities was almost as great. While the effect of this decline must not be exaggerated, since it was spread over a number of years and shifted by sales and purchases so that it was shared by a large number of people, nevertheless it had a profound influence on French attitudes and explains the persistence of the hope of complete restoration of the franc.

A second reason for the delay in stabilization was the condition of the internal debt, which was peculiar to the French situation. The large mass of short-time credits, frequently mentioned herein, made the situation difficult to handle from a technical point of view. Until some plan of consolidation and amortization could be instituted, it was impossible to count on a balanced budget and freedom from future inflation. Such a plan required a strong political majority, a consistent and uninterrupted financial program, and heavy taxation. When these conditions were realized in 1926, the *caisse d'amortissement* became a possibility, and the menace of the *bons de la défense* diminished. It is frequently stated that an internal debt is no problem, since it merely requires the shifting of wealth from one person to another within the state, and no loss of real wealth. This is undoubtedly true under normal conditions and in the long run. But when, as in the case of France, this redistribution of wealth threatens the continuity of the political régime and disturbs the relations between classes and parties, it constitutes a problem of the first magnitude. Certainly it was a factor in delaying the final solution of the exchange problem.

Then, in the third place, the external debts of France were troublesome. They interfered, not so much because there was urgent need of payment, as because they prevented securing the foreign credits which were considered necessary for stabilization. It is true that the large private debts, accumulated since the war, tended to be offset by the credits which French citizens gained during the period of the *flight from the franc*. But, although France probably reconstituted a large part of the foreign holdings sold during the war, the nature of the new credits was such that they did not offer much support to the franc in case of stabilization; they were, on the contrary, indications of distrust and of the *sauve qui peut* spirit which hampered government action. The debt of France to the United States, moreover, was for a time a definite barrier to loans from that quarter. Although such loans became superfluous after the Bank of France had built up its large holdings of dollar and pound credits in 1927, they would have made possible a quicker adjustment of the whole problem had they been available earlier.

These three factors are the inevitable outgrowth of the war and reconstruction expenditures. It was the budget deficits which led to depreciation, and therefore to the heavy losses sustained by the *rentier*. It was the cost of reconstruction which increased the internal debt, and made it impossible to discharge external debts. If the severe crises attributable to government embarrassment in handling the debt and the budget in 1924 and 1926 could have been avoided, if the budget could have been passed with reasonable speed in 1925, there is no reason to suppose that France would have found stabilization impossible in 1925 or 1926. It is important, then, to realize that the French difficulties were a combination of the exceptionally heavy postwar burdens and a political system unadapted to handling such difficult problems.

THE FINAL PANIC [1]

The last plunge of the franc in 1926 led almost inevitably to the recovery which followed so quickly. This incident has

[1] See *supra,* Chapter V, pp. 193–198.

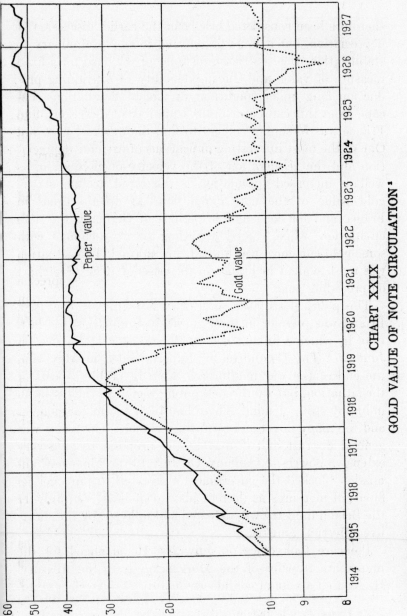

CHART XXIX

GOLD VALUE OF NOTE CIRCULATION [1]

[1] See appendix for figures.

therefore been considered briefly in the earlier discussion of depreciation, but it must be referred to as a preliminary to stabilization. It is a striking instance of the need for a fixed measure of value and the impossibility of continuing production long under conditions of violent fluctuations. Escape from this can be made in a number of directions, and France was fortunate enough to find the quickest way out. One of the most interesting indications of extreme depreciation and the acceleration of the velocity of circulation, as well as increased speculation is the rapid decline of the gold value of the note circulation. At certain times in France and for considerable periods in Germany the note circulation, when valued according to its exchange with some gold currency, was much below normal. This situation was most evident in France in the crisis of 1926. (See chart on preceding page.)

The political situation in 1926 was extremely confused. Briand was premier in three successive ministries, the last, that in which Caillaux was made minister of finance on June 25.[1] The Committee of Experts called in May, and the end of the war in Morocco, were favorable aspects of the situation, but the French public was nevertheless in an unhappy state of mind. There had been too many changes and too many novel and confusing schemes. The result was general distrust and dismay at the proposal to give very extensive powers to Caillaux. On July 16 the Finance Commission blocked the government's proposal to put over its financial measures as decrees instead of laws.[2] On July 17 the Briand ministry was defeated and followed by the short-lived Herriot ministry.

Poincaré took office on July 24.[3] He arranged for the immediate transfer of the Morgan funds to the treasury. He secured a vote of confidence on July 27. The clear state-

---

[1] *Le Temps,* June 25, 1926.
[2] New York *Herald Tribune* (July 17, 1926).
[3] *Le Pour et le contre* (August 15, 1926).

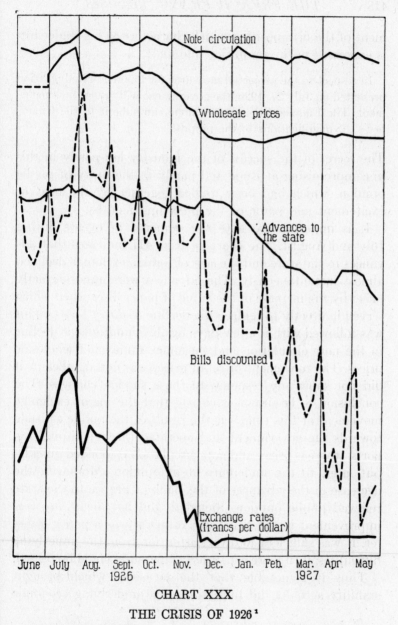

Note circulation

Wholesale prices

Advances to
the state

Bills discounted

Exchange rates
(francs per dollar)

| June | July | Aug. | Sept. | Oct. | Nov. | Dec. | Jan. | Feb. | Mar. | Apr. | May |

1926   1927

CHART XXX

THE CRISIS OF 1926[1]

[1] See appendix for figures.

ment of the firm position which characterized his leadership is expressed in the resolution adopted:

> In respect to the projected measures for financial rehabilitation presented on July 27, 1926, the government will accept no amendment. The Finance Commission alone can submit to the Chamber . . . modifications to the proposals.[1]

The secret of the success of the ministry lay partly in this uncompromising attitude and partly in the unity of public opinion, which had been welded together by the heat of excitement and panic of the preceding months.

It is important to note the sequence of events during July and August. The chart on page 417 indicates that advances to the state and the cost of foreign exchange declined almost instantaneously. The advances were almost exactly offset by the increase of the value of paper discounted which served indirectly to replace the decline of *direct* loans.[2] This was followed within a few days by the simultaneous decline in the note circulation and the index number of wholesale prices. The movement of retail prices was not significant, it did not show any response to these sudden changes. The conclusion to be drawn is clearly that the major exchange movement at this time was the result of the public attitude towards the government and operated through capital exports, whereas prices and note circulation responded quickly, but later, to the undercurrent of opinion. Moreover, the decrease in the advances of the Bank of France to the state relieved public opinion, though it did not mean any real improvement in the situation; rather it was a paper transfer. It was sufficient to divert attention from the underlying difficulties until more constructive measures could be passed.

Thus it is notable that the measures which brought stability actually did little to change underlying economic

---

[1] *Revue de science et de législation financières, loc. cit.*, p. 688.

[2] See *supra*, Chapter VI, pp. 235–237, 240. Some of the ways of securing funds are here described.

conditions. The laws of August 3 and 6 [1] changed few
things, except to alter the method of collecting taxes and to
establish the *caisse de gestion des bons,* which of itself was
important as much because of its moral effect as on account
of any new procedure involved. This last measure was invested with all the solemnity that the government could
secure, since it was realized that the public, seriously
alarmed, needed the encouragement which a vigorous program could arouse. The law was voted in a joint session
of the two branches of the legislature at Versailles. It set
an upper limit to the *bons de la défense* and arranged for
the gradual consolidation, putting at the resources of the
caisse the proceeds of the tobacco monopoly. This separation of the *bons* from the general treasury account had little
real significance in addition to the fact that it showed a
determination to take the floating debt seriously. There was
no net increase in the resources in the hands of the government for the purpose of redeeming or reorganizing the debt.
There was no very great change in taxation, since it was
realized that rates were already heavy enough if the proper
measures were taken to collect the revenues. Moreover, a
period of calm during which business could go on in a
normal fashion was apt to add more to receipts than an
increase in tax rates, which might disturb the existing business situation. A glance at the income from the business
turnover tax shows a notable rise, in part due to the law
which changed the percentage by a small fraction,[2] and in
part to the general improvement of business conditions and
a more careful supervision of tax collection.

Although there was no revolutionary legislation at this
time, the provisions of the law of August 6, allowing the
purchase of exchange and the issue of notes, was very help-

[1] The date of promulgation of the law creating the *Caisse de gestion
des bons* was August 8, *Revue d'économie politique,* vol. xlix, no. 6, p. 1389.

[2] Raymond Poincaré, *Exposé du projet du budget générale de l'exercice
1927, Chambre,* no. 3248, vol. i, 1926, p. 50. The increase expected was three
billion francs.

ful in steadying the franc when it tended to fall too rapidly, and in building up foreign credits which were a psychological and technical aid to later measures.[1] On the whole, however, the general improvement must be attributable to the fact that the new confidence allowed a breathing space,[2] a time of adjustment during which economic life could become productive, taxes be collected, and people go about their ordinary business without abnormal concern over financial problems. This breathing space was the result of the new political situation and the recognized strength of Poincaré. The surprising force which he manifested was due, in part, to personality and, in part, to the fact that he belonged to a political party which had not advocated radical measures such as the capital levy. If one contrasts this with the autumn of 1925, one realizes the difficulties which were implicit in a situation with the majority farther to the left, which had to advocate heavy direct taxation in order to please the Socialists, and yet could not come out squarely for a capital levy for fear of alienating the moderate groups. Poincaré desired and made no such compromise. Moreover, since he was thought to advocate the appreciation of the currency, he kept the support of those large groups who wished a higher franc. At the same time, he did not definitely alienate the industrial interests, since without any definite announcement of a deflationary policy he attained the respite from uncertainty, which business needed.

Thus the very chaos of July led naturally to a general desire for stability which was easily attained by the new ministry. After the sharp fall of the franc, there was a considerable rise, modulated in October and the following months by the pegging operations of the Bank of France.

---

[1] See *supra,* Chapter VI, pp. 261, 262.

[2] Professor Schumpeter used this expression in an interview with the writer and stressed the tremendous moral effect of the leadership of Poincaré.

The value of the currency was regularly fixed in December, 1926 [1] by the purchase of exchange credits at a price fixed by an official of the Bank of France, and subsequently allowed to vary only within narrow limits. Some variation was permitted because it was thought that it would prevent speculators from assuming a permanent value when the government preferred to leave the matter open.

The uncertainty which remained as to the future of the franc was considered by many to be a political expedient designed to lessen hostile attacks on the government. It is obvious that Poincaré used it as a threat, by implication at least, on many occasions. Certainly there was less opposition to the budget than was usual under normal financial conditions. It called for a total of government receipts, including the *caisse de gestion des bons,* of 51,904 million francs,[2] a sum almost twice that collected before 1924.[3] Nevertheless, since this large sum did not require any marked readjustment of taxation, but merely the continuance of normal economic activity, the project did not shake the stability which had lasted for several months. The government seemed to be in a stronger position than ever and maintained its prestige almost unchallenged throughout the year.

THREE WAYS TO STABILITY

There are three different approaches to stability. In the first place, during the times of most violent fluctuations such as those just described, the use of substitutes for the fluctuating money is apt to become evident. This was less true of France than it was of Germany, but even in France the stress of uncertainty began to call out exceptional measures such as those used in times of collapse. Such measures were, in the first place, sliding scales which made it possible

---

[1] See *supra,* Chapter VI. Previous to this time support had been given more by the treasury than by the Bank of France.

[2] *Le Pour et le contre* (January 29, 1927), p. 93.

[3] See *supra,* Chapter IX.

for wages and prices to be altered rapidly with the exchange rates. Then, in the second place, there was some use of foreign money as the unit of account for transactions normally carried on in francs. Farther than this, a third and more crude device to meet the situation was the actual use of foreign currencies as a medium of exchange within the countries. There were traces of all these things in the last months of depreciation in France, though they never came to be recognized generally, and were most of them, in fact, banned by law.

These abnormal economic devices are all a part of the general effort to establish a new basis for stability when the normal one has broken down. They indicate the fact that the influence of value as a guide to production has become impaired, and that order must be restored in some way. The method used, the substitution of a foreign unit of account as a standard, is cumbersome and unnatural, and occurs only where the need has become very great, as in Germany in 1922. Once it has become universal, there is a tendency to arrange the old units in such a way that they can express stable values more simply. This took place in Germany through the introduction of the *renten mark*. The unit was so like the old that the step back to the use of the mark was simple, and the accounting in foreign currencies, an emergency measure at best, was quickly abandoned. France, on the other hand, never carried this practice so far and did not establish a new unit in place of the former franc. There was therefore less real hardship to the creditor than occurred under the German procedure. This first method of reaching stability, through collapse, is a painful and costly way.

The second approach to stability is the slow and difficult one of returning to the former par. This program, practicable in the case of England, was out of the question for France after the extreme depreciation of the years from 1919 through 1924. While such a policy held out certain advantages in demonstrating financial power and in doing justice to a certain class of the population, it occasioned many new injustices while it attempted to right the old. Whereas stability at the existing level was possible without contracting the note issue and even in the face of some increases, a restoration of the former value of the franc would have meant drastic and prolonged deflation. The note circulation had been increased fivefold and more,[1] and to contract the circulation would have meant such increases in taxation as would have enabled the state to pay back thirty billion francs, more or less, to the Bank of France. Since taxation was already heavy, however, it was impossible to contemplate such a step. In addition to this, it would have been necessary to raise the discount rate to attract foreign loans, and this would have tended to depress an industry already hard pressed by a policy of deflation and taxation. There would be no way in which the government could bring about such a great appreciation except through acting on the price level and so on foreign commerce and capital flow, through the discount rate which might have attracted short-time credits, and through direct pegging, which was expensive to the state. A government already charged with heavy burdens could not think of adding to them in this unprecedented fashion.

Moreover, it must be remembered in considering the possibility of increasing the value of the franc that deflation and inflation are not symmetrical. It is not possible to contract a note circulation as fast as to expand it. It is not possible to use the same mechanism or to expect the same results. There are forces which tend to push prices higher; they have been referred to in Chapter VII as resembling a spiral, for prices influence wages and wages prices; thus the interests, motives and desires of the active forces in productive life all move upward.[2] It is always easier to borrow than to repay. The attempt to call in money loans inevitably

[1] See *infra,* appendix.   [2] See *supra,* Chapter VII, pp. 299-301.

means forced liquidations, either on the part of governments or on the part of individuals, and the result is disrupting price declines which are apt to lessen production, and this in its turn drives prices up again. Thus the movement downward is apt to be shortlived; the movement upward goes on for considerable time on its own momentum.

The third approach to stabilization is the acceptance of conditions as they appear in a moment of temporary calm and the attempt to bring all values into adjustment to the temporary equilibrium which may intervene at various times. The longer the temporary respite, the better the chance of consolidating it by official measures. The natural tendencies of prices to adjust themselves to exchange rates, and vice versa, leads to a new harmony unless it is prevented by extra-economic forces. Thus in 1926, in France wholesale prices tended to react to the new exchange rates so that gold prices became stable, and retail prices continued to rise until they had nearly closed the gap opened up by the rapid movement of wholesale prices. This state of affairs came about only after the political situation made further interference in the economic world less likely, after the threat to the note circulation and taxation was less alarming, and the gradual reëstablishment of *laissez faire* allowed the more valued and customary forces to prevail. Stabilization *de facto* thus permitted economic life to return to its usual concerns and the problems of money ceased to interest the general public in an unusual way.

The method of approaching stabilization in France was undoubtedly the one best suited to her needs, granted the difficult months that had preceded and the degree of depreciation of the franc. That there was hardship and injustice involved cannot be denied; but any other step would merely have added to existing wrongs and prolonged the suffering which came with uncertainty and changing values. It must be remembered that some of those who suffered as bond holders had gained as industrialists, and not all the

holders of government securities in 1927 had bought them at
prewar values. Moreover, the important thing in such a situation was to stress, not the return to a condition precisely
like that before the war, but measures which would stimu-
late rather than depress industry, and which would lead to
the greatest possible sum of real wealth in the future. This
seemed to be dependent on cutting down risks and uncertainties and turning men's energies from speculation to production. This state of affairs called for less interference by
the state in economic life and came to pass after the *ability*
of the state to gain control had been clearly demonstrated.

The Experts' Report

The approach to stability, as well as the final legal step,
was dependent on psychological and economic forces. It
is for this reason that the Experts' Report, setting forth
important facts in a clear way, was of real importance. It
is probable that the document exerted considerable influence, although because of the disturbed political situation
and the change of government it was never given much recognition in the official measures taken in 1926. The committee which was formed as the result of the decree of May
31, 1926 under the Briand premiership,[1] completed its
work on July 3. Its recommendations were clear cut and
sane though they were in no sense novel; they brought out
emphatically certain features of the situation which had not
been generally admitted before that date.

In the first place, the report stressed the consequences of
instability, many of which have already been mentioned
here. It commented on the dissipation of capital, the increase of poverty, and the dangers of substituting a speculative spirit for hard work and providence.

In France, a country of moderate incomes, of limited indus-
trialism, a country whose prosperity is based primarily on the

[1] *Rapport du comité des experts, op. cit.,* p. 1.

ability to save, the results of instability are peculiarly grave. If foresight becomes deception, if the lure of speculation and gambling does away with the taste for effort and productive work, we shall see shortly the disappearance of the highest national virtues.[1]

It then stated the impossibility of the complete revalorization of the franc, and recommended instead an early stabilization as a means of general security.

The conditions were as clearly set forth as was the end to be attained. The technical requisites were given under six headings: [2]

1. A normal balance of accounts due to a cessation of the excessive short-time capital movements
2. A balanced budget
3. A balanced treasury account
4. The adjustment of external debts
5. The adaptation of economic factors to the new monetary situation
6. The accumulation of a sufficient gold and exchange reserve behind the note issues and commercial paper

The Report then took up the first three of these conditions in considerable detail. The balance of accounts was said to offer no serious obstacle to stabilization. The budget and the treasury were in need of energetic measures. The adjustment of the foreign debts, condition four, they did not discuss, probably because of the delicate political nature of the question. The problem of securing foreign credits, condition six, assumed to be closely linked up with the acceptance of the American debt proposal, like condition four, was left out of the discussion. The fifth condition was one which would come about naturally without any definite effort on the part of the government. Thus the condition of government finance was one which, rightly, demanded the attention of the committee more than any of the other matters.

[1] *Rapport du comité des experts, op. cit.,* p. 8.   [2] *Ibid.,* p. 11.

As to the budget, the conclusion was that there was no serious difficulty in securing a balance with some slight readjustments as soon as early stability was the definite goal. Here the committee sees a closer, more immediate connection between the rising price level and budget deficits than has been traced in this analysis of budget factors.[1] Nevertheless, the importance of working for a balanced budget and stability simultaneously is universally admitted, since the two act on each other at many points. The difficulties of the treasury, which have been described above,[2] it attributed to the need of funds for commercial purposes, and to fear. The solution recommended was, in the main, the recourse to sound budget methods and gradual amortization and refunding of the floating debts. The committee foresaw no serious difficulties in the way of accomplishing this.

In addition to these general recommendations, it urged, in particular, the reduction of government expenditures wherever it was possible, the restoration of the Bank of France to complete independence of action, the freedom of capital movements from legal hindrance, the purchase of gold by the Bank at a price consistent with foreign exchange rates, the gradual reduction of the advances by the Bank to the state, and encouragement of hard work and habits of saving.[3]

The interesting fact to note about this report is that the traditional recommendations for monetary rehabilitation are nowhere stressed. For instance there is no emphatic insistence on deflation, though a certain amount would naturally result from the partial repayment of the advances of the Bank. On the contrary, it is clearly stated that the determination of an upper limit for the note circulation would be superfluous.[4] Then again, there is no insistence on the discount rate as a possible means of strengthening the franc

---

[1] See *supra*, Chapter IX.
[2] See the discussion of the *bons de la défense*, Chapter VI.
[3] *Rapport du comité des experts, op. cit.*, p. 53.   [4] *Ibid.*, p. 46.

and increasing the control by the Bank. Further, it states that the immediate return to a gold basis is entirely unimportant. These things, and the fact that the problem of righting the wrongs of depreciation are subordinated to the technical problems of finding an early and lasting stability at any level, give this report a point of view which is somewhat different from some of the earlier documents. It is interesting to note that many of the recommendations were put into effect very much as they are outlined in the report.

There is clear evidence that the experiences in other countries had given perspective to this committee, struggling with the complexities of stabilization. The process was divided into three periods: [1]

1. Prestabilization
2. Stabilization, in fact
3. Stabilization, in law

The first of these three periods was to be short and was to be characterized mainly by the rigid limitation of the borrowings of the state from the Bank and the building up of the gold reserve. The second was to be characterized by a kind of gold exchange standard, since the Bank was to buy and sell gold and foreign exchange at prices fairly definitely fixed. The third stage was considered easy to accomplish, once the second stage had become a well-established fact. The main problem to be faced at this final period was the extent to which the advances should be reduced and in what form to leave the residue carried forward as a permanent result of the war.

The consequences of such steps as these were clearly set forth in the discussion of the economic depression which was sure to follow such measures. The significant point brought out in this connection was the fact that such a crisis was bound to come even if the money continued to fall in value, that delays, therefore, in stabilizing merely postponed and

[1] *Rapport du comité des experts, op. cit.,* pp. 45–47.

augmented the inevitable liquidation. This fact is the natural result of the characteristics of severe depreciation which have already been pointed out, that is to say, an artificial stability based on various substitute units of account inevitably comes into effect. Nevertheless, there were evidences that such a crisis would not be severe and certain measures could be taken to lessen the ill effects. Such measures were: economy, international adjustments to facilitate foreign commerce, and the better apportioning of the large number of foreign laborers to industrial needs in France.

Although the unexpected events of July, 1926 introduced several new elements into the prestabilization period, the steps taken afterward were, to a striking degree, in line with the outline here made. The only notable addition to what the committee recommended was the exchange purchase mechanism of August 6.[1] This facilitated pegging operations and prevented undue movement of exchange in either direction.

THE DEPRESSION

The depressing effect of stabilization in France was not very great. There was, of course, considerable suffering for a short time, and a few people were reduced to real misery, but if one has in mind the functioning of the economic system as a whole, and ignores the instances of individual distress, it is clear that there was no serious interruption to economic life. There are a number of reasons why this was so, but chief among them was the fact that the panic of 1926 had indicated that the existing situation was not sound, and industry preferred to face the new conditions and try to build up a more lasting basis for prosperity, accepting the temporary reduction of profit and keeping the wheels going as far as was practicable. Moreover, there were no startling innovations to upset the gradual adjustment of 1926 and 1927. Other reasons will be pointed out later

[1] See *supra*, Chapter VI.

after the consideration of the main indications of economic conditions which are available.

The growth of unemployment in 1926 and 1927 was the most striking sign of the depression, but it never attained the alarming proportions characteristic of the English conditions; nor did it last to any notable extent beyond the first year of stable exchange rates. There was no completely satisfactory measure of unemployment. Registration was incomplete, relief figures were not adequate, and the trade union statements cannot be checked. All that one can do is to take the official figures as an index of the general condition, realizing that the actual figures probably showed only a half or a third of existing unemployment. Nevertheless, it seems safe to assume that the total did not exceed one hundred thousand for very long. The figures given out by the French government indicate a maximum of about ninety-seven thousand demands for work which could not be satisfied in February, 1927. This figure was certainly high; it was about eight times that of the same month in 1926. The total declined rapidly, however, through the following months, and was less than thirty thousand in July.[1] The number in receipt of relief in February, 1927 was sixty-four thousand, but this figure, though large enough to indicate a serious situation, was less than the ninety-one thousand receiving relief in March, 1921, the peak of the previous depression.[2]

The upward trend of wages is significant. (See Table XLI.) It is not possible to estimate the considerable amount of underemployment which increased the hardship of these months.[3] It is better to try to judge the situation through a consideration of the volume of production and economic activity, which is a check on this unemployment

[1] See *infra*, appendix.
[2] Reference Service on International Affairs, *European Economic and Political Survey* (Paris, February 15, 1927), pp. 288, 289.
[3] *Journal officiel, Chambre, débats*, January 27, 1928, p. 335.

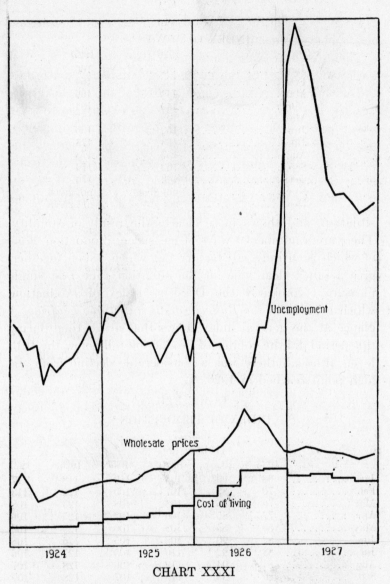

Unemployment

Wholesale prices

Cost of living

1924   1925   1926   1927

CHART XXXI

UNEMPLOYMENT, PRICES AND THE COST OF LIVING [1]

[1] See appendix for figures.

431

TABLE XLI

INDEX OF WAGES [1]

	1926	1927
Jan	132	166
Feb	132	164
Mar	141	166
Apr	144	164
May	148	167
Jun	152	166
Jul	153	173
Aug	157	173
Sep	162	174
Oct	166	176
Nov	not given	not given
Dec	not given	not given

situation, and shows more clearly the result of stability. There are a number of ways of measuring production, none of which is entirely satisfactory but which, taken together, give a fairly clear view of the situation. The best single measure is probably the Dessirier Index of Production, which is given in the *Bulletin de la statistique générale*. A glance at the general index shows that at no time during this period did the volume of production fall below the 1913 level, although there was a considerable decline from the high point reached in 1926.

TABLE XLII

INDEX OF PRODUCTION [2]

1922–27

(1913 = 100)

	1922	1923	1924	1925	1926	1927
Jan	68	90	105	110	118	117
Feb	70	85	107	109	122	113
Mar	76	86	108	108	123	108
Apr	77	85	106	107	125	106
May	80	85	108	106	126	108
Jun	82	90	108	105	126	108
Jul	83	92	110	105	127	106
Aug	84	94	112	106	128	107
Sep	86	95	115	107	128	109
Oct	90	97	117	111	129	110
Nov	92	99	113	116	129	112
Dec	90	102	113	118	123	115

[1] *Bulletin de la statistique générale*, vol. xvi, no. ii, p. 173; vol. xvii, no. ii, p. 184.

[2] See *infra*, appendix.

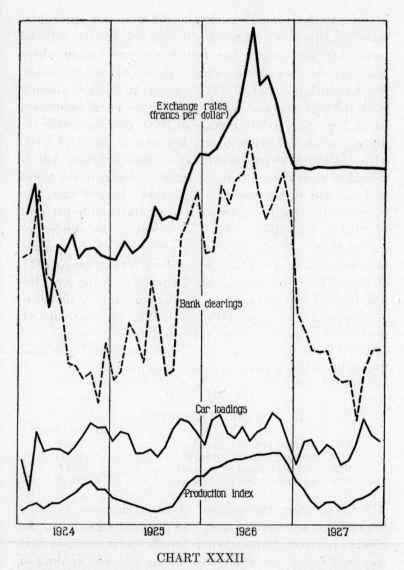

Exchange rates
(francs per dollar)

Bank clearings

Car loadings

Production index

1924   1925   1926   1927

CHART XXXII

ECONOMIC ACTIVITY AND THE DOLLAR EXCHANGE RATE[1]

[1] See appendix for figures.

If one examines more closely the different industries governed by this index, it is evident that the textiles suffered more than any other. The figures are given under three headings, the mechanical industry, which did not fall below one hundred per cent of 1913, though it declined sharply from the high average of 130 in 1926; the metal industries, which kept close to the average of 1925; and the textile industry, which fell below ninety per cent of the 1913 level. This marked a serious condition in that industry, but it should be remembered that the textile industry in the world at large was in an unsettled condition.[1] In any case, the index for the textile industries rose to ninety-nine per cent of 1913 in November, 1927.[2] Then again, the number of car loadings, a fairly significant indication of the volume of production, stayed at about the same level through 1925, 1926, and 1927, but was slightly higher than in the years before that.[3] A consideration of the fluctuation of bank clearings shows a very marked decline in 1927, but this must be attributed in large measure to the falling off of speculation, rather than to the lessening of normal commercial activities. The following comparison is significant.

TABLE XLIII

BANK CLEARINGS[4]

		Million Francs
1923	Average monthly clearings	19,888
1924	Average monthly clearings	30,671
1926	July, high point of the year	55,843
1927	September, low point of year	20,593

After September the volume of bank clearings shows a gradual upward trend, which was partial indication of the general recovery, although it is hardly to be expected that they will equal the large sums during the wild trading of

[1] *Bulletin de la statistique générale,* vol. xvii (October–December, 1927), p. 1.
[2] *Monthly Supplement, Bulletin de la statistique générale* (Paris, January, 1928), p. 2.
[3] See *infra,* appendix.   [4] See *infra,* appendix.

1926. It is sometimes hard to interpret these figures because of the many changes which the French banking system has undergone in the past fifteen years. The value of securities floated on the French market is an indication of some of the factors which influenced the fluctuations of bank clearings.[1] Then again, the yield of the business turnover tax, which

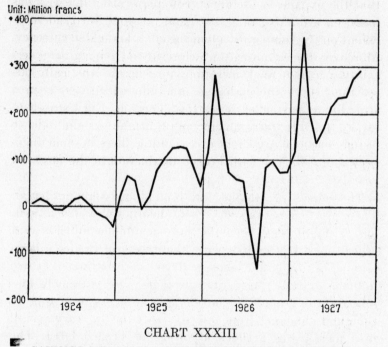

CHART XXXIII

SAVINGS DEPOSITS IN EXCESS OF WITHDRAWALS[2]

showed the activity of economic affairs, pointed to a fairly prosperous condition in 1927.[3]

The changes in export trade are surprising in view of the fears of a marked decline after stabilization. The figures show, on the contrary, a fairly steady growth after the first unfavorable reaction at the end of 1926. This decline,

[1] See *infra,* appendix.   [2] See *supra,* Chapter IX.
[3] See appendix for figures.

moreover, was due mainly to the deflation of franc values
and not to any notable decrease in tonnage. The net result
of the trade situation was that for the first time in many
years the balance of trade was favorable to France in 1926,
and this favorable excess was slightly greater in 1927.[1] This
fact, which was contrary to some forecasts, goes to prove
that the expansion of French commerce after the war was
based on a number of factors, and not to any considerable
extent on the temporary advantage of a low-value currency.
Moreover, the advantages which resulted from a greater certainty in commercial operations in general, practically offset the loss of the exchange premium which had been a
stimulus to particular industries. There is every reason to
expect that French commerce will continue to be in balance
or may even show a slight excess unless there is some unexpected interference with French production in the next few
years.

The effects of stability on production were not great.
There are four reasons why the difficulties were not as serious as might have been the case in other countries or at
other times. In the first place, there were in France a large
number of immigrant laborers. These were estimated at two
millions in 1925. Since these workers were extremely mobile, returning home in considerable numbers from time to
time and changing from industry to industry, they served
in a measure as a shock absorber for French labor. The
government took steps to check the numbers coming in so
that they would not compete with French workers. Then, in
the second place, industries had been accumulating entirely
unprecedented sums as profits and undivided surplus during
the years of speculative changes. These funds made it possible for them to go on producing during the times when
profits were scarce, and steadied the economic situation.
Thirdly, the workers who had been earning high wages during the war and postwar years had raised their standard of

[1] See *supra,* Chapter I.

living in many respects. This meant that they had bought articles of better quality and found themselves better clothed and better supplied, so that they could stand a temporary slack time with less acute suffering. This fact has been noted also in connection with American labor during the years of depression after the armistice. A fourth fact, which has already been discussed in the description of French life in general, is that many workers cultivated gardens, even owned their own houses and farms in some cases, and so were less subject to the ill effects of industrial fluctuations. Careful observers who were in France during these years of depression noted certain signs of poverty and want, but felt convinced that recovery would soon come to a nation so well adapted to bear these shocks of financial changes. The general improvement of the situation is indicated by the marked increase of savings in 1927.[1]

The Stabilization of 1928

The final act of stabilization of June 25, 1928, merely perpetuated the existing state of affairs, and increased confidence and economic activity.[2] Thus the franc which had been worth about 20 cents before the war came to have a fairly steady value of 3.93 cents after the war. This change of ratio, which seems so marked when the comparison is made directly between the two periods, really brought no change at the time when it was recognized by law.[3] The adjustment had been so complete during the fifteen years that the new government measures simply confirmed what had been already widely accepted. In fact, after stabilization as before, the gold value of prices, the most definite phase of value which can be measured, had not changed since 1914 more than in the United States and in other countries.

[1] See *infra*, appendix.

[2] R. Poincaré, *Exposé des motifs du projet de loi monétaire, Journal officiel, lois et décrets*, June 24, 1928, p. 7068.

[3] F. Maroni, "Après la réforme monétaire," *La Situation économique et financière* (June 29, 1928), p. 401.

Stabilization at the existing rate of exchange was therefore welcomed in all quarters as the proper and desirable solution of the monetary problem.[1] Those who still hoped to secure compensation for the decline in government securities and other values, were far outnumbered by those who wished to gain regularity and predictability in exchange transactions. There was, indeed, little to concern the average business man, except the fact that he need not worry any longer about sudden changes of export and import prices nor make abnormal efforts to build up bank balances abroad.

To the student of monetary theory, on the other hand, there are four main points of interest in the provisions for stabilization. In the first place, it is significant that by the act of stabilization France passed almost imperceptibly to a full gold standard in place of the limping standard which had existed before the war. Then, in the second place, the new law did away with the former system of fixing the upper limit of the note circulation at a definite figure, and substituted the minimum ratio of gold to sight liabilities as the determinant. In the third place, in contrast to the procedure in other countries, France secured no large foreign loans to facilitate stabilization. And, finally, as has been said above, the legal act of stabilization brought no adverse economic reaction, but rather hastened the recovery of industry which was, already, fairly general.

It would be a mistake to exaggerate the first point. Although it was the first time in the history of France when there had been a full gold standard,[2] the part played by silver before the war had been a minor one, and the place of gold coinage in the future will probably be less in all countries than it was formerly. Nevertheless, this step is in the direction of simpler more flexible monetary procedure

[1] J. M. Keynes, "The Stabilization of the Franc," *The New Republic* (July 18, 1928), p. 218.

[2] R. Poincaré, *Exposé des motifs, loc. cit.*, p. 7069.

and also makes it possible to keep Paris more closely linked
with London and New York because of greater similarity in
banking method. The flow of gold to France in the early
months of 1928 led to fears that further purchases might
bring a general scramble for the world's gold supply.[1] The
purchases of metal had been occasioned more by efforts of
the Bank of France to keep the franc steady in face of speculation for a rise, than by the desire to increase reserves.
There was, in fact, no need to increase holdings once the
rate of exchange for the franc had been fixed and speculators had become less anxious to buy francs. There was no
immediate likelihood of circulating gold, though the law
included the provision that the Bank should assure con-
vertibility and that it should replace the metal and paper
currency, to and including the 20 franc note, by other money
before the end of 1932.[2] The date of the manufacture of
gold coin was to be fixed by decree. Fifteen years of the use
of paper money had pretty well accustomed the French to
do without gold, and there was no indication of any great
impatience to put it in circulation again. The large reserves
held by the Bank of France, over a billion dollars worth [3]
was well above the 35 per cent gold cover required by the
new law. The position of the Bank was extremely strong,[4]
but a certain delay in putting gold in circulation was wise in
view of the economy which results from a sparing use of
the metal, and the danger which might arise if there were
any sudden increase in the demand for gold coin. Thus, gold
became more important as it was the sole value behind the

[1] R. Poincaré, "Discours devant la Chambre," *Le Temps* (June 23, 1928), p. 3.

[2] *Journal officiel, lois et décrets*, June 25, 1928, pp. 7085, 7086.

[3] *Le Pour et le contre* (July 22, 1928), p. 699. The Bank statement for July 19 gave 29,403 million francs in addition to gold credits abroad.

[4] Frédéric Jenny, *Le Temps*, Economique et financière (July 2, 1928). "La situation de l'institut d'émission est, de ce fait, des plus brilliantes." J. M. Keynes, *The New Republic* (July 18, 1925), p. 218. "The Bank of France emerges much stronger than the Bank of England."

money, and less important in that it was not demanded for
hand to hand circulation in the same way as before the war.

The change in the manner of fixing the maximum for the
note circulation, was probably a step in advance. Before
1914, the number of notes was limited by law, with frequent
increases as the limit tended to be reached. The system
worked pretty well, but was subject to the criticism that it
threw the matter into Parliament, and made it possible for
sudden stringencies to disturb business if there seemed to
be threat of delay in raising the limit. The new principle
was to limit the notes by keeping a certain minimum ratio
between the sight liabilities—notes and deposits—and gold.
This principle, similar to that governing the Federal Reserve notes, has been adopted in several countries since the
war, and seems to be gaining ground over the more rigid
systems. It throws more responsibility on the Bank management and less on the law maker. It was an advance
toward greater elasticity and simplicity in banking procedure.

From a political point of view the absence of foreign
loans, the third notable aspect of the stabilization program,
is particularly interesting, because it recalls the difficulties
over the debt to the United States. Ever since the failure of
the Caillaux mission in 1925, and the delay in regard to the
Bérenger debt agreement, there had been much controversy
as to how the franc could be stabilized without the ratifica-
tion of the debt accord. It would have been unwise to
request stabilization loans, if there were likelihood of
Washington opposing the participation of Wall Street in
such loans. The Experts' Report had favored action on the
debt accord and the recourse to loans in New York and
London. When such loans proved unnecessary, the whole
troublesome question was avoided.[1] It is true that Ger-

[1] It should be noted in this connection that France was making payments to the United States, although she had not bound herself to make
such payments.

many, also, had kept the rentenmark stable for several months without foreign help, but the subsequent arrangement for a large loan under the Dawes Plan consolidated the situation. England, Belgium and Italy all had outside support even though they did not need to draw extensively on credits granted. The French position was strengthened by the large amounts of credit which had been accumulated by private individuals abroad,—thus, those who had at one time been called traitors because they had accelerated the "flight from the franc," offered the means of support for stabilization, since their foreign credits constituted a potential demand for francs.[1] Meanwhile government resources were augmented by the flotation of consolidation loans.[2] In addition to the greater political freedom this gave France, it gratified the national pride and helped to lessen the disappointment of those who had hoped for an increase in the value of the franc. During the most severe crises, some had talked in a vague way of a "Dawes Plan for France" and the popular reply had been that France would save herself; certainly, in the final act of stabilization, she was highly successful.

The general economic situation, the fourth subject of comment, needs no detailed discussion here. The state of foreign commerce, production, the budget, and the Bank was most favorable at the time the measure was passed and there was no notable interruption after June 25. There were of course adjustments which had to be made, but there was no general crisis, no widespread difficulty which could be attributed to stabilization.

---

[1] *Journal officiel, débats, Sénat,* 2 séance, June 24, 1928, p. 1002. M. Chéron here comments on the various recommendations of the Experts' Committee and how, in general, they were fulfilled. In place of the foreign long time credits advised, short time credits were readily available.

[2] R. Poincaré, *Le Temps* (June 23, 1928), p. 5. The 1927 six per cent loan yielded 18,224 million francs and the 1928 five per cent yielded 20,850 millions.

It is unfortunate that stabilization of the franc had to wait so long. If it could have been done sooner, a higher exchange value could have been chosen and this would have lessened the hardship which fell on the *rente* holders. If the situation had been in hand earlier, much ill-feeling and several distressing panics could have been avoided. The good and ill effects of a *laissez faire* policy are here seen. In the course of the struggle the strong came out fairly well, but the weak suffered many hardships. Then, as is frequent in the case of trial and error procedure, the final step to bring financial life to order was sure and reasonable. Real tendencies had indicated themselves so clearly that the law could take them into proper account. There are many to condemn the French government for its dilatory policy, and few to justify the delay and uncertainties which occurred.

Stabilization took money out of politics and ended one of the most interesting cases of depreciation that has ever taken place. Those who are familiar with the history of money realize that there have been successive steps downward in the relation of most currencies to gold. Wars, changes in banking methods, the adjustment of the physical size of the unit and other causes have been responsible. Those who are less familiar with the problem of money value, are surprised that a unit can lose four-fifths of its value and still be an effective medium of exchange. It is possible, of course, that the size of the unit, the absolute purchasing power in gold or goods, affects in some way the habits of consumption, investment and exchange of a nation. However this may be, the ratio of money to gold, and even the ratio to goods, is relatively unimportant if this ratio is steady. It is only harmful to have a different relationship, while the change is taking place, and if it occurs rapidly. Thus, France is as well off with a franc worth four cents as she was when it was worth twenty cents, once stability and regularity have been reëstablished.

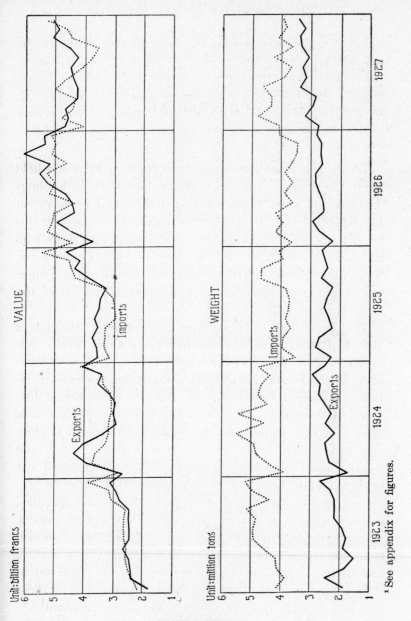

VALUE

Unit: billion francs

WEIGHT

Unit: million tons

Exports

Imports

Imports

Exports

1923   1924   1925   1926   1927

[1] See appendix for figures.

CHART XXXIV

FRENCH COMMERCE, 1923 TO 1927[1]

443

CHAPTER XI

Conclusions

THOSE who bought francs at two cents in 1926 and held them for a short time saw the value of their holdings doubled and their hopes of French financial recovery an accomplished fact. It is true that there were many reasons for not buying francs, reasons which frightened those who had seen the collapse of the mark and other currencies. Nevertheless, the underlying economic condition of France was sound and there was steady improvement after the sharp crisis of 1926.

The franc had declined almost constantly through a period of twelve years. There had been sharp breaks, followed by short periods of recovery, with a net loss of four-fifths of the prewar gold value of the franc. Such depreciation was bound to bring great changes in economic life. Some of these were unfavorable but some were favorable since they were in line with beneficial tendencies in production and consumption. This was true in France more than in other countries because prior to the war France had just begun to adapt herself in a slight degree to large-scale production and to the general attitude of mind which prevailed in most western European countries. Thus, readjustments, which were unavoidable after severe depreciation, tended to hasten the adaptation of French economic life to modern conditions. It was natural, therefore, that the final act of stabilization in June, 1928, increased the optimism of those who had seen the rapid recovery of the preceding months.[1]

[1] *The Manchester Guardian,* "The Franc" (June 25, 1928), p. 8. "France has no unemployment, her industry has been modernized and is competing more effectively than ever before with that of other countries . . ."

444

Conclusions as to the effects of depreciation and predictions as to the economic future fall naturally under two headings, first, those which are concerned immediately with practical affairs and, second, those which deal mainly with theory. A proper appreciation of the practical aspects of the French situation must be based more on a familiarity with actual conditions than on a study of documents and academic opinions. A correct analysis of the bearing of recent events on economic theory, on the other hand, calls for a wide historical knowledge which few possess. It is possible, however, to note briefly a few of the outstanding characteristics of French life, and point to the shift of emphasis in economic principles without claiming a full knowledge of either fact or theory.

In 1928, France possessed about the same material wealth as she did before the war. The losses caused by the hostilities were approximately offset by the gain in territories, rich in mineral and industrial resources. An accurate statement of the war balance sheet of France is, of course, impossible until the reparation question has been finally settled.

The more indirect effects of the war through depreciation, taxation, debt increases, and the redistribution of wealth in general, cannot be disposed of in such summary fashion. The loss in financial prestige, for instance, which has been mentioned above, was considerable, but France was never one of the important international money markets. The loss in her investments abroad had been great but there are indications that a considerable portion of these have been replaced out of postwar profits invested in other countries. The less obvious, and, at the same time, more serious harm, wrought by violent shifts in the distribution of wealth through the depreciation of government securities and the unequal incidence of taxation, cannot be measured and appraised. It must be taken into account even though it is recognized as intangible. In fact, it is probable, that such injuries were the more serious in that they were so hard to anticipate and measure. Despite severe losses, however, it is evident that France recovered with surprising rapidity. She emerged from the trying months of preliminary stabilization into a period of sound prosperity.[1]

A study of the particular financial measures adopted and of their after effects, leads to the conclusion that this recovery is to be attributed more to the general intelligence and energy of the nation than to carefully wrought plans and consistent financial policies. It is true that during the war there was little room for choice of method, particularly during the early months. Loans, inflation, and foreign aid were, to a considerable degree, inevitable. Taxation was difficult and any considerable restriction of expenditures was practically impossible. Thus, to a certain extent, budget deficits as well as the increase in the internal debt must be considered unavoidable.

The history of war finance, reconstruction, and reparation is full of strange contrasts. There was much extravagance and mismanagement in the rebuilding of the destroyed villages, but, on the other hand, the return to normal life in the invaded regions was remarkable. Those who saw the extent of the damage did not believe that villages could rise so quickly from the ruins, then again, the confusion and conflict in regard to reparation is hard to understand in retrospect. There is little doubt that France stood in the way of her own best interests in refusing for several years to look at the problem with a reasonable consideration of the basic importance of German recovery.[2] The emotions and disappointments which are the aftermath of war are a partial explanation of the frequent misunderstandings.

The technical measures which were used to support the franc, at times when financial difficulties threatened its

[1] *The Economist* (London, June 23, 1928), p. 1286. "France now that the worst of her post-war troubles are over, will henceforward play a much larger rôle as a producing and exporting country than she did before the war."

[2] Charles Rist, *Les Finances de guerre d'Allemagne* (Paris, 1921).

destruction, were frequently inadequate and ill advised. This was true in part because French traditions and institutions were not fitted for the ready control of runaway money. It is notable that centralized control of banking was almost entirely lacking, that the discount rate had never become an effective instrument of credit control, that currency was used in transactions where credit would have been used in other countries, and that there had been too much dependence on internal government loans. These facts made it more difficult to use the discount rate as a weapon against depreciation. Moreover, attempts at deflation, because they were ill-timed and too little coördinated with the government policy as to loans, led to future difficulties and, therefore, to further depreciation of the franc. Thus the attempt to control values through the medium of banks was fruitless and often led to severe crises which shook the French financial structure. In other countries and at other times, the situation might have worked out differently. Actually, in France, the plans of finance ministers usually availed little and did not lead to heroic effort and vigorous measures in taxation until the threat of catastrophe brought painful realization of the need for government revenues.

Political difficulties were in most cases at the bottom of these economic disturbances and they did not cease with stabilization. The traditional division into many parties and the uncertainty of political majorities, made the formulation of financial programs an extremely delicate matter. It became evident, eventually, that recovery was dependent on a temporary fusion of interests such as would make possible a strong and continuous policy.

The surprising thing about the history of depreciation in France is that through almost all the financial storms, production continued with little interruption. Both internal commerce and foreign trade developed in a slow but fairly steady fashion. Except for the depression of 1921, and that of 1927, there was practically no recession either in economic activity or in the further development of material resources. Thus, the financial crises were not the result of general economic difficulties, but rather, of the problems of distribution of wealth particularly as they are connected with taxation and the internal debt.

The slow adaptation of taxation to the urgent needs of the government is the natural sequel to a long series of events which had disturbed French life for more than a hundred years. The struggle between classes, the frequent changes in political systems, and the general distrust which resulted from revolutions and wars, made it difficult to handle public finance in the best technical manner. The extreme emergency of the war hastened the evolution of the fiscal system at some points, while it retarded it at others. The shift from indirect to direct taxation was halted by the dependence of the government on indirect taxes which tended to adjust themselves automatically to price changes, although, on the other hand, the need for more funds led to heavy levies on inherited wealth and high incomes. This latter tendency, in so far as it was evident, was merely a continuation of the prewar development and was in line with a general simplification of the whole financial procedure.

Another significant change in France, as in a number of other countries was the higher standard of living of the lower income classes, a change which frequently comes with rapidly fluctuating prices. Although this has been deplored by some, as causing extravagance and impairing the habits of thrift and economy, it is probable that it will lead to an enlargement and enrichment of French life. Along with this, there are indications of greater flexibility in industrial methods and a broader viewpoint on the part of the small producer and merchant. Though some of these changes are most evident in their materialistic aspects in the first instance, they lead almost inevitably to broader sympathies and interests with the passage of time. Consequently, in spite of the real havoc wrought by depreciation, a consideration of the general tendencies of French economic life over a period of fifteen years must end on a cheerful note. There are signs of vigor and a healthy adaptation to present-day conditions.

When one turns from the actual state of affairs in France to points of theory raised in explanation of the depreciation of the franc, certain modifications and qualifications of some of the existing doctrines seem called for. It is true that the fifteen years under consideration were exceptional in many respects. It is even more true, that one cannot carry over conclusions based on "short-run" relationships to "long-run" situations. Nevertheless, it is necessary to take account of such striking exceptions before formulating economic "laws." This is particularly true in the use of the quantity theory, the purchasing power parity doctrine, and theories regarding speculation. In France experience shows that the main effort to protect the franc had to be devoted, not to controlling the quantity of money directly, but to straightening out the budget tangle, and this required certain very important political adjustments. Moreover, attempts made in France to steady values through the direct control of money and credit failed miserably. Then again, the exchange value of the franc did not influence very directly the flow of commodity trade, nor did commerce react on the internal value situation very quickly. Thus, it is necessary to qualify and limit the meaning of the quantity theory as an explanation and as a guide to practical action. There was no clear line of causality in France, running from the volume of purchasing power to price levels and, thence, to the flow of foreign trade and the shifting of credit balances between countries. Changes, when they were in harmony with each other were in some cases simultaneous, while in some instances they acted in ways quite contrary to certain abstract theories.

On the other hand, the ready response of the various economic factors to political and financial events in France, seems to offer clear evidence of the power of speculation, using the term in the broadest sense. Of course it is possible for those who prefer to put the main stress on purchasing power to say that speculation was merely anticipating the future increases in purchasing power which would result from a political upset or national bankruptcy. Such an interpretation, however, does violence to the point of view actually existing in France and misrepresents the more powerful forces at work. For instance, a wave of distrust sweeping through financial centers sometimes made it possible for a slightly unfavorable turn of financial life to be the occasion for a very unfavorable budget situation and, thus, an increase in the means of payment through government borrowings. At another time, a much more serious gap between government expenditures and receipts, even one great enough to cause a large increase in borrowing, would not lead to a corresponding change in prices, and might even be offset in a short time by deflation, because it had not led to adverse speculation. The crux of the matter does not lie in whether or not the changes in purchasing power affected the price level, for few will deny that in one form or another, an increasing means of payment and a rising price level go together. But the crux lies in whether or not favorable speculation can make a difference in delaying or definitely preventing price and exchange increase, and whether or not a loss of confidence can lead to a marked rise in values accompanied by or followed by an increase in money. Conclusions as to this matter based on a study of the franc, are that speculation is an important force, guided by a multitude of factors, and not mainly by the quantity of money, that speculation for short periods can hold a weak currency above the value justified by economic conditions, that speculation can depress values so that the readjustment of all other economic factors will be downward and the net loss due to the temporary attack on a currency may never be completely regained.

"Speculation" is a word used in many ways and suggesting many different agents and influences. It is here taken to mean the tide of opinion and the general state of public confidence which can influence values, as well as some of the more technical implications of the word. Its influence is traced through two main channels. In the first place, it is effective through the shifting of balances in and out of France, or what is known as the "flight from the franc." This tendency is hard to measure because of the difficulty of discovering the ownership of bank balances, and because many credits and deposits can never be traced to their source. Nevertheless, the general forces at work are well known and the importance of these capital movements in all cases of severe depreciation are so generally recognized as to need no proof. Then, in the second place, speculation acts within a country through the shrinkage or expansion of the value of government securities as well as affecting people's desire to hold money. In the case of France, changes in the value of government securities were particularly important, because the treasury depended to a considerable extent on *bons de la défense nationale*. For this reason, any sudden wave of pessimism led to a withdrawal of funds from the treasury, and very directly to the issue of new notes by the Bank of France, notes which might not have been needed if the public had been less susceptible to the rumors and vicissitudes which were characteristic of the postwar years.

There is no real conflict between this interpretation of the French case and the most commonly accepted theories of the relation between money and prices. There is, however, a difference in emphasis which would lead one to work in a practical situation, not directly through money and credit, but indirectly through whatever factor was disturbing the institutions which issued money and credit. That is, in

France it was more important to secure political unity than
it was to pay back the advances of the Bank of France to the
State. It was more important to put the treasury accounts
in order by cutting down expenses and collecting the taxes
which had been voted than it was to increase the discount rate. Indeed, decreasing the note circulation may have
caused later depreciation, and the increase in the discount
rate accentuated unfavorable speculation. Thus, paradoxically, the deflation voted in 1920 caused the inflation in
1925.

It is perfectly possible to harmonize events in France with
the broader formulations of the quantity theory. In fact,
it is not possible to question seriously the formulas which
take account of the influence of money together with the
rapidity of its circulation, or those which state that incomes
spent are the important forces behind value changes. It
must be remembered, however, that in handling emergencies
such as the panics of 1924 and 1926 those in authority in
France could not focus on the long run adjustments, but had
to seek out those things which would stay the tide rushing
so destructively against the franc. They had to fight for
the breathing space which would make it possible for the
usual relationships to be reëstablished. Only when a normal
state of mind had been attained, could the instruments of
economic control work in the expected manner, only when
the fever had subsided could those who were speculating
see clearly the nature of long-run values and act for their
own best interests.

France achieved this breathing space. Moreover, she
avoided the extremes of collapse and destructive deflation.
Productive life has been fairly normal despite the distressing
crises in finance. It is astonishing to find the power of recovery so great, and there is reason to hope that the constructive forces now evident in some parts of French industrial life have created a sound basis for enduring financial
stability.

APPENDIX

THE DOLLAR EXCHANGE RATES ON THE PARIS BOURSE[1]

Daily 1919

	January[2]		February		March	
	Low	High	Low	High	Low	High
1	5.425	5.475	5.425	5.475	5.425	5.475
2	5.425	5.475	....	....	....	....
3	5.425	5.475	5.425	5.475	5.425	5.475
4	5.425	5.475	5.425	5.475	5.425	5.475
5	....	....	5.425	5.475	5.425	5.475
6	5.425	5.475	5.425	5.475	5.425	5.475
7	5.425	5.475	5.425	5.475	5.425	5.475
8	5.425	5.475	5.425	5.475	5.425	5.475
9	5.425	5.475	....	....	....	....
10	5.425	5.475	5.425	5.475	5.425	5.475
11	5.425	5.475	5.425	5.475	5.425	5.475
12	....	....	5.425	5.475	5.425	5.475
13	5.425	5.475	5.425	5.475	5.425	5.475
14	5.425	5.475	5.425	5.475	5.500	5.550
15	5.425	5.475	5.425	5.475	5.650	5.750
16	5.425	5.475	....	....	....	....
17	5.425	5.475	5.425	5.475	5.700	5.880
18	5.425	5.475	5.425	5.475	5.680	5.760
19	....	....	5.425	5.475	no $ quotation	
20	5.425	5.475	5.425	5.475	5.740	5.790
21	5.425	5.475	5.425	5.475	5.725	5.775
22	5.425	5.475	5.425	5.475	5.770	5.820
23	5.425	5.475	....	....	....	....
24	5.425	5.475	5.425	5.475	5.790	5.840
25	5.425	5.475	5.425	5.475	5.795	5.845
26	....	....	5.425	5.475	5.875	5.925
27	5.425	5.475	5.425	5.475	5.920	5.970
28	5.425	5.475	5.425	5.475	5.950	6.020
29	5.425	5.475	....	....	6.055	6.105
30	5.425	5.475	....	....	....	....
31	5.425	5.475	....	....	6.045	6.095

[1] *La Cote officielle,* Journal official, Paris, daily issues. For January 1, 1919, to September 10, 1919, and from January 28, 1924, a series of figures for quotations on the Bourse printed in this official source, the high and low are given here. For the other days averages are given in *La Cote officielle.*

[2] Quotations were the same from January 1 till March 13.

THE DOLLAR EXCHANGE RATES ON THE PARIS BOURSE

Daily 1919

	April		May		June	
	Low	High	Low	High	Low	High
1	6.050	6.100	....	....	....	....
2	6.000	6.050	6.035	6.085	6.225	6.275
3	5.930	5.980	6.045	6.095	6.365	6.415
4	5.825	5.875	....	....	6.435	6.485
5	5.895	5.945	6.115	6.165	6.440	6.490
6	....	....	6.135	6.185	6.445	6.495
7	5.855	5.905	6.115	6.165	....	....
8	5.860	5.910	6.095	6.145	....	....
9	5.955	6.005	6.140	6.190	....	....
10	5.980	6.050	6.140	6.190	6.415	6.465
11	5.990	6.040	....	....	6.400	6.450
12	6.010	6.060	6.155	6.205	6.385	6.435
13	....	....	6.220	6.270	6.305	6.355
14	5.925	5.975	6.265	6.315	....	....
15	5.960	6.010	6.285	6.335	....	....
16	5.975	6.025	6.365	6.415	6.305	6.355
17	5.975	6.025	6.425	6.475	6.465	6.515
18	....	....	....	....	6.480	6.530
19	....	....	6.475	6.525	6.435	6.485
20	....	....	6.525	6.575	6.400	6.450
21	....	....	6.620	6.670	....	....
22	5.995	6.045	6.570	6.690	....	....
23	6.005	6.055	6.525	6.575	6.350	6.400
24	6.045	6.095	6.465	6.515	6.395	6.445
25	6.085	6.135	....	....	6.460	6.510
26	6.055	6.105	6.555	6.605	6.455	6.505
27	....	....	6.530	6.580	6.450	6.500
28	6.055	6.105	6.350	6.470	....	....
29	6.020	6.070	....	....	....	....
30	6.030	6.080	6.275	6.325	6.435	6.485
31	....	....	6.320	6.370	....	....

THE DOLLAR EXCHANGE RATES ON THE PARIS BOURSE

Daily 1919

	July Low	July High	August Low	August High	September* Low	September* High
1	6.445	6.495	7.255	7.305	8.095	8.145
2	6.455	6.505	....	....	8.145	8.195
3	6.550	6.610	....	....	8.145	8.195
4	6.665	6.715	7.335	7.385	8.195	8.245
5	....	....	7.420	7.470	8.255	8.305
6	....	....	7.570	7.760	....	....
7	6.785	6.835	7.640	7.950	....	....
8	6.900	6.950	7.695	7.745	8.300	8.350
9	6.815	6.865	....	....	8.340	8.390
10	6.845	6.895	....	....	8.370	
11	6.820	6.870	7.625	7.675	8.405	
12	....	....	7.625	7.675	8.565	
13	....	....	7.735	7.785	....	
14	....	....	7.770	7.820	....	
15	6.880	6.930	....	....	8.930	
16	6.990	7.040	....	....	9.135	
17	7.170	7.220	....	....	9.150	
18	7.050	7.100	7.870	7.920	8.740	
19	....	....	7.985	8.035	8.850	
20	....	....	8.140	8.210	....	
21	no $ quotation		8.175	8.225	....	
22	7.080	7.130	8.145	8.195	8.850	
23	7.085	7.135	....	....	8.700	
24	7.095	7.145	....	....	8.610	
25	7.115	7.165	8.080	8.130	8.350	
26	....	....	8.070	8.120	8.100	
27	....	....	8.035	8.085	....	
28	7.160	7.210	7.895	7.945	....	
29	7.245	7.295	8.050	8.100	7.600	
30	7.235	7.285	....	....	8.485	
31	7.230	7.280	....	....	....	

* The manner of quoting the rates changed in September.

THE DOLLAR EXCHANGE RATES ON THE PARIS BOURSE

Daily   1919

(Average)

	October	November	December
1	8.505	....	9.865
2	8.445	....	9.985
3	8.445	8.855	10.300
4	8.415	9.040	10.330
5	....	9.045	10.500
6	8.370	8.955	10.780
7	8.350	8.960	.....
8	8.420	9.015	11.240
9	8.480	....	11.885
10	8.495	9.160	11.825
11	8.540	9.320	11.595
12	....	9.540	11.350
13	8.600	9.340	11.425
14	8.725	9.620	.....
15	8.775	9.420	11.135
16	8.730	....	10.030
17	8.665	9.475	10.320
18	8.625	9.610	11.275
19	....	9.675	11.180
20	8.665	9.710	10.860
21	8.695	9.685	.....
22	8.670	9.615	10.690
23	8.675	....	10.355
24	8.670	9.600	10.500
25	8.660	9.600	.....
26	....	9.685	10.525
27	8.615	9.735	10.545
28	8.675	9.715	.....
29	8.810	9.755	10.745
30	8.835	....	10.745
31	8.840	....	10.995

THE DOLLAR EXCHANGE RATES ON THE PARIS BOURSE

Daily 1920

(Average)

	Jan	Feb	Mar	Apr	May	June
1	.....	.....	14.255	14.735	.....	12.965
2	10.810	13.530	14.085	.....	.....	12.730
3	10.755	14.390	14.205	.....	16.650	12.980
4	.....	14.740	14.170	.....	16.295	13.010
5	10.755	15.000	13.935	.....	16.450	.....
6	10.750	14.500	.....	14.750	16.445	.....
7	10.980	14.960	.....	15.340	16.000	12.980
8	11.165	.....	14.030	15.260	.....	12.995
9	11.170	14.485	13.820	15.810	.....	12.960
10	11.140	14.415	13.440	.....	15.755	13.060
11	.....	14.470	13.030	.....	15.210	13.215
12	11.150	14.215	13.415	16.970	14.940	.....
13	11.200	14.335	.....	17.050	.....	.....
14	11.245	14.110	.....	16.025	15.265	13.225
15	11.440	.....	13.610	16.790	15.255	13.090
16	11.565	14.215	13.585	16.460	.....	12.825
17	11.570	14.400	13.450	.....	14.580	12.650
18	.....	14.315	13.625	.....	13.740	12.505
19	11.540	13.845	13.680	16.220	13.440	.....
20	11.705	13.140	.....	15.990	14.270	.....
21	11.915	.....	.....	16.420	13.900	12.530
22	12.145	.....	14.275	16.610	.....	12.115
23	11.910	14.300	14.930	16.635	.....	11.630
24	12.075	14.245	14.550	.....	.....	11.970
25	.....	14.095	14.330	.....	13.270	12.030
26	12.520	14.320	14.400	16.955	12.465	.....
27	12.890	14.295	.....	17.080	13.130	.....
28	13.405	.....	.....	16.775	13.750	.....
29	13.190	.....	14.480	16.390	.....	12.105
30	13.175	.....	14.905	16.665	.....	12.165
31	13.220	.....	14.970	.....	12.800	12.150
				.....		.....

THE DOLLAR EXCHANGE RATES ON THE PARIS BOURSE

Daily 1920

(Average)

	July	Aug	Sep	Oct	Nov	Dec
1	12.100	.....	14.345	14.950	.....	16.510
2	11.940	13.035	14.390	14.845	.....	16.450
3	.....	13.325	14.475	.....	15.965	16.565
4	.....	14.040	.....	15.015	16.205	16.655
5	11.600	13.940	.....	14.940	16.630	.....
6	11.645	13.930	14.450	14.955	16.555	16.795
7	11.745	.....	14.620	14.965	.....	17.065
8	12.150	.....	14.825	14.980	17.190	16.775
9	11.790	14.060	14.745	14.985	17.290	17.040
10	.....	13.960	14.855	.....	17.190	17.070
11	.....	13.760	.....	15.195	.....	17.070
12	11.840	13.695	.....	15.300	17.290	.....
13	11.925	13.820	15.130	15.190	17.170	17.170
14	.....	.....	15.610	15.215	.....	17.210
15	12.080	.....	15.450	15.325	17.400	17.070
16	11.865	.....	15.260	15.400	17.320	16.905
17	.....	13.710	15.090	.....	16.630	16.400
18	.....	13.815	.....	15.450	16.215	16.735
19	12.055	14.025	.....	15.555	16.795	.....
20	12.235	14.120	14.325	15.460	16.635	17.115
21	12.275	.....	14.705	15.420	.....	16.770
22	12.705	.....	14.955	15.465	16.240	16.905
23	13.140	14.155	14.575	15.490	16.095	16.835
24	.....	14.560	14.840	.....	16.400	16.950
25	.....	14.610	.....	15.495	16.715	.....
26	12.960	14.190	.....	15.615	16.515	.....
27	12.725	14.350	15.010	15.760	16.430	17.095
28	12.775	.....	14.915	15.715	.....	17.210
29	13.085	.....	14.915	15.655	16.600	17.135
30	13.075	14.520	15.080	15.755	16.495	16.865
31	13.105	14.510	.....	.....	.....	16.885

THE DOLLAR EXCHANGE RATES ON THE PARIS BOURSE

Daily   1921

(Average)

	Jan	Feb	Mar	Apr	May	June
1........	.....	14.530	13.875	14.280	.....	11.910
2........	.....	14.310	14.060	14.325	12.915	11.915
3........	17.075	14.225	13.995	.....	12.510	12.010
4........	17.180	14.220	13.835	14.325	12.635	.....
5........	17.020	14.240	13.930	14.285	.....	.....
6........	16.630	.....	.....	14.090	12.112	12.425
7........	16.845	14.250	13.820	13.975	.....	12.535
8........	16.795	14.205	13.950	14.105	.....	12.500
9........	.....	13.965	14.110	14.195	12.235	12.885
10........	16.825	13.890	14.010	.....	11.820	12.785
11........	16.340	13.785	14.030	14.025	11.995	.....
12........	16.280	13.785	14.110	14.035	11.910	.....
13........	16.520	.....	.....	14.125	11.645	12.700
14........	16.380	13.795	14.155	14.070	.....	12.540
15........	16.435	13.570	14.465	14.020	.....	12.430
16........	.....	13.360	14.215	14.035	.....	12.070
17........	16.210	13.560	14.425	.....	11.875	12.080
18........	15.895	13.640	14.360	13.950	11.685	.....
19........	15.845	14.045	14.425	13.745	11.315	.....
20........	15.250	.....	.....	13.700	11.365	12.145
21........	15.065	13.945	14.330	13.750	.....	12.295
22........	14.310	13.790	14.365	13.710	.....	12.520
23........	.....	13.780	14.355	13.705	11.800	12.425
24........	13.955	13.950	14.390	.....	12.000	12.510
25........	13.735	14.120	.....	13.600	11.475	.....
26........	14.120	13.950	.....	13.330	11.775	.....
27........	13.925	.....	.....	13.265	11.890	12.365
28........	14.265	14.040	.....	13.210	.....	12.365
29........	14.245	.....	14.410	13.010	.....	12.380
30........	.....	.....	14.260	12.900	12.245	12.490
31........	13.925	.....	14.240	.....	12.155	.....

THE DOLLAR EXCHANGE RATES ON THE PARIS BOURSE

Daily 1921

(Average)

	July	Aug	Sep	Oct	Nov	Dec
1	12.495	13.040	12.730	.....	.....	13.970
2	12.495	13.160	12.740	.....	13.595	13.670
3	12.455	13.150	12.870	14.130	13.600	13.710
4	12.450	13.035	.....	14.085	13.540	.....
5	.....	12.925	13.015	13.975	13.535	13.605
6	12.565	12.935	13.160	13.755	.....	13.350
7	12.590	.....	13.105	13.825	13.645	13.200
8	12.565	12.750	13.020	.....	13.765	13.185
9	12.565	12.805	13.275	.....	13.750	12.820
10	.....	12.710	13.430	13.660	13.740	12.940
11	12.865	12.770	.....	13.650	13.835	.....
12	12.865	12.815	13.865	13.765	13.865	12.395
13	12.675	.....	13.790	14.010	.....	12.400
14	.....	.....	14.065	13.755	13.880	12.460
15	.....	.....	14.330	.....	13.745	12.355
16	.....	12.880	14.360	.....	13.820	12.840
17	12.675	13.055	14.150	13.775	13.820	12.730
18	12.865	12.870	.....	13.900	13.840	.....
19	12.910	12.980	13.810	14.105	13.845	12.305
20	12.860	12.930	14.130	13.835	.....	12.360
21	12.935	.....	14.285	13.710	13.950	12.430
22	12.915	12.955	14.160	.....	14.200	12.580
23	12.915	13.005	14.060	.....	14.165	12.610
24	.....	12.980	14.020	13.850	14.255	12.575
25	12.940	12.875	.....	13.665	14.280	.....
26	12.925	12.960	13.815	13.635	14.520	.....
27	12.915	12.940	14.105	13.785	.....	12.385
28	12.980	.....	14.020	13.790	14.320	12.365
29	12.980	12.870	14.075	.....	14.465	12.485
30	13.160	12.820	13.990	.....	14.230	12.475
31	.....	12.775	.....	.....	.....	12.310

THE DOLLAR EXCHANGE RATES ON THE PARIS BOURSE

Daily 1922

(Average)

	Jan	Feb	Mar	Apr	May	June
1	.....	12.050	10.850	11.080	10.860	10.985
2	.....	11.925	10.935	.....	10.860	10.975
3	12.455	11.905	10.925	11.005	10.965	.....
4	12.435	11.910	11.040	10.935	10.945	.....
5	12.595	.....	.....	10.905	10.910	.....
6	12.440	11.870	11.025	10.980	.....	10.960
7	12.465	11.845	11.045	10.970	.....	10.960
8	.....	11.790	11.240	10.945	11.020	10.970
9	12.085	11.540	11.125	.....	10.980	11.050
10	12.015	11.560	11.165	10.880	10.910	.....
11	12.095	11.730	11.210	10.850	10.930	.....
12	12.060	.....	.....	10.850	10.955	11.195
13	12.230	11.710	11.320	10.785	.....	11.290
14	12.185	11.570	11.465	.....	.....	11.350
15	.....	11.550	11.235	.....	10.940	11.305
16	12.090	11.555	11.145	.....	10.940	11.380
17	12.155	11.485	11.160	.....	10.985	.....
18	12.240	11.300	11.045	10.735	10.975	.....
19	12.190	.....	.....	10.780	11.035	11.700
20	12.315	10.910	11.150	10.715	.....	11.630
21	12.370	10.935	11.155	10.755	.....	11.550
22	.....	10.985	11.025	10.725	11.125	11.630
23	12.505	10.915	11.065	.....	11.085	11.715
24	12.370	11.045	11.075	10.740	11.090	.....
25	12.245	11.230	11.045	10.720	.....	.....
26	12.275	.....	.....	10.840	10.960	12.060
27	12.245	10.895	11.110	10.845	.....	11.935
28	12.195	10.935	11.190	10.870	.....	11.905
29	.....	.....	11.100	10.920	10.950	12.040
30	12.160	.....	11.100	.....	10.945	11.995
31	11.970	.....	11.080	.....	10.955	.....

THE DOLLAR EXCHANGE RATES ON THE PARIS BOURSE

Daily 1922

	July	Aug	Sep	Oct	Nov	Dec
1	.....	12.195	12.895	.....	.....	14.230
2	.....	12.320	.....	13.175	14.335	14.200
3	11.980	12.265	.....	13.210	14.540	.....
4	12.060	12.185	12.845	13.190	14.575	14.310
5	12.195	.....	12.845	13.095	.....	14.340
6	12.260	.....	12.660	13.175	14.820	14.315
7	12.695	12.250	12.725	.....	15.590	14.165
8	.....	12.280	12.910	.....	16.060	14.085
9	.....	12.410	.....	13.195	15.565	14.170
10	12.800	12.535	.....	13.285	15.235	.....
11	12.370	12.370	13.095	13.245	.....	14.220
12	12.225	.....	13.055	13.240	.....	14.070
13	12.120	.....	13.145	13.190	14.735	14.060
14	.....	.....	13.300	.....	14.960	13.930
15	.....	.....	13.155	.....	14.950	13.700
16	.....	12.555	.....	13.310	14.655	13.260
17	12.115	12.655	.....	13.350	14.410	.....
18	11.935	12.465	13.270	13.415	14.225	13.120
19	11.820	.....	13.215	13.525	.....	13.560
20	11.940	.....	13.120	13.450	14.105	13.475
21	11.830	12.510	13.055	.....	13.510	13.500
22	.....	12.585	13.135	.....	14.120	13.455
23	.....	12.710	.....	13.835	13.970	13.500
24	11.780	12.875	.....	14.010	13.960	.....
25	11.835	13.105	13.000	14.075	14.000	.....
26	12.050	.....	13.140	14.605	.....	13.525
27	12.070	.....	13.165	14.435	14.195	13.755
28	12.075	12.960	13.220	.....	14.545	13.905
29	.....	12.970	13.225	.....	14.400	13.785
30	.....	13.000	.....	14.455	14.370	13.700
31	12.390	13.135	.....	14.260	.....	.....

THE DOLLAR EXCHANGE RATES ON THE PARIS BOURSE

Daily 1923

	Jan	Feb	Mar	Apr	May	June
1........	.....	16.845	16.410	.....	14.835	15.365
2........	13.550	16.345	16.510	.....	14.890	.....
3........	13.835	15.620	16.470	15.175	15.105	.....
4........	14.085	.....	.....	15.520	14.960	15.625
5........	14.435	15.960	16.355	15.235	.....	15.545
6........	14.215	15.620	16.425	15.110	.....	15.485
7........	.....	15.970	16.525	15.140	15.175	15.530
8........	14.675	16.215	16.535	.....	15.095	15.530
9........	14.720	16.065	16.580	14.840	15.185	.....
10........	14.550	16.110	16.560	14.950	.....	.....
11........	14.475	.....	.....	15.100	15.190	15.565
12........	14.245	16.190	16.470	15.005	.....	15.575
13........	14.270	16.245	16.555	14.930	.....	15.605
14........	.....	16.635	16.520	15.045	15.060	15.795
15........	14.455	16.415	16.275	.....	14.945	15.760
16........	14.740	16.585	15.775	15.040	15.000	.....
17........	14.935	16.775	15.990	15.120	15.040	.....
18........	15.295	.....	.....	15.345	15.000	16.060
19........	15.000	16.580	15.730	15.010	.....	16.090
20........	15.185	16.430	15.370	15.000	.....	16.055
21........	.....	16.230	14.920	15.065	.....	16.065
22........	15.670	16.450	14.950	.....	15.045	16.210
23........	15.340	16.440	15.250	14.965	15.005	.....
24........	15.515	16.550	15.425	14.925	15.055	.....
25........	15.515	.....	.....	14.750	15.130	16.175
26........	15.585	16.400	15.690	14.895	.....	16.320
27........	15.795	16.210	15.015	14.760	.....	16.370
28........	.....	16.390	15.115	14.730	15.080	16.315
29........	16.185	.....	15.095	.....	15.135	16.395
30........	16.425	.....	.....	14.775	15.160	.....
31........	16.890	.....	.....	.....	15.215	.....

THE DOLLAR EXCHANGE RATES ON THE PARIS BOURSE

Daily 1923

	July	Aug	Sep	Oct	Nov	Dec
1.........	.....	17.290	.....	16.370	.....	18.550
2.........	16.815	17.450	.....	16.770	17.245	.....
3.........	16.890	17.355	17.680	16.955	17.450	18.480
4.........	16.755	.....	17.730	17.165	.....	18.790
5.........	17.055	.....	17.930	16.815	17.295	18.580
6.........	17.255	17.250	18.040	.....	17.375	18.430
7.........	.....	17.430	18.080	.....	17.545	18.830
8.........	.....	17.485	.....	16.745	17.405	18.790
9.........	17.380	17.485	.....	16.535	17.720	.....
10.........	17.030	17.575	17.835	16.420	17.850	18.710
11.........	16.775	.....	17.365	16.440	.....	18.755
12.........	16.765	.....	17.235	16.415	18.100	18.750
13.........	17.060	18.015	17.420	.....	17.875	18.880
14.........	.....	18.255	17.170	.....	18.195	18.825
15.........	.....	.....	.....	16.310	18.475	18.885
16.........	17.065	18.235	.....	16.320	18.880	.....
17.........	17.220	18.105	17.225	16.655	18.985	18.930
18.........	17.070	.....	17.330	16.705	.....	19.080
19.........	16.925	.....	17.060	16.695	19.230	19.155
20.........	17.040	17.960	16.880	.....	18.590	19.450
21.........	.....	17.865	16.960	.....	18.520	19.450
22.........	.....	17.660	.....	17.160	18.335	19.800
23.........	16.795	17.830	.....	17.465	18.615	.....
24.........	16.745	17.840	16.215	17.205	18.535	.....
25.........	16.940	.....	15.920	17.280	.....	.....
26.........	16.845	.....	16.190	17.120	18.165	19.965
27.........	16.870	17.565	16.285	.....	18.435	19.620
28.........	.....	17.530	16.295	.....	18.630	19.160
29.........	.....	17.600	.....	17.170	18.655	19.610
30.........	17.035	17.775	.....	16.945	18.650	.....
31.........	17.130	17.765	.....	16.965	.....	.....

THE DOLLAR EXCHANGE RATES ON THE PARIS BOURSE

Daily 1924

	January* High	January* Low	February High	February Low	March High	March Low
1........	.....		21.360	21.210	.....	.....
2........	19.920		21.220	21.185	.....	.....
3........	20.535		.....	.....	24.070	23.900
4........	20.570		21.520	21.420	24.800	24.700
5........	20.580		21.620	21.505	24.720	24.550
6........	.....		21.550	21.470	24.760	24.635
7........	19.880		21.485	21.450	26.260	25.820
8........	20.555		21.815	21.785	.....	.....
9........	20.415		22.225	22.150	.....	.....
10........	20.445		.....	.....	27.050	26.870
11........	20.850		22.020	21.930	27.200	26.950
12........	21.195		22.170	22.130	24.900	24.700
13........	.....		22.260	22.070	23.100	22.740
14........	22.800		22.670	22.540	21.650	21.450
15........	22.345		22.550	22.460	.....	.....
16........	21.340		22.820	22.740	.....	.....
17........	21.245		.....	.....	20.500	20.200
18........	21.995		23.410	23.300	19.980	19.720
19........	21.895		24.450	23.950	19.630	19.500
20........	.....		24.120	23.720	19.690	19.600
21........	22.490		23.920	23.650	19.200	19.140
22........	22.115		23.320	23.100	.....	.....
23........	22.170		23.190	23.150	.....	.....
24........	22.385		.....	.....	18.150	17.730
25........	22.130		22.820	22.550	18.590	18.500
26........	22.310		23.460	23.190	18.525	18.520
27........	.....		23.920	23.700	18.410	18.380
28........	21.830	21.720	24.270	23.980	18.220	18.180
29........	21.720	21.530	24.000	23.830	.....	.....
30........	21,975	21.890	.....	.....	.....	.....
31........	21.665	21.525	.....	.....	18.240	18.200

*The manner of quoting the rates changed again in January.

THE DOLLAR EXCHANGE RATES ON THE PARIS BOURSE

Daily 1924

	April High	April Low	May High	May Low	June High	June Low
1........	17.950	17.900	15.520	15.500	.....	.....
2........	17.150	16.890	15.450	15.400	20.690	20.430
3........	17.300	16.830	.....	.....	19.840	19.380
4........	17.420	17.350	.....	.....	19.720	19.540
5........	.....	.....	15.510	15.500	20.235	20.010
6........	.....	.....	15.500	15.480	19.990	19.860
7........	17.120	17.080	15.380	15.230	.....	.....
8........	17.160	17.130	16.200	15.820	.....	.....
9........	16.680	16.610	17.070	16.870	.....	.....
10........	16.800	16.500	.....	.....	19.960	19.875
11........	17.040	16.960	.....	.....	19.300	18.840
12........	.....	.....	17.850	17.430	19.000	18.790
13........	.....	.....	18.150	17.900	18.920	18.575
14........	16.690	16.600	17.100	16.990	.....	.....
15........	16.400	16.270	17.300	16.880	.....	.....
16........	16.230	16.100	17.590	17.340	18.170	17.945
17........	16.150	16.020	.....	.....	18.690	18.435
18........	.....	.....	.....	.....	18.720	18.680
19........	.....	.....	18.000	17.910	18.600	18.510
20........	.....	.....	19.010	18.850	18.540	18.380
21........	.....	.....	18.540	18.180	.....	.....
22........	15.560	15.320	17.850	17.770	.....	.....
23........	15.100	14.820	18.800	18.425	18.520	18.430
24........	15.620	15.480	.....	.....	19.050	18.800
25........	15.920	15.800	.....	.....	19.120	19.040
26........	.....	.....	18.410	18.260	18.970	18.940
27........	.....	.....	18.730	18.560	19.000	18.900
28........	15.580	15.370	18.910	18.860	.....	.....
29........	15.470	15.430	.....	.....	.....	.....
30........	15.500	15.490	19.370	19.260	18.950	18.925
31........	.....	.....	.....	.....	.....	.....

THE DOLLAR EXCHANGE RATES ON THE PARIS BOURSE

Daily 1924

	July High	July Low	August High	August Low	September High	September Low
1........	19.360	19.258	19.760	19.590	18.550	18.500
2........	19.460	19.430	.....	.....	18.460	18.430
3........	19.610	19.450	.....	.....	18.650	18.525
4........	19.710	19.600	18.970	18.770	18.920	18.860
5........	.....	.....	18.675	18.335	18.945	18.865
6........	.....	.....	18.280	18.030	.....	.....
7........	19.770	19.660	18.450	18.315	.....	.....
8........	19.530	19.490	18.870	17.730	19.010	18.960
9........	19.740	19.540	.....	.....	19.180	19.120
10........	19,620	19.590	.....	.....	18.960	18.870
11........	19,625	19.570	17.580	17.350	18.800	18.670
12........	.....	.....	17.910	17.590	18.700	18.570
13........	.....	.....	18.220	18.055	.....	.....
14........	.....	.....	18.000	17.970	.....	.....
15........	19.380	19.325	.....	.....	18.810	18.660
16........	19.555	19.475	.....	.....	18.910	18.820
17........	19.470	19.425	.....	.....	18.730	18.600
18........	19.730	19.670	18.200	18.020	18.820	18.795
19........	.....	.....	18.490	18.315	18.940	18.870
20........	.....	.....	18.640	18.520	.....	.....
21........	19.375	19.345	18.590	18.460	.....	.....
22........	19.410	19.360	18.520	18.475	18.890	18.860
23........	19.390	19.350	.....	.....	19.005	18.985
24........	19.560	19.480	.....	.....	18.985	18.945
25........	19.495	19.460	18.550	18.380	18.955	18.920
26........	.....	.....	18.510	18.445	19.020	19.000
27........	.....	.....	18.460	18.380	.....	.....
28........	19.790	19.620	18.580	18.540	.....	.....
29........	19.800	19.745	18.470	18.460	19.070	19.050
30........	19.945	19.920	.....	.....	19.095	19.000
31........	20.095	20.050	.....	.....	.....	.....

THE DOLLAR EXCHANGE RATES ON THE PARIS BOURSE

Daily   1924

	October High	October Low	November High	November Low	December High	December Low
1	18.880	18.825	.....	.....	18.490	18.415
2	18.980	18.930	.....	.....	18.255	18.160
3	19.010	18.980	19.075	19.030	18.230	18.205
4	.....	.....	19.095	19.070	18.180	18.150
5	.....	.....	19.140	19.090	18.365	18.290
6	19.065	19.025	19.145	19.100	18.570	18.535
7	19.063	19.043	19.080	19.030	.....	.....
8	19.210	19.155	19.130	19.090	18.490	18.400
9	19.375	19.250	.....	.....	18.490	18.455
10	19.500	19.250	19.030	19.000	18.595	18.540
11	.....	.....	.....	.....	18.600	18.680
12	.....	.....	18.920	18.880	18.820	18.675
13	19.045	18.960	18.980	18.900	18.705	18.685
14	19.060	18.970	18.895	18.820	.....	.....
15	19.200	19.120	18.930	18.920	18.630	18.605
16	19.250	19.130	.....	.....	18.610	18.560
17	19.190	19.100	19.030	18.980	18.740	18.695
18	.....	.....	19.110	19.040	18.735	18.690
19	.....	.....	19.110	19.065	18.580	18.500
20	19.225	19.190	19.070	19.033	18.550	18.520
21	19.240	19.135	18.895	18.830	.....	.....
22	19.090	19.020	18.850	18.030	18.5675	18.550
23	19.145	19.055	.....	.....	18.590	18.565
24	19.175	19.140	18.910	18.855	18.580	18.575
25	.....	.....	19.010	18.945	.....	.....
26	.....	.....	18.990	18.920	18.550	18.540
27	19.230	19.190	18.845	18.810	18.530	18.530
28	19.160	19.120	18.710	18.670	.....	.....
29	19.110	19.060	18.615	18.550	18.500	18.475
30	19.100	19.060	.....	.....	18.4725	18.435
31	19.135	19.100	.....	.....	18.4775	18.440

THE DOLLAR EXCHANGE RATES ON THE PARIS BOURSE

Daily 1925

	January		February		March	
	High	Low	High	Low	High	Low
1........	.....	.....	.....	.....	.....	.....
2........	18.415	18.380	18.485	18.465	19.655	19.550
3........	18.450	18.430	18.500	18.480	19.870	19.740
4........	.....	.....	18.480	18.460	19.720	19.650
5........	18.630	18.510	18.520	18.480	19.650	19.595
6........	18.630	18.590	18.580	18.555	19.470	19.440
7........	18.565	18.520	18.575	18.560	19.360	19.280
8........	18.580	18.530	.....	.....	.....	.....
9........	18.670	18.650	18.645	18.615	19.400	19.280
10........	18.680	18.640	18.690	18.645	19.530	19.488
11........	.....	.....	18.680	18.655	19.385	19.320
12........	18.670	18.600	18.680	18.635	19.495	19.388
13........	18.705	18.685	18.850	18.825	19.430	19.380
14........	18.765	18.720	19.290	19.240	19.400	19.390
15........	18.675	18.605	.....	.....	.....	.....
16........	18.493	18.468	19.200	19.010	19.480	19.430
17........	18.585	18.550	19.050	18.960	19.370	19.335
18........	.....	.....	19.000	18.900	19.220	19.170
19........	18.450	18.380	19.220	19.135	19.320	19.275
20........	18.585	18.530	19.160	19.130	19.295	19.225
21........	18.548	18.505	19.090	19.060	19.275	19.265
22........	18.480	18.450	.....	.....	.....	.....
23........	18.490	18.465	19.225	19.190	19.298	19.210
24........	18.530	18.513	19.250	19.240	19.150	19.125
25........	.....	.....	19.380	19.275	19.140	19.085
26........	18.550	18.510	19.490	19.450	19.070	19.040
27........	18.560	18.540	19.533	19.490	18.870	18.825
28........	18.460	18.4325	19.570	19.480	19.000	18.940
29........	18.483	18.4575	.....	.....	.....	.....
30........	18.500	18.470	.....	.....	18.945	18.920
31........	18.450	18.435	.....	.....	18.790	18.680

THE DOLLAR EXCHANGE RATES ON THE PARIS BOURSE

Daily 1925

	April High	April Low	May High	May Low	June High	June Low
1........	19.110	19.040	19.120	19.050	.....	.....
2........	19.325	19.190	.....	.....	20.180	20.155
3........	19.530	19.430	.....	.....	20.170	20.130
4........	19.405	19.320	19.130	19.105	20.390	20.535
5........	.....	.....	19.090	19.075	20.570	20.515
6........	19.430	19.310	19.200	19.140	.....	.....
7........	19.560	19.460	19.280	19.230	.....	.....
8........	19.415	19.350	19.180	19.150	20.790	20.715
9........	19.540	19.480	.....	.....	20.433	20.340
10........	.....	.....	.....	.....	20.353	20.325
11........	.....	.....	19.230	19.220	20.530	20.510
12........	.....	.....	19.155	19.135	20.720	20.670
13........	.....	.....	19.250	19.220	.....	.....
14........	19.500	19.410	19.185	19.160	.....	.....
15........	19.500	19.460	19.225	19.190	20.780	20.740
16........	19.325	19.270	.....	.....	20.940	20.890
17........	19.030	18.910	.....	.....	20.950	20.890
18........	19.080	19.020	19.300	19.260	21.290	21.200
19........	.....	.....	19.340	19.315	21.190	21.155
20........	19.130	19.070	19.465	19.430	.....	.....
21........	19.150	19.110	.....	.....	.....	.....
22........	19.210	19.160	19.500	19.455	21.520	21.440
23........	19.290	19.250	.....	.....	21.450	21.260
24........	19.200	19.160	.....	.....	21.550	21.470
25........	19.260	19.235	19.550	19.510	21.735	21.540
26........	.....	.....	19.810	19.750	21.875	21.705
27........	19.310	19.260	20.045	19.970	.....	.....
28........	19.260	19.235	19.935	19.870	.....	.....
29........	19.123	19.090	19.958	19.905	21.860	21.790
30........	19.170	19.150	.....	.....	22.160	22.105
31........	.....	.....	.....	.....	.....	.....

THE DOLLAR EXCHANGE RATES ON THE PARIS BOURSE

Daily 1925

	July High	July Low	August High	August Low	September High	September Low
1........	22.380	22.310	.....	.....	21.310	21.295
2........	21.990	21.915	.....	.....	21.300	21.295
3........	21.430	21.140	21.120	21.100	21.343	21.335
4........	.....	.....	21.095	21.078	21.340	21.320
5........	.....	.....	21.315	21.230	.....	.....
6........	21.065	20.928	21.340	21.295	.....	.....
7........	21.475	21.420	21.345	21.290	21.330	21.320
8........	21.465	21.420	.....	.....	21.313	21.285
9........	21.310	21.185	.....	.....	21.265	21.220
10........	21.320	21.285	21.400	21.378	21.280	21.250
11........	.....	.....	21.330	21.290	21.325	21.290
12........	.....	.....	21.450	21.380	.....	.....
13........	.....	.....	21.445	21.415	.....	.....
14........	.....	.....	21.428	21.420	21.300	21.273
15........	21.330	21.270	.....	.....	21.200	21.180
16........	21.175	21.130	.....	.....	21.270	21.215
17........	21.300	21.260	21.480	21.455	21.220	21.205
18........	.....	.....	21.570	21.390	21.175	21.130
19........	.....	.....	21.300	21.285	.....	.....
20........	21.225	21.205	21.355	21.340	.....	.....
21........	21.200	21.160	21.310	21.300	21.105	21.070
22........	21.240	21.205	.....	.....	21.160	21.125
23........	21.310	21.250	.....	.....	21.150	21.125
24........	21.205	21.170	21.250	21.220	21.150	21.135
25........	.....	.....	21.275	21.268	21.120	21.100
26........	.....	.....	21.435	21.410	.....	.....
27........	21.175	21.140	21.295	21.265	.....	.....
28........	21.180	21.150	21.320	21.310	21.150	21.135
29........	21.115	21.100	.....	.....	21.155	21.145
30........	21.065	21.030	.....	.....	21.155	21.145
31........	21.110	21.095	21.335	21.305	.....	.....

THE DOLLAR EXCHANGE RATES ON THE PARIS BOURSE

Daily   1925

	October		November		December	
	High	Low	High	Low	High	Low
1........	21.135	21.120	.....	.....	25.460	25.350
2........	21.390	21.300	.....	.....	26.200	25.800
3........	.....	.....	24.830	24.500	26.350	26.100
4........	.....	.....	24.865	24.750	26.210	25.930
5........	21.610	21.570	25.410	25.000	.....	.....
6........	21.680	21.655	25.060	24.750	.....	.....
7........	21.680	21.625	24.820	24.700	26.020	25.860
8........	21.630	21.595	.....	.....	26.160	25.970
9........	21.630	21.605	25.280	25.180	26.710	26.650
10........	.....	.....	25.150	25.110	26.480	26.420
11........	.....	.....	.....	.....	26.990	26.580
12........	21.770	21.730	25.100	24.900	.....	.....
13........	21.990	21.930	24.600	24.530	.....	.....
14........	22.260	22.180	24.855	24.845	27.880	27.590
15........	22.400	22.170	.....	.....	27.880	27.720
16........	22.580	22.485	24.920	24.870	27.490	27.180
17........	.....	.....	25.040	25.015	27.650	27.550
18........	.....	.....	24.990	24.935	26.960	26.650
19........	22.790	22.730	25.350	25.250	.....	.....
20........	22.700	22.610	25.255	25.130	.....	.....
21........	22.665	22.650	25.600	25.510	26.870	26.715
22........	23.190	23.070	.....	.....	27.320	27.110
23........	23.940	23.620	25.900	25.780	27.100	26.850
24........	.....	.....	26.030	25.910	27.190	27.000
25........	.....	.....	26.830	26.580	.....	.....
26........	24.450	23.600	26.640	26.330	.....	.....
27........	23.960	23.840	25.810	25.680	.....	.....
28........	24.245	24.140	25.830	25.800	27.500	27.410
29........	23.820	23.670	.....	.....	27.030	26.940
30........	23.820	23.750	25.740	25.590	26.420	26.340
31........	.....	.....	.....	.....	26.860	26.730

THE DOLLAR EXCHANGE RATES ON THE PARIS BOURSE

Daily 1926

	January		February		March	
	High	Low	High	Low	High	Low
1........	.....	.....	26.610	26.590	27.010	26.900
2........	.....	.....	26.745	26.700	27.200	27.010
3........	.....	.....	26.670	26.630	26.820	26.750
4........	26.080	25.980	26.655	26.645	26.910	26.820
5........	26.490	26.320	26.680	26.665	26.910	26.850
6........	26.120	25.900	26.700	26.690	27.760	27.680
7........	26.140	26.020	.....	.....	.....	.....
8........	26.035	25.940	26.960	26.860	27.930	27.820
9........	.....	.....	27.160	27.070	27.630	27.500
10........	.....	.....	27.370	27.255	27.470	27.400
11........	26.285	26.120	27.225	27.140	27.580	27.555
12........	26.520	26.185	27.180	27.135	27.510	27.380
13........	26.860	26.660	27.065	27.060	27.570	27.540
14........	26.690	26.630	.....	.....	.....	.....
15........	26.695	26.540	27.260	27.170	27.980	27.680
16........	.....	.....	27.560	27.535	27.780	27.660
17........	.....	.....	27.565	27.550	27.960	27.920
18........	26.590	26.465	27.550	27.485	28.030	27.910
19........	26.740	26.660	28.045	27.960	28.150	26.020
20........	26.780	26.680	28.090	28.000	28.400	28.330
21........	26.840	26.657	.....	.....	.....	.....
22........	26.755	26.705	27.880	27.780	28.360	28.240
23........	.....	.....	27.890	27.660	28.490	28.330
24........	.....	.....	27.455	27.250	28.720	28.620
25........	26.930	26.825	27.470	27.385	28.590	28.540
26........	26.990	26.930	27.410	27.180	29.100	28.720
27........	26.820	26.730	27.270	27.215	29.080	29.000
28........	26.700	26.630	.....	.....	.....	.....
29........	26.600	26.520	.....	.....	29.520	29.030
30........	.....	.....	.....	.....	29.160	28.900
31........	.....	.....	.....	.....	28.900	28.620

THE DOLLAR EXCHANGE RATES ON THE PARIS BOURSE

Daily   1926

	April		May		June	
	High	Low	High	Low	High	Low
1........	28.905	28.790	.....	.....	30.810	30.570
2........	.....	.....	.....	.....	30.650	30.410
3........	.....	.....	30.555	30.480	31.500	31.150
4........	.....	.....	30.590	30.555	32.440	32.170
5........	.....	.....	31.730	31.535	.....	.....
6........	28.820	28.740	32.250	31.630	.....	.....
7........	28.730	28.620	31.900	31.675	32.970	32.320
8........	28.860	28.730	.....	.....	33.900	33.340
9........	29.260	29.110	.....	.....	33.700	33.400
10........	29.220	29.110	32.060	31.755	33.920	33.500
11........	.....	.....	32.010	31.900	34.570	34.270
12........	29.260	29.140	31.940	31.900	.....	.....
13........	28.940	28.760	.....	.....	.....	.....
14........	29.235	29.120	32.620	32.120	35.800	35.490
15........	29.620	29.420	.....	.....	36.150	35.580
16........	29.750	29.620	.....	.....	35.550	35.280
17........	29.900	29.750	33.440	32.940	35.350	34.980
18........	.....	.....	34.700	34.350	36.300	36.000
19........	29.700	29.560	35.380	34.840	.....	.....
20........	30.365	30.250	33.720	33.500	.....	.....
21........	30.040	29.890	32.780	31.800	35.140	34.780
22........	29.870	29.760	.....	.....	35.860	35.560
23........	30.080	30.030	.....	.....	35.220	35.060
24........	29.770	29.720	.....	.....	34.880	34.630
25........	.....	.....	30.320	30.225	34.290	33.880
26........	29.860	29.800	30.800	30.730	.....	.....
27........	30.050	29.965	30.225	30.020	.....	.....
28........	30.220	30.130	31.350	31.100	34.520	34.370
29........	30.350	30.250	.....	.....	35.020	34.830
30........	30.490	30.380	.....	.....	35.700	35.520
31........	.....	.....	31.040	30.820	.....	.....

THE DOLLAR EXCHANGE RATES ON THE PARIS BOURSE

Daily 1926

	July High	July Low	August High	August Low	September High	September Low
1........	36.900	36.610	.....	.....	33.800	33.530
2........	37.390	37.000	39.170	37.600	33.350	33.110
3........	.....	.....	37.800	37.380	34.150	33.910
4........	.....	.....	35.270	34.750	.....	.....
5........	37.070	36.700	35.630	34.950	.....	.....
6........	37.600	37.200	33.250	32.200	34.010	33.935
7........	37.450	37.000	.....	.....	33.990	33.880
8........	39.010	38.300	.....	.....	33.945	33.810
9........	38.500	38.150	34.340	33.960	34.900	34.720
10........	.....	.....	35.530	35.120	35.050	34.970
11........	.....	.....	36.250	35.880	.....	.....
12........	39.880	39.480	36.480	36.100	.....	.....
13........	39.580	.....	36.625	36.420	34.760	34.710
14........	.....	.....	.....	.....	35.340	35.210
15........	40.590	40.200	.....	.....	35.080	34.880
16........	42.950	42.300	.....	.....	35.180	35.080
17........	.....	.....	36.770	36.680	35.620	35.435
18........	.....	.....	35.520	34.860	.....	.....
19........	47.300	36.220	34.870	34.520	.....	.....
20........	49.220	47.850	35.400	35.320	35.815	35.740
21........	46.950	46.350	.....	.....	36.100	35.850
22........	44.800	44.000	.....	.....	36.540	36.410
23........	43.800	42.870	35.580	35.010	35.960	35.820
24........	.....	.....	35.440	35.230	36.180	35.930
25........	.....	.....	35.010	34.900	.....	.....
26........	39.120	38.830	35.180	34.975	.....	.....
27........	40.920	40.400	35.030	34.880	36.050	35.835
28........	42.170	41.820	.....	.....	35.790	35.625
29........	42.860	41.930	.....	.....	35.765	35.700
30........	41.900	41.540	34.740	34.715	35.320	35.230
31........	.....	.....	34.240	33.980	.....	.....

THE DOLLAR EXCHANGE RATES ON THE PARIS BOURSE

Daily   1926

	October		November		December	
	High	Low	High	Low	High	Low
1........	35.565	35.515	.....	.....	27.050	26.860
2........	.....	.....	.....	.....	26.330	26.080
3........	.....	.....	31.100	30.950	26.360	25.720
4........	35.740	35.510	29.990	29.630	25.180	24.950
5........	35.370	35.245	30.700	30.320	.....	.....
6........	34.880	34.730	30.210	30.140	25.360	24.960
7........	34.850	34.680	.....	.....	25.840	25.450
8........	34.760	34.680	30.600	30.440	25.980	25.350
9........	.....	.....	30.840	30.705	25.500	25.010
10........	.....	.....	31.150	30.860	25.780	25.570
11........	34.830	34.680	.....	.....	25.340	25.230
12........	34.890	34.800	30.090	29.760	.....	.....
13........	35.240	35.080	30.390	30.220	25.050	24.935
14........	35.010	34.960	.....	.....	25.240	25.040
15........	34.780	34.700	29.940	29.780	25.220	25.050
16........	.....	.....	30.040	29.830	24.960	24.930
17........	.....	.....	29.255	29.070	25.020	24.940
18........	34.690	34.510	29.060	28.810	24.970	24.940
19........	34.280	34.220	28.440	28.270	.....	.....
20........	33.880	33.550	26.900	26.370	24.940	24.620
21........	33.080	32.890	.....	.....	24.900	24.740
22........	33.670	33.470	28.520	28.050	25.160	25.060
23........	.....	.....	28.550	28.270	25.190	.....
24........	.....	.....	28.970	28.500	25.213	25.208
25........	32.810	32.660	28.000	27.760	.....	.....
26........	32.640	32.360	27.750	27.360	.....	.....
27........	32.770	32.655	27.920	27.720	25.273	25.255
28........	32.750	32.660	.....	.....	25.233	25.225
29........	32.070	31.800	27.320	26.950	25.240	25.235
30........	.....	.....	27.220	26.900	25.250	25.243
31........	.....	.....	.....	.....	25.290	25.285

THE DOLLAR EXCHANGE RATES ON THE PARIS BOURSE

Daily 1927

	January High	January Low	February High	February Low	March High	March Low
1........	.....	.....	25.254	25.254	25.560	25.553
2........	.....	.....	25.254	25.254	25.566	25.563
3........	25.315	25.305	25.254	25.254	25.580	25.565
4........	25.315	25.305	25.254	.....	25.578	25.570
5........	25.370	25.315	25.254	25.254	25.573	25.568
6........	25.338	.....	.....	.....	.....	.....
7........	25.308	25.303	25.255	25.254	25.575	25.570
8........	25.280	25.278	25.255	25.254	25.560	25.558
9........	.....	.....	25.255	25.255	25.570	25.568
10........	25.240	25.225	25.255	25.255	25.565	25.560
11........	25.220	25.213	25.255	25.255	25.558	25.565
12........	25.190	25.188	25.255	25.255	25.560	.....
13........	25.185	25.170	.....	.....	.....	.....
14........	25.165	25.160	25.254	.....	25.563	25.560
15........	25.150	.....	25.255	25.254	25.553	25.548
16........	.....	.....	25.255	25.255	25.550	25.545
17........	25.140	25.138	25.255	25.255	25.548	25.543
18........	25.145	25.135	25.255	25.255	25.543	25.540
19........	25.198	25.190	25.255	.....	25.543	25.540
20........	25.180	25.175	.....	.....	.....	.....
21........	25.223	25.220	25.256	25.255	25.543	25.540
22........	25.250	25.245	25.256	25.255	25.545	25.543
23........	.....	.....	25.256	25.256	25.538	25.535
24........	25.235	25.233	25.256	25.256	25.535	.....
25........	25.280	25.270	25.256	25.256	25.540	25.538
26........	25.323	25.320	25.256	.....	25.538	.....
27........	25.355	25.350	.....	.....	.....	.....
28........	25.368	.....	25.256	25.256	.....	.....
29........	25.380	25.378	.....	.....	.....	.....
30........	.....	.....	.....	.....	.....	.....
31........	25.393	25.390	.....	.....	.....	.....

THE DOLLAR EXCHANGE RATES ON THE PARIS BOURSE

1914-1918, and 1927 [1]

Monthly

	1914		1915		1916	
	Low	High	Low	High	Low	High
Jan	5.165	5.195	5.100	5.250	5.835	5.895
Feb	5.165	5.195	5.255	5.305	5.835	5.895
Mar	5.160	5.190	5.280	5.330	5.940	6.000
Apr	5.1375	5.1675	5.300	5.350	5.905	5.965
May	5.1325	5.1625	5.365	5.465	5.895	5.955
Jun	5.1333	5.165	5.450	5.550	5.880	5.940
Jul	5.135	5.165	5.650	5.700	5.875	5.935
Aug	5.100	5.140	5.900	6.000	5.860	5.920
Sep	no quot.	no quot.	5.700	5.800	5.820	5.880
Oct	5.100	5.250	5.915	6.015	5.810	5.860
Nov	5.020	5.170	5.855	5.955	5.810	5.860
Dec	5.090	5.240	5.800	5.900	5.810	5.860

	1917		1918		1927
	Low	High	Low	High	
Jan	5.810	5.860	5.675	5.725	25.26
Feb	5.810	5.860	5.675	5.725	25.48
Mar	5.810	5.860	5.675	5.725	25.55
Apr	5.675	5.725	5.675	5.725	25.53
May	5.675	5.725	5.675	5.725	25.53
Jun	5.675	5.725	5.675	5.725	25.54
Jul	5.675	5.725	5.675	5.725	25.55
Aug	5.675	5.725	5.470	5.520	25.52
Sep	5.675	5.725	5.445	5.495	25.50
Oct	5.675	5.725	5.445	5.495	25.47
Nov	5.675	5.725	5.425	5.475	25.45
Dec	5.675	5.725	5.425	5.475	25.40

[1] Source: *L'Economiste Française*, 1914-1926. *Bulletin de la Statistique générale de la France*, 1927.

NOTE CIRCULATION OF THE BANK OF FRANCE

1914–1918

Monthly

(In millions of francs)

	1914	1915	1916	1917	1918
Jan	5,894	10,474	13,858	17,328	23,534
Feb	5,764	10,962	14,295	17,889	24,308
Mar	5,743	11,177	14,952	17,460	25,179
Apr	6,038	11,584	15,278	19,010	26,395
May	5,812	11,828	15,435	19,479	27,303
Jun	5,852	12,105	15,806	19,823	28,550
Jul	6,683	12,593	16,091	20,202	29,148
Aug	....	12,050	16,425	20,569	29,434
Sep	....	13,458	16,714	20,995	29,922
Oct	....	13,868	16,589	21,705	30,782
Nov	....	14,287	16,119	22,691	29,072
Dec	10,043	13,310	16,679	22,337	30,250

Source: U. S. Senate, *Foreign Currency and Exchange Investigation*, Washington, 1925, vol. i, pp. 470, 471.

NOTE CIRCULATION OF THE BANK OF FRANCE

(In millions of francs)

1918				1919			
Jan 3	22,789	Jul 4	28,952	Jan 2	31,055	Jul 3	34,753
10	22,983	11	29,090	9	31,567	10	35,008
17	23,063	18	29,111	16	31,700	17	34,977
24	23,163	25	29,148	23	31,794	24	34,932
31	23,534			30	31,983	31	35,025
Feb 7	23,740	Aug 1	29,321	Feb 6	32,367	Aug 7	35,258
14	23,821	8	29,477	13	32,507	14	35,152
21	23,986	16	29,408	20	32,492	21	35,064
28	24,308	22	29,424	27	32,716	28	35,090
		29	29,434				
Mar 7	24,650	Sep 5	29,727	Mar 6	33,092	Sep 4	35,456
14	24,744	12	29,764	13	33,234	11	35,681
21	24,825	19	29,788	20	33,262	18	35,655
28	25,179	26	29,922	27	33,372	25	35,787
Apr 4	25,848	Oct 3	30,225	Apr 3	33,736	Oct 2	36,256
11	26,087	10	30,540	10	33,998	9	36,726
18	26,232	17	30,631	17	33,975	16	36,799
25	26,395	24	30,721	24	33,978	23	36,769
		31	30,782			30	36,974
May 2	26,733	Nov 7	30,820	May 1	34,100	Nov 6	37,419
10	27,012	14	30,571	8	34,429	13	37,395
16	27,004	21	30,192	15	34,324	20	37,427
23	27,073	28	29,072	22	34,134	27	37,424
30	27,303			30	34,061		
Jun 6	28,012	Dec 5	28,733	Jun 5	34,371	Dec 4	37,756
13	28,232	12	29,028	12	34,449	11	37,678
20	28,414	19	29,271	19	34,450	18	37,378
27	28,550	26	30,250	26	34,442	26	37,275

(See weekly statements of the Bank of France, *L'Economiste Française, Le Pour et le contre,* and other periodicals, and official sources.)

NOTE CIRCULATION OF THE BANK OF FRANCE

(In millions of francs)

1920				1921			
Jan 2	37,660	Jul 1	37,763	Jan 6	38,590	Jul 7	37,667
8	38,010	8	38,012	13	38,463	15	37,555
15	37,901	15	38,011	20	38,153	21	37,270
22	37,679	22	37,765	27	37,913	28	36,941
29	35,582	29	37,696				
Feb 5	38,042	Aug 5	38,213	Feb 3	38,205	Aug 4	37,365
12	37,987	12	38,046	10	38,272	11	37,226
19	37,958	19	37,900	17	38,072	18	36,983
26	37,889	26	37,904	24	37,808	25	36,783
Mar 4	38,356	Sep 2	38,333	Mar 3	38,146	Sep 1	37,025
11	38,465	9	38,622	10	38,366	8	37,254
18	38,160	16	38,666	17	38,245	15	37,128
25	37,569	23	38,690	24	38,133	22	36,921
		30	39,208	31	38,435	29	37,129
Apr 1	37,334	Oct 7	39,567	Apr 7	38,696	Oct 6	37,792
8	37,507	14	39,527	14	38,529	13	37,612
15	37,434	21	39,290	21	38,282	20	37,407
22	37,327	28	39,084	28	38,211	27	37,154
29	37,688						
May 6	38,249	Nov 4	39,646	May 6	38,833	Nov 3	37,522
14	38,138	12	39,619	12	38,742	10	37,376
20	38,051	18	39,256	19	38,455	17	36,719
27	37,915	25	38,807	26	38,233	24	36,336
Jun 3	38,173	Dec 2	38,573	Jun 2	38,392	Dec 1	36,489
10	38,157	9	37,920	9	38,375	8	36,666
17	37,842	16	37,509	16	37,972	15	36,407
24	37,544	23	37,444	23	37,494	22	36,246
		30	37,902	30	37,422	29	36,487

NOTE CIRCULATION OF THE BANK OF FRANCE

(In millions of francs)

	1922				1923		
Jan 5	37,421	Jul 6	36,798	Jan 4	37,426	Jul 5	37,661
12	37,123	13	36,501	11	37,387	12	37,400
19	36,785	20	36,369	18	37,081	19	37,233
26	36,432	27	36,049	25	36,780	26	36,929
Feb 2	36,060	Aug 3	36,399	Feb 1	37,083	Aug 2	37,339
9	36,704	10	36,449	8	37,409	9	37,426
16	36,434	17	36,221	15	37,176	16	37,265
23	36,150	24	36,050	22	37,055	23	37,111
		31	36,384			30	37,364
Mar 2	36,258	Sep 7	36,959	Mar 1	37,434	Sep 6	37,998
9	36,225	14	36,607	8	37,822	13	37,703
16	35,660	21	36,585	15	37,555	20	37,607
23	35,281	28	36,602	22	37,221	27	37,625
30	35,528			29	37,187		
Apr 6	36,153	Oct 5	37,514	Apr 5	37,824	Oct 4	38,529
13	36,035	12	36,418	12	37,296	11	38,489
20	35,951	19	37,128	19	36,823	18	38,086
27	35,787	26	36,693	26	36,547	25	37,670
May 4	36,178	Nov 2	36,847	May 3	36,902	Nov 2	37,848
11	36,122	9	36,914	11	36,964	8	38,041
18	35,847	16	36,321	17	36,692	15	37,439
26	35,674	23	35,789	24	36,386	22	37,158
		30	36,114	31	36,740	29	37,329
Jun 1	35,982	Dec 7	36,383	Jun 7	36,945	Dec 6	37,939
8	36,317	14	36,070	14	36,701	13	37,547
15	36,028	21	36,049	21	36,621	20	37,629
22	35,852	28	36,359	28	36,689	27	37,905
29	36,039						

NOTE CIRCULATION OF THE BANK OF FRANCE

(In millions of francs)

	1924				1925			
Jan	3	39,114	Jul 3	40,115	Jan 2	40,885	Jul 2	43,799
	10	39,172	10	40,224	8	40,830	9	44,493
	17	38,678	17	40,155	15	40,797	16	44,532
	24	38,329	24	40,081	22	40,601	23	44,220
	31	38,834	31	40,324	29	40,515	30	44,496
Feb	7	39,174	Aug 7	40,571	Feb 5	40,858	Aug 6	45,333
	14	38,932	14	40,399	12	40,777	13	44,906
	21	38,894	21	40,250	19	40,771	20	44,785
	28	39,344	28	40,034	26	40,791	27	44,701
Mar	6	40,266	Sep 4	40,399	Mar 5	40,886	Sep 3	45,445
	13	39,929	11	40,314	12	40,870	10	45,685
	20	39,905	18	40,244	19	40,880	17	45,613
	27	39,949	25	40,338	26	40,892	24	45,556
Apr	3	40,213	Oct 2	40,533	Apr 2	40,903*	Oct 1	46,353
	10	40,145	9	40,648	9	43,004*	8	47,165
	17	39,943	16	40,569	16	42,959	15	46,913
	24	39,824	23	40,459	23	42,662	22	46,599
			30	40,528	30	43,049	29	46,678
May	1	40,020	Nov 6	40,705	May 7	43,408	Nov 5	48,011
	8	39,928	13	40,635	14	42,991	12	47,681
	15	39,739	20	40,530	22	42,749	19	47,943
	22	39,402	27	40,447	28	42,702	26	48,085
	30	39,556						
Jun	5	39,965	Dec 4	40,700	Jun 4	43,648	Dec 3	49,183
	12	39,896	11	40,567	11	43,387	10	49,536
	19	39,742	18	40,518	18	43,053	17	49,627
	26	39,664	26	40,603	25	43,000	24	49,933
							31	51,085

* This large increase is due to the correct statement of the Bank of France which had given a false impression for several of the preceding weeks.

NOTE CIRCULATION OF THE BANK OF FRANCE

(In millions of francs)

1926				1927			
Jan 7	51,982	Jul 1	53,914	Jan 6	54,305	Jul 7	53,951
14	51,328	8	54,861	13	53,515	15	53,490
21	50,817	15	54,917	20	52,811	21	53,131
28	50,618	22	55,006	27	52,172	28	52,756
		29	56,022				
Feb 4	51,471	Aug 5	57,259	Feb 3	52,626	Aug 4	53,694
11	50,089	12	56,271	10	52,643	11	53,282
18	50,962	19	55,659	17	52,153	18	52,925
25	50,991	26	55,147	24	51,697	25	52,672
Mar 4	52,065	Sep 2	55,346	Mar 3	52,462	Sep 1	53,266
11	51,951	9	55,458	10	52,764	8	54,117
18	51,699	16	54,913	17	52,273	15	53,892
25	51,492	23	54,507	24	51,912	22	53,773
		30	55,010	31	52,385	29	54,156
Apr 1	52,127	Oct 7	55,994	Apr 7	53,351	Oct 6	55,887
8	52,851	14	55,432	14	52,883	13	55,404
15	52,443	21	54,988	21	52,550	20	55,005
22	52,014	28	54,578	28	52,210	27	54,700
29	52,208						
May 6	53,181	Nov 4	55,651	May 5	53,319	Nov 3	55,855
14	52,653	12	54,927	12	52,618	10	55,909
20	52,658	18	54,064	19	52,157	17	55,443
27	52,735	25	53,263	27	51,801	24	54,962
Jun 3	53,390	Dec 2	53,332	Jun 2	52,328	Dec 1	55,465
10	53,353	9	53,294	9	52,786	8	56,233
17	53,033	16	52,563	16	52,381	15	55,811
24	53,073	23	52,234	23	52,107	22	55,806
		30	52,907	30	52,786	29	56,551

GOLD VALUE OF NOTE CIRCULATION
1913–1927
Monthly
(In millions of dollars)

	1913	1914	1915	1916	1917	1918	1919	1920
Jan	1,139	1,135	2,021	2,370	2,963	4,107	5,869	3,187
Feb	1,120	1,112	2,094	2,430	3,059	4,254	6,003	2,667
Mar	1,082	1,103	2,112	2,519	3,157	4,406	5,907	2,701
Apr	1,086	1,168	2,178	2,551	3,298	4,619	5,671	2,355
May	1,064	1,128	2,200	2,601	3,399	4,778	5,382	2,601
Jun	1,042	1,135	2,179	2,671	3,449	4,996	5,390	2,973
Jul	1,096	1,370	2,241	2,719	3,515	5,101	5,040	3,065
Aug	1,044	....	2,067	2,784	3,558	5,269	4,478	2,722
Sep	1,062	....	2,288	2,850	3,622	5,461	4,209	2,643
Oct	1,118	....	2,357	2,837	3,776	5,618	4,296	2,552
Nov	1,085	....	2,420	2,756	3,937	5,344	3,974	2,332
Dec	1,097	....	2,276	2,852	3,898	5,554	3,444	2,244

	1921	1922	1923	1924	1925	1926	1927
Jan	2,438	2,973	2,457	1,184	2,192	1,903	2,076
Feb	2,711	3,156	2,279	1,739	2,093	1,870	2,046
Mar	2,702	3,198	2,350	1,870	2,148	1,781	2,051
Apr	2,766	3,303	2,438	2,453	2,247	1,712	2,045
May	3,200	3,253	2,440	2,290	2,144	1,699	2,028
Jun	3,020	3,157	2,311	2,082	1,993	1,487	2,066
Jul	2,885	2,971	2,175	2,065	2,116	1,337	2,064
Aug	2,854	2,896	2,111	2,186	2,102	1,611	2,065
Sep	2,703	2,804	2,204	2,138	2,155	1,557	2,123
Oct	2,694	2,704	2,241	2,120	1,972	1,702	2,147
Nov	2,616	2,477	2,061	2,136	1,825	1,957	2,159
Dec	2,861	2,629	1,990	2,193	1,896	2,092	2,226

Source: 1913-1924, U. S. Senate *Foreign Currency and Exchange Investigation, op. cit.*, vol. i, pp. 480, 481. 1925-1927, compiled from figures of daily exchange rates, and Note Circulation of Bank of France, from *Le Pour et le contre*.

ADVANCES TO THE STATE BY THE BANK OF FRANCE

(In millions of francs)

	1922				1923			
Jan	5	24,150	Jul	6	23,700	Jan	4	23,300	Jul	5	23,900

1922					1923			
Jan 5	24,150	Jul 6	23,700	Jan 4	23,300	Jul 5	23,900
12	23,800	13	23,500	11	23,300	12	23,600
19	23,350	20	23,400	18	23,100	19	23,300
26	23,000	27	23,000	25	23,100	26	23,000
Feb 2	23,500	Aug 3	23,600	Feb 1	23,400	Aug 2	23,700
9	23,200	10	23,500	8	23,400	9	23,400
16	22,900	17	23,500	16	23,300	16	23,400
23	22,500	24	23,300	22	23,200	23	23,400
		31	23,900			30	23,400
Mar 2	22,400	Sep 7	23,900	Mar 1	23,700	Sep 6	23,900
9	21,900	14	23,900	8	23,500	13	23,800
16	21,200	21	24,100	15	23,400	20	23,700
23	21,500	28	24,000	22	23,300	27	23,700
30	21,500			29	23,100		
Apr 6	22,200	Oct 5	24,500	Apr 5	23,600	Oct 4	23,900
13	22,200	12	24,200	12	23,200	11	23,700
20	22,300	19	24,000	19	22,800	18	23,500
27	22,100	26	23,600	26	22,500	25	23,400
May 4	22,800	Nov 2	23,900	May 3	23,000	Nov 2	23,400
11	22,600	9	23,700	11	22,800	8	23,100
18	22,600	16	23,000	17	22,800	15	22,900
26	22,450	23	22,600	24	22,600	22	22,800
		30	22,900	31	23,000	29	22,800
Jun 1	23,100	Dec 7	23,200	Jun 7	23,100	Dec 6	23,200
8	23,100	14	22,900	14	23,100	13	23,100
15	23,000	21	23,400	21	23,100	20	23,100
22	23,100	28	23,600	28	23,100	27	23,300
29	23,300						

(See weekly statements of the Bank of France, *L'Economiste Française*, and other periodicals, and official sources.) These are new advances and are exclusive of 200,000,000 francs which appear in the balances of the bank as a separate item.

ADVANCES TO THE STATE BY THE BANK OF FRANCE

(In millions of francs)

	1924				1925			
Jan 3	23,100	Jul 3	23,100	Jan 2	21,800	Jul 2	27,700
10	22,900	10	23,000	8	21,700	9	27,400
17	22,800	17	22,900	15	21,500	16	27,850
24	22,600	24	22,700	22	21,400	23	27,400
31	22,800	31	23,000	29	21,200	30	27,250
Feb 7	23,100	Aug 7	23,000	Feb 5	21,900	Aug 6	28,200
14	22,900	14	22,900	12	21,900	13	28,100
21	22,900	21	22,900	19	21,900	20	28,000
28	23,100	28	22,800	26	21,900	27	27,750
Mar 6	23,100	Sep 4	23,100	Mar 5	21,900	Sep 3	28,800
13	23,000	11	23,000	12	21,800	10	28,650
20	22,900	18	23,000	19	21,800	17	28,800
27	22,700	25	23,000	26	21,800	24	28,900
Apr 3	23,000	Oct 2	23,100	Apr 2	21,900	Oct 1	30,350
10	22,800	9	22,900	9	22,000	8	30,800
17	22,700	16	22,800	16	22,350	15	30,500
24	22,700	23	22,700	23	22,700	22	30,350
		30	22,700	30	23,250	29	29,950
May 1	23,000	Nov 6	23,100	May 7	23,850	Nov 5	31,400
8	22,800	13	23,000	14	23,950	12	31,350
15	22,700	20	22,900	22	24,100	19	31,600
22	22,700	27	22,600	28	23,850	26	31,950
30	22,700						
Jun 5	23,000	Dec 4	23,000	Jun 4	25,200	Dec 3	33,500
12	23,000	11	22,700	11	25,200	10	33,700
19	23,000	18	22,400	18	25,250	17	34,000
26	23,000	26	22,600	25	25,650	24	34,650
						31	35,950

ADVANCES OF THE BANK OF FRANCE TO THE STATE

(in millions of francs)

1926				1927	
Jan 7	35,550	Jul 1	37,350	Jan 6	35,000
14	34,850	8	37,700	13	34,550
21	34,800	15	37,800	20	33,650
28	34,200	22	38,350	27	32,550
		29	37,450		
Feb 4	34,100	Aug 5	37,850	Feb 3	31,900
11	34,650	12	37,300	10	31,000
18	34,600	19	36,950	17	30,500
25	34,500	26	36,450	24	29,600
Mar 4	35,700	Sep 2	37,350	Mar 3	29,500
11	35,450	9	37,000	10	29,300
18	35,250	16	36,850	17	28,900
25	35,000	23	36,400	24	28,100
		30	36,650	31	28,150
Apr 1	36,250	Oct 7	36,950	Apr 7	28,150
8	36,250	14	36,300	14	28,150
15	35,650	19	36,150	21	29,300
22	35,300	28	35,750	28	29,300
29	35,150				
May 6	35,250	Nov 4	36,550	May 5	29,300
14	34,850	12	36,050	12	28,900
20	35,100	19	35,850	19	27,400
27	35,900	25	35,700	27	26,600
Jun 3	36,900	Dec 2	36,700	Jun 2	27,100
10	36,400	9	36,700	9	27,200
17	36,400	26	36,450	16	26,950
24	36,600	23	36,450	23	26,650
		30	36,000		

MISCELLANEOUS ASSETS OF THE BANK OF FRANCE

1926, 1927

(Weekly)

	1926				1927		
Jan 7	3,312	Jul 1	2,948	Jan 6	5,931	Jul 7	23,518
14	3,677	8	3,704	13	6,125	14	23,460
21	3,707	15	3,214	20	6,524	21	24,177
28	3,561	22	3,376	27	7,225	28	24,551
		29	4,233				
Feb 4	3,183	Aug 5	3,689	Feb 3	7,192	Aug 4	23,853
11	3,487	12	4,535	10	8,517	11	23,960
18	3,467	19	4,043	17	9,053	18	23,677
25	3,529	26	4,503	24	9,075	25	23,965
Mar 4	3,158	Sep 2	3,787	Mar 3	8,887	Sep 1	23,565
11	3,640	9	4,575	10	9,308	8	24,302
18	3,367	16	4,454	17	9,784	15	23,938
25	3,502	23	4,602	24	10,733	22	23,795
		30	4,072	31	11,104	29	23,733
Apr 1	3,187	Oct 7	5,311	Apr 7	12,607	Oct 6	24,758
8	3,586	14	4,984	14	11,442	13	24,526
15	3,567	21	5,009	21	11,284	20	24,219
22	3,612	28	5,062	28	12,526	27	24,000
29	3,353						
May 6	4,339	Nov 4	4,189	May 5	14,301	Nov 3	23,912
13	3,581	12	4,985	12	16,179	10	24,459
20	3,543	18	4,866	19	18,074	17	24,489
27	3,599	25	4,832	27	19,018	24	24,628
Jun 3	3,220	Dec 2	4,388	Jun 2	19,704	Dec 1	24,561
10	3,655	9	5,137	9	20,484	8	25,512
17	3,498	16	4,892	16	21,300	15	25,320
24	3,303	23	4,738	23	22,015	22	25,793
		30	5,010	30	22,321	29	26,551

Source: *Le Temps, Le Pour et le contre,* and other periodicals.

BILLS DISCOUNTED BY THE BANK OF FRANCE

1923 to 1924

Weekly

(In millions of francs)

1923				1924			
Jan 4	3,449	Jul 5	3,007	Jan 3	4,314	Jul 3	4,728
11	2,686	12	2,313	10	3,546	10	4,865
18	2,660	19	2,453	17	3,589	17	4,719
25	2,662	26	2,475	24	3,670	24	4,699
				31	4,198	31	5,135
Feb 1	3,090	Aug 2	3,040	Feb 7	3,605	Aug 7	4,565
8	2,652	9	2,471	14	3,576	14	4,511
15	2,761	16	2,405	21	3,461	21	4,398
22	2,684	23	2,312	28	3,891	28	4,407
		30	2,634				
Mar 1	3,205	Sep 6	2,206	Mar 6	4,388	Sep 4	5,125
8	2,684	13	2,260	13	4,501	11	4,016
15	2,754	20	2,373	20	5,072	18	3,889
22	2,470	27	2,512	27	5,361	25	3,986
29	2,686						
Apr 5	3,129	Oct 4	3,847	Apr 3	5,947	Oct 2	4,890
12	2,359	11	3,101	10	4,993	9	4,999
19	2,533	18	3,032	17	4,697	16	4,893
26	2,641	25	3,089	24	4,604	23	4,973
						30	5,452
May 7	3,239	Nov 2	4,017	May 1	5,006	Nov 6	5,855
14	2,558	8	3,321	8	4,227	13	4,636
21	2,403	15	3,352	15	4,368	20	4,727
28	2,414	22	3,304	22	4,056	27	4,811
		29	3,726	30	4,486		
Jun 7	2,344	Dec 6	3,181	Jun 5	4,992	Dec 4	5,597
14	2,263	13	3,185	13	3,731	11	4,659
21	2,161	20	3,272	19	3,705	18	4,902
28	2,487	27	3,664	26	3,704	26	5,242

Source: Morgan Bank, *Statistical Atlas* (Paris, unpublished), p. 12a.
The figures include discounts by the central bank and its branches.

BILLS DISCOUNTED BY THE BANK OF FRANCE

1925 to 1926

(Weekly)

(In millions of francs)

1925				1926			
Jan 2	6,060	Jul 2	4,339	Jan 7	4,735	Jul 1	5,841
8	5,948	9	3,355	14	3,287	8	4,874
15	5,982	16	3,205	21	2,967	15	5,231
22	5,526	23	3,048	28	3,397	22	5,220
29	5,908	30	3,640			29	6,712
Feb 5	6,303	Aug 6	3,209	Feb 4	4,358	Aug 5	7,866
12	4,811	13	3,251	11	3,119	12	5,988
19	5,007	20	3,250	18	3,139	19	5,976
26	5,111	27	3,497	25	3,374	26	5,753
Mar 5	6,468	Sep 3	4,432	Mar 4	4,256	Sep 2	6,535
12	6,062	10	3,357	11	3,139	9	5,065
19	5,757	17	3,183	18	3,239	16	4,760
26	5,558	24	3,213	25	3,312	23	4,864
						30	5,884
Apr 2	6,570	Oct 1	3,879	Apr 1	4,376	Oct 7	4,802
9	6,181	8	2,847	8	3,347	14	5,027
16	5,550	15	2,952	15	3,484	21	4,691
23	5,374	22	2,798	22	3,412	28	5,388
30	5,962	29	3,590	29	4,191		
May 7	4,873	Nov 5	4,473	May 6	3,906	Nov 4	6,334
14	4,705	12	3,301	14	4,437	12	4,303
22	4,290	19	3,395	20	4,545	18	4,265
28	4,596	26	3,597	27	4,588	25	4,424
Jun 4	5,186	Dec 3	4,706	Jun 3	5,718	Dec 2	5,322
11	3,828	10	3,663	10	4,683	9	3,806
18	3,746	17	3,432	17	4,488	16	3,616
25	3,836	24	3,696	24	4,745	23	3,646
		31	4,188			30	4,440

BILLS DISCOUNTED BY THE BANK OF FRANCE

1927

(Weekly)

(In millions of francs)

Jan	6	5,166	Apr	7	2,242	Jul	7	1,433	Oct	6	1,222
	13	3,585		14	2,472		15	1,619		13	1,344
	20	3,594		21	2,186		21	1,332		20	1,414
	27	3,596		28	3,023		28	1,760		27	1,635
Feb	3	4,380	May	5	3,194	Aug	4	2,388	Nov	3	2,466
	10	3,216		12	1,940		11	1,448		10	1,535
	17	3,058		19	2,095		18	1,482		17	1,443
	24	3,230		27	2,206		25	1,729		24	1,796
Mar	3	3,678	Jun	2	2,760	Sep	1	2,105	Dec	1	2,230
	10	2,938		9	1,785		8	1,327		8	1,374
	17	2,728		16	1,673		15	1,414		15	1,398
	24	2,898		23	1,832		22	1,245		22	1,243
	31	3,401		30	2,495		29	1,923		29	2,171

FRENCH BUDGET

1913–1927

(In billions of francs)

Year	Receipts	Expenditures	Deficit or Excess
1913	5.1	5.1	− 0.03
1914	4.2	10.4	− 6.2
1915	4.1	22.1	− 18.0
1916	4.9	36.8	− 31.9
1917	6.2	44.7	− 38.5
1918	6.8	56.7	− 49.9
1919	11.6	54.2	− 42.6
1920	20.1	58.1	− 38.0
1921	23.1	51.1	− 28.0
1922	24.2	48.9	− 24.7
1923	27.7	45.8	− 18.1
1924	31.1	40.2	− 9.1
1925	29.5	34.2	− 4.7
1926	45.1	44.9	+ 0.2
1927	43.7	42.7	+ 1.0

Sources: 1913, U. S. Senate *Foreign Currency and Exchange Investigation, op. cit.,* p. 493. 1914–1924, Clémentel, *Inventaire,* pp. 14, 21. 1925, *Revue d'économie politique,* March–April, 1927, pp. 309, 312. 1926, Receipts *Ibid.,* p. 312. Expenditures, Poincaré, *Exposé des motifs,* 1927, no. 3248, p. 115. 1927, J. P. Morgan, *Statistical Atlas* (New York, unpublished).

GOVERNMENT EXPENSES

1924–1926

1926 (Provisional)

(In millions of francs)

Nature of Expenses	1924 Credits Voted	1925 Provisional Situation	1926 Budget Project
I. Public Debt			
General Budget	11,631	15,484	15,881
Special Budget	3,991	.....	.....
Total	15,622	15,484	15,881
II. Debt Viagère			
General Budget	1,442	3,776	5,144
Special Budget	1,771	.....	.....
Total	3,213	3,776	5,144
III. Military Expenses			
General Budget	5,924	5,624	5,502
Special Budget	30	.....	.....
Total	5,954	5,624	5,502
IV. Civil Expenses			
General Budget	9,528	9,336	10,119
Special Budget	1,520	.....	.....
Total	11,048	9,336	10,119
Grand Total	35,837	34,220	36,646

Source: Henry Chéron, *Rapport au Sénat*, no. 84, February 22, 1925.

YIELD OF THE BUSINESS TURNOVER TAX

Receipts by Months

(In millions of francs)

	1920	1921	1922	1923	1924	1925	1926	1927
Jan		184	192	231	303	430	498.4	855.4
Feb		152	165	202	289	340	451.1	707.4
Mar		148	169	218	303	333	395.0	604.8
Apr		158	183	249	346	395	537.3	767.1
May		147	180	239	343	390	509.9	770.0
Jun		147	189	241	321	351	545.8	639.8
Jul	2.6	146	197	259	380	376	690.9	793.3
Aug	3.7	147	188	257	334	369	726.1	696.0
Sep	293	157	187	259	323	349	703.8	619.3
Oct	234	168	208	294	429	376	856.7	776.6
Nov	205	172	210	289	369	424	823.1	710.7
Dec	203	173	213	278	350	400	729.8	665.0
Totals[1] ..	942	1,911	2,281	3,015	4,090	4,535	7,467.9	8,605.4

[1] Totals are not identical in each case with the sums of the monthly figures given as the thousands are omitted in the latter. The totals are from official figures for the years.

(Figures taken from the Files of the *Institut de Statistique de l'Université de Paris* and the *Bulletin de la statistique générale*.)

YIELD OF THE TAX ON BOURSE OPERATIONS

Receipts by Months

1919–1927

(In thousands of francs)

	1919	1920	1921	1922	1923
Jan	229	1,118	2,499	1,635	3,727
Feb	335	1,234	2,105	1,553	5,563
Mar	270	1,962	1,486	1,437	5,373
Apr	326	2,069	1,517	1,445	4,205
May	476	2,209	1,668	1,544	4,025
Jun	471	1,713	1,385	1,718	3,972
Jul	527	1,866	1,477	1,829	3,958
Aug	550	1,755	1,159	2,171	3,761
Sep	708	1,951	1,454	2,772	3,861
Oct	1,123	2,711	1,389	2,769	3,930
Nov	1,083	2,724	1,409	3,761	4,479
Dec	1,028	3,277	1,742	3,321	5,645

	(In thousands of francs)		(In millions of francs)	
	1924	1925	1926	1927
Jan	6,356	8,439	20.7	26.2
Feb	8,669	8,986	19.3	32.4
Mar	9,220	9,142	18.8	29.3
Apr	8,283	7,793	19.6	35.9
May	7,381	7,293	29.2	35.3
Jun	7,777	9,098	42.5	26.3
Jul	7,483	*14,483	50.9	22.4
Aug	6,544	10,749	45.7	22.3
Sep	5,793	10,607	31.4	21.4
Oct	7,838	13,448	39.1	32.6
Nov	8,863	22,142	38.3	32.5
Dec	8,377	26,548	31.3	30.8

* This increase is in part due to the change in the rate of taxation, from .50 to .60 a 1,000 frs.—Law of July 13, 1925. Figures taken from the *Institut de Statistique de l'Université de Paris* and *Bulletin de la statistique générale*, 1926, 1927.

THE DETAIL OF THE INTERNAL DEBT

October 31, 1925

(In millions of francs)

I. Perpetual Debt.

Rentes, 3% perpetual	19,740
Rentes, 5% 1915 and 1916 perpetual......................	18,855
Rentes, 4% perpetual, 1917	9,005
Rentes, 4% 1918 perpetual	20,619
Rentes, 6% perpetual, 1920	27,505
Rentes, 4% perpetual, 1925	5,934
Rentes, Alsace-Lorraine	73
Permanent Advances by the Bank of France................	200
Total....................	101,931

II. Rentes, Obligations, etc., with fixed maturity.

Rentes, 3% redeemable	2,741
Rentes, 3½% redeemable	12
Rentes, 5% redeemable	15,733
Capitalized annuities	11,250
Capitalized income granted to war victims...............	9,884
Obligations of State Railways...........................	1,569
Issues of the Crédit National 1919, 1920, 1924..........	9,544
Total...	50,733
Subtract Rentes, 5% redeemable which are in possession of the State.......................................	4,506
Balance	46,227

III. Short Term Debt.

Obligations, Défense Nationale: sexennals 1919...........	425
Décennals 1919–29........	7,208
Décennals 1922–32........	254
Sexennals 1925–31........	1,683
Bons du Trésor, 2 years 1921, not redeemed...............	1
3 and 5 years 1922......................	4,322
3, 6, and 10 years 1923 (I and II series)....	15,508
10 years 1924	4,836
Issues of Crédit National 1921, 1922, 1923................	12,551
Total......................................	46,786

IV. Floating Debt.

Treasury Bills, ordinary	3,623
National Defense Bills	46,659
Advances of the Bank....................................	29,950
Deposits	7,716
Postal checks accounts..................................	916
Total......................................	88,864

Summary:

Perpetual Debt	101,931
Rentes, Obligations, etc., with fixed maturity...........	46,227
Short Term Debt...	46,788
Floating Debt	88,864
Grand Total...................................	283,810

Source: Henry Chéron, *op. cit.*, February 22, 1925.

BANK CLEARINGS BY MONTHS

Through the Paris Clearing House

1913, 1914, 1919–1925

(In millions of francs)

	1913	1914	1919	1920
Jan	1,582	1,621	3,763	10,914
Feb	1,522	1,574	3,611	11,685
Mar	1,543	1,765	4,136	14,126
Apr	1,581	1,669	4,734	14,705
May	1,492	1,699	5,265	14,084
Jun	1,692	1,746	5,470	13,783
Jul	1,467	1,762	5,856	13,920
Aug	1,212	....	5,738	13,913
Sep	1,500	....	7,507	13,521
Oct	1,639	....	7,927	14,147
Nov	1,412	....	8,296	16,105
Dec	1,796	....	10,536	16,220
Total	18,375	11,837	72,839	167,123
Monthly Average ..	1,531	1,691	6,069	13,926

	1921	1922	1923	1924	1925
Jan	16,426	12,229	18,864	36,847	23,913
Feb	14,187	11,746	18,997	37,252	24,650
Mar	14,477	12,286	20,376	46,651	29,170
Apr	15,599	9,860	18,252	34,643	27,889
May	15,976	11,805	16,995	33,705	25,390
Jun	15,144	11,856	19,062	31,058	33,895
Jul	10,946	13,487	19,122	25,229	29,454
Aug	12,135	12,789	19,855	25,017	24,283
Sep	14,383	12,586	19,020	24,019	24,716
Oct	11,583	14,451	23,674	24,532	39,811
Nov	12,621	18,794	22,980	21,979	42,105
Dec	13,711	15,756	21,515	27,126	46,379
Total	167,158	167,645	238,666	368,058	371,656
Monthly Average	13,928	13,970	19,889	30,671	30,971

Source: *Bulletin de la statistique générale de la France* and files of the *Institut de Statistique de l'Université de Paris.*

ORDINARY SAVINGS BANKS OPERATIONS

Monthly statements of the operations of the ordinary Savings Banks
with the *Caisse des Depots et consignations*

(Millions of francs)

	1924			1925		
Month	Deposits During the Month	Withdrawals During the Month	Differences Between Deposits and Withdrawals	Deposits During the Month	Withdrawals During the Month	Differences Between Deposits and Withdrawals
Jan	24	20	+ 4	43	22	+ 21
Feb	50	35	+ 15	89	21	+ 68
Mar	40	32	+ 8	73	17	56
Apr	31	37	— 6	33	35	— 2
May	26	33	— 7	61	36	+ 25
Jun	28	27	+ 1	96	16	+ 80
Jul	39	24	+ 15	119	15	+104
Aug	40	20	+ 20	146	21	+125
Sep	30	27	+ 3	137	9	+128
Oct	22	38	— 16	139	14	+125
Nov	21	45	— 24	101	19	+ 82
Dec	20	60	— 40	73	28	+ 45
Total...	371	398	— 27	1110	253	+857

	1926			1927		
Month	Deposits During the Month	Withdrawals During the Month	Differences Between Deposits and Withdrawals	Deposits During the Month	Withdrawals During the Month	Differences Between Deposits and Withdrawals
Jan	124	9	+115	126	6	+120
Feb	292	12	+280	377	19	+358
Mar	182	12	+170	212	15	+197
Apr	95	21	+ 74	156	19	+137
May	83	22	+ 61	185	19	+166
Jun	86	30	+ 56	228	14	+214
Jul	45	98	— 53	250	17	+233
Aug	50	179	—129	250	15	+235
Sep	112	28	+ 84	286	13	+273
Oct	127	29	+ 98	310	19	+291
Nov	101	27	+ 74	...	...	...
Dec	102	27	+ 75	...	...	...
Total...	1399	494	+905	2380	156	+2224

Source: The statistical service of J. P. Morgan and Company (New
York).

DEMAND LIABILITIES

Of Four French Banks Publishing Monthly Statements
(In millions of francs)

	1920	1921	1922	1923
Jan	.....	13,131	13,367	14,096
Feb	13,366	13,247	13,137	13,863
Mar	12,787	12,945	12,836	13,912
Apr	13,323	13,440	13,506	13,815
May	13,870	13,551	13,389	14.094
Jun	13,387	12,629	14,036	14.248
Jul	13,433	13,024	13,546	14.132
Aug	13,192	12,856	13,340	14,333
Sep	13,587	12,974	13,602	15,158
Oct	13,985	13,513	13,946	14,418
Nov	14,064	13,122	13,538	14,243
Dec	13,270	13,319	13,966	14,945

	1924	1925	1926	1927
Jan	15,145	14,996	20,732	22,760
Feb	15,578	15,119	20,910	23,659
Mar	15,457	15,312	20,475	25,159
Apr	15,191	15,345	20,516	24,637
May	14,973	16,422	21,436	24,753
Jun	15,358	16,880	22,418	25,090
Jul	15,641	17,604	23,335	26,172
Aug	16,114	17,733	22,693	24,467
Sep	15,435	18,900	22,123	24,554
Oct	15,308	18,996	23,120	25,716
Nov	15,860	19,321	22,101	25,505
Dec	14,853	19,943	22,469	26,405

The four banks are the *Société générale, Crédit Lyonnais, Comptoir d'escompte de Paris, Société générale de crédit industriel et commercial.*

INDEX OF PRODUCTION

1919–1927

1913 = 100

(By months)

	1919	1920	1921	1922	1923
Jan	58	65	64	68	90
Feb	58	65	59	70	85
Mar	58	65	56	76	86
Apr	60	65	53	77	85
May	61	62	51	80	85
Jun	62	64	51	82	90
Jul	64	63	50	83	92
Aug	63	64	50	84	94
Sep	61	66	50	86	95
Oct	61	70	49	90	97
Nov	62	69	56	92	99
Dec	64	68	64	90	102

	1924	1925	1926	1927	1928
Jan	105	110	118	117	...
Feb	107	109	122	113	...
Mar	108	108	123	108	...
Apr	106	107	125	106	...
May	108	106	126	108	...
Jun	108	105	126	108	...
Jul	110	105	127	106	...
Aug	112	106	128	107	...
Sep	115	107	128	109	...
Oct	117	111	129	110	...
Nov	113	116	129	112	...
Dec	113	118	123	115	...

Source: *Bulletin de la statistique générale de la France*, Dessirier Index, October, 1924, p. 106, and April, 1926, p. 305; 1927, vol. xvi, p. 350.

DEMANDS FOR EMPLOYMENT NOT SATISFIED

1924–1927

Monthly

	1924	1925	1926	1927
Jan	12,089	13,030	12,863	73,506
Feb	11,278	12,807	11,368	96,670
Mar	10,129	13,838	10,213	80,741
Apr	10,412	11,666	10,369	68,614
May	8,038	10,997	8,883	48,241
Jun	9,154	10,321	8,272	32,622
Jul	8,653	10,548	7,682	29,264
Aug	9,358	9,196	8,597	29,576
Sep	9,536	10,104	11,753	27,896
Oct	10,505	11,208	11,759	25,817
Nov	11,886	11,923	16,126	26,587
Dec	9,901	9,276	23,985	27,603

Source: *Bulletin du Ministre du Travail*, 1924, pp. 118, 233, 357; 1925, pp. 20, 133, 275, 376; 1926, pp. 58, 180; 1927, pp. 332, 333.
1928 *Bulletin de la statistique générale de la France, supplément mensuel*, April, 1928.
Jan 31,967   Feb 30,356

PRODUCTION OF COAL AND LIGNITE

(Not including the Saar)

In thousands of tons

1919–1925

	1919	1920	1921	1922	1923	1924	1925
Jan	2,473	2,200	2,428	2,670	2,670	3,148	3,762
Feb	2,244	1,973	2,204	2,502	2,502	2,479	3,649
Mar	2,125	1,541	2,320	2,764	2,764	3,012	3,773
Apr	1,745	1,817	2,316	2,479	2,479	3,000	3,641
May	1,733	1,056	2,162	2,595	2,595	3,129	3,693
Jun	858	2,301	2,408	2,551	2,551	3,326	3,496
Jul	1,430	2,358	2,328	2,525	2,525	3,215	3,784
Aug	1,782	2,371	2,455	2,665	2,665	3,405	3,691
Sep	1,838	2,403	2,489	2,720	2,720	3,321	3,837
Oct	2,065	2,436	2,589	2,824	2,824	3,690	4,103
Nov	1,983	2,374	2,574	2,800	2,800	3,506	3,675
Dec	2,066	2,444	2,703	2,821	2,821	3,347	3,850

Source: Files of the *Institut de Statistique de l'Université de Paris*.

CAR LOADINGS

Monthly
1920–1923

	1920	1921	1922	1923
Jan	30,121	33,398	39,726	55,052
Feb	31,454	35,255	42,057	55,464
Mar	28,429	33,935	43,270	56,971
Apr	33,369	35,353	41,827	54,931
May	21,063	33,991	42,617	54,272
Jun	35,018	36,153	42,919	56,758
Jul	34,334	34,256	43,140	55,073
Aug	35,425	37,181	43,623	54,964
Sep	36,189	39,503	46,808	59,025
Oct	37,512	42,769	49,482	60,517
Nov	37,627	43,247	48,624	61,976
Dec	34,447	43,271	48,408	57,995

1924–1927

	1924	1925	1926	1927
Jan	57,362	61,361	60,808	56,663
Feb	61,609	63,352	66,179	61,967
Mar	63,228	62,990	67,329	61,880
Apr	59,126	58,944	63,193	58,817
May	59,777	58,946	62,075	60,858
Jun	59,597	59,683	64,856	59,494
Jul	58,708	58,037	61,478	56,549
Aug	60,303	60,143	63,487	57,386
Sep	62,812	64,107	64,600	61,032
Oct	65,471	66,542	67,923	66,507
Nov	64,256	65,957	66,125	62,963
Dec	64,284	63,437	60,775	61,456

Source: *Institut de Statistique*, Paris, and *Bulletin de la Statistique Générale de la France*. Alsace-Lorraine is included in 1923, 1924, 1925, but not in 1922.

STEEL PRODUCTION

1920 to 1925

In thousands of tons

	1920	1921	1922	1923	1924	1925
Jan	195	268	315	408	541	608
Feb	194	264	317	290	555	569
Mar	188	251	367	316	573	607
Apr	186	257	324	355	567	587
May	172	244	364	388	598	596
Jun	244	245	358	427	555	600
Jul	255	223	369	400	565	625
Aug	277	232	397	452	582	617
Sep	300	236	407	446	598	632
Oct	324	260	430	476	609	668
Nov	314	277	410	493	558	647
Dec	312	302	415	526	605	...

Production of 1919 (in thousands of tons) was
1st semester 1,004   2nd semester 1,182

Figures from the Files of the *Institut de statistique de l'Université de Paris.*

INDEX OF QUOTATIONS OF 3 PER CENT BONDS OF SIX FRENCH RAILROADS

Base 1901–1910

Monthly

1923–1927

	1923	1924	1925	1926	1927
Jan	70.5	66.1	52.7	50.8	62.9
Feb	70.3	66.0	47.1	51.8	60.6
Mar	72.0	64.3	51.7	49.9	70.7
Apr	70.5	64.2	52.3	49.0	...
May	70.2	61.5	48.4	49.5	...
Jun	70.0	62.3	44.4	47.7	...
Jul	70.7	63.9	55.7	48.9	...
Aug	71.5	64.3	52.9	49.7	...
Sep	70.5	59.6	52.7	48.9	...
Oct	71.8	58.4	49.3	51.9	...
Nov	66.1	53.6	44.2	55.2	...
Dec	65.6	53.0	46.7	59.8	...

Source: *Bulletin de la statistique générale de la France,* 1923-27.

THREE PER CENT *RENTES* ON THE PARIS *BOURSE*

Relative Price, Base 1901–1910

1919 to 1922

On the 15th of the Month

	1919	1920	1921	1922
Jan	65.0	59.8	60.2	57.4
Feb	65.5	59.0	59.7	58.7
Mar	64.3	60.0	59.4	58.2
Apr	63.8	58.1	57.4	58.9
May	63.3	60.8	58.4	58.9
Jun	64.0	57.9	57.3	58.9
Jul	62.5	59.8	57.6	60.2
Aug	62.4	57.2	57.6	61.5
Sep	62.6	55.3	57.3	61.3
Oct	61.6	56.5	55.3	59.6
Nov	61.3	57.4	56.0	60.7
Dec	60.7	50.5	55.8	60.2

Figures for January and February are interpolated from a series taken from Morgan & Co., Paris, Unpublished Statistical Papers. An adjustment of .50 is made because their quotations are slightly lower where figures are given for the same date.

Source: *Institut de statistique générale de la France. Bulletin de la statistique générale de la France.*

1923–1927

	1923	1924	1925	1926	1927
Jan	59.2	55.1	49.4	50.2	55.6
Feb	59.8	57.6	49.1	49.8	53.3
Mar	58.4	56.1	47.7	48.3	58.9
Apr	58.9	54.7	45.9	48.1	...
May	58.9	53.5	45.5	48.7	...
Jun	56.7	53.7	43.8	48.2	...
Jul	58.9	53.0	50.7	48.5	...
Aug	58.6	54.6	47.2	50.9	...
Sep	58.1	53.4	48.9	49.4	...
Oct	56.8	51.0	46.9	50.7	...
Nov	55.6	51.5	46.8	50.9	...
Dec	54.3	50.8	50.9	56.1	...

INDEX OF VALUES OF 13 BANK SHARES

Base 1901–1910

Monthly

1923–1927

	1923	1924	1925	1926	1927
Jan	150	180	160	183	238
Feb	162	184	153	178	247
Mar	157	169	155	172	277
Apr	157	168	152	176	...
May	158	165	145	178	...
Jun	162	168	142	186	...
Jul	165	172	150	222	...
Aug	167	172	151	233	...
Sep	165	173	154	235	...
Oct	167	171	148	223	...
Nov	172	167	147	217	...
Dec	176	162	185	220	...

Source: *Bulletin de la statistique générale de la France.*

SECURITY VALUES
SUEZ CANAL

Relatives, Base 1901-1910

Monthly

1923–1927

	1923	1924	1925	1926	1927
Jan	176	229	379	588	609
Feb	183	314	442	571	621
Mar	176	227	418	585	585
Apr	190	251	441	587	...
May	195	307	459	617	...
Jun	204	317	562	721	...
Jul	210	331	512	781	...
Aug	221	326	534	640	...
Sep	202	334	510	740	...
Oct	198	366	554	712	...
Nov	216	344	578	599	...
Dec	224	385	622	599	...

Source: *Bulletin de la statistique générale de la France,* 1923-27.

INDEX OF 23 INDUSTRIAL STOCKS

Relatives, Base 1901-1910

Monthly

1923–1927

	1923	1924	1925	1926	1927
Jan	194	265	255	252	301
Feb	201	282	251	257	305
Mar	196	254	254	247	331
Apr	201	258	255	247	...
May	204	260	242	253	...
Jun	217	260	248	277	...
Jul	229	270	264	325	...
Aug	237	268	264	307	...
Sep	225	269	258	324	...
Oct	231	276	252	313	...
Nov	244	265	258	285	...
Dec	248	258	261	273	...

Source: *Bulletin de la statistique générale de la France*, 1926-27.

SHARES OF TEN METALLURGICAL COMPANIES

Index of Quotations

Relatives, Base 1901-1910

1919–1925

	1919	1920	1921	1922	1923	1924	1925
Jan	179	220	190	143	185	184	124
Feb	169	225	169	133	172	179	117
Mar	163	268	172	129	170	185	115
Apr	162	281	169	121	171	158	109
May	178	280	156	126	163	159	109
Jun	173	252	142	121	155	149	103
Jul	170	248	132	116	175	150	114
Aug	175	238	156	132	193	151	122
Sep	189	219	151	136	186	147	116
Oct	215	202	149	141	177	149	111
Nov	223	188	144	150	170	136	106
Dec	223	197	148	154	175	120	104

Source: *Institut de Statistique de l'Université de Paris.*

VALUE OF FRENCH SECURITIES FLOATED ON THE PARIS BOURSE

(In millions of francs)

1924–1927

	1924			1925		
	Actions	*Obligations*	Total	*Actions*	*Obligations*	Total
Jan	195.8	3053.9	3249.7	206.8	23.0	229.8
Feb	222.9	34.3	257.2	204.4	11.4	215.8
Mar	480.7	114.8	595.5	305.8	40.2	346.0
Apr	275.7	49.9	325.6	192.8	121.2	314.0
May	327.4	167.0	494.4	351.3	62.5	413.8
Jun	320.0	487.5	807.5	394.8	269.4	664.2
Jul	210.7	44.8	255.5	149.9	33.6	183.5
Aug	119.6	10.1	129.7	102.1	16.3	118.4
Sep	358.4	142.4	500.8	150.7	23.6	174.3
Oct	370.0	99.7	469.7	117.5	490.0	607.3
Nov	361.4	24.5	385.9	235.8	22.0	257.8
Dec	404.2	14.8	419.0	197.9	10.3	208.2

	1926			1927		
	Actions	*Obligations*	Total	*Actions*	*Obligations*	Total
Jan	141.7	123.3	265.0	225.0	201.2	426.2
Feb	213.3	142.7	356.0	232.4	18.7	251.1
Mar	264.9	95.7	360.6	458.5	182.1	640.6
Apr	199.6	38.1	237.7	318.5	121.0	439.5
May	310.6	902.9	1213.5	570.5	774.3	1344.9
Jun	284.5	211.6	495.9	381.2	207.7	588.9
Jul	161.1	113.7	274.8	219.1	296.5	515.6
Aug	254.3	9.7	264.0	182.8	142.5	325.4
Sep	157.2	15.9	173.1	172.3	226.8	399.1
Oct	247.8	94.4	342.2	498.3	478.0	976.3
Nov	518.2	131.7	649.9	293.2	325.4	618.5
Dec	266.6	41.3	307.9	595.8	394.5	990.3

Source: *Bulletin de la statistique générale de la France*, 1924-1927.

WHOLESALE PRICES

(July, 1914 = 100)

	1914	1915	1916	1917	1918	1919	1920
Jan	....	....	....	....	319.5	355	497
Feb	....	....	....	....	326.1	348	533
Mar	....	132.3	189.9	233.6	334.0	344	566
Apr	....	....	....	....	340.5	339	600
May	....	....	....	....	342.6	332	562
Jun	....	140.3	192.4	271.8	335.7	336	503
Jul	100.0	....	....	....	344.5	356	506
Aug	....	....	....	....	357.8	355	512
Sep	102.2	147.5	192.7	285.9	362.7	367	537
Oct	....	....	....	....	367.6	390	512
Nov	....	....	....	....	365.5	413	470
Dec	112.8	166.7	207.8	279.0	360.4	432	444

	1921	1922	1923	1924	1925	1926	1927
Jan	415	320	395	505	525	647	635
Feb	385	313	431	555	526	649	645
Mar	367	314	433	510	524	645	655
Apr	354	320	423	459	523	664	650
May	336	323	415	468	531	702	642
Jun	332	332	417	475	554	754	636
Jul	337	332	415	491	569	854	633
Aug	339	338	421	487	569	785	631
Sep	351	336	433	496	567	804	613
Oct	338	344	429	507	584	767	600
Nov	339	359	452	514	618	700	607
Dec	333	370	468	518	646	641	617

Source: *Bulletin de la statistique générale de la France*, April, 1919, p. 296; October, 1918, p. 145; October, 1919, p. 206.

RETAIL PRICES

(July, 1914 = 100)

	1914	1915	1916	1917	1918	1919	1920
Jan	...	...	...	...	...	248	290
Feb	...	122	137	139	191	226	297
Mar	...	...	...	...	...	248	339
Apr	...	...	...	...	...	257	358
May	...	116	135	147	218	268	378
Jun	...	...	...	...	...	263	369
Jul	100	...	...	...	...	261	373
Aug	...	122	132	183	206	238	373
Sep	...	...	...	...	...	259	407
Oct	...	...	...	...	...	283	420
Nov	...	120	138	184	237	280	426
Dec	...	...	...	...	...	285	424

	1921	1922	1923	1924	1925	1926	1927
Jan	410	319	309	376	408	480	592
Feb	382	307	316	384	410	495	585
Mar	358	294	321	392	415	497	581
Apr	328	304	320	380	409	503	580
May	317	317	325	378	418	522	589
Jun	312	307	331	370	422	544	580
Jul	306	297	321	360	421	574	557
Aug	317	289	328	366	423	587	539
Sep	329	291	339	374	431	590	532
Oct	331	290	349	383	433	624	520
Nov	326	297	355	396	444	621	500
Dec	323	305	365	404	463	599	523

Source: *Bulletin de la statistique générale de la France,* April, 1918, p. 260; April, 1919, p. 310; October, 1919, p. 206.

WHOLESALE PRICES

Weekly

July, 1926, to December, 1927

1926			1927				
Jul	3	786	Jan	1	640	Jul 2	632
	10	810		8	639	9	628
	17	837		15	641	16	631
	24	848		22	640	23	633
	31	854		29	636	30	633
Aug	7	775	Feb	5	635	Aug 6	628
	14	789		12	640	13	629
	21	784		19	643	20	632
	28	786		26	647	27	632
Sep	4	779	Mar	5	650	Sep 3	628
	11	785		12	656	10	627
	18	794		19	654	17	626
	25	798		26	651	24	617
Oct	2	803	Apr	2	653	Oct 1	613
	9	791		9	650	8	610
	16	791		16	648	15	610
	23	782		23	652	22	603
	30	767		30	650	29	600
Nov	6	746	May	7	647	Nov 5	602
	13	736		14	647	12	602
	20	710		21	646	19	603
	27	700		28	643	26	606
Dec	4	660	Jun	4	643	Dec 3	613
	11	648		11	638	10	613
	18	640		18	635	17	610
	25	640		25	637	24	612
						31	617

Source: *Bulletin de la statistique générale de la France, Supplément mensuel*, 1926, 1927, and January, 1928.

INDEX NUMBER OF WHOLESALE PRICES

General and by Classes

of the *Bulletin de la Statistique Générale de la France.*

(Base 1901–1910 = 100)

1922

End of Month	General Index	Foodstuffs Average	Vegetable	Animal	Sugar Coffee Cocoa	Average	Mineral Metal	Textiles	Miscel.
Jan	363	349	347	364	325	373	309	424	385
Feb	354	349	345	358	337	359	290	404	376
Mar	355	367	342	402	345	346	290	382	361
Apr	363	388	372	427	339	343	294	374	356
May	366	387	371	427	336	349	299	395	356
Jun	376	395	381	429	354	361	306	436	355
Jul	376	382	351	423	359	371	318	459	359
Aug	383	379	351	417	357	387	330	493	366
Sep	381	368	335	408	353	391	334	495	375
Oct	390	362	339	402	329	412	370	521	381
Nov	407	384	346	430	366	426	366	548	399
Dec	418	404	360	457	386	430	373	553	401

(Industrial Materials columns: Average, Mineral Metal, Textiles, Miscel.)

Source: *Bulletin de la statistique générale de la France, 1922, January, 1923.*

INDEX NUMBER OF WHOLESALE PRICES

General and by Classes

of the *Bulletin de la Statistique Générale de la France*

(1914 = 100)

1923

End of Month	General	Foodstuffs				Industrial Materials			
	Index	Average	Vegetable	Animal	Sugar Coffee Cocoa	Average	Mineral Metal	Textiles	Miscel.
Jan	395	361	313	376	412	427	385	499	406
Feb	431	395	322	406	519	465	444	517	441
Mar	433	390	324	400	505	473	474	506	449
Apr	423	387	313	399	511	459	435	496	447
May	415	378	302	395	498	451	419	502	433
Jun	417	382	346	387	459	451	409	509	436
Jul	415	377	330	380	467	449	419	492	438
Aug	421	376	322	390	450	464	440	520	441
Sep	433	401	332	408	526	462	429	520	444
Oct	429	386	343	402	448	467	438	539	442
Nov	452	404	358	414	487	494	461	592	456
Dec	468	422	375	437	493	509	477	613	466

For the first nine months these figures were converted from the original figures in the *Bulletin de la statistique Générale* on the base 1901-1910.

INDEX NUMBER OF WHOLESALE PRICES

General and by Classes

(1914 = 100)

1924

End of Month	General	Foodstuffs					Industrial Materials		
	Index	Average	Vegetable	Animal	Sugar Coffee Cocoa	Average	Mineral Metal	Textiles	Miscel.
Jan	505	441	399	437	550	560	525	693	500
Feb	555	484	441	444	682	617	592	745	555
Mar	510	455	434	430	563	558	488	678	529
Apr	459	423	392	424	491	492	431	594	467
May	468	425	423	401	488	506	440	654	458
Jun	475	428	421	406	492	517	456	650	474
Jul	491	436	416	423	514	539	479	677	493
Aug	487	431	408	427	492	536	474	672	491
Sep	496	440	425	441	469	545	458	704	502
Oct	507	445	451	434	458	562	484	701	526
Nov	514	449	460	442	437	572	498	719	527
Dec	518	447	457	446	423	581	523	722	530

INDEX NUMBER OF WHOLESALE PRICES

General and by Classes

(1914 = 100)

1925

End of Month	General	Foodstuffs				Average	Industrial Materials		
	Index	Average	Vegetable	Animal	Sugar Coffee Cocoa		Mineral Metal	Textiles	Miscel.
Jan	525	455	484	435	437	587	516	717	552
Feb	526	457	482	429	464	586	526	715	547
Mar	524	450	465	433	452	590	505	724	561
Apr	523	449	469	429	448	589	508	731	553
May	531	470	503	447	446	584	510	705	557
Jun	554	486	529	448	477	614	550	739	577
Jul	569	497	514	480	498	631	562	755	597
Aug	569	490	491	480	513	638	577	762	601
Sep	567	482	485	467	507	643	581	761	609
Oct	584	480	490	466	492	675	651	763	626
Nov	618	500	516	476	515	722	674	875	658
Dec	646	528	531	514	542	751	692	898	697

INDEX NUMBER OF WHOLESALE PRICES

General and by Classes

1914 = 100

1926

	General	Foodstuffs		Sugar Coffee Cocoa	Industrial				National	Imports
	Average	Vegetables	Animal		Average	Mineral and Metal	Textile	Miscel.		
Jan	647	531	538	511	562	748	698	887	695	...	...
Feb	649	535	534	515	582	749	719	872	693	...	...
Mar	645	537	539	516	580	740	718	862	680	...	...
Apr	664	561	583	514	624	753	726	876	696	...	...
May	702	597	637	525	673	794	757	933	971	...	...
Jun	754	646	731	533	717	848	838	971	781	...	...
Jul	854	703	788	552	861	985	1025	1147	863	...	1074
Aug	785	672	745	544	804	885	919	940	831	733	902
Sep	804	706	801	554	846	889	941	939	827	722	912
Oct	768	695	790	568	773	831	855	823	822	743	808
Nov	698	643	687	570	714	747	788	706	747	744	701
Dec	641	597	603	550	692	678	726	626	680	699	628

Source: *Bulletin de la statistique générale de la France, 1926, and January, 1927.*

INDEX NUMBER OF WHOLESALE PRICES
General and by Classes
1914 = 100
1927

	General	Foodstuffs			Sugar Coffee Cocoa	Average	Industrial Mineral and		Miscel.	National	Imports
		Average	Vegetables	Animal			Metal	Textile			
Jan	635	605	624	544	705	662	683	628	668	640	624
Feb	645	616	634	560	706	671	690	656	667	643	650
Mar	655	629	633	596	696	678	685	700	660	647	667
Apr	650	632	670	580	666	666	654	696	655	648	653
May	642	617	666	552	653	664	643	691	660	639	646
Jun	636	598	645	536	632	669	638	723	656	623	659
Jul	633	585	617	529	637	677	639	757	652	611	674
Aug	631	573	611	517	614	682	619	783	660	603	681
Sep	613	546	558	508	605	672	602	766	658	582	669
Oct	600	519	541	466	591	670	590	745	673	564	663
Nov	607	532	545	485	609	673	595	729	687	575	664
Dec	617	553	552	524	619	673	601	713	693	593	660

Source: *Le Pour et le contre, Le Bulletin de la statistique générale* and other periodicals.

COST OF LIVING

1922 to 1925

Index for Paris of the Statistique Générale

July 1914 = 100

			General Average				General Average
1920,	1st	quarter.......	295	1924,	1st	quarter......	365
	2nd	"	341		2nd	"	366
	3rd	"	363		3rd	"	367
	4th	"	370		4th	"	377
1921,	1st	quarter.......	338	1925,	1st	quarter.......	386
	2nd	"	307		2nd	"	390
	3rd	"	295		3rd	"	401
	4th	"	297		4th	"	421
1922,	1st	quarter.......	291	1926,	1st	quarter.......	451
	2nd	"	302		2nd	"	485
	3rd	"	289		3rd	"	539
	4th	"	300		4th	"	545
1923,	1st	quarter.......	324	1927,	1st	quarter.......	524
	2nd	"	334		2nd	"	525
	3rd	"	331		3rd	"	507
	4th	"	345		4th	"	498

Sources: *Bulletin de la Statistique générale,* Vol. xvi, No. 1, p. 56. *Le Pour et le contre,* 13 Feb, 1927, p. 139; 12 June, 1927, p. 521; 18 Sept, 1927, p. 790; 10 Oct, 1927, p. 874; 13 Jan, 1928, p. 66.

WHOLESALE PRICES

Quarterly

End of 1922 to 1926

Base 1901 to 1910

	1922	1923			
	4th	1st	2nd	3rd	4th
General average	405	475	474	479	509
Foodstuffs average	383	450	450	453	478
Raw material, average	422	495	493	500	535
Wheat	358	387	407	385	406
Flour	347	386	402	382	391
Rye	354	428	383	396	458
Barley	305	336	337	352	371
Oats	345	380	376	334	339
Corn (maize)	441	482	490	488	529
Potatoes	209	203	276	388	369
Rice	429	555	459	513	619
Average of the group	349	395	391	405	435
Beef 1st quality	354	371	451	436	451
Beef 2nd quality	339	351	466	435	447
Mutton 1st quality	485	506	518	515	546
Mutton 2nd quality	420	493	519	467	502
Pork	523	590	588	588	578
Salted meat	515	586	589	589	580
Butter	396	484	290	365	463
Cheese	405	459	422	442	539
Average of the group	430	480	481	480	513
Sugar, raw	590	963	1003	998	927
Sugar, refined	396	531	562	535	539
Coffee	287	319	285	288	341
Cocoa	170	182	171	167	161
Average of the group	361	499	505	497	492

45 Commodities used by the *Bulletin de la statistique générale* in their **index number.**

WHOLESALE PRICES

Quarterly (*Continued*)

	1922	1923			
	4th	1st	2nd	3rd	4th
Pig iron	351	546	617	589	589
Billets	334	438	461	435	433
Copper	264	335	316	317	311
Tin	327	431	405	427	513
Lead	470	594	511	542	662
Zinc	426	409	409	472	501
Coal	417	442	456	455	455
Average of the group..	370	468	453	463	495
Cotton	631	814	782	864	1155
Flax	616	681	639	635	658
Hemp	338	383	413	424	530
Jute	639	696	599	477	506
Wool	508	598	683	769	791
Silk	514	634	655	669	686
Average of the group..	541	634	628	640	721
Hides (salted)	283	345	350	307	306
Skins	219	226	223	241	253
Grease	329	401	383	421	455
Oil (colza)	544	686	702	699	720
Oil (linseed)	562	695	718	759	785
Alcohol	388	336	346	331	353
Petroleum	392	390	390	424	452
Soda carbonate	362	373	353	344	352
Soda nitrate	319	410	373	390	410
Benzol	713	773	873	818	802
Wood	564	593	607	607	620
Rubber	52	71	68	75	64
Average of the group..	394	442	449	451	464

WHOLESALE PRICES

Quarterly (Continued)

	1924				1925			
	1st	2nd	3rd	4th	1st	2nd	3rd	4th
General average ..	592	529	556	581	595	607	643	698
Foodstuffs average.	544	503	515	529	537	554	579	594
Raw material, average	630	550	589	623	641	650	695	780
Wheat	433	421	461	531	576	570	566	586
Flour	422	409	443	498	545	552	540	562
Rye	494	461	534	627	668	674	603	578
Barley	471	498	531	544	536	514	517	515
Oats	370	377	405	476	516	562	572	556
Corn (maize)	659	557	587	686	704	739	763	755
Potatoes	511	601	359	366	400	498	435	412
Rice	764	679	728	704	685	749	828	1013
Average of the group	515	500	506	554	579	607	603	622
Beef 1st quality...	466	522	520	539	524	561	574	552
Beef 2nd quality..	483	533	545	566	528	564	571	571
Mutton 1st quality	575	577	611	608	583	630	619	599
Mutton 2nd quality	542	521	558	571	538	575	552	570
Pork	588	553	581	547	525	557	684	663
Salted meat	580	545	573	544	516	557	653	631
Butter	504	354	381	464	537	416	437	516
Cheese	553	425	458	486	493	473	583	665
Average of the group	536	504	528	541	531	542	584	598
Sugar, raw	1216	947	869	624	678	715	773	734
Sugar, refined	634	536	517	432	424	439	467	455
Coffee	434	379	466	545	542	515	590	672
Cocoa	191	165	181	212	221	222	256	274
Average of the group	619	507	508	454	466	472	523	534

WHOLESALE PRICES

Quarterly (*Continued*)

	1924				1925			
	1st	2nd	3rd	4th	1st	2nd	3rd	4th
Pig iron	567	540	451	432	471	493	493	493
Billets	440	439	422	373	393	417	417	440
Copper	377	305	334	349	359	364	412	494
Tin	702	489	594	650	667	697	782	1028
Lead	882	649	770	947	931	898	1058	1233
Zinc	601	453	512	568	605	611	701	918
Coal	472	468	468	468	468	468	468	470
Average of the group	577	478	507	541	556	564	619	725
Cotton	1187	978	930	834	858	895	932	918
Flax	956	966	1119	1103	1023	880	966	960
Hemp	669	725	725	812	906	894	890	861
Jute	683	574	728	866	963	1221	1238	1719
Wool	1021	879	1005	1131	1028	909	903	1048
Silk	734	590	590	572	569	600	724	841
Average of the group	875	785	849	886	891	900	942	1058
Hides (salted) ...	388	303	324	425	440	418	446	477
Skins	267	253	280	337	331	310	338	353
Grease	557	404	498	558	541	566	616	702
Oil (colza)	955	817	876	964	1025	996	1101	1181
Oil, linseed	1020	793	918	898	969	1037	1145	1196
Alcohol	412	425	447	498	462	419	408	410
Petroleum	521	475	496	475	507	514	518	548
Soda carbonate ...	380	369	355	367	336	341	341	352
Soda nitrate	478	408	433	447	457	486	523	608
Benzol	797	777	747	773	967	1000	1027	1213
Wood	626	626	626	626	642	647	659	707
Rubber	68	54	67	71	97	156	261	342
Average of the group	539	475	506	539	564	574	615	674

Source: *Bulletin de la statistique générale de la France.*

WHOLESALE PRICES

Quarterly (*Continued*)

1926

	1st	2nd	3rd	4th
General average	732	800	922	795
Foodstuffs average	632	712	821	763
Raw material, average.....	813	870	1003	820
Wheat	641	790	979	847
Flour	620	769	979	882
Rye	609	799	1014	977
Barley	519	639	775	768
Oats	581	662	655	616
Corn (maize)	759	860	1012	833
Potatoes	436	595	582	701
Rice	1052	1201	1559	1111
Average of the group....	652	789	944	842
Beef 1st quality.........	587	621	606	621
Beef 2nd quality.........	585	636	621	600
Mutton 1st quality........	651	662	712	718
Mutton 2nd quality.......	582	556	646	651
Pork	747	838	888	831
Salted meat	679	733	733	643
Butter	563	488	588	748
Cheese	654	611	610	710
Average of the group....	631	643	675	690
Sugar, raw	850	954	1176	1064
Sugar, refined	497	546	726	755
Coffee	740	897	1049	740
Cocoa	289	378	511	446
Average of the group....	594	694	865	751

WHOLESALE PRICES

Quarterly (*Continued*)

1926

	1st	2nd	3rd	4th
Pig iron	571	613	819	857
Billets	493	545	652	618
Copper	528	605	720	527
Tin	1113	1267	1571	1227
Lead	1234	1267	1654	1138
Zinc	913	982	1185	868
Coal	520	561	662	730
Average of the group	768	834	1037	852
Cotton	950	1048	1239	693
Flax	953	1075	1185	813
Hemp	837	784	829	762
Jute	1845	1829	1704	1003
Wool	1029	1206	1445	1170
Silk	889	958	1110	907
Average of the group	1084	1150	1252	891
Hides (salted)	524	564	684	606
Skins	383	358	433	426
Grease	731	869	991	696
Oil (colza)	1194	1219	1419	1125
Oil (linseed)	1044	1081	1241	830
Alcohol	487	510	595	680
Petroleum	645	809	954	930
Soda carbonate	397	471	577	592
Soda nitrate	669	759	824	678
Benzol	1367	1380	1387	1440
Wood	754	797	977	1001
Rubber	248	210	214	175
Average of the group	704	752	858	765

FREQUENCY TABLE OF WHOLESALE PRICE RELATIVES

Fourth Quarter of 1922 to Fourth Quarter of 1926

Quarterly

Index by	1922	1923				1924			
Hundreds	4th	1st	2nd	3rd	4th	1st	2nd	3rd	4th
0	1	1	1	1	1	1	1	1	1
1	1	1	1	1	1	1	1	1	..
2	5	2	4	2	1	1	1	1	1
3	18	13	10	12	9	4	6	5	5
4	8	11	12	13	10	11	13	12	11
5	8	9	7	7	12	10	11	12	11
6	3	5	5	4	5	6	4	2	6
7	1	1	3	2	3	4	3	5	2
8	..	1	1	2	1	1	2	2	4
9	..	1	..	1	1	2	3	2	2
10	..	..	1	..	..	2	..	1	..
11	..	..	..	..	1	1	..	1	2
12	..	..	..	..	..	1	..	..	..
Total	45	45	45	45	45	45	45	45	45
General average	405	475	474	479	509	592	529	556	581

Index by	1925				1926			
Hundreds	1st	2nd	3rd	4th	1st	2nd	3rd	4th
0	1	..	..	..	..	..	..	..
1	..	1	1	..	..	..	..	1
2	1	1	2	1	2	1	1	..
3	4	3	2	3	2	2	..	..
4	8	10	9	8	4	2	1	2
5	15	12	11	11	10	7	5	2
6	6	6	6	5	8	8	8	11
7	1	3	5	4	5	7	5	9
8	1	4	2	2	3	5	4	8
9	5	2	3	3	3	3	5	3
10	3	2	2	3	3	3	3	3
11	..	..	2	2	2	..	4	4
12	..	1	1	2	1	5	2	1
13	..	..	..	..	1	1	1	1
14	..	..	..	..	..	..	2	1
15	..	..	..	..	..	..	2	..
16	..	..	..	..	..	..	1	..
17	..	..	..	1	..	..	1	..
18	..	..	..	..	1	1	..	..
Total	45	45	45	45	45	45	45	45
General average	595	607	643	698	732	800	922	795

PURCHASING POWER PARITIES

1914–1927

Year	Quarter	Francs per Dollar	Year	Quarter	Francs per Dollar
1914........	1st	5.29	1916........	1st	8.21
	2nd	5.29		2nd	8.14
	3rd	5.39		3rd	7.85
	4th	5.71		4th	7.54
1915........	1st	6.56	1917........	1st	7.28
	2nd	7.08		2nd	7.43
	3rd	7.36		3rd	7.39
	4th	8.03		4th	8.04

PURCHASING POWER PARITIES

Francs per Dollar

	1918	1919	1920	1921	1922
Jan	8.82	9.06	10.83	12.41	11.79
Feb	8.89	9.13	11.67	12.21	11.25
Mar	9.06	8.89	12.30	12.03	11.21
Apr	9.08	8.65	12.44	12.15	11.39
May	9.14	8.34	11.55	11.76	11.10
Jun	8.93	8.40	10.52	11.86	11.24
Jul	8.91	8.53	10.67	12.14	10.87
Aug	9.07	8.32	11.25	12.08	11.07
Sep	9.02	8.89	12.06	12.64	11.15
Oct	9.24	9.38	12.33	12.08	11.60
Nov	9.14	9.67	12.20	12.21	11.70
Dec	8.97	9.83	12.59	12.08	12.03

	1923	1924	1925	1926	1927
Jan	12.85	17.01	16.99	21.45	22.02
Feb	13.93	18.55	16.96	21.65	22.79
Mar	13.83	17.24	16.84	22.02	23.31
Apr	13.53	15.77	17.32	22.74	23.36
May	13.51	16.18	17.72	23.93	23.05
Jun	13.85	16.64	18.23	25.64	22.84
Jul	13.97	16.95	18.39	29.32	22.58
Aug	14.27	16.47	18.34	27.25	22.22
Sep	14.27	16.92	18.34	27.66	
Oct	14.27	16.95	19.17	26.52	
Nov	15.11	17.04	20.25	24.24	
Dec	15.75	16.75	21.39	22.53	

FRENCH FOREIGN COMMERCE

Value and Weight of Exports and Imports

Yearly, 1913–1927

(000 omitted)

	Value			Weight		
	Export	Import	Excess	Export	Import	Excess
1913....	6,880	8,421	— 1,541	220,745	442,204	—221,559
1914....	4,869	6,402	— 1,533	126,638	334,346	—107,708
1915....	3,937	11,036	— 7,099	40,911	330,493	—289,582
1916....	6,215	20,640	—14,425	37,300	400,906	—363,606
1917....	6,013	27,554	—21,541	30,111	348,326	—318,215
1918....	4,723	22,306	—17,583	37,182	293,517	—256,335
1919....	11,880	35,799	—23,919	55,644	384,472	—328,828
1920....	26,895	49,905	—23,010	128,552	505,379	—376,827
1921....	19,773	22,068	— 2,295	160,350	400,621	—240,271
1922....	21,379	23,930	— 2,551	226,429	514,182	—287,753
1923....	30,433	32,689	— 2,256	249,099	548,647	—299,548
1924....	41,468	39,928	+ 1,540	293,871	565,914	—272,043
1925....	45,755	44,095	+ 1,660	303,871	474,433	—170,562
1926....	59,535	59,615	+ 20	324,291	455,134	—130,843
1927....	55,225	52,853	+ 2,372	380,510	493,589	—113,079

Source: *Statistique Mensuelle du Commerce Extérieur de la France.*

FRENCH FOREIGN TRADE

1914, 1915

Monthly

(000 omitted)

1914

	Value (francs)			Weight (metric quintals)		
	Imports	Exports	Excess	Imports	Exports	Excess
Jan ...	739,357	403,914	—335,461	33,895	11,651	—22,244
Feb ...	773,593	592,543	—181,050	40,572	16,272	—24,300
Mar ..	778,280	629,803	—148,477	41,438	13,348	—28,090
Apr ...	722,915	587,869	—135,046	37,500	23,014	—14,486
May ..	685,263	622,283	— 62,980	37,528	19,010	—18,518
Jun ...	701,368	545,786	—155,582	40,748	17,973	—22,775
Jul ...	591,313	481,716	—109,597	28,397	8,348	—20,049
Aug ...	240,773	230,456	— 10,317	11,996	4,038	— 7,958
Sep ...	256,127	155,291	—100,836	11,200	3,155	— 8,045
Oct ...	239,523	183,403	— 56,120	14,690	3,099	—11,591
Nov ..	266,781	170,127	— 96,654	15,067	2,497	—12,570
Dec ...	406,858	265,643	—141,215	21,315	4,233	—17,082

1915

	Value (francs)			Weight (metric quintals)		
	Imports	Exports	Excess	Imports	Exports	Excess
Jan ...	549,967	197,354	—262,613	17,276	2,376	—14,900
Feb ...	697,372	284,569	—412,803	20,737	3,087	—17,650
Mar ..	865,021	343,010	—522,011	26,805	4,026	—22,779
Apr ...	925,990	334,055	—591,935	25,996	4,137	—21,859
May ..	833,839	320,790	—513,049	25,754	3,328	—22,426
Jun ...	1,044,943	327,750	—717,193	29,006	4,128	—24,878
Jul ...	990,149	312,266	—677,883	30,662	3,303	—27,359
Aug ...	1,064,041	337,974	—726,067	31,423	4,133	—27,290
Sep ...	987,555	335,120	—652,435	31,563	2,855	—28,708
Oct ...	1,031,548	334,350	—697,198	32,492	2,831	—29,661
Nov ..	853,062	388,989	—464,073	28,665	3,283	—25,382
Dec ...	1,283,307	421,142	—861,165	30,114	3,424	—26,690

Source: U. S. Senate, *Foreign Currency and Exchange Investigation,* vol. i, p. 483.

FRENCH FOREIGN TRADE

Monthly
(000 omitted)
1916

	Value (francs)			Weight (metric quintals)		
	Imports	Exports	Excess	Imports	Exports	Excess
Jan ...	1,180,417	324,614	— 855,803	26,178	2,660	—23,518
Feb ...	1,351,526	471,916	— 879,610	28,236	3,133	—25,103
Mar ..	1,382,322	485,716	— 896,606	28,500	3,327	—25,173
Apr ...	1,571,139	521,092	—1,050,047	31,801	3,448	—28,353
May ..	1,694,452	460,418	—1,234,034	35,032	3,403	—31,629
Jun ...	1,525,574	555,575	— 969,999	34,907	3,495	—31,412
Jul ...	1,898,045	464,112	—1,433,933	36,696	3,044	—33,652
Aug ...	2,117,932	420,690	—1,697,242	38,862	2,845	—36,017
Sep ...	1,803,971	466,587	—1,337,384	38,069	2,672	—35,397
Oct ...	1,844,503	608,205	—1,236,298	37,645	2,946	—34,699
Nov ..	2,054,851	895,829	—1,159,022	30,787	3,370	—27,417
Dec ...	2,215,687	539,840	—1,675,847	34,193	2,957	—31,236

1917

	Value (francs)			Weight (metric quintals)		
	Imports	Exports	Excess	Imports	Exports	Excess
Jan ...	2,179,304	372,999	—1,806,305	26,454	2,040	—24,414
Feb ...	2,644,904	446,377	—2,198,527	29,405	2,373	—27,032
Mar ..	3,035,549	575,241	—2,460,308	31,730	2,621	—29,109
Apr ...	1,764,479	484,615	—1,279,864	25,625	2,746	—22,879
May ..	2,069,645	531,021	—1,538,624	30,494	2,890	—27,604
Jun ...	2,482,513	573,336	—1,909,177	32,057	2,701	—29,356
Jul ...	2,796,251	656,960	—2,139,291	35,060	2,661	—32,399
Aug ...	2,949,682	676,653	—2,273,029	33,776	2,709	—31,068
Sep ...	1,829,308	429,302	—1,400,006	27,169	2,752	—24,417
Oct ...	2,146,980	420,309	—1,726,671	25,350	2,978	—22,372
Nov ..	1,868,459	398,687	—1,469,772	25,806	1,727	—24,079
Dec ...	1,786,981	447,288	—1,339,693	25,400	1,913	—23,487

Source: U. S. Senate, *Foreign Currency and Exchange Investigation,* vol. i, p. 483.

FRENCH FOREIGN TRADE

Monthly

(000 omitted)

1918

	Value (francs)			Weight (metric quintals)		
	Imports	Exports	Excess	Imports	Exports	Excess
Jan ...	1,591,325	378,244	—1,213,081	19,522	2,338	—17,184
Feb ...	1,785,135	401,546	—1,383,589	22,416	3,402	—19,014
Mar ..	1,996,912	458,259	—1,538,653	21,972	3,168	—18,804
Apr ...	1,839,064	348,582	—1,490,482	25,555	3,753	—21,802
May ..	1,729,254	468,429	—1,260,825	25,656	3,601	—22,055
Jun ...	1,864,614	424,041	—1,440,573	23,666	3,505	—20,161
Jul ...	1,964,475	408,797	—1,555,678	29,705	4,984	—24,721
Aug ...	1,852,164	449,860	—1,402,304	27,148	3,012	—24,136
Sep ...	1,615,545	376,185	—1,239,360	23,660	3,852	—19,808
Oct ...	1,685,375	343,245	—1,342,130	18,775	2,563	—16,212
Nov ..	1,580,370	338,413	—1,241,957	21,295	1,534	—19,761
Dec ...	2,802,144	327,135	—2,475,000	34,147	1,460	—32,687

1919

	Value (francs)			Weight (metric quintals)		
	Imports	Exports	Excess	Imports	Exports	Excess
Jan ...	1,739,985	490,465	—1,249,520	17,534	1,667	—15,867
Feb ...	2,472,686	508,657	—1,964,029	22,768	1,299	—21,469
Mar ..	3,195,639	666,456	—2,529,183	26,601	2,073	—24,528
Apr ...	3,015,630	599,391	—2,416,239	24,243	2,049	—22,194
May ..	2,560,573	711,517	—1,849,056	24,327	2,705	—21,622
Jun ...	3,128,978	790,711	—2,338,267	31,626	2,114	—29,512
Jul ...	2,899,449	1,009,205	—1,890,244	31,459	3,313	—28,146
Aug ...	2,730,406	966,816	—1,763,590	29,785	2,802	—26,983
Sep ...	2,824,074	960,999	—1,863,075	30,110	2,661	—27,449
Oct ...	2,830,350	1,028,933	—1,801,417	30,307	3,608	—26,699
Nov ..	2,811,659	928,850	—1,882,809	22,278	2,776	—19,502
Dec ...	5,589,838	3,217,600	—2,372,238	93,434	28,577	—64,857

Source: U. S. Senate, *Foreign Currency and Exchange Investigation*, vol. i, p. 484.

FRENCH FOREIGN TRADE

Monthly

(000 omitted)

1920

	Value (francs)			Weight (metric quintals)		
	Imports	Exports	Excess	Imports	Exports	Excess
Jan ...	3,577,085	1,245,400	—2,331,685	26,622	4,492	—22,130
Feb ...	4,454,448	2,150,784	—2,303,664	34,387	10,259	—24,128
Mar ..	5,225,921	2,100,860	—3,125,061	42,084	8,989	—33,095
Apr ...	4,865,959	2,110,093	—2,755,066	39,003	10,364	—28,639
May ..	4,005,824	1,842,674	—2,163,150	39,102	7,578	—31,524
Jun ...	4,417,561	2,805,512	—1,612,049	43,908	13,553	—30,355
Jul ...	4,102,825	2,097,415	—2,005,410	50,276	10,567	—39,709
Aug ...	3,958,570	2,881,016	—1,077,554	42,240	12,786	—29,454
Sep ...	3,697,498	2,413,141	—1,284,357	42,825	10,929	—31,896
Oct ...	3,593,510	3,016,917	— 576,593	44,726	12,771	—31,955
Nov ..	3,677,284	1,962,130	—1,715,154	44,617	14,587	—30,030
Dec ...	4,328,412	2,268,096	—2,060,316	55,589	11,677	—43,912

1921

	Value (francs)			Weight (metric quintals)		
	Imports	Exports	Excess	Imports	Exports	Excess
Jan ...	2,374,333	1,781,552	—592,781	40,791	12,065	—28,726
Feb ...	1,708,457	1,646,703	— 61,754	28,492	15,868	—12,624
Mar ..	1,813,182	1,595,295	—217,887	29,861	11,891	—17,970
Apr ...	1,731,271	1,814,977	+ 83,706	28,611	12,483	—16,128
May ..	1,501,551	1,546,349	+ 44,798	24,675	12,455	—12,220
Jun ...	1,566,223	1,645,485	+ 79,262	22,574	14,402	— 8,172
Jul ...	1,384,253	1,514,008	+129,755	24,520	13,492	—11,028
Aug ...	1,594,127	1,624,476	+ 30,349	30,366	11,962	—18,404
Sep ...	1,951,841	1,647,221	—304,620	42,121	12,965	—29,156
Oct ...	2,103,888	1,607,958	—495,930	37,667	13,383	—24,284
Nov ..	1,761,358	1,640,618	—120,740	42,214	15,562	—26,652
Dec ...	2,577,424	1,707,870	—869,554	48,729	13,822	—34,907

Source: U. S. Senate, *Foreign Currency and Exchange Investigation,* vol. i, p. 484.

FRENCH FOREIGN TRADE

Monthly

(000 omitted)

1922

	Value (francs)			Weight (metric quintals)		
	Imports	Exports	Excess	Imports	Exports	Excess
Jan ...	1,459,526	1,535,587	+ 76,061	33,810	15,543	—18,267
Feb ...	1,833,409	1,739,454	— 93,955	41,047	15,186	—25,861
Mar ..	1,940,844	1,763,180	—177,664	44,544	15,934	—28,610
Apr ...	1,751,338	1,897,481	+146,143	37,971	17,726	—20,245
May ..	1,798,421	1,778,264	— 20,157	43,868	15,482	—28,386
Jun ...	1,851,983	1,551,130	—300,853	43,128	18,003	—25,125
Jul ...	1,996,607	1,532,357	—464,250	42,203	17,372	—24,831
Aug ...	1,973,982	1,806,432	—167,550	44,708	17,968	—26,740
Sep ...	1,881,123	1,858,758	— 22,365	41,517	24,151	—17,366
Oct ...	2,081,481	2,071,825	— 9,656	45,354	24,743	—20,611
Nov ..	2,348,843	1,683,405	—665,438	45,761	20,245	—25,516
Dec ...	3,012,771	2,319,054	—693,717	50,271	19,046	—31,225

1923

	Value (francs)			Weight (metric quintals)		
	Imports	Exports	Excess	Imports	Exports	Excess
Jan ...	2,135,999	1,802,590	—333,409	41,077	18,943	—22,134
Feb ...	2,340,428	2,378,128	+ 37,709	38,600	24,903	—13,697
Mar ..	2,479,000	2,380,430	— 98,570	41,019	18,226	—22,793
Apr ..	2,549,583	2,441,522	—108,061	41,324	15,108	—26,216
May ..	2,524,206	2,663,896	+139,690	45,102	18,761	—26,341
Jun ...	2,630,268	2,482,297	—147,911	48,994	17,836	—31,158
Jul ...	2,632,268	2,412,361	—219,907	49,246	19,171	—30,075
Aug ...	2,625,243	2,486,351	—138,892	48,152	21,741	—26,411
Sep ...	2,604,026	2,483,855	—120,171	50,473	21,457	—29,016
Oct ...	3,060,415	2,808,235	—252,180	43,834	21,701	—22,133
Nov ..	3,160,504	2,941,386	—219,118	49,451	23,089	—26,362
Dec ...	3,826,834	3,113,874	—712,960	51,650	26,629	—25,021

Source: U. S. Senate, *Foreign Currency and Exchange Investigation*, vol. i, p. 484.

FRENCH FOREIGN TRADE

(000,000 omitted)

1924

	Value (francs)			Weight (metric quintals)		
	Imports	Exports	Excess	Imports	Exports	Excess
Jan	2,888	2,700	—188	39,268	17,679	—21,589
Feb	3,714	3,918	+204	43,952	23,254	—20,698
Mar	3,623	4,355	+732	48,219	24,842	—23,377
Apr	3,292	4,027	+735	49,244	24,996	—24,248
May	3,183	3,369	+186	54,849	21,708	—23,141
Jun	3,179	2,922	—257	45,818	24,676	—21,142
Jul	3,100	3,014	— 86	54,097	23,171	—30,926
Aug	3,072	2,967	—105	44,568	24,984	—19,584
Sep	3,157	3,184	+ 27	47,323	27,088	—20,235
Oct	3,398	3,532	+144	46,601	26,827	—19,774
Nov	3,415	3,433	+ 18	43,597	29,489	—14,108
Dec	4,118	4,042	— 76	47,314	25,124	—22,190

1925

	Value (francs)			Weight (metric quintals)		
	Imports	Exports	Excess	Imports	Exports	Excess
Jan	3,173	3,563	+390	35,215	23,324	—11,891
Feb	3,346	3,595	+249	39,723	28,429	—11,294
Mar	3,307	3,762	+455	39,471	27,078	—12,393
Apr	3,051	3,558	+507	36,577	22,969	—13,608
May	2,969	3,640	+671	38,195	24,294	—13,901
Jun	2,991	3,507	+516	37,304	25,778	—11,526
Jul	3,034	3,484	+450	37,092	24,418	—12,674
Aug	3,297	3,258	— 35	38,088	22,930	—15,158
Sep	4,317	3,850	—467	46,506	26,673	—19,833
Oct	4,476	4,375	—101	46,434	24,526	—21,908
Nov	4,574	4,193	—381	39,584	25,365	—14,219
Dec	5,446	4,629	—817	40,067	26,476	—13,591

FRENCH FOREIGN TRADE

(000,000 omitted)

1926

	Value (francs)			Weight (metric quintals)		
	Imports	Exports	Excess	Imports	Exports	Excess
Jan	4,483	3,868	—615	36,294	22,713	—13,581
Feb	5,245	4,409	—836	41,453	27,518	—13,872
Mar	5,095	4,960	—135	39,461	29,185	—10,276
Apr	5,020	4,353	—667	41,829	25,932	—15,897
May	4,390	4,461	+ 71	36,070	26,250	— 9,820
Jun	5,181	4,672	—509	38,940	27,450	—11,490
Jul	5,016	5,244	+228	36,080	28,690	— 7,390
Aug	5,235	5,543	+308	38,830	28,599	—10,231
Sep	4,625	5,197	+572	36,488	26,290	—10,198
Oct	5,106	6,103	+997	34,884	26,890	— 7,994
Nov	4,994	5,329	+335	34,417	26,693	— 7,724
Dec	5,123	5,395	+272	40,389	28,088	—12,301

1927

	Value (francs)			Weight (metric quintals)		
	Imports	Exports	Excess	Imports	Exports	Excess
Jan	4,079	4,708	+619	40,642	27,914	—12,728
Feb	4,780	4,597	—183	47,804	32,093	—15,111
Mar	4,414	4,694	+280	43,633	29,515	—14,118
Apr	4,298	4,255	— 43	43,329	28,353	—14,976
May	4,989	4,281	—708	46,096	33,854	—12,242
Jun	4,558	4,417	—141	39,056	31,587	— 7,469
Jul	4,068	4,499	+431	36,544	33,017	— 3,527
Aug	3,771	4,287	+516	42,152	30,613	—11,539
Sep	3,572	4,545	+973	36,204	33,396	— 2,808
Oct	4,476	5,050	+574	40,947	33,776	— 7,171
Nev	4,632	4,871	+239	38,096	32,160	— 5,936
Dec	5,216	5,020	—106	39,083	34,232	— 4,851

ESTIMATES OF DEVASTATION

and Reconstruction Completed to 1924

	Devastated Number	Completed Number	Per Cent	To Be Completed Number	Per Cent
Population and Dwellings					
Houses	741,933	605,989	81.67	133,944	18.33
Temporary dwellings..	190,312	182,844	96.07	7,468	3.93
Population (Aug 1st, 1914, 4,650 thousands)	2,075,067	4,263,677	90.69	436,506	9.31
Agricultural Situation					
Land, releveled (acres)	8,170,630	7,268,600	88.96	902,030	11.04
Arable land (acres) ..	4,752,997	4,420,892	93.00	332,905	7.00
Cattle	834,933	529,940	63.47	304,993	36.53
Horses, donkeys, mules	375,393	299,697	79.83	75,696	20.17
Sheep and goats......	890,794	429,003	47.11	461,971	52.79
Hogs	331,656	183,720	55.39	147,936	44.61
Industrial Situation					
Factories and plants..	22,900	20,872	91.14	2,028	8.86
Coal mines and collieries	200	145	72.50	55	27.50
Public Utilities					
Highways and roads (miles)	36,472	36,321	72.16	10,151	27.84
Bridges and tunnels..	6,125	4,800	78.36	1,325	21.64
Trunk lines, rail (miles)	1,493	1,493	100.00	.....	....
Local railways (miles)	1,496	1,367	91.37	129	8.83
Local railways, tunnels, bridges and viaducts	998	888	88.97	110	11.03

1924—80 per cent completed.

Source: U. S. Consul General, Paris, *Reports;* compare E. Michel, *La situation financière et l'achèvement de la reconstitution, au 31 décembre, 1925* (Paris, 1925).

BIBLIOGRAPHY

JOURNALS AND PERIODICALS

Aftalion, Albert, *Monnaie, prix et change;* Sirey, Paris, 1927. (Most of the material here given appeared in the *Revue d'économie politique*, 1925-26.)

Allix, Edgar, *Traité élémentaire de la science des finances et de la législation financière française;* Rousseau, Paris, 1921.

—— "Les deux projets financiers devant le Parlement," *Revue politique et parlementaire*, January, 1926.

Allix, Edgar, and Lecerclé, Marcel, *L'Impôt sur le revenu;* Rousseau, Paris, 1926.

Angell, James W., *The Theory of International Prices;* Harvard University Press, Cambridge, Mass., 1926.

—— "Monetary Theory," *The Quarterly Journal of Economics*, 1925.

Arnauné, Auguste, *La Monnaie;* Seventh edition, Alcan, Paris, 1926.

Auld, George T., *Reparations and the Policy of Repudiation, Foreign Affairs*, September 15, 1923.

Baruch, Bernard, *The Making of the Reparations and Economic Sections of the Treaty;* Harpers, New York, 1920.

Batsell, W. R., *The Debt Settlement and the Future;* Lecram Press, Paris, 1927.

Bayart, Pierre, "La Stabilisation française;" *Revue des sciences économiques*, No. 3 (April, 1917, Liège).

Bérenger, Henry, "L'Accord franco-american sur les dettes de guerre," *L'Europe nouvelle*, 9th year, no. 429, May 8, 1926, Paris.

Bergmann, Karl, *History of Reparations;* E. Benn, London, 1927.

Bogart, E. L., *Direct and Indirect Costs of the Great War;* Oxford University Press, London, 1919.

Bonnet, George-Edgar, *Les Expériences monétaires contemporaines;* Collection Arnaud Colin, Paris, 1926.

Buty, Robert, *Le Vote du budget et l'amelioration des méthods du travail parlementaire;* Les Presses Universitaires, Paris, thesis, 1926.

Cahill, J. R., *The Economic Conditions in France, revised to June, 1924;* London, 1924. British Overseas Trade Report.

Cahill, J. R., *Economic and Industrial Conditions in France, 1925-1926;* London, 1927. British Overseas Trade Report.

Calmette, Germain, *Recueil de documents sur l'histoire des réparations, 1919-May 5, 1921;* A. Costes, Paris, 1924.

Casamajor, Jean, *Le Marché à terme des changes en France;* Dalloz, Paris, 1924.

Cassel, Gustav, *Money and Foreign Exchange After 1914;* Macmillan, New York, 1923.

Charbonnet, G., *La Politique financière de la Banque de France pendant la guerre;* Cadoret, Bordeaux, 1922.

Chéron, Henry, *Rapport au Sénat,* February 22, 1926, No. 84.

—— *Rapport au Sénat,* No. 225, April 4, 1926.

—— *Rapport au Sénat,* No. 656, December 10, 1926.

Clémentel, Etienne, *Inventaire de la situation financière au début de la treizième législature;* Imprimerie nationale, Paris, 1924.

Commerce Year Book, 1926, United States Department of Commerce, Washington, 1927.

Dausset, Louis, *L'Information,* noon edition, November 28, 1925.

Dawes Report, *Reparation,* Part V, World Peace Foundation, vol. vi, 1923, no. 5, Boston, 1925.

De Bernonville, L. Dugé, "Essaie d'un indice pondéré des prix de gros en France," *Bulletin de la statistique générale,* January-March, 1928.

de Bordes, J. van Walré, *The Austrian Crown;* P. S. King, London, 1924.

Décamps, Jules, *Les Changes étrangers;* Paris, 1922.

—— *La Situation monétaire et l'avenir du franc;* Speech to L'Union républicaine, December 19, 1924, Paris, 1925.

Dessirier, Index of Production; *Bulletin de la statistique générale,* October, 1924.

Documents parlementaires *Chambre* annexe no. 5455, 1919; annexe no. 5771, 1919; annexe no. 537, 1924; annexe no. 88, 1925; no. 1088; annexe no. 2180, 1925.

—— projet du budget, for respective years.

—— *Sénat* annexe no. 537, 192; annexe no. 225, 1926; annexe no. 84, 1926; annexe no. 656, 1926.

Duchemin, Olivier, *Le Journal des débats,* January 5, 1926.

Experts' Report, *Rapport du comité des experts;* May, 1926, Paris.

Fisk, Harvey E., *French Public Finance;* Bankers Trust Company, New York, 1922.

Fisk, Harvey E., *Inter-Ally Debts;* Bankers Trust Company, New York, 1924.

Fourgeaud, André, *La Dépréciation et la révalorisation du mark Allemand;* Payot, Paris, 1926.

François-Marsal, F., "French Finance and the Franc," *Foreign Affairs,* New York, January, 1927.

Frayssinet, Pierre, *La Politique monétaire de la France, 1924-1928;* Sirey, Paris, 1923.

Germain-Martin, *Les Finances publiques de la France et la fortune privée, 1914-1925;* Payot, Paris, 1925.

Gregory, T. E., *Foreign Exchange;* Oxford, 1925, 3rd edition.

Hawtrey, R. G., *Currency and Credit;* 2nd edition, Longmans, Green, London, 1923.

—— *Monetary Reconstruction;* Longmans, Green, London, 1923.

Herriot, Edouard, "The Program of Liberal France," *Foreign Affairs,* June, 1924.

Institute de statistique, "Etude des cycles économiques," *Supplément au indices du mouvement général des affaires,* 4th year, January, 1926.

Jenny, Frédéric, *Le Temps, Economique et financière;* July 2, 1928.

Jèze, Gaston, *Cours de science des finances et de législation financière française;* Paris, 1925, Giard.

—— *Les Finances de guerre;* Giard et Brière, Paris, 1920.

Katzenellenbaum, S. S., *Russian Currency and Banking, 1914-1924;* P. S. King, London, 1925.

Kemmerer, E. W., *Poland, Report of Commission of the American Financial Experts,* published by the Ministry of Finance, Warsaw, 1926.

Keynes, J. M., *Monetary Reform;* Harcourt, Brace and Company, New York, 1924.

—— "Balance of British Trade," *Economic Journal,* vol. xxxvii, no. 84, December, 1927.

—— "Some Facts and Later Reflections About the Franc," *The Nation,* London, January 30, 1926.

—— "The Stabilization of the Franc," *The New Republic,* 1928.

Lachapelle, Georges, *Revue d'économie politique,* vol. xxxix, March, April, 1925.

Lagneau, J., *La Législation relative à l'exportation des capitaux;* Paris, 1925.

Lambert, Louis, *Le Credit national pour faciliter la réparation;* Picart, Paris, 1925.

L'Annuaire statistique de la France.

Lasch, Georges, *De la répercussion de la valeur monétaire sur la dette publique et privée;* imprimerie des dernières nouvelles, Strasbourg, 1924.

Laurès, J., *Le Problème des changes;* Dalloz, Paris, 1926.

Layton, W. T., and Rist, Charles, *The Economic Situation of Austria,* Report to the Council of the League of Nations; Geneva, 1925.

League of Nations, *Memorandum on Currency and Central Banks, 1913-25;* Geneva, 1926. vol. ii.

Lecerclé, Marcel, and Allix, Edgar, *L'Impôt sur le revenu;* Rousseau, Paris, 1926.

Lewinsohn, Richard, *Histoire de l'inflation;* traduit par H. Simondet, Payot, Paris, 1926.

Lockhart, Jacques, *Le Marché des changes de Paris,* thesis, Les Presses universitaires, Paris, 1927.

Loi des finances de 1925, Bureau de statistique et de législation comparée, Imprimerie nationale, 1925.

Lorin, Jean, *Les Banques françaises de dépôt pendant la guerre;* Thesis, Les Presses universitaires, Paris, 1923.

Loucheur, Louis, "Exposé des motifs du projet du budget," *Documents, parlementaires,* Chambres no. 2180. Paris, 1925.

Lowell, A. L., *Greater European Governments;* Harvard University Press, Cambridge, Mass., 1918.

Lewis, Cleona (see H. G. Moulton), *The French Debt Problem;* Macmillan, New York, 1925.

March, Lucien, *Mouvement des prix et des salaires pendant la guerre;* Presses universitaires de France, Paris, 1922.

Maroni, F., "Revue financière" (weekly); *Journal des débats.*

Meynial, Pierre, *Créances et dettes internationales;* Dalloz, Paris, 1926.

—— "'The French Debt Problem' et le déséquilibre du budget"; *Revue d'économie politique,* November, December, 1925.

—— "La Balance des comptes"; *Revue d'économie politique,* March, April, 1927.

Michel, E., *La Situation financière et l'achèvement de la recon-*

stitution, au 31 décembre, 1925; Berger-Levrault, Paris, 1925.

Morgan and Company, *Statistical Atlas,* unpublished, Paris.

Moulton, H. G., and Cleona, Lewis, *The French Debt Problem;* Macmillan, New York, 1925.

Mourré, Baron, *Revue d'économie politique,* vol. 35, 1921.

National Industrial Conference Board, *Inter-Ally Debts,* New York, 1925.

Nogaro, Bertrand, *La Monnaie et les phénomènes contemporaines;* Giard, Paris, 1924.

———— *Finances et politique;* Giard, Paris, 1927.

Olivier, Maurice, *Les Nombres indices de la variation des prix;* Thesis, Giard, Paris, 1926.

Oualid, William, *L'Europe nouvelle,* February, 1919, vol. ii, no. 7.

Pallain, Georges, "Compte rendu de la Banque de France, 1915," *Bulletin de statistique et de législation comparée,* February, 1916.

Peel, Hon. George, *The French Financial Crisis;* London, 1925.

Pigou, A. C., "Inflation," *Economic Journal,* vol. xxvii, December, 1917.

Polier, Léon, *L'Europe nouvelle,* vol. ii, 1919.

Poincaré, Raymond, "Exposé des motifs du projet du budget, 1927," *Chambre,* annexe no. 3248.

———— "Exposé des motifs du projet du budget, 1928," *Chambre,* annexe no. 4310.

———— "Discours," *Le Temps,* June 23, 1928.

Projet du Budget (for respective years, see *Journal officiel*).

Ribot, A., "Exposé des motifs du projet du budget, 1914," *Bulletin de statistique et de législation comparée.*

Rist, Charles, *La Déflation en pratique;* Giard, Paris, 1924.

———— *Finances de guerre de l'Allemagne;* Payot, Paris, 1921.

Rosenthal, Narcisse, *La Politique d'escompte de la Banque de France depuis 1914;* published by La France de Nice et du Sud-Est, 1926.

Schacht, Hjalmar, *The Stabilization of the Mark;* The Adelphia Company, New York, 1927.

Seligman, E. R. A., *Essays in Taxation and Public Finance;* Macmillan, New York, 1926.

———— *Political Science Quarterly,* March, 1924.

Service d'études de la Banque de France.

Simondet, H., see Lewinsohn.

Stamp, J. C., "National Wealth and the Income of the Chief Powers," *Journal Royal Statistical Society*, July, 1919.

Statistique mensuelle du commerce extérieur de la France.

Taussig, F. W., "Is Market Price Determinate?" *Quarterly Journal Economics*, May, 1921.

———— *International Trade;* Macmillan, New York, 1927.

United States Senate, Commission of Gold and Silver Inquiry, Report, pursuant of resolution 469, 67th Congress, Entitled, "Foreign Currency and Exchange Investigation," Serial 9, vols. i and ii, by John Parke Young, Washington, 1925.

Wolff, Robert, *Note sur le système monétaire français;* Gauthiers-Villars, Paris, 1927.

Young, Allyn A., *Economic Problems New and Old;* Houghton Mifflin, Boston, 1927. See also *Foreign Affairs*, March, 1924.

Young, John Parke, U. S. Senate Commission of Gold and Silver Inquiry Report, "Foreign Currency and Exchange Investigation."

JOURNALS AND PERIODICALS

Agence économique et financière, 26 Boulevard Poissonnière, Paris, 1926.

Bulletin de la statistique générale de la France.

Bulletin de statistique et de législation comparée.

Compte rendu de la Banque de France (yearly).

The Economic Journal.

The Economist (London).

Figaro.

Foreign Affairs.

Herald Tribune.

Journal de Genève.

Journal des economistes.

Journal des débats, "Revue financière" (every Monday).

Journal officiel; Débats; Chambre, Sénat; Lois et décrêts.

L'Annuaire Statistique.

La Cote officiel.

La France économique et financière.

L'Echo de Paris.

L'Economiste français.

L'Europe nouvelle.

L'Homme libre.

L'Intransigeant.
Le Matin.
Le Pour et le contre.
Le Quotidien.
Le Temps.
The London Times.
Manchester Guardian.
New York Herald, Paris edition.
The London Times.
The New Republic.
Paris Midi.
Quarterly Journal of Economics.
Reference Service on International Affairs, Paris.
Revue d'économie politique.
Revue de science et de la législation financières.
Service d'études de la Banque de France.
Statistique mensuelle du commerce extérieur de la France.

INDEX

INDEX

financial policy, 12, 330, 345; influence of bankers on, 354; influence of new personality on, 341; internal struggles, 9, 12, 13; money removed from, 44; political system, 12, 13; reflects in exchange values, 363; reparation policy, 6, 7, 130, 330; taxation struggles, 199, 201, 372, 373, 376, 377; unstable, 12.

Post, Telegraph and Telephone, estimate of deficit, 385.

Post-War Problems, contributing causes, 110.

Pound Sterling (See also *Amsterdam, Great Britain*), fluctuations in value, 80.

Prediction, 332; measurement of exchange fluctuation, 339.

"Prediction Became Impossible," 334-40.

Premium on Franc, 34, 94, 95.

Price Control, 85, 104, 105, 106, 349.

Price Indices, Wholesale and Retail (See also *Price Relatives, Prices, Purchasing Power Parities,* 99, 100, 104, 107; base of French, 304; basis for par, 23; constituents of, 311, 312; rise of wholesale index (1914-19), 206; study of (Oliver), 304; table (1914-19), 100; use of retail versus wholesale, 23, 24; wholesale and retail (1926), 197; wholesale index, 315.

Price Relatives (See also *Price Indices*), frequency distribution, 303, 304; skewed curves, 310; symmetry of, 310; table, "Price Relatives Classified by Direction of Movement," 314.

Prices (See also *Crises, Cyclical Price Movement, Demand, Depreciation, Exports, Foreign Exchange Rates, Imports, Income, Inflation, Production, Profits, Purchasing Power Parities, Quantity Theory of Money, "Relation of Prices and Commerce," Speculation, Stability, Commerce and Prices, Summary of Price Changes, Wages*), 510-27; adjustments of, 271; affected by psychological factors, 42; changes, 21, 265-68; 318; collapse 145-47, (1920), 148; credits, effect on, 17, 18, 88; cyclical movement, 278-282; decline, 296; deflation, 138; discount rate related to price level, 111; dominated by exchange movements, 157; effect of commerce, 123; effect of government interference on, 278; effect of inconvertibility on, 88; effect of weakness of government on, 19; equation of exchange, 17; export and import, 438; fluctuation of, 28, 45, 265-321, 397; food, 146; gold value of, 146, 437; international, 138, 145; in United States, 144; lag in, 105, 424; maladjustment, 142; movement of index number, 276; net changes one hundred years, 269, 270; post-war movements, 44; quantity theory, 16-20, 273, 274; relation to budget deficits, 387; relation to commodities, 58; relation to exchange rates, 18, 25, 89, 269, 310; relation to means of payment, 16; relation to velocity of circulation, 18; results of changes in, 270, 271; retail, 99, 302, 391; rise of, 139, 140, 141, 148, 268, 272, 278, 279; Table, "Wholesale Indices," 145; wartime, 277; wholesale, 99, 125, 178, 291, 389, 418.

Private Credits (See also *Credit*), 102, 103, 340.

Private Finance, not favorable to long war, 66.

Private Financiers (See also *Speculation*), influence on demand and supply of foreign credit, 328.

Production (See also *Bank Clearings, Dessirier Index, Industry, Recovery, Steel, Textiles*), 502-5; as aspect of exchange problem, 331; car loadings, 147, 434; changes due to depreciation, 1; conservatism, 75; decline (1920-21), 147; domination by large corporations, 1; expansion forecast, 139; factor in stabilization, 441; index (1926), 197; maintained during war, 104; means of stimulation of, 217; not entirely disrupted by financial disorganization, 323; political obstacles to, 66; Table, "Index of Production," 432; Table, "Index of Production (1921-23)," 285; use of inflation, 111; volume of, 130, 169, 170, 285, 430; war limitations, 104.